REBELS
AT THE GATE

Lee and McClellan
on the Front Line
of a Nation Divided

W. HUNTER LESSER

SOURCEBOOKS, INC.®
NAPERVILLE, ILLINOIS

Published by Sourcebooks, Inc.
P.O. Box 4410, Naperville, Illinois 60567-4410
(630) 961-3900
FAX: (630) 961-2168
www.sourcebooks.com

Library of Congress Cataloging-in-Publication Data

Lesser, W. Hunter.
  Rebels at the gate / by W. Hunter Lesser.
    p. cm.
  Includes bibliographical references and index.
  ISBN 1-57071-747-8 (alk. paper)
  1. United States—History—Civil War, 1861–1865—Campaigns. 2.
Virginia—History—Civil War, 1861–1865—Campaigns. 3. West
Virginia—History—Civil War, 1861–1865—Campaigns. 4. Virginia—
History—Civil
War, 1861–1865. 5. West Virginia—History—Civil War, 1861–1865. I. Title.
  E470.2.L48 2004
  973.7'3'09755—dc22

                                                2003027656

              Printed and bound in the United States of America
              QW   10   9   8   7   6   5   4   3   2   1

To Walt and Ellie, who lit the flame,
and to Leann, who patiently nurtured it.

ACKNOWLEDGMENTS

There is great power in the written word. I have always found that evident when reading a tattered Civil War–era diary or letter. The faded sweep of pencil and ink yields haunting voices from the past—voices that ring with great dramatic power. A journey to the ghost-filled grounds of which they speak may almost bring the dead to life.

It has been my privilege to walk with such ghosts in the preparation of this book. Some of their words have never before been published. All quotations and dialogue from letters, diaries, and other sources have only been modified for clarity, without use of the term "[sic]" to denote quirks in spelling and punctuation. I did not wish to stifle the power and meaning of their words.

Many among the living (and a few now sadly deceased) have generously helped along this journey. While all cannot be named, I would be remiss not to acknowledge the following:

Historians Richard L. Armstrong and Joe Geiger Jr. unselfishly opened their extensive files of manuscripts and printed material from the Western Virginia campaign—material gleaned from myriad libraries and archives that saved me countless hours and miles of travel. Their research skills far overshadow my own, and I owe them both an enormous debt of gratitude. Richard's hospitality included a quiet workspace at his place of employment, the Bath County, Virginia, Sheriff's Department: a holding cell.

Another talented and tireless researcher, Gary Ecelbarger, often shared discoveries while combing the archives for his own book projects. His energy and insight never fail to amaze me. Max Arbogast, an avid student of Robert E. Lee's nadir on Cheat Mountain, shared references, field trips, and ideas about what really happened in that rugged wilderness during 1861.

I am especially indebted to Donald L. Rice, for his trailblazing work on the Western Virginia campaign; and to Jessie Beard Powell, matron of Travellers Repose, for her insights on the Yeager family and the war in their midst. Heartfelt thanks as well to members of the Rich Mountain Battlefield Foundation, the Laurel Mountain Reenactment Foundation, Monongahela National Forest, and others engaged in preserving and interpreting sites of the first campaign.

Other authors, historians and friends shared research, manuscripts and inspiration—or led me to "hallowed grounds." They include William Acree, Randy Allan, Jeffrey Barb, Phyllis and Peter Baxter, Mark E. Bell, Richard Beto, Robert Black, Matthew Burton, Lars Byrne, Steve Chandler, Larry Corley, Jon Csicsila, Steve Cunningham, Reuben Currence, Jeffrey B. Davis, Terry Del Bene, Robert Denton, Robert Duncan, Alta Durden, Julia Elbon, Scott Francis, Carroll M. Garnett, Clarence Geier, Dean Harry, Jack and Janet Isner, Mark Jaeger, Katherine Jourdan, Mike Ledden, Terry Lowry, Kim and Stephen McBride, Stuart McGehee, Tim McKinney, Bill McNeel, Harry Mahoney, Mark Mengele, Martin C. Miller, Paul Mullins, Michael Pauley, Johnnie Pearson, Michael Phillips, Franz Pogge, Gerald Ratliff, Gilbert T. Renaut, Joe and Mary Moore Rieffenberger, Ed Riley, Hugh and Ruth Blackwell Rogers, Robert and Anita Schwartz, R. Wayne Scott, Darrell See, Bill Smedlund, Joy Stalnaker, Matthew Switlik, Gail Tacy, Mark and Diane Tennant, Don Teter, Victor Thacker, William E. Thompson, Darley Ware, Robert Whetsell, Beth A. White, Richard Wolfe, and Eddie Woodward.

The following libraries and archives were generous in sharing their treasures for this story. Without exception, I found their staffs to be marvelously helpful: Alexander Mack Memorial Library; Allegheny Regional Family History Society Library; Bath County (VA) Library; Central West Virginia Genealogy and History Library; Duke University Library; Emory University Library; Georgia Department of Archives and History; Huntington Library; Indiana Historical Society; Indiana State Library; Library of Congress; Lilly

Library, Indiana University; Mary Baldwin College Archives; Museum of the Confederacy, Eleanor S. Brockenbrough Library; National Archives; Ohio Historical Society; Randolph County (WV) Historical Society; Shepherd College, George Tyler Moore Center for the Study of the Civil War; Stanford University Libraries, Department of Special Collections; Tennessee State Library and Archives; University of Virginia Library; Upshur County (WV) Historical Society; Virginia Historical Society; Virginia Military Institute Archives; West Virginia State Archives and West Virginia University Libraries. A special thanks to staff of the Elkins-Randolph County Public Library and Davis and Elkins College Library in my hometown—always willing to summon books from the stacks or find them by interlibrary loan.

I am indebted to author John Waugh, and to my literary agent Mike Hamilburg, both of who have kindly guided me through the mysteries of publishing. Gladys Walker, an accomplished writer who happens to be my aunt, also provided wise counsel. My editors at Sourcebooks, Hillel Black and Laura Kuhn, deserve much praise. Hillel skillfully trimmed the manuscript and added clarity, while making me think I'd somehow done it myself. Laura fine-tuned the result with a sharp eye for detail, and, with the production team at Sourcebooks, brought it to fruition.

Edwin C. Bearss, National Park Service Chief Historian Emeritus, graciously read the manuscript and shared his unmatched insight. I thank him for long ago recognizing the importance of this story.

And finally, I offer very special thanks to my family; all were ever supportive and understood the need for solitude. I cannot properly express my love and gratitude for the contributions they made as their husband, son, brother, and in-law journeyed through the past.

TABLE OF CONTENTS

Some Civil War "Firsts" in Western Virginia, 1861

- First enlisted man in United States service killed by a Confederate soldier: T. Bailey Brown, May 22, 1861.
- First regiment mustered on Southern soil for defense of the Union under President Lincoln's call for troops: First (U.S.) Virginia Infantry, May 23, 1861.
- First campaign of the Civil War: Federal troops under General George McClellan invade Virginia, May 27, 1861.
- First trains used to carry soldiers to battle on American soil, May, 1861.
- First land battle of the Civil War: Philippi, June 3, 1861.
- First Federal officer wounded by a Confederate: Colonel Benjamin Kelley, June 3, 1861.
- First amputation of the Civil War: James E. Hanger, June 3, 1861.
- First Union government restored in a Confederate state: Wheeling, June 20, 1861.
- First use of the telegraph by an American army in the field: June 1861.
- First general killed in the Civil War: Robert S. Garnett, C.S.A., July 13, 1861.
- First time Robert E. Lee leads troops into battle as a commanding general: September 1861.

PRELUDE
THE DELECTABLE
MOUNTAINS

"I see that region as a veritable realm of enchantment; the Alleghenies as the Delectable Mountains. I note again their dim, blue billows, ridge after ridge interminable, beyond purple valleys full of sleep, 'in which it seemed always afternoon.' Miles and miles away, where the lift of earth meets the stoop of sky, I discern an imperfection in the tint, a faint graying of the blue above the main range—the smoke of an enemy's camp."

—Ambrose Bierce

At 4:30 A.M. on the morning of April 12, 1861, a single mortar shell arched through the night sky near Charleston, South Carolina, and burst into flames over the Federal garrison at Fort Sumter. It was the opening shot of an unparalleled war. Thousands of Americans would rush to arms in a dreadful clash of brothers. Few imagined the terrible cost of dividing a nation.

This is the story of the beginning of America's Civil War. The first battles of that war, after Fort Sumter's nearly bloodless fall, were fought on Virginia soil. Virginia was the pivotal state. A message from her borders caused the first gun to be fired at Fort Sumter, and it was a Virginian who declined the honor of igniting that first gun.

Virginia, the "Mother of Presidents," home to the authors of the Declaration of Independence and the United States Constitution, would be home to nearly 60 percent of the conflict. Four anguished years would pass before the war ended on her doorstep, at a rural courthouse called Appomattox.[1]

But Virginia was also divided. Her internal strife—the agrarian, slave-holding east versus an industrial, free-soil west—mirrored the epic struggle between North and South. Against this backdrop, in the year 1861, Union and Confederate troops waged the war's first campaign.

Embattled Virginia thus became a proving ground. Amid her rugged mountains, a Federal army, led by George B. McClellan, grappled with Confederates directed by Robert E. Lee. Here, in a campaign of notable "firsts," McClellan won the Union's inaugural victories and rocketed to fame. Here armies and leaders were forged, and future battlefields were determined.

Virginia was a key battleground in 1861. Union forces wrested nearly one-third of her landmass from the Confederacy—along with control of the Baltimore and Ohio Railroad, a vital Northern link. The result was all-important. Union victories in the mountains of Virginia diverted war east to the Shenandoah Valley rather than to the upper Ohio Valley and Midwest. The first campaign profoundly shaped America's Civil War. Yet it was overshadowed by the cataclysmic battles to follow and has been nearly forgotten.

While the soldiers clashed, Virginia Unionists waged an extraordinary political fight, creating a loyal state government to oppose the Confederate one in Richmond. From that contest a new state was born—cleaved from Virginia in a defiant act to sustain the Union. West Virginia's name belies her ancient ties. In the following pages, her territory prior to statehood in 1863 is called by its historic name, "Western Virginia."[2]

My involvement with this story began as a youth, fired by the discovery of a dirt-encrusted bullet on the crest of Rich Mountain, scene of a battle that propelled General McClellan to the national stage. A decades-long treasure hunt began as musty manuscripts, diaries, letters, and chronicles were uncovered. From the poignant words of soldiers and civilians, the drama unfolded.

═══ ▲ ═══

Between the Shenandoah Valley of Virginia and the Ohio River stands a chain of lofty sentinels known as the Allegheny Mountains. Stretching from Pennsylvania to Virginia, they are among the tallest mountains in the east. Capped by erosion-resistant sandstones, the Alleghenies rise to heights of nearly five thousand feet.

These mountains were sculpted by water, and storms regularly sweep their crests. Rains pelting the western slopes drain north or west into the Ohio River. Water on the eastern slopes—perhaps a few feet away—flows north into the Potomac, making the region a birthplace of rivers.

Along the eastern flank, long, linear peaks overlook the Shenandoah Valley. The Blue Ridge, Piedmont, and Tidewater sections lay farther east. To the west is the trans-Allegheny, a region of deeply eroded hills remarkably alike in elevation, part of an unglaciated plateau that stretches to the Ohio River.

The Alleghenies are a land of transition. Many plant and animal species found here reach their northern or southernmost limits of distribution. Climatically, the highest peaks are like northern New England or eastern Canada, their summits crowned by a remnant forest of spruce and fir, cranberry bogs, and varying or "snowshoe" hares (brown in summer, white in the winter).[3]

The Alleghenies have been a formidable barrier to human settlement. The name itself may derive from the Delaware Indian term *Eleuwi-guneu*, meaning "endless" mountains. Native Americans first traversed the region more than ten thousand years ago. They were semi-nomadic hunters and gatherers, and the environment that met their eyes was dramatically unlike today: spruce and pine forests, tundra and grasslands—a legacy of receding glaciers. As the climate warmed, native peoples thrived amid rich hardwood forests, building cultures of increasing complexity. But contact with western explorers ultimately brought disease and warfare that decimated the native populations.

The first European to reach the Alleghenies is unknown. Englishmen Thomas Batts and Robert Fallam explored beyond the Virginia Piedmont in 1671, noting trees marked by earlier visitors. Lieutenant Governor Alexander Spotswood of Virginia glimpsed the Alleghenies during an expedition from Williamsburg to the Shenandoah Valley in 1716. Spotswood was joined by a band of cavaliers, slaves, Indian guides, and mules laden with casks of choice Virginia wine and champagne. His "Knights of the Golden

Horseshoe" merrily toasted their discoveries. The adventure enticed others to come west.

Early settlers breached the forbidding mountains by tracing the Potomac River and its tributaries. To encourage them and contest French expansion in the Ohio Valley, the Colony of Virginia offered one thousand acres to land speculators for each family placed west of the Blue Ridge. Those settlers were not to be resident Virginians; many came from Maryland, Pennsylvania, and New Jersey.[4]

An English nobleman, Thomas, Sixth Lord Fairfax, influenced westward expansion. His claim, the Northern Neck Proprietary, encompassed all territory between the headsprings of the Rappahannock and Potomac Rivers—more than five million acres. A survey by the Crown in 1746 established Lord Fairfax's southwestern boundary. The party labored over mountains and through nearly impenetrable swamps and laurel thickets to mark the Potomac headspring with the famous "Fairfax Stone."

Thomas Lewis, chronicler of the expedition, reported that "Never was any poor Creaturs in Such a Condition as we were in nor Ever was a Criminal more glad By having made his Escape out of prison as we were to Get Rid of those Accursed Lorals..." But Lewis also wrote of fine grazing land and magnificent forests, "Exceding well timbred with Such as very Large Spruce pines great multituds of Each and Shugartrees Chery trees the most and finest I ever Saw Some three or four foot Diameter." Reports like this sparked an influx of settlers to the eastern foot of the Alleghenies by the 1750s. Lord Fairfax began to issue leases; a young surveyor named George Washington laid out many of the tracts.[5]

As intrepid pioneers crossed the Alleghenies and established residence in fertile valleys to the west, the French—struggling with Britain for control of the Ohio Valley—exploited Indian fears. Vicious raids began to threaten settlements on the frontier. That violence, coupled with the defeat of British General Edward Braddock's army in 1755 near Fort Duquesne (present-day Pittsburgh), ignited the French and Indian War.

Young George Washington was placed in command of Virginia's militia as settlers fled back across the mountains. He called for a chain of forts along the eastern ramparts of the Alleghenies, defenses that often provided a false sense of security. Near one, a horrified visitor discovered the bodies of three massacre victims. He wrote that they had been "scalped, and after thrown into a fire, [their] bodies were not yet quite consumed, but the flesh on many part of them, we saw the clothes of these people yet bloody, and the stakes, the instruments of their death still bloody & their brains sticking on them."[6]

British arms finally drove the French from their northern strongholds; war ended in 1763 with the Treaty of Paris. France ceded all Ohio Valley claims to the Crown. The Indians were not so pacified. Britain sought to appease the tribes with the Proclamation of 1763, forbidding settlement west of the Alleghenies. Land speculators balked, however, and treaties with the Iroquois and Cherokee reopened most of trans-Allegheny Virginia by 1770.

Settlers again pushed across the mountains. In a move foreshadowing events of 1861, the Grand Ohio Company pressed claims in 1769 to make the western settlements part of a proposed fourteenth colony. The new colony—to be named Vandalia in honor of Queen Charlotte, who claimed descent from the Vandals—was to include all of trans-Allegheny Virginia and a portion of western Pennsylvania and Kentucky. Impending conflict between England and her American colonies doomed the plan.[7]

Trans-Allegheny colonists on the front lines in the French and Indian War now fought as rearguard in the American Revolution. British troops disbanded garrisons in the Ohio Valley, leaving the frontier defenseless. By 1777, the British had pressured many Native American tribes to action, enticing them with payment for scalps. The "bloody year of the three 7s" was a period of unprecedented violence on the Allegheny frontier. Indian war parties from as far away as Detroit were dispatched in a murderous reign of terror.[8]

Atrocities were committed by both sides in that bloody year of sevens. The venerated Shawnee chief Cornstalk bravely entered a Virginia garrison at Point Pleasant on the Ohio River that spring to make peace. Cornstalk was imposing, a magnificent orator who spoke impeccable English. But when a militiaman's scalped corpse was found outside the fort, enraged soldiers murdered the noble chief.

The Revolutionary War ended with the British surrender at Yorktown in 1781, yet bloodshed in the west continued as most of the Indians were driven out. A new wave of European immigrants swept across the Alleghenies. They came for reasons monetary and political, and by 1790 some fifty-five thousand of them lived in Western Virginia.[9]

The seven decades between this surge of immigration and the outbreak of war at Fort Sumter brought significant economic growth to the trans-Allegheny region. Settlers followed well-worn Indian trails through the mountains to build cabins and farms. In autumn, pack-horse caravans laden with pelts, tallow, ginseng, and home-brewed whiskey headed back across the mountains to trade. Grist mills and saw mills sprang from the wilderness as settlements grew into communities.

Fledgling industries in salt, iron, pottery, and glass required improved transportation. Goods could be floated to market on major rivers in the Ohio Valley, but trade across the mountains remained difficult. River communities such as Wheeling, Parkersburg, and Charleston grew in size and stature while isolated settlements within the interior changed slowly.[10]

Virginia's legislature addressed the problem in 1816 by creating a fund for internal improvements and a Board of Public Works. A surge of road building followed. Important routes were laid out by a talented French engineer named Claudius Crozet. These "turnpikes" were so named because a pike blocked the road at points for the collection of tolls and was "turned" upon payment.

The James River and Kanawha Turnpike, completed by 1830, traversed the southern Alleghenies, bearing west from Covington in the Valley of Virginia through Lewisburg, Gauley Bridge, and

Charleston to Guyandotte on the Ohio River. By 1838, the Northwestern Turnpike crossed the northern end of Virginia, connecting Winchester in the Shenandoah Valley with Parkersburg on the Ohio River. Its completion fostered the growth of towns such as Romney, Grafton, and Clarksburg. The Staunton-Parkersburg Turnpike, lying between the two earlier routes, was finished by 1847, winding over the mountains from Staunton in the Shenandoah Valley through Monterey, Beverly, and Weston to Parkersburg along the Ohio.

Interlacing country roads, often impassible for much of the year, linked these three major east-west thoroughfares. One important north-south route was the Weston and Gauley Bridge Turnpike, joining the Staunton-Parkersburg Turnpike with the James River and Kanawha Turnpike. Another, the Beverly and Fairmont Road, connected the Northwestern and Staunton-Parkersburg Turnpikes by 1850.

The new roads had a dramatic effect on commerce. Wagons of all descriptions creaked along their routes. Rumbling stagecoaches—often called "shake guts"—brought weary travelers to bustling taverns. Large droves of cattle and sheep filled the roads as they were herded to market.[11]

But the heyday of turnpikes was short-lived. Track for the Baltimore and Ohio Railroad, a brainchild of Maryland businessmen, had been laid to Wheeling by 1852. Three-quarters of its route lay across northern Virginia. The Baltimore and Ohio was an engineering marvel, traversing the most rugged terrain yet faced by railroad builders in America. For a time it was the only rail link to the nation's capital. A branch line, the Northwestern Virginia Railroad, reached Parkersburg in 1857, connecting that Ohio River town to the main line at Grafton. The railroad spawned a new era of development. Virginians touched by it were bound into closer social and political union with the Northern states.[12]

═══ ▲ ═══

As population and commerce grew in the trans-Allegheny region, so did sectional differences with eastern Virginia. The Allegheny crests marked a boundary of contrasting economies. To the east lay fertile soils and a climate suitable for the production of staple crops on large plantations, requiring the labor of slaves. Rugged terrain and variable climate precluded a plantation economy in much of the west. Hardscrabble subsistence farms dotted the western landscape; diverse natural resources encouraged industrial development with less need for slavery.

The people were of different stock. German, Scotch-Irish, and Welsh settlers were drawn to the trans-Allegheny region. Most shared an egalitarian culture quite unlike the English Piedmont and Tidewater aristocrats of eastern Virginia.

By 1860, the forty-eight counties that would become Western Virginia contained 376,677 residents, about one-quarter of Virginia's population. The region was mostly rural, with some mountainous areas completely uninhabited. Only seven towns had populations of one thousand or more. Wheeling, the largest by far with fourteen thousand residents, was a major industrial and trading center on the Ohio River, strongly linked to northern interests by geography. Parkersburg, also on the Ohio (1860 population: 2,493), had been the scene of a frenetic oil boom in 1859 and was the western terminus of the Northwestern Turnpike, the Staunton-Parkersburg Turnpike, and the Northwestern Virginia Railroad. Charleston (1860 population: 1,520), the economic hub of the Kanawha Valley, had no railroad, but maintained trade with Cincinnati and Louisville via the Great Kanawha River, while the James River and Kanawha Turnpike gave it stronger ties to eastern Virginia. Railroad and turnpike communities such as Grafton, Fairmont, Weston, Beverly, Lewisburg, and Harpers Ferry were mere villages.[13]

Virginia was also divided by slavery. The first African slaves arrived at Jamestown in 1619—a year before the Pilgrims landed at Plymouth. By 1860, there were 490,865 slaves in the Commonwealth. Few westerners owned them. The 18,371 slaves residing in forty-eight western counties that year made up less than

4 percent of Virginia's total. The slave population in Western Virginia actually decreased in the decade leading to the Civil War—portals to a growing "Underground Railroad" were enticingly near.[14]

Virginia's constitution, adopted in 1776, strongly favored the east. Voting rights were limited to white male "freeholders" (property owners). The General Assembly and courts appointed state and county officials. Each county was given two delegates to the General Assembly, regardless of size or population. Western Virginia received only four of the twenty-four state senatorial districts. Easterners controlled the government, leading to complaints of an all-powerful "Richmond Junta."

Little tax money was spent west of the Alleghenies. Urging reform, Thomas Jefferson noted the gross inequities of Virginia's constitution as early as 1782: "The majority of the men in the state who pay and fight for its support are unrepresented in the legislature." Westerners talked of revising the state constitution—and of carving Virginia in two.[15]

Reform efforts led to a constitutional convention at Richmond in 1829. Representation and suffrage were the key issues. Western delegates sought representation on the basis of white population; easterners desired representation based on slave property as well. Led by former Presidents James Madison, James Monroe, and Chief Justice John Marshall, the east granted few concessions. Poor white farmers of the trans-Allegheny were looked on as mere peasants, occupying a niche similar to Tidewater slaves—unworthy to vote.

Shenandoah Valley counties, formerly allied with the west, joined eastern Virginia to protect slave property. The resulting constitution further isolated the west. A *Wheeling Gazette* writer urged westerners to call their own convention for "a division of the state—peaceably if we can, forcibly if we must."[16]

On August 13, 1831, a "wild fanatical Baptist preacher" named Nat Turner and sixty Negro followers went on a murderous rampage, killing more than fifty whites in Southampton County, Virginia. Fear of additional slave uprisings sparked a great national debate. Abolitionists sought to end the "peculiar institution," yet southerners defended it as a right ordained by God. One year later, the grandson of Thomas Jefferson offered a resolution in the Virginia General Assembly to gradually emancipate the slaves. After much debate, it was defeated.

As discontent rose in the trans-Allegheny, Virginians gathered in the "Reform Convention" of 1850. Compromise was finally reached on the issue of representation; all white males over twenty-one years of age were given the right to vote. For the first time, Virginians—rather than their General Assembly and the courts— would elect the governor and state and local officials. Westerners claimed a triumph for democracy, but easterners won preferential taxation of slaves—and prohibition of legislative emancipation.[17]

As the convention closed, President John Y. Mason exhorted the members to allay sectional strife: "May you long live to see this ancient commonwealth united and happy at home, honored and respected abroad." It was not to be. The issue of slavery continued to fester. On the evening of October 16, 1859, it exploded. John Brown, an aging abolitionist from "bleeding Kansas," led a raid on the United States armory at Harpers Ferry, Virginia. His goal was to arm the slaves and lead them in revolt.

Slaves failed to respond, but the angry townspeople of Harpers Ferry and vicinity surrounded Brown's small band in the armory fire engine house. Brown's raid ended on the morning of October 18 when a company of Marines under U.S. Army Colonel Robert E. Lee stormed his stronghold. Brown was captured and taken to nearby Charles Town, Virginia, to stand trial for treason. There, on December 2, 1859, under tight security, he was hanged.[18]

John Brown's raid polarized the nation. Pledging to halt the further spread of slavery, Abraham Lincoln was elected president in 1860. South Carolina promptly separated from the Union, fol-lowed by Mississippi, Florida, Alabama, Georgia, Louisiana, and Texas in early 1861. The die was cast upon bombardment of Fort Sumter. Virginia now moved toward secession. The Alleghenies, a towering barrier in war and peace, were about to become the flashpoint in a great Civil War.

PART I

▲

IMPENDING STORM

▼

Chapter 1
A Very God of War

"There are multitudes of brave men in the West, but no soldiers."
—George B. McClellan

A dapper young figure paced the Ohio Statehouse floor on April 23, 1861. His step was firm, graceful, and deliberate. He was darkly handsome and wore a goatee and an earnest look. Although "rather under the medium height," he was heavily muscled with broad shoulders and a barrel chest. He looked capable of great physical feats. It was said he could bend a quarter between thumb and forefinger—or heave a two-hundred-fifty-pound man over his head.[19]

He was George B. McClellan, the new major general of Ohio Volunteers.

General McClellan faced a daunting task. His charge was to build an army from the raw recruits streaming into the capital city of Columbus, in answer to President Abraham Lincoln's call for seventy-five thousand troops to put down the rebellion of Confederate states. But a convention in neighboring Virginia, angered by that call, had passed an Ordinance of Secession. With Virginia soon to join the Confederacy, Ohio and the other mid-western states lay vulnerable to attack.

The United States's regular army could offer little aid. In 1861, it numbered barely seventeen thousand and was scattered across the continent. Loyal states were left to respond to the crisis on their own—to finance, organize, and equip the troops collected under Lincoln's call. But the states were ill prepared. Politicians, rather than soldiers, often headed their untrained militias. Northern governors, including Ohio's William Dennison, urgently sought out experienced military men to lead the new state troops.[20]

Prominent citizens of Ohio had recommended a former army captain, the West Point–trained George McClellan. He was "a man of remarkable ability," then-president of the eastern division of the Ohio and Mississippi Railroad. Governor Dennison examined a report McClellan had written on European military organization and saw he was "chock full of big war science."

Dennison hastily requested an interview, for McClellan was a hot commodity—the Northern states with the largest military contingents were all bidding for his services. Telegrams intimated that the governor of New York was to make an offer. A prestigious command in McClellan's native Pennsylvania was anticipated. In fact, the young railroad executive was bound for Harrisburg to discuss the matter when he received the summons from Dennison. Convinced that a desirable appointment was at hand, McClellan stopped in Columbus.[21]

Jacob D. Cox, a new brigadier general in the Ohio service, met him at the railway station. "His whole appearance was quiet and modest," recalled Cox of McClellan, "but when drawn out he showed no lack of confidence in himself. He was dressed in a plain traveling suit, with a narrow-rimmed soft felt hat. In short, he seemed what he was, a railway superintendent in his business clothes." He came off as "a very charming man, and his manner of doing business impressed every one with the belief that he knew what he was about."

Governor Dennison outlined the predicament. Ohio's army needed to be built from scratch. There was little military experience on staff—a skilled leader was needed to take charge. McClellan offered keen insight. Given a few weeks' preparation, he vowed the state forces could be made ready for active service. When Dennison solicited his advice for defending Cincinnati, McClellan instructed the governor, "There is only one safe rule in war—i.e. to decide what is the very worst thing that can happen to you, & prepare to meet it."

Dennison offered the Ohio command; McClellan promptly accepted. Within hours, the governor strong-armed a bill through the legislature to secure his man. On April 23, 1861, thirty-four-year-old George McClellan became a major general of Ohio Volunteers. His selection was viewed as "full of promise and hope." Great deeds were expected of young McClellan. It seemed, according to Cincinnati journalist Whitelaw Reid, that "a very god of War" had leaped "out of the smoke and coal dust of the Ohio and Mississippi Railroad Office." [22]

▲

That "very god of War" was born George Brinton McClellan on December 3, 1826, the son of a distinguished Philadelphia surgeon. A child of privileged society, he conversed in Latin and French by the age of ten and enrolled at the University of Pennsylvania at thirteen. His interests soon gravitated to the military. Ancestral McLellans of Scotland had fought with the Stuart kings, and a great-grandfather had earned a general's star in the American Revolution.

McClellan entered the U.S. Military Academy prior to his sixteenth year. He was a popular figure. One classmate wrote that he bore "every evidence of gentle nature and high culture, and his countenance was as charming as his demeanor was modest and winning." McClellan graduated second in the West Point class of 1846—convinced he should have ranked first. He was commissioned a brevet second lieutenant in the elite Company of Engineer Soldiers.[23]

War with Mexico loomed. Accompanied by a black servant loaned from his Alabama brother-in-law, McClellan sailed to the Rio Grande in September 1846 and joined legendary General-in-Chief Winfield Scott in the advance to Mexico City. The young lieutenant promptly showed his mettle. At Puebla, he captured a Mexican cavalry officer; while conducting reconnaissance at Contreras, two horses were killed under him. Once felled by a grapeshot, McClellan arose with only a bruise—the hilt of his sword had absorbed the blow. A brevet promotion was his for "gallant and meritorious conduct."[24]

McClellan further distinguished himself under fire while erecting batteries for Captain Robert E. Lee. Shortly after daylight on September 14, 1847, the American flag waved over Mexico City. To his brother, McClellan wrote:"Thank God! our name has not suffered, so far, at my hands." His courage and initiative were rewarded with a second brevet promotion. Captain George McClellan returned to Philadelphia a hero.[25]

Plumb assignments followed. McClellan translated a French manual on bayonet tactics. He joined an expedition under Randolph Marcy to discover the sources of the Red River and explored the Cascade Range in 1853 for a transcontinental railroad route. He toured Europe to study armies during the Crimean War. Captain McClellan was a rising star. Adapting a Russian manual for horse-soldiers, he also invented the famous McClellan saddle—standard issue until the horse became obsolete. All this from an officer who never served a day in the cavalry.[26]

Yet in 1857, McClellan resigned from the army to become chief engineer for the Illinois Central Railroad. The autonomy and doubling of his salary may have prompted the move. Within a year, he rose to vice president of the railroad, working with men of influence, among them a gangly, backwoods barrister named Abraham Lincoln. McClellan, however, preferred Stephen A. Douglas in the 1858 Illinois senatorial race, and traveled with him by private rail car to one of the Lincoln–Douglas debates.

On May 22, 1860, McClellan married explorer Randolph Marcy's daughter Ellen. In August of that year, he accepted a post as superintendent of the Ohio and Mississippi Railroad and soon became president of the eastern division in Cincinnati—one of the highest-paid railroad executives in America. The war of 1861 interrupted his idyllic life. McClellan believed radical Northern abolitionists and fire-eating Southerners bore equal responsibility for the crisis, but when Fort Sumter was fired on, his choice was clear: "The Govt. is in danger, our flag insulted & we must stand by it." George McClellan was a talent in great demand. And now he paced the Statehouse floor as a major general of Ohio Volunteers.[27]

= ▲ =

Ohio's quota of soldiers under President Lincoln's call was thirteen regiments, more than ten thousand men. Recruiting was easy—volunteers came forth in astonishing numbers. They paraded through the streets of Columbus, overwhelmed private homes, and spilled into the Statehouse. Catching the spirit, members of the legislature pirouetted at evening drill.

Amid this patriotic groundswell, McClellan penned a letter to General-in-Chief Winfield Scott. He vowed that Ohio could supply fifty thousand men to the cause. "I have never seen so fine a body of men collected together," McClellan wrote. "The material is superb, but has no organization or discipline....I find myself, general, in the position of a commander with nothing but men—neither arms or supplies....You can imagine the condition in which I am without a single instructed officer to assist me." He pledged to protect Cincinnati and the Ohio River line. He would create a "secret service" to gather intelligence. He requested experienced officers and regular troops. The letter was delivered by special messenger; telegraph and mail links to Washington had been cut off by Maryland secessionists, and would remain so for more than a week.[28]

McClellan next inspected the State Arsenal. Only a few boxes of rusty smoothbore muskets were discovered—no cartridge boxes, belts, or other accouterments. In one corner stood two or three worn-out six-pounder field guns, badly honeycombed from years of firing salutes. In another corner lay a mildewed heap of artillery harnesses. There was little else. McClellan dryly remarked, "A fine stock of munitions on which to begin a great war!"

The young general began the enormous task of organization. Detailed schedules and estimates of ordinance were created. It was labor at which he excelled. "Feel in my own element," McClellan wrote on April 24, but the mood soon turned bittersweet. A misdirected telegram arrived from Governor Curtin, offering command of Pennsylvania's troops. Had it come two days sooner, McClellan would have gladly accepted. Instead, he gracefully responded that the Ohio forces "need my services & I am bound by honor to stand by them." That wayward telegram would prove fateful to McClellan's rise.[29]

"The general government and the Northern States were utterly unprepared for war," McClellan recorded in his memoirs. "We in the West were therefore left for a long time without orders, advice, money, or supplies of any kind, and it was clear that the different States must take care of themselves and provide for their own means of defense."

His task was compounded by the overwhelming response to President Lincoln's call. Ohio's quota of ten thousand recruits was reached in a matter of days. When thousands more appeared, Governor Dennison accepted them all. Ohio soon had twenty-two regiments in service—thirteen of three-month volunteers under Lincoln's call, plus nine state militia units. All would later be recast as three-year Federal regiments, creating major administrative headaches.[30]

A camp of instruction was needed for the volunteers. McClellan chose sprawling fields along a bend of the Little Miami River near Cincinnati, naming it Camp Dennison in the governor's honor. The first trainload of troops to arrive there on April

30 was met by a dynamic West Point engineer by the name of William S. Rosecrans. Brandishing a compass and chain, Captain Rosecrans laid off the ground for regimental camps and saw to it that wooden shelters were erected. Cincinnati became General McClellan's new headquarters.[31]

During that hectic first week, McClellan composed an extraordinary letter to General-in-Chief Winfield Scott, outlining "a plan of operations intended to relieve the pressure upon Washington and tending to bring the war to a speedy close." The region north of the Ohio and between the Mississippi and the Alleghenies formed "one grand strategic field," McClellan observed, "in which all operations must be under the control of one head...." The implication was that *he* would be that head.

McClellan proposed to cross the Ohio River, invading Western Virginia via the Great Kanawha Valley, then continuing east across the Alleghenies to Richmond. "I know there would be difficulties in crossing the mountains," he admitted, "but would go prepared to meet them." If Kentucky assumed a hostile posture, he would invade that state. Then he would march on Nashville, eventually uniting with an eastern army moving on Pensacola, Mobile, and New Orleans to end the conflict decisively.

McClellan's letter was noteworthy as the first documented strategy to prosecute the war. It was also brash advice from the Union Army's youngest general to a warrior forty years his senior. General Scott fingered its weaknesses: McClellan's reliance on the three-month volunteers—men whose term of service would expire by the time they were fully engaged, and dependence on "long, tedious and break-down" marches across the mountains. Scott then revealed his own proposal "to envelope the insurgent States and bring them to terms." This "Anaconda Plan" consisted of a blockade of Southern ports coupled with an advance down the Mississippi River to New Orleans. Diplomatically, Scott advised that McClellan might "take an important part" in the effort.[32]

On May 3, McClellan was placed in command of the Department of the Ohio, comprising the states of Ohio,

Indiana, and Illinois. A portion of Pennsylvania and Western Virginia north of the Great Kanawha and west of the Greenbrier River were soon added. The young general promptly opened communication with the governors of his new department, all of whom were raising troops. He petitioned General Scott for officers and ordinance, including heavy artillery and armored gunboats. The general-in-chief could not do enough. Governor Dennison and the Ohio legislature came to the rescue, passing bills and appropriating monies for arms, ammunition, clothing, and equipment.

McClellan repeatedly pressed for experienced officers, detained those temporarily assigned, and grabbed others who happened to pass through Cincinnati. "I do not expect your mantle to fall on my shoulders, for no man is worthy to wear it," wrote McClellan to General Scott, "but I hope that it may be said hereafter that I was no unworthy disciple of your school. I cannot handle this mass of men, general; I cannot make an army to carry out your views unless I have the assistance of instructed soldiers....I cannot be everywhere and do everything myself. Give me the men and I will answer for it that I will take care of the rest."

McClellan's "implicit confidence" in Winfield Scott proved tenuous. A rift was developing between the two. When Scott denied a request to organize cavalry and artillery units, McClellan ignored him. To obtain cannons, he nabbed three companies of the Fourth U.S. Artillery traveling on assignment. Scott reluctantly allowed them to stay, but when McClellan sent an officer to Washington with additional demands, the general-in-chief thundered, "I know more about artillery than Gen. McClellan does, and it is not for him to teach me."[33]

"The apathy in Washington is very singular & very discouraging," McClellan confided to Governor Dennison. "I can get no answers except now & then a decided refusal of some request or other—perhaps that is a little exaggerated, but the upshot of it is that they are entirely too slow for such an emergency, & I almost regret having entered upon my present duty."

Ignoring the fact that experienced officers were needed elsewhere, McClellan won a number of desirables, including his father-in-law, Randolph Marcy, as chief of staff; the talented Seth Williams as adjutant-general; and no less a mustering officer than Robert Anderson—the heroic defender of Fort Sumter. But one veteran West Point man got no consideration at all. Twice he visited McClellan's headquarters in quest of a staff position and left word, without reply. McClellan knew the man, and likely remembered his reputation as a drinker. The scorned officer was Ulysses S. Grant.[34]

A twenty-nine-year-old lieutenant of topographical engineers named Orlando Poe had more luck in joining McClellan's staff. Tall and athletic, descended of a legendary Ohio Valley frontiersman, he was sent on a secret reconnaissance into Western Virginia to ascertain "the state of feeling of the inhabitants." Agents were also sent into Kentucky, under direction of Allan Pinkerton, a Chicago private detective retained to head McClellan's intelligence gathering.[35]

There was much concern about Kentucky and Western Virginia. Kentucky's undeclared loyalty had already sparked excitement across the river in Cincinnati. Governor Beriah Magoffin had ignored Lincoln's call for volunteers, yet it was known that his militia was gathering. To Kentucky's neighbors, Magoffin's posture of "armed neutrality" was troubling.[36]

The situation in Western Virginia was even worse. Confederate troops were known to be mustering there. A tenuous truce was in effect until May 23, when citizens voted on an Ordinance of Secession. Virginians were expected to vote their state out of the Union, yet many in the western counties remained loyal. There was no accounting for what the westerners might do.

To a general poring over maps, the strategic importance of Western Virginia was inescapable. Her boundary traced the Ohio River for nearly two hundred fifty miles. Her panhandle thrust like a dagger into the heart of the North—dividing the loyal Union states nearly in two. Confederate forces might pour across her mountain ramparts to rupture the vital Baltimore and Ohio

Railroad or threaten valuable salt works, coalfields, and oil wells on the unguarded frontier.[37]

Putting aside his maps, General McClellan sifted through letters from loyal Union men bemoaning the state of affairs in Western Virginia. Many urged occupation by Federal troops; others warned that the arrival of Lincoln's soldiers would merely arouse state pride and "throw many wavering men into the rebel ranks."

Among those demanding action was George R. Latham, a Grafton attorney. Latham had converted his law office into a Federal recruiting station. "Can anything be done for us?" he implored. "We are now enrolling men and drilling every day, collecting such arms as may be had...and preparing for a fight....The Union men of [Western] Virginia are becoming more firm every day. They want to see secession put down and the leaders hung." A Wheeling resident agreed: "The people will welcome the presence of U.S. forces. There is *no* doubt on this point....[T]heir spirit and determination in this regard...furnish incontestable evidence that they are *now ripe* for a movement."[38]

Governor Dennison pledged to "defend Ohio beyond rather than on her border." In response to these developments, McClellan placed artillery on the Virginia line. As he prepared for hostilities, a dispatch arrived from the War Department. McClellan's face registered astonishment at the news: he had been appointed a major general in United States service, then the highest rank in the army. Thirty-four-year-old George McClellan had received the ultimate soldier's honor—only the venerable Winfield Scott outranked him now. It was stunning tribute for one so young.[39]

McClellan's agents reported much disloyalty across the Ohio River. But the pleas of loyal Virginia Unionists could not be ignored. "My letters from Wheeling," McClellan informed General Scott, "indicate that the time rapidly approaches when we must be prepared to sustain the Union men there."[40]

CHAPTER 2
BURY IT DEEP
WITHIN THE HILLS

"This difficulty is not going to be settled without a fight."
—Francis H. Pierpont, Virginia Unionist

The election of President Abraham Lincoln in 1860 sparked calls for disunion across the South. A writer in the Richmond *Whig* called it "the greatest evil that has ever befallen this country." Lincoln, the "Black Republican" candidate, had pledged to halt the further spread of slavery. His stance was deemed a threat to the Southern way of life.

Thus Virginia's General Assembly gathered in extra session on January 7, 1861. "Great excitement prevails in the public mind," said Governor John Letcher, "and prudence requires that the representatives of the people of this Commonwealth should…determine calmly and wisely what action is necessary in this emergency." Would Virginia join the Confederate states? "Times are wild and revolutionary here beyond description," warned one legislator. "I fear the Union is irretrievably gone."[41]

A convention of 152 delegates gathered at Richmond on February 13 to decide Virginia's fate. Weeks of debate ensued. Firebrands from the Confederate states of South Carolina, Georgia, and Mississippi stirred passions with eloquent speeches.

"The very air here is charged with the electric thunders of war," observed a Richmond correspondent. "On the street, at the Capitol, in the bar-room, at the dinner-table, nothing is heard but resistance to the general government."[42]

The tone of Lincoln's inaugural speech and unfolding drama at Fort Sumter pushed delegates to act. But loyal Unionists from Western Virginia fought back. The most outspoken of them was Clarksburg attorney John S. Carlile. A native Virginian, former state senator, and member of Congress, Carlile was angular and clean-cut, with a sallow face that belied great resolve. He was passionate, dashing, and magnetic. He was a brilliant orator—dazzling in eloquence and power. A rich, deep voice and "imperturbable coolness" made Carlile the most dangerous Unionist in Richmond. Fearlessly he denounced secession, maddening foes and inducing crowds on the street to burn him in effigy.[43]

Westerners cheered him on. "We have no interest," said one, "in a Convention whose object, and sole object…is to make us rebels and traitors to our country…and place us under the unprotected folds of the slimy serpent of South Carolina." "We have been the 'hewers of wood and drawers of water' for Eastern Virginia long enough," thundered the editor of the *Western Virginia Star*, "and it is time that section understood it." If Virginia chose to unite with the Confederacy, westerners called for a new state "independent from the South, and firm to the Union."[44]

President Lincoln's call for troops on April 15 outraged Virginia secessionists. The mood in Richmond grew ominous. Bonfires blazed in the public square. Thugs spilled into the streets, ripped down National flags, and hoisted secession banners in their place. Angry mobs packed the convention galleries to boo and hiss as Unionists tried to speak.[45]

The Richmond convention abruptly went into secret session. On the morning of April 17, former governor Henry A. Wise sealed Virginia's fate.

Wise drew a large Virginia horse-pistol from his bosom, laid it on the desk before him, and proceeded to harangue the delegates in a "most violent and denunciatory manner." His flowing locks danced wildly. His glaring eyeballs bulged from their sockets. The theatrics were shocking, and hypnotic. Wise cried out that events were transpiring that "caused a hush to come over his soul." Flourishing a pocket watch, he gazed at the hands and declared that the hour had come for Virginia to assert her rights. With bated breath, Wise intoned that state forces—under direction of the ex-governor himself—were marching on the Federal armory at Harpers Ferry and the United States naval yard at Norfolk. Virginia was at war![46]

By day's end, the Richmond convention voted eighty-eight to fifty-five to approve an Ordinance of Secession. "I cannot describe to you the terrible solemnity of the closing scenes of the convention," recalled delegate George Porter. "It was the darkest hour I ever saw. Men wept like children. Our country is hopelessly ruined."

Western delegates had voted overwhelmingly against the ordinance. Now the most vociferous among them feared for their lives. Axe-wielding secessionists stormed the Capitol, toppled its flagpole, and tied the Stars and Stripes to a horse's tail. A lynch mob descended on John Carlile's boarding house as he fled the city.[47]

Richmond's "Secession" convention promptly aligned with the Confederate States of America. Western delegates scrambled home to continue the fight. If the Richmond traitors could secede from the Union, westerners threatened to secede from Virginia.[48]

Ever loyal to the Stars and Stripes, they talked of a new government and a new state. Richmond had never supported them— this was only the latest slander in a century of eastern tyranny. It was time for citizens of the west to look out for themselves. To protect the helpless and sustain the Lincoln government, they would rend Virginia in two.

Mass meetings were called. A gathering on April 22 in Clarksburg, Western Virginia, brought out nearly twelve hundred people. John Carlile fired up the crowd. The citizens of each county were urged to select five or more "of their wisest, best, and discreetest men" as delegates to counteract the Richmond convention.

The "Clarksburg Resolutions" were widely distributed—news of the secession vote at Richmond outraged loyal Unionists.[49]

But the sentiment in Western Virginia was far from unanimous. Only days after the Clarksburg mass meeting, "Southern Rights" advocates gathered in that town to endorse the Secession Ordinance. Loyalty was divided even in counties bordering the Ohio River. A Parkersburg newspaper predicted that Lincoln's "treachery" would cause the people of Western Virginia to "repudiate Unionism."[50]

On Monday, May 13, 1861, a convention of Unionists met in Wheeling. It was a proceeding of dubious legality. Attending were more than four hundred delegates from twenty-seven counties. Some had been chosen at public forums, others had been picked by irregular means—even at secret gatherings in the dead of night. The delegates traveled to Wheeling at their own peril.[51]

Nonetheless, Wheeling was a safe venue. Located on the Ohio River in the panhandle far northwest of Richmond, it was Western Virginia's largest city with fourteen thousand residents. Wheeling was one of the few population centers in the state with an overwhelming majority of Unionists. It was a major manufacturing hub. Large numbers of immigrant workers gave the city a decidedly northern flavor.[52]

The Wheeling convention sparked intense curiosity. Reporters attended from New York, Chicago, Cincinnati, Pittsburgh, and other northern cities. The town was decked out in patriotic splendor—flags by the hundreds waved from the streets. Bands blared as throngs of visitors arrived by steamboat and train in a "spectacle to stir the blood."

The convention opened at Washington Hall; inside, a large stage decorated with bunting overlooked the eager, fluttering mass. Grafton attorney George Latham was made temporary secretary and recorded debate. The bombastic John Carlile rose to call for action. Ignoring arguments that the convention lacked authority, he sought no less than a new state government to shield the people of Western Virginia from the "rattlesnake flag" of the Confederacy.

The convention promptly split into two factions: those advocating deliberation until the May 23 referendum on Virginia secession, and those seeking—without delay—a new state.[53]

Carlile spoke as chief advocate for division of the state. A large banner with the inscription "New Virginia, now or never" served as his backdrop. "Let this Convention show its loyalty to the Union, and call upon the government to furnish them with means of defense, and they will be furnished," he exclaimed. "There are 2,000 Minnie muskets here now; and more on the way, thank God.

"Let us act; let us repudiate these monstrous usurpations; let us show our loyalty to Virginia and the Union at every hazard. It is useless to cry peace when there is no peace; and I for one will repeat what was said by one of Virginia's noblest sons and greatest statesmen, 'Give me liberty or give me death!'" Delegates responded with thunderous cheers.[54]

On May 14, Carlile offered a resolution calling for the dismemberment of thirty-two Virginia counties to form a new state. His plan acknowledged Federal law regarding the creation of a new state from the territory of an existing one. A committee would be appointed to draft a constitution and form of government for "the State of New Virginia."[55]

The proposal raised a firestorm of protest. Opponents warned that it lacked support from the Lincoln administration and would plunge Virginia's western counties into the midst of revolution. Carlile did not flinch. "It is represented that a proposition looking to a separate State government is revolutionary in its character," he said. "I deny it. It is the only legal, constitutional remedy left this people if they do not approve the action of the Virginia Convention.…[I]s there a man here that needs to be told it that the Constitution of the United States provides expressly and in terms plain and unmistakable for the separation of a State and the erection of a new State?"[56]

A tall, raw-boned Morgantown attorney named Waitman T. Willey rose in dissent. The nearly fifty-year-old Willey bore an extensive political résumé. He had been an elector on the

Harrison–Tyler ticket of 1840, a member of the Virginia constitutional convention of 1850–51, a candidate for Congress in 1852, a candidate for Lieutenant Governor in 1859, and a delegate to the Richmond convention. He was a "Wheel-horse" of the old Whig party, staunchly conservative and a slaveholder. Yet Willey was also pious and caring—a man of integrity.

He was modest, even retiring, though blessed with a power of speech "rarely found in man." It was said Willey could move an audience at will, that the sweep of his oratory was "utterly irresistible," that an electric current seemed to dance from the ends of his long, bony fingers.[57]

He was perhaps the only delegate in Wheeling who could fend off John Carlile. Summoning his magnificent gift, Willey assailed the statehood proposal. He styled it "triple treason"—treason against the State of Virginia, treason against the U.S. Constitution, even treason against Virginia's alliance with the Confederacy.[58]

Willey maintained that the Wheeling convention had no legal authority. His discourse stretched into May 15, the convention's third and final day. Willey's "triple treason" argument was hotly debated. Some recalled his behavior at the Richmond convention and thought him a "lukewarm" Unionist at best. Spectators jeered Willey's name, but his forceful filibuster paved the way for another speaker.[59]

That delegate was Francis H. Pierpont. Born in a log cabin at "Forks of Cheat," Monongalia County, Virginia, in 1814, he came from pioneer stock. The corpulent Pierpont was a rugged, self-made man. Even his surname had a robust ring, derived as it was from a medieval stone bridge.[60]

As a youth, Pierpont had labored on a farm. He had walked nearly one hundred eighty miles to attend Allegheny College in Pennsylvania and by 1842 gained admission to the bar. He was a life-long friend of Waitman Willey and shared his Whig politics, but decried slavery as a "social and political evil." Pierpont once defended a free black man charged with aiding slaves on the Underground Railroad. He had endured taunts of "Abolitionist,"

"Black Republican" and "the big-bellied slanderer from Fairmont!"[61]

Pierpont was greatly admired in Wheeling. Now he took Carlile and his noisy supporters to task. He quelled fears that Virginia state troops were marching to break up the convention, reassuring delegates that "there would soon be any amount of men and money" to protect Union men in Western Virginia— Ohio Governor Dennison and General McClellan would see to that.[62]

Frank Pierpont offered a compromise to the advocates of "New Virginia." Article IV of the U.S. Constitution inspired his plan: "The United States shall guarantee to every state in this Union a republican form of government, and shall protect them from invasion; and...against domestic violence." Pierpont used it as a guide to hammer out resolutions in committee. The specter of treason offered by Willey had cooled the ardor of Carlile's supporters—the tide of popular opinion had turned.[63]

Withdrawing his statehood proposal, John Carlile moved to adopt resolutions declaring Virginia's Ordinance of Secession to be "unconstitutional, null and void." Loyal Unionists were urged to condemn the ordinance on May 23 at the polls. If it was ratified, delegates would be appointed to a second Wheeling convention on June 11 to devise measures for the safety and welfare of Virginia's western counties.

The resolutions were adopted; a Central Committee made up of Carlile, Pierpont, Latham, and six others was appointed to represent Virginia's Union interests. Carlile made a conciliatory address, but renewed his commitment to a "New Virginia." "[C]ome life or come death," he avowed to hearty applause, "it shall be accomplished."[64]

Calls rang out for Waitman Willey to speak. Willey had nearly skipped the convention—he suffered from an aching back, and his father was near death. But lingering fears that the charismatic Carlile would push delegates into a rash and illegal act had carried him to Wheeling.[65]

Now Willey rose stiffly and summoned a voice that grew in passion and intensity. When the law failed, when the Constitution was exhausted, and when the Secession Ordinance was ratified—then he would stand with those who demanded a new state. Willey invoked the blessings of God and recited patriotic couplets. His speech literally "brought down the house." It was a masterstroke, the Whig wheel-horse at his finest, charging the audience with an electricity that caused old men to jump and shout like schoolboys.

"Fellow citizens," Willey exclaimed, "it almost cures one's back-ache to hear you applaud the sentiment. But then the time for speaking is done." He squared his jaw and looked over the assembly:

> *Fellow citizens, the first thing we have got to fight is the Ordinance of Secession. Let us kill it on the 23d of this month. Let us bury it deep within the hills of Northwestern Virginia. Let us pile up our glorious hills on it; bury it deep so that it will never make its appearance among us again. Let us go back home and vote, even if we are beaten upon the final result, for the benefit of the moral influence of that vote. If we give something like a decided…majority in the Northwest, that alone secures our rights. That alone, at least secures an independent State if we desire it.*

The convention of Virginia Unionists adjourned in a blaze of wild cheers.[66]

CHAPTER 3
A TOWER OF STRENGTH

"My husband has wept tears of blood over this terrible war, but as a man of honor and a Virginian, he must follow the destiny of his state."

—Mary Custis Lee

It was an agonizing decision, the most difficult of his life. Colonel Robert E. Lee had just resigned from the United States Army. "With all my devotion to the Union," he wrote on April 20, 1861, "and the feeling of loyalty and duty of an American citizen, I have not been able to make up my mind to raise my hand against my relatives, my children, my home."[67]

Two days earlier, Lee had left his Virginia home for Washington to meet with Francis P. Blair Sr., an emissary of President Lincoln. Blair was authorized to offer Lee command of the army of seventy-five thousand called out by Lincoln. It was the opportunity of a lifetime—the supreme honor to which any American soldier could dream. Yet Lee barely hesitated. "I declined the offer...as candidly and as courteously as I could," he recalled, "though opposed to secession and deprecating war, I could take no part in an invasion of the Southern States."[68]

Winfield Scott, the general-in-chief, then summoned Lee. Scott was a giant in stature and reputation. He was a towering six-feet-five-inches tall. He was older than the Constitution, a battlefield hero since Lundy's Lane in the War of 1812, the acknowledged genius of the Mexican War, and the 1852 Whig nominee for president. Winfield Scott was a bona fide American legend.

West Point cadet Grant had called Scott "the finest specimen of manhood my eyes had ever beheld." But that had been many years ago. In 1861, Winfield Scott was nearly seventy-five years old. Known as "Old Fuss and Feathers" for his dress and decorum, he was grossly overweight and in poor health, suffering from dropsy and vertigo—unable to mount a horse or even to walk more than a few steps without aid.[69]

During the Mexican War, Scott had mentored Lee and McClellan. Both had served ably under his critical eye. Yet when asked to pass judgment, Scott had called Lee "the very best soldier I ever saw in the field." He had even suggested that in time of war, the government should insure Lee's life for five million dollars a year.

Now, as war loomed again, Lee faced his aged mentor. "These are times," began Scott, "when every officer in the United States service should fully determine what course he will pursue and frankly declare it."

Lee said nothing.

"Some of the Southern officers are resigning," Scott continued, "possibly with the intention of taking part with their States. They make a fatal mistake. The contest may be long and severe, but eventually the issue must be in favor of the Union."

There was a long, awkward pause. Lee remained silent.

"I suppose you will go with the rest," Scott sighed. "If you propose to resign, it is proper you should do so at once; your present attitude is an equivocal one."

Lee replied in a tone of finality, "The property belonging to my children, all they possess, lies in Virginia. They will be ruined, if they do not go with their State. I cannot raise my hand against my children."[70]

Scott, a native Virginian himself, became deeply emotional. "Lee, you have made the greatest mistake of your life; but I feared it would be so."[71]

Robert E. Lee had agonized over that decision, hoped to delay it until Virginians ratified the Ordinance of Secession. But at any hour he might be ordered to invade his homeland—a duty he could not conscientiously perform. To resign under orders would have been a disgrace. Lee did not approve of secession; he had called it "nothing but revolution." He thought little better of slavery. But like the generations of Lees before him, he was first and foremost a Virginian.

His ancestors had embraced revolutionary causes. In 1776, Richard Henry Lee stood before the Continental Congress to offer a motion for American independence. Robert's own father, "Light Horse Harry" Lee, had fought in the American Revolution for his native Virginia. Would his son now be forced to do the same in yet another revolution?[72]

And so Lee made a fateful choice. Sequestered in an upstairs room at the family home known as Arlington, he began a letter to Winfield Scott. "I shall carry to the grave the most grateful recollections of your kind consideration, and your name and fame will always be dear to me," Lee told the aged general. "Save in defense of my native State, I never desire again to draw my sword." He then drafted a one-sentence letter to Secretary of War Simon Cameron: "I have the honor to tender the resignation of my commission as Colonel of the 1st Regt. of Cavalry."[73]

That same day, April 20, *The Alexandria Gazette* said of Lee, "There is no man who would command more of the confidence of the people of Virginia, than this distinguished officer; and no one under whom the volunteers and militia would more gladly rally. His reputation, his acknowledged ability, his chivalric character, his probity, honor, and—may we add, to his eternal praise—his Christian life and conduct—make his very name a 'tower of strength.'"[74]

On the morning of April 22, Robert E. Lee boarded a train for Richmond. Governor John Letcher had summoned him. Although

Lee probably did not imagine it, he had spent his last night at Arlington.

The reserved Virginia gentleman who shook Governor Letcher's hand that day made quite an impression. "The noblest-looking man I had ever gazed upon," thought one observer. Lee was a robust fifty-four years of age. Standing five-feet-eleven-inches tall, he weighed not 170 pounds, yet an enormous upper body and head made him appear larger. He wore a short mustache, and his dark hair was sprinkled with gray. Lee's brown eyes were animated, but his overwhelming expression was a calm self-assurance.[75]

The governor directly asked Lee to take command of Virginia's military forces, with the rank of major general, and he accepted. For his entire adulthood, Lee had been a soldier—it was the only life he knew. He stood before the Richmond convention the next day, in the shadow of his father, "Light Horse Harry" Lee.

Born Henry Lee III in 1756, Light Horse Harry had been a brilliant if erratic cavalry leader during the American Revolution, had been a member of the Continental Congress and governor of Virginia. But he had also been a foolish speculator, and fled the country in disgrace. He had died far from his family in 1818, remembered mainly for a eulogy to his friend George Washington: "First in war, first in peace, and first in the hearts of his countrymen."[76]

Those very words were now paraphrased as tribute to his son Robert, Virginia's new major general. Lee followed with a modest speech. On April 23, 1861—the very day that Major General George McClellan began the Herculean task of organizing Ohio troops—Major General Robert E. Lee took command of the military forces of Virginia.[77]

Lee and McClellan faced many of the same problems. Each sought to mobilize an army made up of raw volunteers. McClellan received scant assistance from Lincoln's War Department, nor could Lee count on the fledgling Confederate government then headquartered in Montgomery, Alabama. McClellan's efforts were greatly facilitated by Ohio's government and citizens, however, while Lee worked in a state divided by sentiment. The South had no standing army. While McClellan had the luxury of an implied truce until Virginia's May 23 ratification vote, Lee toiled under a greater sense of urgency.

President Lincoln's April 15 decree gave Confederate forces twenty days "to disperse and return peaceably to their respective abodes." The implied threat gave Lee less than two weeks to organize. His policy was strictly defensive—"to resist aggression and allow time to allay the passions and permit Reason to resume her sway." He was fortunate to obtain Robert S. Garnett as adjutant general. Garnett had been commandant of cadets at the U.S. Military Academy during Lee's tenure as superintendent in the early 1850s. A fellow Virginian, Garnett was a trusted and talented soldier.

Lieutenant Colonel John A. Washington, a Lee relative and great-grandnephew of the first president of the United States, served as the general's *aide-de-camp*. Lieutenant Colonel George A. Deas and Walter H. Taylor also joined Lee's staff. Taylor was a razor-sharp twenty-two-year-old militia officer who quickly made himself indispensable at headquarters.[78]

As Lee assembled a military staff, his mind drifted to family matters. His wife Mary, a descendent of Martha Washington, had inherited the Arlington homeplace. Lee recognized it as strategic ground, likely to become the scene of conflict. He wrote Mary and their four daughters soon after arrival in Richmond, "You have to move, & make arrangements to go to some point of safety which you must select." Priceless Washington family heirlooms were to be safeguarded. Recalling the embarrassing legacy of his father, Lee redoubled efforts to secure his own debts.[79]

Lee's sons enlisted in Virginia's army. The eldest, Custis—ranked first in the West Point class of 1854—signed up as a captain of engineers. William Henry Fitzhugh, or "Rooney" Lee joined as a cavalry officer. Only the general's teenage son Robert E. Lee Jr. was held back. "I could not consent to take boys from their school & young men from their colleges & put them in the ranks at the beginning of a war when they are not wanted & when there are men enough for the purpose," Lee wrote. "The war may last 10 years. Where are our ranks to be filled from then?"[80]

Lee's pessimism was not well received. Conventional wisdom suggested the conflict would be brief. Walter Taylor believed the general stood alone in "having expressed his most serious apprehensions of a prolonged and bloody war." Lee emphasized "the magnitude of the impending contest" and the "inevitable suffering, sacrifice, and woe."[81]

Even impressionable youth did not escape Lee's gloom. One day an indulgent father brought his five-year-old son to headquarters. At Lee's insistence, the pair was admitted, and the little boy ended up sitting on the general's knee.

"What is General Lee going to do with General Scott?" demanded the father.

The youth, obviously coached in advance, replied, "He is going to whip him out of his breeches."

Lee's manner stiffened. He placed the youngster on his feet and eyed him intently. Then he began to speak, looking toward the father rather than the son. "My dear little boy," he said, "you should not use such expressions. War is a serious matter and General Scott is a great and good soldier. None of us can tell what the result of the contest will be."[82]

Left alone until the Confederate government moved from Montgomery, Alabama, to Richmond in late May, Lee worked feverishly to mobilize Virginia forces. Governor Letcher issued a call for volunteers. Walter Taylor marveled at the energy of Lee and Garnett as they organized, armed, and equipped the troops. Their labors would eventually result in nearly forty thousand soldiers, one hundred fifteen pieces of field artillery, numerous fortified coastal defenses, and warships for Virginia.

Lee faced troubling strategic questions: How could Northern sea power be neutralized? How could Virginia forces be distributed to meet an invasion that might come simultaneously from the north, east, *and* west? He sent a capable Mexican War veteran, William B. Taliaferro, to guard the important naval post at Norfolk and directed a well-regarded militia colonel named Thomas J. Jackson to do the same at Harpers Ferry. Jackson was also ordered to "make diligent inquiry as to the state of feeling in the north-western portion of the State."[83]

Formerly a West Point classmate of George McClellan and a Virginia Military Institute professor, Jackson seemed a good choice for the job; Western Virginia was his boyhood home. He had grown up on the West Fork River in Lewis County. The industrious Jackson warned of "great disaffection" in Virginia's western counties. "Grafton should be occupied at once," he entreated, recognizing the strategic importance of that railroad town.[84]

Jackson's energy drew Lee's interest. The village of Grafton, a collection of railroad shops at the junction of the Baltimore and Ohio with its Parkersburg branch, the Northwestern Virginia Railroad, was key to the control of Western Virginia. The railroad was in a precarious position. B&O President John W. Garrett strived to maintain the appearance of neutrality; both the Virginia government and the Lincoln administration threatened retaliation if troops were carried by his railroad. General Lee hoped to exploit the standoff by collecting forces nearby.[85]

Lee ordered Major Francis M. Boykin Jr., a VMI graduate, to muster volunteers at Grafton, and directed Major Alonzo Loring, a Wheeling iron-works official, to do likewise in the panhandle region. But neither had success in recruiting. "The feeling in nearly all of our counties is very bitter, and nothing is left undone by the adherents of the old Union to discourage those who are disposed to enlist in the services of the State," Major Boykin reported on May 10. Expressing little hope of recruiting a sizeable force, he warned, "This section is verging on a state of actual rebellion."[86]

Perplexed by these developments, Lee ordered Colonel George A. Porterfield, a VMI-trained Mexican War veteran, to assume command at Grafton. Volunteers and wagons of ordnance and provisions were dispatched across the mountains to his aid. On May 14, Colonel Porterfield stepped from the train at Grafton to a rather cold reception. Not a single volunteer was at hand. The colonel was curtly directed to the nearby villages of Fetterman and Pruntytown, where Confederate recruits were said to be gathering. There he found a few hundred men, not the outpouring Lee had anticipated. Porterfield expressed "serious disappointment" in a letter to his commander: "I have found great diversity of opinion and much bitterness of feeling among the people of this region."[87]

The reports baffled General Lee. Raised in the tidewater as a blue-blooded Virginian, he could not fathom the mood of the west. To Colonel Porterfield he wrote, "I cannot believe that any citizen of the State will betray its interests." Meanwhile, volunteers rallied to the blue and gray.[88]

CHAPTER 4
THE GIRL I
LEFT BEHIND ME

"Very often it was that father and sons of the same family differed in political opinions to the extent sometimes of making bitter enemies of those who were a little while ago of one family and one blood."
—John Henry Cammack, C.S.A.

"I have volunteered in the Confederate Army," James E. Hall wrote in the first entry of his war diary. Hall, a twenty-year-old farm boy from Barbour County, Virginia, proudly rushed to arms. Young men like him across the South were pulled into the vortex of secession.[89]

The typical volunteer of 1861 "was a fearfully and wonderfully gotten up representative of the Sons of Mars in the first flush of his war fever," recalled another Virginia Confederate. Marcus Toney of Tennessee believed the war would consist of a single battle "in which one Southern man would whip five Yankees with corn-stalks, England would intervene, peace would be declared, and we should return home." Sam Watkins, a Tennessee Confederate, recalled that nearly everyone "was eager for the war, and we were all afraid it would be over and we not be in the fight."[90]

Many enlisted out of duty to their native state. "I was a Virginian as were my people, and when my State went to war, I

saw no other course open but to follow the fortunes of the old
Dominion," wrote John Cammack of Harrison County. War
seemed inevitable after Lincoln's call for seventy-five thousand
troops to "coerce" the Southern states. A great number joined "in
defense of our firesides, and the Confederate States of America."[91]

Few brought up the issue of slavery. Of those who did, Marcus
Toney's view was typical: "I do know that the abolitionists of the
North had so outraged the feelings of the Southern people that
we felt we did not want any further affiliation with them." Toney
offered another compelling reason to enlist during the heady
days of 1861: "The young ladies were as enthusiastic as the young
men; and if they found a fellow luke warm, he was threatened
with a petticoat and was not allowed to hang up his hat in their
father's hall."[92]

"No male, physically and mentally able to do service, would
stay out," recalled a Virginian. "Boys of tender years enlisted with
the approval of fathers and mothers, and in some instances were
even urged to do so. No critical or even cursory examination was
applied." The minimum age of enrollment was eighteen, but
younger recruits like sixteen-year-old John Cammack stepped into
line—along with drummers of remarkably tender age.[93]

The term of service was usually one year. Volunteers enrolled in
companies of seventy-five to one hundred men. The members of
a company elected their officers and were led by a captain.
Confederate companies often took patriotic, chivalrous, or fear-
some names. Among those defending Western Virginia were the
Pendleton Minutemen, Southern Right Guards, Pocahontas
Rescues, Appomattox Invincibles, Upshur Grays, Kanawha
Riflemen, Elk River Tigers, Buckingham Leeches, and Flat Top
Copperheads.[94]

New recruits were schooled on the drill field. Their instructors
were not always experienced soldiers. A company of young students from Virginia's Hampden-Sydney College marched under
the leadership of the college president, Reverend Dr. John
Atkinson. One of his "Hampden-Sydney Boys" recalled drilling in

the basement of the seminary building during a rainstorm: "Dr. Atkinson marched the front line straight into [a] wall, where the men were forced to press their faces into the bricks until he could figure what order to give next!"[95]

Southern recruits donned a variety of uniforms. The Confederate Congress decreed that "volunteers shall furnish their own clothes and, if mounted men, their own horses and horse equipments." Styles were dictated by popular fashion. "We went in heavy on fancy caps, wavelocks and other...stately head-gear," recalled a Virginian who thought "big boots, the higher the better," were essential. "We wore all sorts of clothing," wrote a Tennessee volunteer. The contrast was marked—from gaily decorated militia and cadet uniforms to bearded mountain men in hunting shirts and coonskin caps.[96]

Wealthy Southerners often donated money to equip the troops. John Worsham's Virginia company had "a fine cadet gray uniform. It consisted first of a frock coat which had a row of Virginia fire-gilt buttons on its front. Around the cuff of the sleeve was a band of gold braid....The pants had a black stripe about one and a quarter inches wide along the outer seams. The cap was made of the same cadet gray cloth, trimmed with black braid....Our knapsacks were a specialty. They were imported from Paris....We also imported our canteens."[97]

"The knapsack was a terror," recalled another Virginian. It overflowed with myriad items, making the owner a veritable "beast of burden." The haversack, or shoulder bag, "always had a good stock of provisions, as though a march across the Sahara might at any time be imminent."

Each member of John Worsham's company had "a fatigue jacket...white gloves, several pairs of drawers, several white shirts, undershirts, linen collars, neckties, white vest, socks, etc.—filling our knapsack to overflowing. Strapped on the outside were one or two blankets, an oil-cloth and extra shoes. Most of the knapsacks weighed between thirty and forty pounds, but some were so full that they weighed fifty pounds!"[98]

The Confederacy faced a chronic shortage of firearms. Recruits were encouraged to bring "smooth bores, shot guns or rifles" from home. Virginia mountaineers sometimes brought hunting rifles far more accurate than the muskets issued by the Confederate states.[99]

The members of Isaac Hermann's First Georgia Infantry received a typical weapon of 1861: "muskets converted into percussion cap…from old revolutionary flint and steel guns, possessing a kicking power that would put 'Old Maude' to shame." Recruits often got muskets with the archaic flintlock mechanism. Some were loath to accept them. An officer protested the inferior arms given his company directly to General Lee. "Sir," Lee was said to have replied, "your people had better write Mr. Lincoln and ask him to postpone this thing for a few months until you can get ready."[100]

Many Confederates sported a huge side knife. Hammered from old steel by local blacksmiths or imported from Europe, a "Bowie" knife or dagger seemed just the thing for hand-to-hand fighting. The boys all had "big knife fever," recalled a Tennessee volunteer. "Our large bloody-looking knives were the only things possessing much similarity, and a failure to have one of these pieces of war cutlery dangling at your side was almost a certain sign of weakness in the knees."[101]

The few cavalry companies mustered at this early date toted handguns, old "pepper box" pistols, shotguns, and antique sabers. Confederates in every branch of service rounded up whatever could be had, and then departed for a camp of instruction.

For many Virginians, the destination was Richmond (population: 37,000), the South's third-largest city. Chaos reigned as volunteers spilled in. Rustic backwoodsmen gawked at huge crowds in front of the state capitol while dignitaries such as Governor Letcher and President Jefferson Davis spoke.[102]

Two miles west of the city, at Camp Lee, many got their first lesson in soldiering. Drillmasters from the Virginia Military Institute guided recruits through their paces, a scene that played out in camps of instruction throughout the South. Young women often came out to witness the drilling. John Worsham thought "they seemed to enjoy it as much as we did their presence."

"The men formed messes," Worsham recalled, "each consisting of about ten men and each employing a Negro man as cook. We got on nicely, as we thought. The regular rations were issued to us; but in order to become accustomed by degrees to eating them, we sent the cook or some other member of the mess into town to get such articles as the market afforded." Marcus Toney recalled, "[W]e were novices as to cooking and washing. We knew that water and flour mixed made batter, and we knew that meat when fried made gravy; so with this much of the art acquired, we had fried dough, or what the boys called flapjacks. As to the washing—well, let that pass."[103]

A Virginian described the schedule at Camp Lee: "We have drills of one hour each day and also a dress parade at 6 in the evening, between times we have to cook, wash, go after provisions, sweep and clean up in front of our bunks and (last but not least) we have to stand guard, having often to shoulder our muskets and march at least 5 miles to stand guard, way below Richmond. So you see we are kept pretty busy."[104]

The novel discipline sparked rebellion. Cosmopolitan Richmond was most alluring to the recruits at Camp Lee. The fancy uniforms of John Worsham's company gave them the appearance of officers, a trait sometimes used to slip out of camp. "[W]e would march boldly by a sentinel on duty at one of the many openings around the grounds, give him the salute, and he would present arms as we passed out," the fun-loving Worsham recalled.[105]

The specter of death also appeared. Recruits were accidentally shot, drowned, hit by trains, or bitten by rattlesnakes. Measles, normally a harmless childhood disease, had serious complications for the rural men never before exposed. "Many cases of measles, and many fatal, took place," wrote Marcus Toney from Camp Cheatham, Tennessee, "and the doleful dirge of the dead march often touched our hearts." But a sense of duty kept most

Confederates in line. "A soldier's life is a hard one," admitted a young Virginian, "yet I would be cheerful and contented were it fifty times as bad for I believe we are engaged in one of the noblest causes on earth, namely the defense of our country, our liberty and the protection of our parents, wives and children, and all that is dear to a man."[106]

Regiments were formed, consisting of ten companies led by a colonel. John Worsham recalled the formation of his regiment, the Twenty-first Virginia Infantry, at Camp Lee: "We were mustered into service for one year...on the capitol square....Each boy under twenty-one, and there were many, brought a written permit from parent or guardian....The regiment numbered about 850, rank and file."[107]

They came from a variety of backgrounds. "The pulpit, the bench, the bar, the farm, the anvil, the shop and every other calling was represented," noted one recruit. The Forty-fourth Virginia Infantry, a typical regiment at Camp Lee, boasted a makeup of 36 percent farmers, 19 percent laborers, 16 percent carpenters and tradesmen, 12 percent students, 8 percent clerks and merchants, 4 percent doctors, lawyers, and ministers with a balance of apprentices and county officials.[108]

"Soldiers were coming into Richmond from all directions," marveled John Worsham. "The streets were filled with marching men and the sound of the drum was heard every hour of the day and night." Raw recruits mustered in as new regiments marched out for the seat of war—all to the frantic "waving of handkerchiefs by the dames and maidens and the huzzas of the men and boys."[109]

By contrast, the mood was somber in much of Western Virginia. Private John Cammack heard few cheers while mustering at his county seat of Clarksburg, Harrison County. Cammack's "Harrison Rifles" shared the town with a company of Union recruits. Old friends and neighbors were now forced to choose sides. To avoid conflict, they drilled at the courthouse on alternate days, locking their weapons in the county jail at night.

"One of the most remarkable things that I have ever known of occurred there," recalled Cammack of his departure. "The Union

Companies came around, most of them willing to talk and such expressions as these could be heard; 'Well Tom, you're going South I see. Well, goodbye, I guess the next time I see you will be in battle.' 'So long, you'll catch the devil when we do get to fighting, alright, all right.'...Many of the men shook hands with their foes and sometimes there were kindly expressions of good bye."[110]

Most Southerners could hardly have imagined it. The adoring citizens of Richmond followed Confederate troops everywhere; "fair maidens" waved and solicited uniform buttons as souvenirs. "Such requests could not be refused," avowed a gallant volunteer. "So far was it carried that some of our uniforms were quite disfigured before we reached our destination."[111]

The pageantry climaxed with the presentation of banners. John Worsham of the Twenty-first Virginia recalled the drama: "Quite a stir was created in camp one day by the announcement that a flag would be presented to Company B. This was a very handsome silk flag. Made by the ladies of Baltimore, it 'ran the blockade' into Richmond and was presented to the company by President Jefferson Davis. He made one of his brilliant speeches in the presence of the regiment and a large number of visitors from Richmond, most of them ladies. The occasion passed off with great enthusiasm." Bestowal of a flag on Sam Watkins's First Tennessee Infantry "fairly ma[d]e our hair stand on end with intense patriotism, and we wanted to march right off and whip twenty Yankees."[112]

"We are anxious to meet the foe," wrote a Virginia Confederate, "for we have them to whip, and the sooner we do it, the sooner we will be able to return to the dear loved ones at home."

Sixteen-year-old Marcus Toney left for war to the tune of "The Girl I Left Behind Me." "I was too young to be leaving a girl behind me," he recalled, "so I marched out with a light step and joyous heart, not dreaming of the shock of battle....I looked to the right as we were passing the girls, and saw tears gathering in many eyes."[113]

——— ▲ ———

In the meantime, Northern volunteers rushed to President Lincoln's call. It seemed everyone wanted to be a soldier, to posture heroically and be adored. Recruiting progressed with marvelous "rapidity and ease." Speeches and patriotic music roused large crowds until prospects bolted forward at the call, "Who will come up and sign the roll?" Billy Davis, a diminutive twenty-three-year-old dry goods clerk from Hopewell, Indiana, recalled his enlistment: "I know that I felt a trembling sensation when writing my name. Don't believe I ever felt so attached to the old flag as I do today."

Like the Confederates, they were citizen-soldiers. Prominent men organized the regiments and were elected to command. "Hosts of charlatans and incompetents were thus put into responsible places at the beginning," recalled General Jacob Cox of Ohio, "but the sifting work went on fast after the troops were once in the field."[114]

The states of Ohio and Indiana provided most of the Federals bound for Western Virginia in 1861. Governor Oliver P. Morton of Indiana was no less active than Ohio's Dennison in organizing troops. The first enlistments were for three months. Most expected to be home in a few weeks, covered with glory, for it was "only a breakfast job."[115]

Love of country compelled many to enlist. To Billy Davis of Indiana, the "all absorbing question" was "shall this union, this government of the people, live or perish." An Ohio Buckeye spoke for most in his belief that "no State had a right to secede...and that the Union must and shall be preserved." Some enrolled for monetary reasons—the pay for an infantry private started at thirteen dollars a month, not an insubstantial sum. A few were motivated by the abolition of slavery. Others were lured by that most compelling of incentives: "If a fellow wants to go with a Girl now he had better enlist," swore one Indiana Hoosier. "The girls sing 'I am Bound to be a Soldier's Wife or Die an Old Maid.'"[116]

Immigrants joined the Union army in great numbers. Notable were the Germans of Cincinnati, Ohio. Many had soldiered in Europe or trained in the paramilitary Turner Society. Turners flourished in a large German quarter of Cincinnati known as "over the Rhine." During an immense gathering there on April 17, 1861, attorney Johann Stallo brought the crowd to its feet with a pledge of loyalty to the Stars and Stripes. An all-German regiment was proposed.

The rolls were filled in a single day. One young recruit remembered his enlistment: "A justice of the peace...swore us in at once. He wrote my good German name with heart-rending mistakes. Only the first letter and the last were right; all others wrong. I pointed out the flaw to him. He answered calmly: 'That doesn't matter a bit! You are sworn and registered by that name, and it will be yours until you are mustered out of the service again.'"

The Germans elected Johann Stallo's law partner Robert McCook as their colonel. One of a large Ohio family of military distinction known as the "Fighting McCooks," he was the lone Anglo-American in the regiment. Modestly styling himself the "clerk for a thousand Dutchmen," McCook took command of a regiment of Germans fighting for the Union—the Ninth Ohio Volunteer Infantry.[117]

Loved ones stitched clothing, socks, and quilts for the Northern volunteers prior to tearful departures. Friends presented Billy Davis with a pocket revolver, admonishing that he might "get into close quarters and need it." Davis and a comrade visited a portrait studio to have their "ambrotype taken." Posed sternly before the camera with a Bible in one hand, a revolver or Bowie knife in the other, they represented any number of soldiers, North or South.

Finally, the Union recruits boarded trains for a camp of instruction. The destination for many Hoosiers was Camp Morton in Indianapolis, and for many of the Buckeyes, Camps Dennison and Harrison near Cincinnati. Every stop created pandemonium. An Ohio volunteer watched citizens swarming the depot "with hot coffee, cigars, cider, and it appeared they could not do enough for us....When we left the ladies were at all the windows and on the houses...waving handkerchiefs and huzzahing. I never saw such a time and all along the road it is the same."

Ebenezer Hannaford of the Sixth Ohio Infantry recalled a bevy of young ladies who entered the trains and "adroitly managed to let the cars carry them off. Despite their protestations, it was easy to see that the girls were happy as little birds. Of course the good-by and kissing part of the programme was repeated *ad libitum*." Gushed a comrade, "Hurrah! who wouldn't be a soldier?"[118]

Recruits were given a physical on the Indianapolis state fair-grounds at Camp Morton. Doctors scrutinized the teeth; soldiers needed them to tear open the paper cartridges used in loading a musket. Lack of a single front tooth caused a member of Billy Davis's regiment to be sent home. Davis himself was nearly rejected as undersized, but most were sworn into United States service.

An Indiana volunteer thought the schedule in camp was "bound up pretty tight...we have to toe the mark." Reveille was at five o'clock, and the order of the day was drill. "After breakfast we went out and drilled, or tried to," wrote Billy Davis. "The Sergeants took out squads and drilled, while the officers studied. They do almost as well as the officers, we are all as awkward as can be." Strapping farm youths accustomed to the plow sometimes found the terms "right" and "left" incomprehensible—for them it was necessary to substitute the familiar commands for steering oxen: "gee" and "haw."[119]

In contrast, Germans of the Ninth Ohio Regiment drilled under an exacting Prussian drillmaster who barked commands in their native tongue. A Cincinnati newspaper reported what every-one at Camp Dennison knew about the Germans: "Training inces-santly, exploiting boundless tenacity, they have already achieved extraordinary precision and skill. An old English-speaking officer said recently that the Ninth is one of the best regiments he had ever seen."[120]

Living quarters varied. Some of the Hoosiers at Camp Morton slept in animal stalls on the fairgrounds or in tents. At Ohio's Camp

Dennison, the wooden shanties constructed by William Rosecrans underwent dramatic improvement. Ebenezer Hannaford wrote how they were "transformed into the likeness of pleasant country cottages, by means of lattice-work porches, cornices of various patterns, pigeon-houses, and similar ornamentation." Nearly every dwelling had a distinctive sign, with titles like the "Astor House," the "Major Anderson," "Stars and Stripes," "Barnum's Museum," or the "Canary Bird Nest."[121]

Cooking details were formed, but the roads to Camps Dennison and Harrison were dotted with carriages, "protruding from which might be seen baskets and bottles, all filled with the good things of this life." A special train accommodated visitors. Since "admission was open to all, and few came empty-handed, soldier-life at Camp Harrison became simply a kind of protracted picnic." Roared an Irish volunteer overcome by the bounty, "If this be war, God grant we may niver have pace."[122]

Liquid spirits were mostly forbidden. "They [are] not going to let the boys swair or drink any," reported an Indiana volunteer. Testified an Ohio recruit, "We don't drink any beer here, or any drinks—only coffee and water." Others hinted of more potent libations. "Canteens were furnished to day, are of tin covered by a coarse cloth," noted Billy Davis. "Some of the boys think them good for Buttermilk, Cider or something stronger." Davis's leather-bound journal reported that members of his regiment had gone to town one evening; "Some returned drunk, others are out." The following day's entry: "At breakfast time the missing boys returned....They are still drunk."[123]

Punishment might include extra duty or time in the guard-house. For stealing, insubordination, and other infractions, recruits would be shaved bald, marched through camp with a humiliating sign, chained to a log, or strapped to the wheel of a gun carriage. For dire offenses like murder, the soldier might face a firing squad or hanging.[124]

The Union volunteers of 1861 wore all manner of uniforms—from the gaudy, outlandish fezzes and bloomers of Zouaves to plain civilian garb. Ebenezer Hannaford's company of the Sixth Ohio Infantry wore a "distinctive pattern, in gray cloth," bought with private contributions. The Seventh Indiana Regiment was in camp for nearly a month before they received uniforms. "The color is gray," noted Billy Davis, "and quite neat when a fellow gets a fit, but such fortunate ones are few."

There was no standard uniform color during the first months of war. "Militia gray" was popular in the North. Some Confederate troops wore blue. The familiar blue uniform did not become standard Union issue until 1862, a situation that led to tragic errors.[125]

Early Union volunteers often received the same arm as their enemy—antiquated muskets firing a huge .69 caliber ball. More than one groused that his weapon "had not been shot since the war with England." A description of arms for the Fourteenth Indiana Infantry appeared in the *Indianapolis Journal*: "Over 200 men in the regiment are armed with percussion-locked muskets altered from the old fashioned flintlock and the remainder are provided with the latest pattern of smooth bore muskets." Flanking companies and sharpshooters received the more accurate British Enfield rifles. "The Regiment took 120 rounds of ammunition for each man," concluded the *Journal*, "sufficient quantity to do a vast amount of execution on the rebels."[126]

General McClellan arrived to review the troops at Indianapolis, fanning rumors of departure for the seat of war. The excitement swelled as muskets were loaded and fired for the first time. Billy Davis lay on his bunk afterward with Bible in hand, lingering over the inscription by a young lady. "Friend Billy;" it read, "You go to fight for us, we will pray for you, may you fight bravely, and should you fall may you die happy."[127]

CHAPTER 5
MCCLELLAN
EYES VIRGINIA

"I hope to secure Western Virginia to the Union."
—George B. McClellan to Abraham Lincoln

A column of volunteers marched at the Wheeling Island fair-grounds. They were soldiers of Virginia, cast from a different mold. Scorned by their own state, these recruits drilled for Mr. Lincoln's army instead. They made up the First Virginia Volunteer Infantry—a United States regiment formed on Confederate soil.

Although residents of Ohio and Pennsylvania swelled their ranks, a large number hailed from the Virginia panhandle. At least one company, the "Iron Guards," came from the mills of Wheeling. These blue-collar Unionists did not look much like soldiers. They lacked uniforms and accouterments of any kind. The citizens of Wheeling had donated blankets, and each man clasped an old Springfield musket—courtesy of the state of Massachusetts—for the United States government was disinclined to send arms to Virginians.[128]

Colonel Benjamin Franklin Kelley led the First Virginia Volunteers. A native of New Hampshire, Kelley had spent much of his life in the Virginia panhandle. He was a tall and commanding fifty-four years of age, with rugged good looks, thick hair, shaggy brows, and a goatee. Kelley's erect carriage suggested a martial background; he was in fact a graduate of Vermont's celebrated Partridge Military Academy, and had once been an officer of Wheeling militia. He was employed as a freight agent for the Baltimore and Ohio Railroad in Philadelphia when war broke out. A call by Virginia residents brought the patriotic Kelley back to Wheeling, and there he took command of a Union regiment unique in every way.[129]

━━━━ ▲ ━━━━

Less than one hundred miles southeast, Confederate volunteers under Colonel George Porterfield gathered on the B&O Railroad at Fetterman, just outside of Grafton. The vital rail junction at Grafton gave Porterfield much concern. The town was poorly sited for defense, and its citizens were unsympathetic. Grafton was populated by immigrant Irish railroad laborers with little taste for secession. "I do not like the place," grumbled a Confederate recruit. "No cheers greet us here; no secession banners wave."[130]

Rumors of a plot to poison the Rebels swirled at Grafton. A bevy of young girls dressed in red, white, and blue were known to promenade there. Perhaps most repugnant of all was a large United States flag rippling over the main street. George Latham, temporary secretary of the Wheeling Convention, was responsible for that flag. Trading his pen for a sword, the twenty-nine-year-old attorney had raised a company of Union recruits known as the "Grafton Guards." He awaited only the May 23 vote on secession to offer their services to Federal authorities in Wheeling.[131]

Taunted by Captain Latham's banner, some two hundred Confederate volunteers under Captain John A. Robinson of the "Letcher Guards" marched into Grafton on May 22 to remove it. Among them was John Cammack: "As we were moving onto the west end of town we heard a tremendous noise of shouting which we thought was joy at our coming. It was not. Nearly the whole population was out on the streets, but they were not cheering. They were shouting and cursing and abusing us dreadfully."

Captain Robinson ordered two men to tear down the "damn rag." An outraged Unionist hurled a chair, knocking the captain from his horse. Robinson arose in a huff, about to give the order to fire when he spied Latham's men—on rooftops, at windows, and in doorways with guns leveled—ready to pour out a deadly volley. The perplexed Confederates fell back. Latham's flag was untouched.

As if on cue, that pesky bevy of girls appeared, waving little Union flags as they serenaded the passing Rebels. Defiantly, Captain Robinson halted his men. The angry crowd hissed and jeered. "We were held for about an hour on the platform of the old railroad hotel," recalled a terrified John Cammack, "and it seemed to me we had an officer for about every six men and all of them begging the men not to shoot. Practically the whole town was out in the street above us cursing and calling us ugly names. I think that was about the longest hour I ever spent."[132]

Bloodshed was averted—by a matter of hours.

That afternoon, two members of the Grafton Guards, Daniel Wilson and Thornsberry Bailey Brown, notified other Unionists in the area of Latham's imminent departure. Emboldened, Brown and Wilson returned by way of Confederate-occupied Fetterman. Near 9 P.M., they approached the intersection of the Northwestern Turnpike and the B & O Railroad on the edge of town.

"Halt," cried a sentinel from the darkness. Brown and Wilson could make out three figures—Captain Robinson's Confederates. A second warning rang out. The pair drew close enough to recognize Daniel Knight, a well-known troublemaker. Brown had once disarmed him in an ugly altercation, and Knight had vowed revenge. The thought of Daniel Knight blocking access to a public highway infuriated Brown.

"Damn him, what right has he to stop us," exclaimed Brown. He drew a revolver and fired—shearing the lobe from Knight's right ear. Knight staggered, leveled a flintlock musket, and discharged the contents into Brown's chest. Brown collapsed; blood poured from three gaping wounds near his heart. Wilson turned and fled.

Bailey Brown was dead—the first enlisted man in United States service to be killed by a Confederate soldier. His death on May 22, 1861, preceded by two days that of Union Colonel Elmer Ellsworth, the well-known Northern martyr shot down in Alexandria while removing a Confederate flag. Brown's blood-stained corpse was handed over to his friends and put on display at the Grafton Hotel. The event sparked a commotion. Hundreds came to view the fallen hero—and to vote in the long-awaited referendum on Virginia's Ordinance of Secession.[133]

To many citizens, the May 23 referendum was mere formality, a vote to legalize acts previously consummated in Richmond. Virginia had already formed an alliance with the Confederacy. But John Carlile, Frank Pierpont, George Latham, and other members of the Wheeling Central Committee encouraged Unionists to resist at the polls—to take a "firm, stern and decided stand" against the ordinance.

The election came off in relative calm, although it was influenced by soldiers' bayonets. Balloting was done by voice, a fact that likely kept many from expressing their true feelings. To no one's surprise, eastern Virginia counties overwhelmingly approved the Ordinance of Secession, while many western counties voted strongly against it. Governor Letcher gave the results as 125,950 to 20,373 in favor of secession, but admitted that returns from numerous western counties had not been received. The western vote was never fully ascertained. It was clearly divided; majorities for secession were later reported in the eleven western counties of Barbour, Braxton, Calhoun, Clay, Gilmer, Nicholas, Pocahontas, Randolph, Roane, Tucker, and Webster.[134]

In the wee hours after the referendum, Captain George Latham and his "Grafton Guards" flagged a train bound for Wheeling. On May 25, they were mustered into service as Company B, Second (U.S.) Virginia Volunteer Infantry—the first Union company recruited from Virginia's interior. Porterfield's Confederates occupied Grafton that same day.[135]

Confederate soldiers closed in on the Fairmont home of Frank Pierpont as he, too, hopped a train for Wheeling. There, members of the Central Committee chided him for missing the vote. "The time for voting is past," snapped Pierpont. "I move that Mr. Carlile be sent, at once, to Washington, to demand troops to drive the Rebels out of Western Virginia."

Carlile did just that, taking a train through Pennsylvania and Maryland to avoid trouble. He arrived at the White House late on May 24, left his card, and was soon called in to see the president.

"Well," Lincoln said, "Mr. Carlile, what is the best news in Western Virginia?"

"Sir, we want to fight. We have one regiment ready, and if the Federal Government is going to assist us we want it at once."

Lincoln replied softly, "You shall have assistance."[136]

━━━━ ▲ ━━━━

Winfield Scott cabled General McClellan on May 24: "We have certain intelligence that at least two companies of Virginia troops have reached Grafton, evidently with the purpose of overawing the friends of the Union in Western Virginia. Can you counteract the influence of that detachment?" From a military conference in Indiana, McClellan replied, "Will do what you want. Make it a clean sweep if you say so."[137]

Federal troops were loaded aboard railcars and dispatched to points on the Ohio River opposite Wheeling and Parkersburg. Spies kept the Confederates well informed of McClellan's movements. To contest the advance, Colonel Porterfield burned some railroad bridges. Under his orders, a squad of Confederates moved by rail on the night of May 25 to fire two wooden spans on the B&O Railroad between Mannington and Farmington, about thirty-five miles northwest of Grafton. Colonel William J. Willey led the bridge-burners. Confederate Colonel Willey's surname was no coincidence—he was the half-brother of staunch Unionist Waitman Willey.[138]

General McClellan was "maturing plans" at Camp Dennison on May 26 when he learned of the bridge burnings. Destruction of the railroad was an overt act of war. The vandals must be stopped, and loyal Unionists rescued from tyranny. McClellan's duty was clear—his army would invade Virginia.

Loyal Virginia regiments led the invasion. McClellan wired orders for Colonel Ben Kelley's First Virginia Infantry and Company A of the Second Virginia Infantry at Wheeling to move on Grafton. Kelley's objective was to restore damaged bridges and prevent further destruction of the railroad. He was to await reinforcements if substantial resistance was met. McClellan cautioned him to "run no unnecessary risk, for it is absolutely necessary that we should not meet even with a partial check at the onset." The Sixteenth Ohio Infantry, Colonel James Irvine commanding at Bellaire, Ohio, crossed the river as Kelley's support.

In concert with Kelley's advance from Wheeling, Colonel James Steedman's Fourteenth Ohio Infantry crossed the Ohio River at Parkersburg and boarded the Northwestern Virginia Railroad, bound east for Grafton. The Eighteenth Ohio Infantry and two guns of the First Ohio Light Artillery followed.[139]

To clarify the purpose of his invasion, General McClellan crafted an address to the troops. From the dining-room table of his Cincinnati home, with ladies chatting in the background, McClellan assumed the bombastic style of Napoleon:[140]

> *Soldiers!—You are ordered to cross the frontier and enter upon the soil of Virginia. Your mission is to restore peace and confidence, to protect the majesty of the law, and to rescue our brethren from the grasp of armed traitors. You are to act in concert with Virginia troops and to support their advance. I place under the safeguard of your honor, the persons and property of the Virginians....If you are called upon to overcome armed opposition, I know that your courage is equal to the task;—but remember that your only foes are the armed traitors....When, under your protection, the loyal men of Western Virginia have been enabled to organize and arm, they can protect themselves, and you can then return to your homes with the proud satisfaction of having saved a gallant people from destruction.[141]*

He also issued a proclamation to the people of Western Virginia:

Virginians!—The General Government has long enough endured the machinations of a few factious rebels in your midst. Armed traitors have in vain endeavored to deter you from expressing your loyalty at the polls...they now seek to inaugurate a rein of terror, and thus force you to yield to their schemes, and submit to the yoke of the traitorous conspiracy, dignified by the name of the Southern Confederacy. They are destroying the property of citizens of your State and ruining your magnificent railways.... The General Government cannot close its ears to the demand you have made for assistance. I have ordered troops to cross the Ohio River. They come as your friends and brothers,—as enemies only to the armed rebels who are preying upon you....Now, that we are in your midst, I call upon you to fly to arms and support the general government. Sever the connection that binds you to traitors; proclaim to the world that the faith and loyalty as long boasted by the Old Dominion, are still preserved in Western Virginia, and that you remain true to the stars and stripes.[142]

In his proclamation, McClellan assured slaveholders that any insurrection by their slaves would be crushed "with an iron hand." By those words, he publicly committed a Union army to protect slavery. No comment was forthcoming from Lincoln or his administration.[143]

The departure of Colonel Kelley's First (U.S.) Virginia Infantry in the early morning hours of May 27 brought out hundreds of Wheeling residents. The soldiers wore blue jeans and work clothes—Kelley's coat may have been the only piece of military garb in the regiment. In lieu of cartridge boxes, ammunition was stuffed into pockets. When the colonel ordered an inspection of arms, he was dismayed to learn that many had loaded their pieces backwards—placing the ball in the muzzle and ramming it down with the powder charge on top! The charges were carefully withdrawn, and the men instructed in the proper way to load and fire.[144]

Kelley commandeered the railroad telegraph office to preserve secrecy, but crowds of waving Virginians along the tracks proved there was little deception. Pressing on to the burned bridges over Buffalo Creek, Kelley's Federals were greeted by armed citizens who exposed a number of secessionists for arrest. The vandalized bridges proved to be of iron; flames had destroyed only the wooden sills and crossties. Repair crews set to work with a vengeance. Within forty-eight hours of departure, Kelley's men had secured the tracks to Fairmont.[145]

The Confederates at Grafton were thrown into a dither—the enemy was collecting in force on the railroad not twenty miles away. On May 28, with no hope of reinforcement, Colonel Porterfield ordered his 550 men to withdraw. News of the evacuation spurred Colonel Kelley forward. With a full brigade behind him, Kelley steamed into Grafton on the afternoon of May 30 without firing a shot.[146]

The advance from Parkersburg did not match Kelley's pace. Colonel Steedman's Fourteenth Ohio Infantry moved with all the caution McClellan had ordered. The Northwestern Virginia Railroad led them through a maze of wooded hills, deep cuts, and tunnels by the score—every turn a likely point of ambush. Vandalized bridges caused further delay. Steedman's force took four days to make the eighty-mile trip by rail, not reaching Clarksburg until the afternoon of May 30. The advance would have taken longer had not a dashing volunteer *aide-de-camp* named Frederick Lander intervened. When an Indiana colonel at Parkersburg refused to move his regiment for fear of a collision, Lander boarded the engine himself and reached Grafton on June 2 without incident.[147]

Cheered by the news, General McClellan cabled the War Department from his Cincinnati headquarters: "It is a source of very great satisfaction to me that we have occupied Grafton without the sacrifice of a single life." Next was to drive Rebel forces across the Alleghenies, freeing Western Virginia of their influence. McClellan fixed his gaze on Colonel Porterfield's Confederates, at a place called Philippi.[148]

PART II

FIRST CLASH
OF ARMIES

CHAPTER 6
THE PHILIPPI RACES

"And boom went the cannon balls, crashing through the huts and stirring out the rebels like a stick thrust into a hornet's nest."
—Whitelaw Reid, *Cincinnati Daily Gazette*

Philippi was a town with passionate ties to the Confederacy. It was located just fifteen miles south of the railroad at Grafton, on the Beverly-Fairmont Road, leading toward the heart of Virginia. Philippi was the Barbour County seat. Nestled in a romantic little valley, it was ordinarily a quiet place. But Colonel Porterfield's beleaguered Confederates made the town their headquarters, and General McClellan's army had come to drive them out. If Federal troops were to reclaim Western Virginia and rally her loyal Unionists, the Rebels at Philippi must go. By fate, Philippi was about to host the first land battle of the Civil War.[149]

A tedious ferry crossed the Tygart Valley River at Philippi until 1852, with construction of the Monarch of the River. The Monarch was a huge covered bridge. It was more than three hundred feet long, double-spanned, and fashioned almost entirely of wood—framed by massive, rough-hewn logs fitted and pegged in a sturdy arch pattern. A Beverly carpenter named Lemuel Chenoweth had erected the Monarch. He was a man with little formal education, but a natural genius in architecture. Chenoweth reportedly won his first bridge-building contract in a novel way. When the Virginia Board of Public Works invited engineers to submit plans for bridges on the Beverly-Fairmont Road, he journeyed nearly two hundred miles on horseback to Richmond. Packed in his saddlebags was a scale-model bridge of hickory wood.

At Richmond, Chenoweth watched elegant presentations by experts of the day, with sophisticated bridge models of cables and cantilevers. When finally called, the long-haired country carpenter rose and assembled his plain wooden model. He placed the completed little span between two chairs, stood on top, and walked its length. "Gentlemen, this is all I have to say," Chenoweth declared. It was enough to win the contract.

The Philippi covered bridge was a boon to transportation and a community landmark. Astonished youngsters who watched it take form later played around the veiled interior. Spying herds of cattle driven along the road to market, they would race inside the span, clamber up the broad wooden arches, and perch triumphantly while bawling animals crowded through below.[150]

But in the spring of 1861, there was a feeling of greater excitement. Young men who had once frolicked inside the Monarch now joined Confederate soldiers gathering in its shadow at Philippi. A "Palmetto" flag, raised in sympathy to South Carolina's departure from the Union, had flown over the courthouse since January. Philippi was proud of its reputation as "the strongest secession town in Western Virginia."[151]

Taking Philippi as his headquarters, Colonel George Porterfield appealed for Confederate recruits. His broadsides pledged to shield the people from "invasion by foreign forces," called on them to "Strike for your State! Strike for your liberties! Rally! Rally at once in defense of your mother!" But the colonel's pleas drew limited numbers—a ragtag gaggle of volunteers. Many of the recruits were mere boys. One company, the "Upshur Grays," had just four members older than twenty-three years of age; their captain, John Higginbotham, was only eighteen.[152]

These young Confederates sorely lacked the tools of war. Most carried old flintlock or converted muskets; a few had no weapons at all. There was little ammunition, about five cartridges per man. Unable to equip two volunteer horse companies, Colonel Porterfield reluctantly sent them home. "The exaggerated idea went forth that an army was in our midst," declared one Confederate at Philippi.[153]

An ordnance officer was detailed to scavenge for gunpowder. Lead pipe was pulled up and melted into bullets. The volunteers rolled homemade cartridges and cleaned rusty muskets. As wildflowers bloomed and spring foliage filled the hillsides, a force of about six hundred infantry and one hundred seventy-five horse soldiers gathered at Philippi.[154]

The Confederates had few tents. Most lodged in the courthouse and dwellings around town. Meals were often taken with the citizens. "Philippi was a pandemonium," recalled one soldier. "No order, our drill foolishness. The whole thing a holiday, full of disorder, uproar, speeches and intense excitement." This sad state of affairs did not inspire confidence in Colonel Porterfield's ability to command. One soldier described him as "a polished Virginia gentleman, but as ignorant of war as a mule is of the Ten Commandments."[155]

Porterfield's officers routinely took "French leave," coming and going as they pleased. Captain Daniel Stofer, a corpulent Pocahontas County attorney, was known for speechmaking. One fine evening, Stofer led his "Pocahontas Rescues" onto the courthouse lawn and began to regale the crowd. Nattily dressed in a black, long-tailed coat, he was plum-faced and jovial: "Many a cup of good cheer had evidently been tendered him by patriotic hands." In a booming voice, "Count" Stofer promised to thrash any Unionists who might be foolish enough to appear. "Gentlemen," he exclaimed, "I could take a peach tree switch and whip all of Lincoln's 75,000 Yankees if they invade Virginia."[156]

════ ▲ ════

A peach tree switch was needed, for on the evening of June 1, trains bearing more than two thousand Indiana volunteers rolled into Grafton, less than a day's march from Philippi. At their head was Union General Thomas A. Morris, a stolid man, grave in countenance and demeanor. Morris was an able soldier, West Point class of 1834, modest and steady. Like McClellan, he had been a railroad president, called back as a brigadier general of Indiana volunteers. For most of his five decades, Morris had been an avid hunter. Now as the ranking officer in Western Virginia, he prepared to track down the Rebels.[157]

Morris arrived to find Colonel Kelley readying an attack on Philippi. Taking Kelley into a council of war, he embellished the plan as a two-pronged movement—adding the newly arrived regiments to entrap Porterfield's command. He also added the fickle element of timing.

On June 2, Colonel Kelley led two Federal columns against the enemy. Each consisted of about fifteen hundred men, traveling south on opposite banks of the Tygart Valley River. Kelley's column boarded an eastbound train at Grafton around 9 A.M., reportedly bound for Harpers Ferry. Just six miles out at Thornton, however, Kelley's First Virginia, the Ninth Indiana, and six companies of the Sixteenth Ohio Infantry left that train and marched for Philippi, twenty-two miles south on "a road but little traveled."[158]

Colonel Ebenezer Dumont, sallow, dyspeptic, and rather eccentric, led the second column. Dumont's piping voice gave him a whimsical air, but he was a capable former Indiana legislator and Mexican War veteran. His march on the Beverly-Fairmont Road to Philippi would be just twelve miles, under cover of night. At 8:30 that evening, Dumont's Seventh Indiana Infantry took a train six miles west, left the cars at Webster, and joined five companies of the Fourteenth Ohio Infantry, six companies of the Sixth Indiana Infantry, and two guns of the First Ohio Light Artillery for the assault.

Dumont's orders were to engage the Rebels at dawn—just as Kelley cut off their southern retreat on the Beverly-Fairmont

Road. The two Federal columns were to arrive in Philippi at precisely 4 A.M. on June 3. If all went according to plan, Porterfield's Confederates wouldn't have a prayer.[159]

The Federals began their first march of the war. Drizzling rain soon turned into a downpour. The night was pitch black. Soldiers traced their progress by the steady flashes of lightning. The raging storm turned narrow country roads into slippery quagmires. Troops slogged over hill and vale, bent against the pounding rain.

An eerie red light glowed at the head of Colonel Dumont's column, emanating from a large ruby lantern carried by Lieutenant Benjamin Ricketts to guide the men. Ricketts had protested the order—that light would signal the enemy! He "didn't want a record in history as the first man killed." But the Confederates in Philippi already knew that something was astir.[160]

Two young Fairmont lasses, Abbie Kerr and Mollie McLeod, had counted the number of soldier-filled railroad cars passing their town. Estimating that five thousand Federal troops were bound for Grafton, the beguiling pair rode at dawn on June 2 to warn Porterfield's Confederates. Their arrival sparked a sensation in Philippi. Citizens scurried about, piled belongings into wagons, and rode away in droves. Colonel Porterfield ordered his men to "be ready to move on a moment's notice." He then called a council of war.[161]

Rain slammed against the windows at headquarters as Confederate officers expressed their desire to fall back. But Colonel Porterfield urged delay. He spoke of the thirty-mile march to Beverly through that withering storm—a punishing ordeal that would break down green troops and ruin meager supplies. It seemed best to wait out the tempest. No army would be out on such a night.

Colonel Porterfield chose to await the dawn. To avoid surprise, his cavalry would scout the approaches to Philippi. An officer of the day would post sentinels around the town. In the carnival atmosphere there, guard duty had been neglected in the past—the colonel himself had found sentinels asleep at their posts.

It so happened that Captain Stofer was officer of the day as Federal troops converged on Philippi. Unfortunately for the Confederates, Stofer must have been hard at the bottle. Around 9 P.M., a sentinel observed him weaving about, stammering, and highly animated. Nothing more was seen of him that night.[162]

Meanwhile, the sentinels kept watch in a drenching rain. Their ammunition, stuffed into wet coat pockets in lieu of cartridge boxes, was soon rendered useless. The rain poured down with a vengeance. As midnight approached, the sodden sentinels and cavalrymen left their posts for dry beds. "Hell," exclaimed one Confederate as he took shelter, "any army marching tonight must be made up of a set of damned fools!"[163]

▲

Out in raven darkness on the Beverly-Fairmont Road, Colonel Ebenezer Dumont scowled at his watch. The mud-spattered Federal column trailing him was behind schedule, nearly five miles from Philippi, with little more than an hour to make up the distance. Colonel Dumont gave orders to quicken the pace. Weary soldiers fainted and collapsed by the roadside.

Dumont had one comfort: leading his column was Frederick W. Lander, a man hungry for adventure. Lander was a thirty-nine-year-old Massachusetts native, robust, flamboyant, and absolutely fearless. His looks and temperament were that of a grizzly bear. Lander was a renowned transcontinental explorer. Among his many adventures was the Pacific Railroad Survey of 1853. When a young lieutenant named George McClellan declined to cross the snow-blanketed Cascade Mountains, Lander had forged ahead on his own. He later married British actress Jean Davenport, the Shirley Temple of her day.

Lander was a romantic poet—as happy lecturing on the fine arts as he was to duel with Bowie knives. When war came, his offer to serve McClellan "in any capacity, at any time, and for any duty" without rank or pay, was gladly accepted. Lander became a volunteer *aide-de-camp*, holding only the honorary title of "Colonel" as he charged through the darkness toward Philippi.[164]

Colonel Kelley could have used Lander on his own march. Kelley's route was far longer than Dumont's, and despite leaving hours ahead, he too was behind schedule. Kelley's guide, a woodsman named Jacob Baker, led the column astray at a narrow crossroads east of Philippi. As Baker followed the right fork, Kelley—sensing treachery—ordered Colonel Robert Milroy's Ninth Indiana Infantry to take the left fork—one that presumably would come out on the Beverly-Fairmont Road south of Philippi, square across the Confederate line of escape.[165]

Meanwhile, Colonel Dumont's column was fast closing on Philippi. Less than two miles from town, the First Ohio Light Artillery wheeled to the front. Lander guided them to the crest of Talbott Hill, an eminence overlooking the sleepy village. Dense fog obscured the town as two bronze six-pounders were unlimbered and rolled into position. Now Lander waited for dawn, for Kelley's arrival, and for a shot signaling the artillery to open fire. Lander disliked waiting; it went against his very nature. He began to pace behind the guns, taunted by a row of white tents visible through the mist below.[166]

Ironically, a woman fired the first shot. As Colonel Dumont's infantry marched by a house on the way to Lander, their clatter awoke an elderly secessionist, Mrs. Thomas Humphreys. Mrs. Humphreys eyed the shiny brass "U.S." buckles on their belts with great concern, for she had a son in Colonel Porterfield's army. Quickly saddling a horse, she placed her twelve-year-old boy Oliver aboard and sent him off to warn the Confederates. Dumont's men promptly pulled the youth from his mount. Mrs. Humphreys rushed from the house, throwing rocks and sticks until the soldiers released her child. She lifted Oliver back into the saddle, but they snatched him off again. Mrs. Humphreys drew a pistol from her bosom and fired.

That harmless shot caught Colonel Lander's attention. Still pacing along the brow of Talbott Hill, he impatiently watched the break of dawn. The rain had eased. A veil of fog lifted from the valley below. The town of Philippi was now visible—the courthouse, the meandering river, the sturdy Monarch, and that beckoning row of tents. Where was Kelley? The hour to attack was past. Movement could be seen on the streets—the Rebels were beginning to stir.

Lander swept the hills with a spyglass as Mrs. Humphreys's echoing pistol shot reached his ears. It wasn't the long-awaited signal, but it was close enough. Lander snapped erect and roared the order for which those anxious cannoneers had been waiting—"Fire!"[167]

A young immigrant named Lewis Fahrion discharged the first bronze gun, landing a ball squarely among the white tents five hundred yards below. As the cannons opened, Colonel Dumont's infantry stormed down a winding road toward the covered bridge. "Close up, boys! Close up!" Dumont squealed as they ran. "If the enemy were to shoot now, they couldn't hit one of you!" Colonel Kelley's men could be seen on a hillside just across the river—fifteen minutes behind, and on the wrong end of town. As the six-pounders boomed, Kelley's men dashed forward, "yelling like fiends incarnate."[168]

The Confederates were taken completely by surprise—jolted from bed by the novel sound of artillery. Some thought it was musketry from their own pickets. "There's a man who's not afraid to burn powder," marveled one Southerner as the cannons roared.[169]

Confederate soldiers rushed into the streets. Balls dropped among the tents as cavalrymen tumbled out, scrambling to catch loose horses. "Out they swarmed, like bees from a molested hive," wrote an Ohio gunner. "This way and that the chivalry flew, and yet scarcely knew which way to run." Men and horses bolted up Main Street, "almost trampling each other in their efforts to get away." It was a "genuine shirt-tail retreat."[170]

"I never saw such a sight before in my life," marveled a Federal soldier. They fled "pell-mell helter skelter without boots, hats, coats or pants." One poor fellow was seen hopping along with one leg in his breeches. Trying to dress on the fly, he lost his balance and ended up face down in the street. Teamsters cut horses loose from the wagons and galloped off "for dear life."[171]

As the Confederates stampeded out of Philippi, Kelley's Virginians poured in. Their entry was symbolic—"loyal" Virginians in pursuit of their "traitorous" brothers. All the commotion finally aroused Colonel Porterfield, who gamely tried to rally his men. "Where are those soldiers fleeing to?" he cried in vain as the street emptied. "Halt them!"[172]

Atop Talbott Hill, Colonel Lander watched the drama unfold. He chafed in the saddle as Dumont's men surged through the covered bridge below. The winding road into town was jammed with troops, but Lander could not stand idle. Putting spurs to his horse, the intrepid Lander plunged down the steep hillside "at a breakneck gallop." Wide-mouthed cannoneers peered over the brink as he leaped a fence and thundered into the bridge, hard on the heels of charging Federal infantry. "Lander's ride" was declared a singular feat of daring and horsemanship.[173]

Colonel Ben Kelley joined Lander in the charge through Philippi. Riding at a full gallop, Kelley pulled a pistol and shot at the fleeing Rebels—until he toppled from his horse with a bullet through the breast. A crowd of Federal soldiers rushed to Kelley's aid, surrounding a burly Confederate quartermaster named William Sims as he cowered behind a wagon, still clutching an old-fashioned horse pistol. "This is the man who shot our Colonel!" cried one as they prepared to spit him with bayonets.

Colonel Lander rode up and ordered them to desist. "This man is a prisoner of war, and to kill him is murder," Lander shouted. "Go after the enemy." He directed the soldiers to carry their badly wounded colonel into a nearby house. Just about then, Colonel Milroy's Ninth Indiana Regiment appeared on a hill overlooking Philippi, too late to cut off the last Confederates streaming down the road to Beverly, thirty miles southeast.[174]

Of the retreat—775 Confederates fleeing before Kelley's force of nearly three thousand men—Virginian John Cammack wrote, "[T]here was nothing left for us to do but to get out of town quickly. We would all have been captured that day were it not for the fact that the flanking columns missed their way and the attack on our flank and rear was not made."[175]

Most of the Confederates regained their composure and retreated in good order. A few never looked back. Citizens along the way testified that "brave cavaliers came up to their doors begging for pairs of breeches to cover their nakedness." Captain Stofer escaped in the bed of a wagon, deathly pale and vomiting. The rest of Colonel Porterfield's band spilled into Beverly that evening, jaded from the long retreat.[176]

Colonel Kelley's men were too exhausted from their all-night march to pursue them. Without cavalry, the Federals were content to halt at Philippi and claim victory. "I must confess that I never saw a flight...executed with more despatch," Colonel Dumont offered in tribute to the departed Rebels. "They're not much for fight, but the devil on a run!" A new term was coined; those panic-stricken Confederates had not just bolted out of town—they had "skedaddled." Kelley's troops dubbed it "The Philippi Races."[177]

Dumont wistfully added that the Rebels had scampered off so fast, "but little execution could be done." The artillery hurled only about six rounds. A scattered volley and some random shots of musketry were thrown in for good measure. Nobody was killed, save an Indiana volunteer who slipped on a log and accidentally shot himself during the night march.[178]

That didn't stop the extravagant body counts. General Morris estimated "from fifteen to forty" Confederate dead. Not to be outdone, a Confederate reported that the Yankees had cannonaded their own men by mistake—nearly one hundred new graves covered the ground in Philippi! "It is very certain that somebody was hurt, and right badly too," a Wheeling reporter weighed in. "A leg, which had been torn off by a cannonball, was picked up in the camp. There was a great deal of blood upon the ground, and all along the road in the direction of the flight."

In fact, there were a grand total of five wounded Federals, two crippled Confederates, and a handful of prisoners at Philippi.

Members of the First Virginia Infantry accounted for all the Union wounded. Most notable was Colonel Kelley himself.[179]

A large pistol ball felled Kelley. Indiana private Ambrose Bierce described the wound as "spang through the breast, a hole that you could have put two fingers in. And, bless my soul! how it bled!" Dr. George New of the Seventh Indiana Infantry gravely pronounced the wound a mortal one. "I expect I shall have to die," Kelley replied stoically. General McClellan fired off a telegram from Cincinnati upon learning the news: "Say to Colonel Kelley that I cannot believe it possible that one who has opened his course so brilliantly can be mortally wounded....If it can cheer him in his last moments tell him I cannot repair his loss and I only regret that I cannot be by his side to thank him in person. God bless him."

Even as newspapers reported his death, Ben Kelley was making a dramatic recovery. McClellan happily recommended a promotion. Sixty days after his wounding, Kelley would be back on duty with a new brigadier general's star.[180]

Unlike Kelley, two Confederate cavalrymen were shot down in relative obscurity. The unclaimed leg reported at Philippi must have belonged to James E. Hanger, an eighteen-year-old member of the Churchville Cavalry. Billeted in the hayloft of the Garrett Johnson barn, Hanger was awakened by the first blasts of Federal cannon fire. At the third fire, a six-pound solid shot crashed through the barn, struck a post, and ricocheted upward, shattering his left leg. The horrified youth pulled himself back into the loft and lay there until discovered.

Hanger was carried to the Philippi Methodist Episcopal Church, where Dr. James Robison of the Sixteenth Ohio Infantry cut off his mangled limb about seven inches below the hip—without benefit of anesthesia. It was the first amputation of the war.[181]

Captain Fauntleroy Daingerfield was "honored" with the second. Although badly wounded in the knee by a musket ball, he managed to escape. At the Logan house in Beverly, Dr. John Huff removed Daingerfield's splintered leg with a butcher knife and carpenter's saw, the only instruments on hand. While both victims recuperated, the inventive James Hanger used a penknife and barrel staves to devise an artificial leg. It worked so splendidly that Hanger would later make wooden limbs for Captain Daingerfield and other Confederate amputees.[182]

At Philippi, gleeful Federals rounded up the spoils of war. Kelley's men proudly displayed Colonel Porterfield's large headquarters flag. Another captured banner had been trampled in the retreat—dirty boot marks upon it were pointed out with great amusement. Philippi, long a hotbed of secession, was to be punished. Federal soldiers occupied fine abandoned homes. Furnishings were wrecked, shutters and railings burned. The Stars and Stripes now floated over that former "Secession hole."[183]

Soldiers raided the Bank of Philippi and blew a safe, but found it empty. Another target was the office of *The Barbour Jeffersonian*, a secessionist tabloid. Unable to find the publisher, the Federals smashed his printing press and cast the type into a well. They did find Colonel William J. Willey at Philippi, sick in bed with typhoid fever. Willey masqueraded as his Unionist half-brother Waitman—until a Confederate commission and some incriminating letters were uncovered regarding the "bridge-burning business." He was then placed under arrest.[184]

From headquarters more than three hundred miles west in Cincinnati, General McClellan labeled Philippi a "decisive engagement," the "most brilliant episode of the war thus far." Newspaper columns fueled the drama—Philippi was deemed the first "land battle" of the war. Word of the little skirmish created a "lively sensation" in Washington. Ignored was the fact that Colonel Porterfield's Confederates had escaped to fight another day.[185]

A reporter named Whitelaw Reid thought the Philippi affair had impact beyond numbers. Tall, longhaired, graceful, and intelligent, the twenty-four-year-old Reid was a crack journalist. The *Cincinnati Daily Gazette* hired him to follow Ohio troops into Western Virginia. There were as yet no provisions for war correspondents, but Reid used connections to secure a position with General Morris, a former printer himself. Reid was designated a volunteer aide and given a sword, fatigue cap, and a tent at headquarters.[186]

"It is impossible to convey any adequate idea of the spirit which animates our soldiers here," penned Reid. Raw recruits strutted around Philippi like veterans. "Only ninety six hours before, we had left Indianapolis....Now, we were in rebeldom," boasted a veteran of the affair. "I feel all right, and have come to the conclusion that I can stand almost anything, and go through any privation. I have seen the elephant!"

Newsman Reid believed they had determined the fate of Western Virginia. "The people had been deceived and inflamed by the grossest exaggerations and positive falsehoods," he wrote. "A single success of the rebel army would have fanned to an instant flame all the concealed sparks of disunion...and we would have had to fight [all of] Western Virginia....A majority was with us before, but their faith has been strengthened, the doubtful have been confirmed, and almost hopeless reprobates have been converted into loyal citizens since we 'met them at Philippi.'"[187]

CHAPTER 7
LET THIS LINE BE
DRAWN BETWEEN US

*"There is no man within the limits of this State that is more thoroughly
convinced than I am...of the necessity of this separation.
There is no power on earth that can prevent it."*

—John Carlile, Virginia Unionist

Steamboats chugged across the Ohio River. Packed aboard were
Federal soldiers of Indiana and Ohio, in bright new uniforms of
wool and burnished brass. They were bound for Western
Virginia—the seat of war.

Loyal Virginians mustered into service to join them. Many
would guard the vital Baltimore and Ohio Railroad—General
McClellan's lifeline into Western Virginia. A scarcity of wagons and
teams made it difficult to move far beyond the rails. The troops
remained idle at Philippi for more than a month. Bemoaned
Whitelaw Reid, "[I]t is certain that had the reinforcements and
supplies...been sent forward...at the proper time, our forces,
instead of lying at Philippi...would have driven every rebel in arms
[out of] Northwestern Virginia."[188]

Meanwhile, Federal soldiers picked wild strawberries and
roamed the hills in quest of the elusive secessionists—now known
derisively as "secesh." They viewed the land, if not its people, with

favor. "We are in the midst of a most splendid country," marveled an Ohio soldier. "The Tygart's is indeed a beautiful valley," wrote another, "nestling under the shelter of the Alleghenies, and hemmed in by crested mountains covered with rich forests of oak, chestnut, pine, beech, and a score of other varieties."[189]

The scenery intoxicated a young private named Ambrose Bierce. One of ten children—all with names beginning with the letter "A"— the nineteen-year-old Bierce possessed a tall, muscular frame, squarish jaw, deep-set blue eyes, and undulating golden hair. To escape work as an Elkhart, Indiana, grocery and restaurant clerk, he had joined the Ninth Indiana Infantry. Bierce had a keen eye and a gifted pen—traits that would become his calling. "Nine in ten of us had never seen a mountain, nor a hill as high as a church spire, until we had crossed the Ohio River," he later wrote. "In power upon the emotions nothing, I think, is comparable to a first sight of mountains."[190]

A mustachioed, pipe-smoking youth in his mid-twenties named William B. Fletcher was more captivated by the ladies. Schooled at Harvard and the New York College of Physicians and Surgeons, Fletcher had been outmaneuvered for a medical appointment in the Sixth Indiana Infantry. Unable to find another vacancy, he had reluctantly claimed the post of fife major in that regiment. Dr. Fletcher had no gift for music, but more compelling duty was to come his way.

As the train bearing Fletcher shuddered to a halt near Grafton, young women scurried forward. Wearing pretty white dresses and hand-sewn aprons bearing the Stars and Stripes, they presented bouquets of flowers to soldiers aboard the cars. Fletcher spied a black-haired beauty and called for her apron. Beaming to the flirtatious doctor, she handed over a "very tastefully made up" creation. The design was unique. A Union shield was prominent, and in the center was a single large star—cut neatly in two. One half was labeled "Eastern Va.," the other, "Western Va."[191]

▲

On June 11—eight days after the "Philippi Races"—Virginia Unionists gathered in a second convention at Wheeling to debate the rending of that star. Attending were more than one hundred representatives from thirty-two western counties. Delegates from the eastern Virginia counties of Alexandria and Fairfax had also crossed the mountains to take part. Nearly one third of Virginia's voting population was represented. Duly-elected members of the General Assembly were seated if known to be loyal to the Union, others were chosen by petition.[192]

News-hawk Whitelaw Reid canvassed the delegates as they arrived. "There appears to be no doubt among the leaders," he wrote, "that the Convention will take measures for the immediate establishment of a Provisional State Government that will at once form the nucleus around which the Union men of Virginia may rally. It seems scarcely probable that anything beyond this movement can be accomplished by the Convention, though the feeling for the separation of Western Virginia from the Eastern portion and the formation of a new State is undeniably very strong and constantly strengthening."[193]

The convention was held in open defiance of the Richmond authorities. Officials in many counties sought to repress it. Each delegate took an oath to support the Constitution of the United States—"anything in the Ordinances of the Convention which assembled in Richmond, on the 13th of February last, to the contrary notwithstanding."

Parkersburg attorney Arthur I. Boreman was chosen as president. However, John Carlile and Frank Pierpont were the linchpins of the second Wheeling convention. Waitman Willey, the law- and-order Unionist from Morgantown, was conspicuously absent; both his father and stepmother were seriously ill.[194]

The flamboyant Carlile, chair of the powerful committee on business, offered resolutions of thanks to General McClellan for rescuing the people of Western Virginia and to Colonel Kelley, "Western Virginia's loyal son," for his service and sacrifice. Carlile's passion for a "New Virginia" had not cooled, but Article IV,

Section 3 of the U.S. Constitution loomed as a stumbling block: "no new State shall be formed or erected within the Jurisdiction of any other State...without the Consent of the Legislatures of the States concerned as well as of Congress." The Richmond legislature would never consent to a division of the state; therefore the plan outlined by Frank Pierpont at the First Wheeling Convention guided the delegates.

A *new* Virginia government would be created. All state offices would be declared vacant, the traitors thrown out by proxy and Union men appointed in their place. Loyal Unionists would claim the political framework of a state already recognized by the Federal government—thereby courting favor with a Lincoln administration not anxious to deal with the Rebels. Lincoln himself held the constitutional authority to determine which of two competing parties was the lawful state government. An 1849 Supreme Court case in Rhode Island—*Luther vs. Borden*—had set the precedent.

Once Federal recognition was gained, a "restored" Virginia government could legally accede to the creation of a new state. The strategy was fraught with risk, but even statehood hard-liners saw its virtue.[195]

On June 13, the convention moved to Wheeling's United States Custom House. Inside its magnificent U.S. courtroom, John Carlile reported a "Declaration of Rights of the People of Virginia." Like the declaration of 1776, this document was revolutionary—it charged secessionists with "usurping" the powers of the people of Virginia, forcing them to wage war against the United States, and attempting to subvert the Union to an "illegal confederacy of rebellious States." The Richmond government had failed to protect the rights of the people; therefore it was "the duty of the latter to abolish it."

All acts of the Richmond convention were repealed. All state offices held by secessionists were declared vacant. On June 14, "An Ordinance for the Re-organization of the State Government" directed the convention to elect a governor, lieutenant governor, and a five-member governor's council. A rump legislature, consisting of loyal Unionists elected to Virginia's General Assembly on May 23, would be formed.[196]

Die-hard advocates continued to pursue statehood, but John Carlile skillfully parried them. "In relation to this thing of dividing," he retorted, "I find that even I, who first started the little stone down the mountain, have now to apply the rubbers to other gentlemen who have outrun me in the race, to check their impetuosity."

"Now Sir, let us pursue the policy laid down in the Declaration," Carlile said, "and let us repudiate Letcher and his transfer; let us assemble a Legislature here...and let that Legislature be recognized by the United States Government as *the* Legislature of Virginia....Give us that recognition, and then the separation will come." Then might Western Virginians demand of their brothers and sisters over the mountains, "Let this line be drawn between us."[197]

On June 17, Frank Pierpont made a tone-setting speech prior to a vote on the "Declaration of Rights." Pierpont called their plan the "brightest scheme" for loyal Virginians, one that could be used as a model for other seceded states. He assured the delegates that President Lincoln and the Congress would recognize theirs as the "rightful government" of Virginia. The Declaration of Rights was then approved by a vote of fifty-six to zero. John Carlile hailed it as an omen—there had also been fifty-six signers to the Declaration of Independence.[198]

Delegates voted to adopt the Reorganization Ordinance on June 19. They signed the Declaration of Rights in solemn ritual, added the phrase "Liberty and Union" to Virginia's state seal and proudly forwarded copies to Washington. The "Restored Government" of Virginia was born.[199]

Frank Pierpont was unaminously elected governor the next day. Governor Pierpont began his term with few trappings of rank. His office consisted of a vacant room in the Custom House. A bare table, half quire of paper, pen, and ink were his only furnishings. A friend remarked that he might be the first public official ever to "thank men for putting a rope around his neck."

Pierpont addressed a letter to President Lincoln, writing of events at Wheeling, of the crisis in Virginia, and of the need for Federal troops to maintain law and order. He signed that letter "F.H. Pierpont, Governor of Virginia."[200]

Few American executives ever faced Governor Pierpont's dilemma. The Restored Government had little real authority. Secessionists remained in control of most state and local offices. There were bills to be paid, yet Pierpont's government had no money. Early on the morning of June 24, he sought to withdraw five thousand dollars apiece from two Wheeling banks. When a cashier balked, Pierpont explained the risk in his matter-of-fact way: "If my government succeeds you are sure of your money. If it does not succeed, your money is not worth a bubble." He secured the loans and went on to reap more than $41,000 in Federal notes that Virginia had neglected to appropriate.

Pierpont's fund-raising was capped by a spectacular raid on $27,000 in gold. The Exchange Bank of Weston held that treasure trove, deposited by the state to pay for construction of a "Lunatic Asylum." When rumors reached Pierpont of intentions by that *other* governor of Virginia to seize the gold, he sent John List of Wheeling to claim it for the Restored Government. Colonel Erastus B. Tyler's Seventh Ohio Infantry accompanied List to Weston, snapped up the gold, and escorted it to Clarksburg in a hearse. It was the heaviest guarded "funeral" procession ever seen in Western Virginia.[201]

The Second Wheeling Convention adjourned on June 25, 1861. In twelve days of debate, Virginia Unionists had sketched out a new state government. They would reconvene on August 6 to take up the issue deftly sidestepped—creation of a new state.[202]

A dispatch from Secretary of War Simon Cameron soon brought cherished news to Wheeling. "The President," wrote Cameron, "never supposed that a brave and free people, though surprised and unarmed, could long be subjugated by a class of political adventurers always adverse to them, and the fact that they have already rallied, reorganized their government, and checked the march of these invaders demonstrates how justly he appreciated them."

The letter was addressed to "Hon. Francis H. Pierpont, Governor of the State of Virginia." It was tacit Federal recognition of the Restored Government.[203]

Chapter 8
A Dreary-Hearted General

"I don't anticipate anything very brilliant—
indeed I shall esteem myself fortunate if I escape disaster."
—Robert S. Garnett, C.S.A.

Alarming dispatches poured into Richmond from over the mountains. "The affair at Philippi was a disgraceful surprise," General Robert E. Lee was notified. "The only wonder is that our men were not cut to pieces." Colonel Porterfield's Confederates had fled to Huttonsville, a crossroads hamlet about forty miles south of Philippi. They were not to be blamed for running, insisted one officer. What he blamed them for was that "they didn't stop running when the Yankees stopped."

Virginian John Cammack spoke for many of those demoralized Confederates: "It seems to me that if Colonel Porterfield had set out to help McClellan he could not have done it any more successfully than he did." A respected officer informed Lee, "I am pained to have to express my conviction that Colonel Porterfield is entirely unequal to the position which he occupies."[204]

A court of inquiry charged Porterfield with negligence. However, General Lee ruled out court-martial proceedings. He considered the inquiry punishment enough—hoping "that the sad effects produced by the want of forethought and vigilance…in this case," would be "a lesson to be remembered by the army throughout the war."[205]

Lee faced trials of his own. A June 8 proclamation by the governor handed Virginia's military forces over to the Confederate States and terminated Lee's duty as general-in-chief. Overnight, he became a brigadier general in the Confederate army—the highest rank then existing—but an officer without assignment. Lee remained in Richmond as a personal advisor to Confederate President Jefferson Davis. The dignified president, a longtime friend, supported him with "unqualified confidence."[206]

Something had to be done for Western Virginia before the entire region was lost. In that spirit, Lee turned to his adjutant, Robert Garnett, the only qualified officer not already in the field, and one of the most capable in the Confederacy.

Robert Selden Garnett was forty-one years old, just under six feet tall, trim, and stern. His hair was nearly coal black, worn long on the neck in a style popular with Virginia's elite. His closely cropped beard was slightly grizzled with white. His forehead was high and arching, his darkly handsome features "almost classic in their regularity and mingled delicacy."[207]

Garnett's pedigree was rich in arms and aristocracy. His ancestors included a French general, a countess, and a major general in the War of 1812. His father was a five-term Virginia Congressman, his cousin the personal physician of Jefferson Davis.

Garnett's résumé was stellar. He had graduated at West Point, class of 1841, and served as an instructor of tactics. As an aide to General Zachary Taylor in the Mexican War, he had been twice brevetted for gallantry. In 1849, while shipwrecked during an important mission to California, he designed the state's Great Seal. Garnett returned to West Point as commandant of cadets under Robert E. Lee. In 1857, he married a fair-haired New York socialite named Marianna Nelson and escorted her to Fort Simcoe, Washington Territory.

But Garnett's happiness was short-lived. Returning from an expedition the next year, he found Marianna and an infant son dead of "bilious fever." Described as proud, reserved, and "cold as an icicle," Garnett became "more frozen and stern and isolated than ever." He buried his family, took extended leave, and returned to duty in a Confederate uniform—as adjutant general of Virginia forces.[208]

The army became his life. "In every one else," a fellow officer remarked, "I have seen some mere human traits, but in Garnett every trait was purely military." A future general described him as "brave, intelligent, impartial...truthful and full of energy." That talent was badly needed in Western Virginia—Garnett received a brigadier's star and was sent into the mountains. But he remained a "dreary-hearted man." The night before Garnett left Richmond, a staff officer heard him utter, "They have not given me an adequate force. I can do nothing. They have sent me to my death."[209]

The scene at Huttonsville must have mortified the spit-and-polish Garnett. There he found twenty-three Confederate companies "in a most miserable condition as to arms, clothing, equipment and discipline." From them he formed two regiments—the Twenty-fifth Virginia Infantry, led by Lt. Colonel Jonathan Heck, a Morgantown attorney, and the Thirty-first Virginia Infantry, headed by Lt. Colonel William L. Jackson, a former lieutenant governor of Virginia, with the remainder filling Lt. Colonel George Hansbrough's Ninth Virginia Battalion.[210]

Garnett's directive was to halt the Federal advance into Virginia. He hoped as well to strike the B&O Railroad, an important east-west Union supply line. General Lee's desire had been succinct: "The rupture of the railroad at Cheat River would be worth to us an army."

Two mountain passes were the keys to Garnett's defense—one on the Staunton-Parkersburg Turnpike over Rich Mountain, another sixteen miles north on the Beverly-Fairmont Road at Laurel Hill. He called them the "gates to the northwestern country."

On June 15, Garnett marched north. Lt. Colonel Heck's Twenty-fifth Virginia Infantry, two guns, and a squad of cavalry seized the pass over Rich Mountain. The next day Garnett occupied Laurel Hill with the Thirty-first Virginia Infantry, a company of cavalry and six pieces of artillery. His first impression was disappointing; the pass at Laurel Hill was "not so formidable" as he had been told.

Rich Mountain offered more promising terrain. The Staunton-Parkersburg Turnpike wound through a narrow defile at the mountain's western base. Garnett believed a fortified detachment there should be able to hold back "five times their number." On the slopes, Confederate soldiers built fortifications as he watched. "General Garnett has the confidence of everybody," wrote Lt. Colonel Heck, "He is the very man for the Northwest." In his honor, the works at Rich Mountain were named "Camp Garnett."[211]

Returning to Laurel Hill, the general established headquarters. His tenuous supply line stretched more than one hundred turnpike miles over the mountains to Staunton. Garnett barricaded roads along his flanks and sent out heavy escorts to gather forage as the troops dug in. He found it difficult to obtain reliable intelligence. "The enemy are kept fully advised of our movements...by the country people," he complained, "while we are compelled to grope in the dark as much as if we were invading a foreign country."

Garnett put the volunteers under rigorous drill and instruction. While standing guard one dark night, John Cammack halted Major Joseph Chenoweth, son of the Philippi bridge builder. The two engaged in pleasantries until Chenoweth asked to handle Cammack's musket. When Cammack refused, Chenoweth stormed off in anger. Cammack was relieved to learn he had acted properly; the major had received the arms of two other pickets—landing them in serious trouble.[212]

Reinforcements began to appear in Garnett's camps. From the east came Colonel William B. Taliaferro's Twenty-third Virginia Infantry, Colonel Samuel V. Fulkerson's Thirty-seventh Virginia

Infantry, a portion of the Twentieth Virginia Infantry, and Colonel James N. Ramsey's First Georgia Infantry. The Georgians created a sensation at Camp Laurel Hill. Led by a snappy fife-and-drum corps, they were handsomely uniformed and equipped—with imported cloth, silver, and body servants to attend every need. The veteran Colonel Taliaferro thought they had left home prepared "rather for a gay holiday than for real war."

Local recruiting efforts added few more. By July 1, only twenty-three Confederates had signed up, not enough to make up for discharges. Garnett could muster just 4,500 men, a force President Davis described as "lamentably weak." The dreary-hearted general saw little chance of offering battle. To Lee he confessed, "I cannot operate beyond my present position...with the present force under my command, and I deem it my duty to state the fact....I can only say I shall watch vigilantly, and strike whenever and wherever I can see a reasonable hope of success."[213]

▲

Exaggerated reports of the Confederate buildup had already reached General McClellan's Cincinnati headquarters. McClellan now personally took the field to "dispose of Garnett before he was in condition to do much mischief."

His young wife remained behind in Cincinnati. Mary Ellen McClellan was of modest height and shapely form. Her hair was golden, her eyes a splendid hazel. Her face beamed with affection, intelligence, and determination. She was utterly heartstopping—and six months pregnant. Now, just over a year after their union, George left his "charming Nelly" for the front. Her father, Randolph Marcy, the distinguished soldier and western explorer, accompanied his son-in-law as inspector general. "I *may* yet play my part on the stage of the world's affairs and leave my name in history," George had told his love, "but Nelly whatever the future may have in store for me *you* will be the chief actor in the play." He pledged to write a letter every day during the absence.[214]

On June 20, McClellan boarded a train for Western Virginia. "At every station where we stopped, crowds had assembled to see the 'Young General,'" he wrote Nelly. "Gray-headed old men & women; mothers holding up their children to take my hand, girls, boys, all sorts, cheering and crying, God bless you! I never went thro' such a scene in my life & never expect to go thro' such another one."

Trainloads of soldiers and ordinance were at his heels. McClellan brought nearly twenty thousand men—enough to thrash whatever might be ahead. "I will, without delay, beat them up in their quarters and endeavor to put an end to their attempts in this direction," he told General Scott.[215]

McClellan reached Grafton on June 23, less than fifty miles from the enemy. He found military affairs in confusion. "Everything here needs the hand of the master & is getting it fast," Nellie was informed. His eye was on the B&O Railroad, a vital artery for communication, troops, and supplies. He noted the Tray Run Viaduct at Rowlesburg, one of the most remarkable engineering works on the entire line. The towering viaduct, six hundred feet long and one hundred sixty feet high, spanned a deep gorge by means of slender iron columns. It was located in an isolated setting on Cheat River—the very spot coveted by General Lee. McClellan visited Rowlesburg in person, left one thousand men to guard the viaduct and five times that number to protect his railroad lifeline.[216]

McClellan's intelligence gathering was no more effective than Garnett's, a "peculiar characteristic" of that region. He did know that Confederates held the mountain passes. It was enough to formulate a plan. In a June 23 letter to General-in-Chief Scott, McClellan proposed a march on Beverly, via Clarksburg, Buckhannon, and Rich Mountain, to turn the Rebel position at Laurel Hill. The troops at Philippi under General Morris would follow up any retreat. Having disposed of Garnett, McClellan would dispatch troops to "reassure the Union men."[217]

He scripted another proclamation to rally those Unionists, informing them that his army, led by "Virginia troops," would support loyal civil authorities, that they were enemies to "none but armed rebels and those voluntarily giving them aid." In an address "To the Soldiers of the Army of the West," McClellan admonished his troops to "Bear in mind that you are in the country of friends, not of enemies; that you are here to protect, not to destroy:"

> *Your enemies have violated every moral law; neither God or man can sustain them. They have, without cause, rebelled against a mild and paternal Government; they have seized upon public and private property; they have outraged...Northern men merely because they loved the Union; they have placed themselves beneath contempt, unless they can retrieve some honor on the field of battle. You will pursue a different course. You will be honest, brave, and merciful; you will respect the right of public opinion; you will punish no man for opinion's sake. Show to the world that you differ from our enemies....Soldiers! I have heard that there was danger here. I have come to place myself at your head and to share it with you. I fear now but one thing— that you will not find foemen worthy of your steel.*[218]

Sophia Hawthorn, wife of the celebrated author, compared McClellan's words to the sound of "the silver trumpets of Judah." A letter to Nelly described "crowds of the country people who have heard of me & read my proclamations come in from all directions to thank me, shake me by the hand, & look at their 'liberator, the General!'...Well, it is a proud & glorious thing to see a whole people here, simple & unsophisticated, looking up to me as their deliverer from tyranny."

McClellan's mood was buoyant. To Nelly he boasted, "I hope to thrash the infamous scamps before a week is over—all I fear is that I can't catch them." His soldiers were in fine spirits, too. "They will render a good account of themselves, or I am much mistaken," he told Secretary of the Treasury Salmon P. Chase. "I think we can show that one Southerner is not equal to *more* than three Northern men!"[219]

Foremost in mind were the Germans of the Ninth Ohio Infantry. On June 30, those "Bully Dutchmen" led the Federal march to Buckhannon, twenty-two miles west of Rich Mountain. At their head was William Starke Rosecrans, the engineer who had laid out Camp Dennison, and who was now a brigadier general. The forty-one-year-old Rosecrans was nearly six feet tall, compactly built with an aquiline nose, piercing eyes, a brilliant mind, and a sharp temper.

Rosecrans had graduated fifth in the West Point class of 1842. He had been superintendent of a coal company in Western Virginia, and later, as head of a Cincinnati kerosene refinery, was burned in an explosion that left his face permanently scarred. A devout Catholic, Rosecrans was utterly destitute of pretense. His speech grew nearly to a stutter when excited, and he was "nervous and active in all his movements," never retiring before two o'clock in the morning, very often not until four, and sometimes not at all.[220]

While Federal troops closed on Garnett's army, McClellan also launched steps to "clean out the valley of the Kanawha." He ordered General Jacob Cox at Camp Dennison to move toward Gallipolis, Ohio, with four regiments, in preparation for an advance up the Kanawha River. "Communicate frequently," McClellan directed. "A telegraph line follows me out."[221]

As a former railroad man, George McClellan understood the promise of the telegraph. Railroads used the technology to coordinate traffic, and telegraph lines were in place along the B&O. McClellan appointed Anson Stager, general superintendent of Western Union Telegraph Company, as military director of telegraph lines within the Department of the Ohio. Two experienced men, William S. Fuller and T.B.A. David, were hired as managers. Ignoring skeptics, McClellan detailed Fuller and David to construct a telegraph line along his route of march. It was a novel idea—the telegraph had never followed an American army into battle.

To discourage eavesdroppers, a way was needed to code the messages sent by wire. Stager accomplished this by developing a simple but ingenious cipher. Fittingly, McClellan's code name was "Mecca." Morris was "Venice," and General Scott "Baghdad." Washington was "Nimrod;" Wheeling, "Peter;" Grafton, "Lot;" and so forth. It was the first telegraphic cipher ever used by an army in war.[222]

The telegraph men had no problem keeping up with their general. McClellan did not join Rosecrans in Buckhannon until July 2; the laggard pace was blamed on delays in securing transportation. "I am bothered half to death in getting up supplies," he informed Nelly, "unless where I am in person everything seems to go wrong." He remained at Buckhannon for three more days, refusing to give way to impatience. It was a lesson learned from Winfield Scott—"not to move until I know that everything is ready, and then to move with the utmost rapidity and energy."[223]

Meanwhile, patrols explored the countryside. Among them was the first three-year volunteer cavalry unit in the field, a squad of Pennsylvanians known as the "Ringgold cavalry." The Ringgolds carried huge old flintlock horse pistols. For the first time, those weapons were loaded and primed. First, a small handful of powder was poured in and sealed with newspaper. "On top of this we put eight or ten chunks of lead," recalled trooper John Elwood. "This would fill the gun about one-half the length of the barrel, and, when filled to the muzzle with brick dust, we were ready for the fight." Elwood's pistol went off accidentally, knocking him to the ground with a fearful roar. Stunned, he arose to find a hole in the earth "large enough to bury a good sized dog."[224]

"I doubt whether the rebels will fight," McClellan informed Nelly. "It is possible they may, but I begin to think my successes will be due to manoeuvers, & that I shall have no brilliant victories to record." He assured General Scott that "no prospect of a brilliant victory" would induce him to fight when he might outwit Garnett: "I will not throw these raw men of mine into the teeth of artillery and intrenchments if it is possible to avoid it."

He hoped instead to pull a "Cerro Gordo," duplicating Scott's brilliant flanking movement in the Mexican War. McClellan would send Morris's brigade to "amuse" Garnett at Laurel Hill—making him think the main attack would come there—while he took three brigades and swept around the Confederate left flank at Rich Mountain. He would then march into Beverly, cutting off Garnett's retreat. The Rebels would be captured or destroyed.[225]

A sweltering Independence Day found McClellan reviewing the troops at Buckhannon. Citizens gawked as regiment after regiment passed the bareheaded young general in parade. "Lordy!" exclaimed one mountaineer. "I didn't know there was so many folkses in the world."[226]

McClellan's review of Garnett's numbers was also growing. Magnifying enemy strength would become one of his signature traits. He now estimated that the Rebel general had some ten thousand soldiers—eight thousand at Laurel Hill and two thousand at Rich Mountain. In reality, Garnett possessed half that number. Only 1,300 Confederates were dug in at Rich Mountain; Garnett's total strength would never exceed 5,300 men. While McClellan moved against a Rich Mountain force he outnumbered more than five to one, General Morris was about evenly matched at Laurel Hill.

Had Garnett the numbers McClellan believed, what might keep him from taking the offensive? If he counterattacked and defeated Morris, a race for the railroad would take place at McClellan's rear. "I confess I feel apprehensive unless our force could equal theirs," offered the soft-spoken Morris to his commander.[227]

McClellan's reply was terse. "I am not a little surprised that you feel the defense of Philippi so hazardous and dangerous an operation. If four thousand (nearly) of our men...are not enough to hold the place against any force these people can bring against it, I think we had better all go home at once." He grudgingly sent reinforcements with a warning not to ask for more. McClellan's disdain spilled out in a letter to Nelly: "I have not a Brig Genl worth his salt—Morris is a timid old woman—Rosecranz a silly fussy goose—Schleich knows nothing," he complained.[228]

On July 5, McClellan's know-nothing brigadier, politician Newton Schleich of Ohio, sent fifty men on an unauthorized expedition to Middle Fork Bridge, a covered span midway between Buckhannon and the Rebels at Camp Garnett. When that party lost six men in a firefight the next day, McClellan was livid. General Schleich, Democratic leader in the Ohio Senate, was relieved of command. McClellan's advance guard cleared Middle Fork Bridge on the morning of July 7. "I got my pants and boot-legs riddled with bullets," wrote Confederate Captain John Higginbotham of the skirmish, "but without serious injury in fact 'no meat hurt.'" Not one to shy from a fight, the youthful Higginbotham would prove to be a magnet for Yankee lead.[229]

As McClellan's troops neared the Confederates at Camp Garnett, Lt. Colonel John Pegram arrived at that post with the remainder of his Twentieth Virginia Infantry and took command. Pegram was twenty-nine years old, born of a distinguished tidewater Virginia family, short, goateed, haughty, and handsome. At West Point, J.E.B. Stuart had called him "the best-hearted fellow I ever knew," which perhaps explained Cadet Pegram's first-year collection of more than one hundred demerits. He was said to be the first U.S. Army officer on active duty to offer his sword to Virginia.[230]

Pegram knew next to nothing about Rich Mountain, but a civilian named Jedediah Hotchkiss had recently learned much. Born at Windsor, New York, in 1828, he had moved to Virginia's Shenandoah Valley as a teacher. Hotchkiss was a gifted cartographer. He could walk over a tract once and map it with astounding accuracy. For nearly a week, the bearded professor had been shooting angles and taking elevations around Camp Garnett.[231]

While this talented mapmaker surveyed the laurel thickets of Rich Mountain, General George McClellan surveyed his own chances for winning laurels there. The rugged terrain gave him pause. "There were few regions," he fretted, "more difficult for the operations of large bodies of troops."[232]

McClellan's tone became less confident. "I realize now the dreadful responsibility on me—the lives of my men—the reputation of the country & the success of our cause," he confided to Nelly. "I shall feel my way & be very cautious for I recognize the fact that everything requires success in my first operations." To General Scott he wired, "Enemy said to be entrenched in force in my front. Cannot rely on reports. Will not learn what I have met until the advance guard comes in contact. I will be prepared to fight whatever is in front of me."[233]

On July 9, the young general led three brigades to within sight of Camp Garnett. "We came over the hills with all the pomp and circumstance of glorious war," wrote Lt. Colonel John Beatty, "infantry, cavalry, artillery, and hundreds of army wagons; the whole stretching along the mountain road for miles." The army bivouacked on Roaring Creek flats, just west of the Rebel camp. "These mountain passes must be ugly things to go through when in possession of an enemy," wrote John Beatty as he steeled himself for battle. "I endeavor to picture to myself all its terrors, so that I may not be surprised and dumbfounded when the shock comes." A loud clap of thunder cut short his musings. And then another soft rumbling. "There it goes again!" Beatty jotted in his diary. It was the sound of distant cannon fire.[234]

══════ ▲ ══════

Sixteen miles north, the artillery banged away in front of Garnett's defenses at Camp Laurel Hill. Confederates there held the second turnpike pass. The coveted crossings at Rich Mountain and Laurel Hill were gateways to the heart of Virginia. If the Federals were to claim Western Virginia for the Union and push on toward Richmond, those gates must be secured.

On July 7, nearly four thousand Federal troops under General Morris had marched from Philippi on the Beverly-Fairmont Road to a hamlet named Belington, two miles west of Laurel Hill. Dr. William Fletcher, fife major of the Sixth Indiana Infantry, had crept between the lines to sketch the layout of Confederate defenses. Armed with that intelligence, General Morris pushed forward. Over the next four days, his troops grappled at arm's length with Garnett's army at Laurel Hill.

Morris was only to *amuse* the Rebels, awaiting McClellan's flank movement at Rich Mountain. But the Federal troops at Laurel Hill proved difficult to restrain. "A few dozen of us, who had been swapping shots with the enemies' skirmishers, grew tired of the resultless battle," recalled the Ninth Indiana's Ambrose Bierce, "and by a common impulse—and I think without orders or officers—ran forward into the woods and attacked the Confederate works. We did well enough considering the hopeless folly of the movement, but we came out of the woods faster than we went in—a good deal."[235]

Even a clergyman got into the act. Sergeant Copp, parson of the Ninth Indiana Regiment, was in the midst of a Sunday sermon at Belington when brisk firing broke out in the woods nearby. The parson dropped his Bible, snapped up a rifle, and led his congregation in a charge.

After two days of skirmishing, the Federals won a hotly contested point known as Girard Hill, named for the first Indiana soldier to fall upon its crest. On July 10, Morris planted artillery within range of Garnett's camp and opened fire.[236]

They "shot cannon balls, case shot and canister at us for near ten hours," recalled Confederate James Hall. "We were sheltered from them, however, by the large trees in the woods." Isaac Hermann of the First Georgia Regiment stood guard at Camp Laurel Hill during this fire. Nervously, Hermann collared an officer making the rounds. "Colonel," he implored, "am I placed here as a target to be shot at by those fellows yonder?"

"Take your beat in the ditch," was the reply, "and when you see the smoke, tuck your head below the breastworks." Hermann did so, watching for the smoke of the gun. He learned that the sound took eight seconds to reach him, followed about four seconds later by arrival of the ball—allowing time to hunker down. But the discovery gave small comfort. "I was very willing when relief came, for the other fellow to take my place," recalled Hermann.[237]

The spirited action at Laurel Hill induced General Garnett to believe that McClellan's main force was before him. Lt. Col. Pegram's optimistic dispatches from Rich Mountain intimated the same. Garnett prepared to meet the enemy with cold steel. To Lee he wrote, "My only apprehension is that by the guidance of Union men of the neighborhood they may get in my rear by some path unknown to me."[238]

CHAPTER 9
THE WHOLE EARTH
SEEMED TO SHAKE

"There was...not the slightest possible hint of softness or mildness, not a lineament of beauty remaining, to relieve the harsh, horrid, distorted, agonized faces of the dead of Rich Mountain."
—W.D. Bickham, *Cincinnati Daily Commercial*

General McClellan's regimental bands struck up melodies that drifted over Roaring Creek to the Confederates at Rich Mountain. From the trenches of Camp Garnett, the "Hampden-Sydney Boys" answered in song. But fellow Americans also made ready for war. The general hastily scribbled a note to Nelly on July 10: "The enemy are in sight & I am sending out a strong armed reconnaissance to feel him & see what he is. I have been looking at the camps with my glass—they are strongly entrenched...."[239]

Lieutenant Orlando Poe led the reconnaissance with that crack German regiment, the Ninth Ohio Infantry. The Germans swept forward in crisp lines, driving back enemy pickets until compelled by withering fire to take shelter in a timber barricade about three hundred yards from the Confederate works. Accompanied by Colonel Frederick Lander, Poe began to examine the defenses with a glass. Rifle and cannonballs cracked through the brush as he nervously jotted notes. Poe looked up incredulously as Lander strolled down the road for a closer view. Gunfire slacked off briefly as the fearless colonel doffed his cap and bowed to the enemy.[240]

The Rebel defenses were formidable. Mountain spurs above the turnpike bristled with entrenchments. Impenetrable laurel thickets guarded each flank. The dreadful defile leading to Camp Garnett was choked with timber—a veritable "Valley of Death." The works might be taken by storm, but McClellan fretted over such bloody work. Privately, he feared the result "at least doubtful."[241]

If a frontal assault was required, McClellan looked to his most experienced brigadier, that "silly fussy goose," William Rosecrans. The high-strung Rosecrans was hunting up a young civilian named David Hart. It was rumored that Hart lived nearby and that he "knew the mountains thoroughly" from herding cattle. Late that evening, he was found at the outer picket line and delivered to Rosecrans.

Hart was twenty-two years old, rugged and forthright. He was a strong Unionist, descended from John Hart, a signer of the Declaration of Independence. David's father owned a home beside the turnpike on the summit of Rich Mountain, about two miles behind Camp Garnett. Having returned from visiting relatives, the boy now offered to guide Rosecrans around the Confederate left flank by an obscure path. The path was rugged, David warned, and no artillery could follow. The excitable Rosecrans led Hart straight to McClellan's tent.

It was about ten o'clock in the evening when General McClellan began to question young Hart. David related in simple language all he knew of Rich Mountain and its defenders. McClellan listened raptly as he described the rude path to his father's farm on the summit. The mountain was very steep, David acknowledged, and laurel grew so thick along part of the route that a man could actually walk upon its matted crown.

McClellan interrupted, "Do you say men can walk on the *tops* of the laurel?

"Yes sir," answered David.

"Do you think my army can go up the mountain, over the tops of the laurel?"

"No sir," David replied, "but *I* have done so, and a man *might*, if he would walk slowly and had nothing to carry."

"Tell the truth, my boy."

"I *am* telling you the truth, General."

"But," McClellan shot back, "do you know, if you are not, you will be shot as a spy?"

"I am *willing* to be shot if all I say is not true."[242]

Rosecrans ushered Hart away and offered McClellan a plan. "Now General," he intoned, "if you will allow me to take my brigade I will take this guide and, by a night's march, surprise the enemy at the gap, get possession of it, and thus hold his only line of retreat. You can then take him on the front. If he gives way we shall have him; if he fights obstinately I will leave a portion of the force at the gap and with the remainder fall upon his rear."

McClellan listened in silence. Major Marcy piped up, "General, I think that is a good plan." Nearly an hour passed before the details were arranged. Rosecrans would start before dawn on July 11, following young Hart on a three-hour march to the summit. He expected to reach the Hart farm by 10 A.M. Upon hearing Rosecrans's musketry in rear of the Rebel works, McClellan would launch the frontal assault.[243]

Colonel Isaac Morrow of the Third Ohio Infantry roused his men for battle. It was midnight, recalled John Beatty, "the hour when graveyards are supposed to yawn, and the sheeted dead to walk abroad." Colonel Morrow's speech reflected the funereal character of the hour:

Soldiers of the Third: The assault on the enemy's works will be made in the early morning. The Third will lead the column. The secessionists have ten thousand men and forty rifled cannon. They are strongly fortified....They will cut us to pieces. Marching to attack such an enemy, so entrenched and so armed, is marching to a butcher-shop rather than to a battle...Many of you, boys, will go out who will never come back again.

A chill shot through Beatty as Morrow's words pierced the darkness. It was hard to die so young and far from home. The men kicked campfire embers into a blaze that revealed "scores of pallid faces." Thoughts turned to mothers, wives, and sweethearts. "In short," Beatty declared, "we all wanted to go home." The Confederates also mulled their fate. A brilliant comet was visible in the night sky over Camp Garnett—thought to be an omen of disaster.[244]

General Rosecrans's flank march began at 5 A.M. A drenching rain commenced. Young David Hart led the way, accompanied by Colonel Frederick Lander, now a fixture on any expedition in the mountains. The Eighth, Tenth, and Thirteenth Indiana Infantry regiments, the Nineteenth Ohio Infantry, and Burdsal's Ohio Cavalry made up Rosecrans's brigade—a total of 1,917 men. Each toted a firearm and cartridge box, a haversack with one day's rations, and a canteen of water. Entering the forest in silence, they kept low on the mountain spurs to avoid detection, slogging through laurel thickets on a circuit estimated to be five miles in length. A member of Burdsal's cavalry backtracked every hour with a report for General McClellan.[245]

At Roaring Creek headquarters, McClellan grew restless. By 9 A.M., he sent a mounted courier after Rosecrans—reportedly to call off the attack until a better plan was devised. But the galloping courier blundered into Confederate pickets, was shot from his horse, and was taken in for questioning. From him, Lt. Col. Pegram learned of the flank attack, if not its direction. Pegram believed his flanks were unapproachable. To play it safe, however, he sent Captain Julius DeLagnel, Garnett's chief of artillery, with a cannon and reinforcements to the picket station on top of Rich Mountain.[246]

The 310 Confederates on the summit that day consisted of members of the Twentieth and Twenty-fifth Virginia Regiments, a detachment of the Churchville Cavalry, and the crew of a bronze six-pounder gun led by Lt. Charles Statham of the Lee Battery. The Virginians fashioned crude log breastworks in a gap along the turnpike opposite the two-story Hart farmhouse. Captain DeLagnel, a fourteen-year veteran of the U.S. Army, commanded the post. His orders were to defend it "to the last extremity."[247]

While Rosecrans's brigade marched around the Confederate left flank, Lt. Col. Pegram imagined they were circling his right flank instead. He notified General Garnett at Laurel Hill and sent a messenger to hurry up Colonel William C. Scott's Forty-fourth Virginia Infantry, just in from Staunton. Scott was ordered to guard the Merritt Road, an obscure track intersecting the turnpike from the north, one and a half miles west of Beverly.[248]

The Federals under General Rosecrans clambered up Rich Mountain from the *south*. Their route proved nearly impassable for horses, just as young Hart had claimed. Pausing above a steep gorge at 11 A.M., Rosecrans sent a dispatch to McClellan stating that he would send no more messengers until there was "something of importance to communicate." It was the last word between the two generals that day.

Following a brief rest near the summit, the brigade turned north. Rosecrans was badly off schedule—his three-hour march had stretched to nearly ten. At 2:30 P.M., on the crest of the mountain less than a mile from Hart's, skirmishers of the Tenth Indiana Regiment were fired on by Confederate pickets. Captain Christopher Miller and two other members of the Tenth fell before the Rebels were driven to flight. David Hart had already dropped back into the main Federal column, fearing for his safety. Now he was accused of treachery. "Gentlemen," David replied, "go where I take you and you will not be beaten."[249]

As gunfire echoed from the south, startled Confederates at the Hart house rolled their cannon around and leapt behind logs and boulders in the stable yard. Peering up the mountainside, they watched Federal skirmishers emerge from the woods at a range of three hundred fifty yards. Almost on cue, a heavy rainstorm erupted. The lone Confederate cannon opened with a roar. Lieutenant Statham, commander of the gun, watched his case shot bursting in the midst of the enemy. Urgent cries of Union officers to "close up ranks" spurred him on. Statham poured on the fire at a rate of nearly four shots per minute.

The Tenth Indiana, in advance, was ordered to "lie down" as cannonballs sheared off the treetops. Limbs crashed to the ground. Exploding shrapnel filled the air. David Hart hugged the wet slope for dear life, certain the Rebels had twenty-five or thirty cannon.

Stalled by nature's fury and Statham's artillery, General Rosecrans called up his troops. The Eighth Indiana joined the Tenth in line of battle on his right and center. The Thirteenth Indiana formed on the left, with the Nineteenth Ohio in reserve. From the Confederate works, Captain David Curry of the Rockbridge Guards watched the drama unfold: "As Regt. after Regt. of the enemy came into view, our small force saw it had heavy work before it.…We knew we had no chance to defeat so much superior force, but we believed that our whole force would be brought up from our Camp and that at this point would be fought the battle we had for days been anticipating."[250]

Moving his cannon up the opposite slope to gain elevation, Lieutenant Statham pounded the Union line with short-fused shot. Blast after blast of his gun echoed across Rich Mountain. The confused Yankees fell back. Grimy Confederate defenders waved their hats and rent the air with shouts.[251]

Their cheers were premature. Laboring to reform his green troops, General Rosecrans brought skulkers into line with a sharp rap from the flat of his sword. Union regiments again filled the mountainside, pouring musketry into a line of defenders little more than one hundred yards long. The attack played havoc with Lieutenant Statham's artillery. Terrified horses bolted away with caisson and drivers, leaving only a little ammunition in the limber box. Statham moved the gun downhill beside a log stable, placed his artillery horses behind it for protection, and discharged rounds of canister into Rosecrans's lines.

One of those rounds felled Colonel Lander's horse. Struggling to his feet, the intrepid Lander hopped upon a large rock. Muskets were handed up and he fired them at the Rebel artillerists. "Bang away, you scoundrels!" roared Lander. "We'll come down there and lick you like the devil directly!"[252]

Federal sharpshooters leveled a deliberate volley at some Rebels on the opposite slope, but cleanly missed. A Confederate seemed much amused. He turned around, dropped his pantaloons, and offered a "glaring insult." One of the sharpshooters answered with a "centre shot," leaving the dead Rebel in a rather undignified pose.[253]

Leaden missiles rattled and whined through the underbrush. "[O]ur boys…let into them with their Enfield and Minie rifles," wrote David Hart. "I never heard such screaming in my life." Sharpshooters reaped a fearful toll in the stable yard—Statham's artillerists were dropping fast. Anxious to silence that gun, General Rosecrans gave the order to "fix bayonets." Defenders plainly heard the jangle of cold steel. Rosecrans rode to the head of the Indiana Thirteenth and drew his sword. "Charge bayonets," he screamed. The Federals swept downhill "like a thunderbolt."[254]

Lieutenant Statham loaded canister until he fell wounded near his gun. Captain DeLagnel rushed to the piece and fired three or four rounds before he too was shot down. The searing bronze cannon was silenced at last. By one count, it had fired 165 rounds.[255]

Seven companies of the Nineteenth Ohio Infantry delivered a terrific volley into the Rebels. "The whole earth seemed to shake," David Hart attested. Hot lead whistled through the stable yard, ricocheting wildly off the boulders. A second thunderous volley broke the defenders' resolve. General Rosecrans spurred for the enemy works. A resolute Confederate was killed in the act of firing point-blank at the general. Charging with a terrific yell, Federal troops swarmed across the turnpike, hoisting one poor fellow off the cannon with their bayonets.[256]

Lt. Colonel Pegram arrived from Camp Garnett with fifty men and a second cannon of Captain Pierce Anderson's Lee Battery—

too little, too late. Federals shot the wheel horses of the second
gun, plunging it over an embankment. Indiana troops crowded
over the prize. Pegram, badly hurt by a fall from his horse, joined
the Confederates in retreat. "Trepidation seized me and I ran up
the hill," recalled Willis Woodley of the Upshur Grays, "and every
bullet that passed me knocked up the leaves...which only acceler-
ated my speed. In fact there is no telling how fast a fellow can go
with bullets pattering around his feet."[257]

Unlike Pegram, Colonel Scott's Forty-fourth Virginia Infantry,
570 strong, never reached the fight. Scott—guarding the unused
Merritt Road at the eastern foot of Rich Mountain—had sent
Beverly lawyer John Hughes up the mountain to find out what all
the shooting was about. Hughes, an avowed secessionist from the
Richmond convention, mistook Confederate soldiers for the
enemy and hailed them as a "Northern man." It was a fatal error.
By one count, seventeen bullets riddled his corpse. Scott later
marched to within sight of the battlefield—but deemed discretion
the better part of valor and withdrew.[258]

The Battle of Rich Mountain was over. Flushed with success,
General Rosecrans's troops scattered through the woods after the
enemy. Those 310 Confederates had held their ground for more
than two hours, despite being outnumbered six to one. By all
accounts, they had been a "gallant and determined" foe. Yet their
defeat on the mountaintop foreshadowed the demise of Camp
Garnett and opened the turnpike to Beverly, just five miles east. If
Federal troops reached that town, they could trap General
Garnett's army at Laurel Hill—then march unimpeded toward the
Virginia Central Railroad at Staunton, one hundred five miles
southeast. That railroad led another one hundred and twenty miles
to the Confederate capitol at Richmond.[259]

From the direction of Camp Garnett there was silence.
Contrary to plan, General McClellan had not assailed the
Confederate works. His loss of nerve (another evolving trait) left
General Rosecrans in a tight spot on top of Rich Mountain.
Rosecrans was square between the enemy forces. It was well

after 6 P.M. before his men were gathered—too late for weary troops to fall upon the Confederates nearly two miles below at Camp Garnett. Pointing the captured guns down the pike in opposite directions, Rosecrans braced for a counterattack as darkness settled in.[260]

The hours had passed slowly for McClellan's troops in front of Camp Garnett that day. Heads snapped to attention when shots rang out and the thunderous peal of artillery echoed from the rear of Pegram's fortifications. "Every man sprang to his feet," recalled John Beatty, "assured that the moment for making the attack had arrived. General McClellan and staff came galloping up, and a thousand faces turned to hear the order to advance; but no order was given. The General halted a few paces from our line, and sat on his horse listening to the guns, apparently in doubt as to what to do; and as he sat there with indecision stamped on every line of his countenance, the battle grew fiercer in the enemy's rear."[261]

That firing, distant and stationary, baffled McClellan. "If the enemy is too strong for us to attack," John Beatty wondered, "what must be the fate of Rosecrans's four regiments, cut off from us, and struggling against such odds? Hours passed; and as the last straggling shots and final silence told us the battle had ended, gloom settled down on every soldier's heart, and the belief grew strong that Rosecrans had been defeated, and his brigade cut to pieces or captured."[262]

McClellan saw an officer ride into Camp Garnett, followed by wild cheering that prompted him to write off his quirky brigadier. He made it known that Rosecrans had disobeyed orders, that the "fussy goose" bore responsibility for whatever disaster had occurred. Fearing the worst, McClellan armed his teamsters.[263]

The Confederate officer seen at Camp Garnett was none other than Lt. Colonel John Pegram, returning from the battlefield to rally his men. Pegram led a detachment up the mountain to counterattack, but found them too demoralized to fight. Sending those men through the woods toward Beverly, he stumbled back to Camp Garnett again, not reaching the fortifications until almost midnight. Declaring the situation hopeless, Pegram ordered his troops to abandon their camp.

That night, mapmaker Jed Hotchkiss led nearly six hundred Confederates in single file through the black woods north of the turnpike, bearing east. After resting in his tent for some time, the beleaguered Colonel Pegram sent an orderly to halt the column until he caught up. Unaware of Pegram's meddling in the darkness, Hotchkiss and fifty members of the Twenty-fifth Virginia at the head of the line continued on their way. The rest of the Confederates were soon following Pegram, who had no idea where he was headed.[264]

General Rosecrans learned of the evacuation of Camp Garnett from a prisoner brought in during the night. At daybreak on July 12, Rosecrans led his brigade warily down the turnpike into the enemy camp, taking charge of nearly seventy sick and wounded Confederates. Also seized were two additional cannons, four caissons and ammunition, nineteen thousand cartridges, two stands of colors, a large quantity of clothing, tents, camp equipment, wagons, teams, and personal items.

One of the captured Rebels weighed more than three hundred pounds. The portly officer, captain of the "Hardy Blues," directed his men from the seat of a buggy. He was still on that perch as Federal troops circled round. "I am forced to surrender," he boomed, "because the d____d fools took a bridle path across the mountains. Had they gone by the road, sir, like gentlemen, so I could have used my buggy, I should have accompanied them." A waggish Federal retorted, "Boys, this is old 'Secesh' himself."[265]

A messenger was sent through the abandoned works to notify General McClellan. The general had directed pioneers to cut a road for artillery up the ridge south of Camp Garnett. He was making ready to shell the Rebels when Rosecrans's messenger informed him that they were already gone. A look of amazement came over McClellan's face. It had been nearly fifteen hours since the battle ended.[266]

The news sent cheers roaring down the valley. Bands struck up "Yankee Doodle." McClellan's order to the troops was, "Up tents and after them." The general and his staff rode through the deserted works in a "dazzling display." General Rosecrans received a hero's welcome. His displeasure with the commanding general was only later expressed officially: "General McClellan, contrary to agreement and military prudence, did not attack."[267]

Soon the battlefield was reached. "It is horrible to review the carnage," wrote one Hoosier. The ground was covered with "a large number of horses, cattle, hogs, &c. Trees, stumps and rocks are shattered with bullets. Some cannon balls are sticking in the trees." Broken weapons, clothing, and personal items lay scattered about.[268]

To raw recruits, the toll was shocking. Fellow Americans had suddenly become mortal foes. "It was a bloody affair when we consider the number engaged," wrote Lt. Orlando Poe. "I don't want to witness the effect of *another* battle." By later standards, the casualties were minor. More than twenty-two thousand Americans would be lost on a single day at Antietam in 1862, almost five thousand in barely half an hour at Cold Harbor in 1864. Yet at Rich Mountain in 1861, the twelve Federal soldiers killed and sixty-two wounded, along with the loss of more than eighty Confederates, were no less powerful.

One of every four Confederates at the Hart farm had been killed or wounded. Among them was Private Henry Clay Jackson, a member of the Upshur Grays. Before the fight, young Jackson had boasted that he would "kill a damn Yankee and cut out his heart and roast it." The action had just commenced when he was struck in the throat by a ball and killed, never firing a shot. Captain John Higginbotham, the "lead magnet," escaped with a flesh wound, but field commander Julius DeLagnel was missing and presumed dead.[269]

The dead of both armies were buried on the field. A large trench—reportedly dug before the fight and labeled "For Union men"—was filled with Confederates instead. "The dead presented a ghastly spectacle. I never conceived anything half so hideous. No power of expression is adequate to describe it," wrote William D. Bickham, reporting for the *Cincinnati Daily Commercial*. "They had about twenty five thrown into a ditch," affirmed an Ohio corporal, "and of all the hor[r]id sights I ever looked upon this was the most hor[r]id. They were thrown in without any regard to order or the usual rites of scripture, some with shattered skulls, mangled limbs or ghastly bayonet wounds." A few were naked, recalled a Hoosier sergeant, all "blackened with smoke." Newsman Bickham blanched at the "fearful orifices perforating their heads, through which the brains oozed in sickening clots...Oh horrible! Most horrible!"[270]

The Hart house became a makeshift hospital, filled with "convulsive and quivering" bodies. Wounded Confederates were placed under guard on an upper porch to protect them from the curious. The "bloody-handed surgeons," wrote one observer, "with lint, chords, bandages, saws, scalpels, probes, and bullet forceps, were busy bandaging and dressing what could be saved, and amputating hopelessly shattered and lacerated limbs."

Heartrending groans filled the air. A dying sixteen-year-old boy begged piteously for his mother. General McClellan stepped in to inquire of the wounded, and exited with tears in his eyes. Newsman Bickham wrote, "I shall not attempt to depict the ghastly pictures of horrid wounds and shuddering forms of poor victims, to whom it would have been merciful if they could have died...and yet could not eke out a last suffering gasp."[271]

A divergent scene laid mere steps away. From the brow of Rich Mountain, Federal soldiers beheld a stunning landscape of verdant forests, fields, and ridges. The mountains were "piled peak above peak," marveled one, "like the congealed bellows of a mighty ocean covered with their thousand shaded mantle of emerald leaves." The contrast was breathtaking. "We had just passed through some of the works of sinful man," he wrote, "and we now had an untarnished view of the works of Almighty God. You can better imagine than describe my feelings at this moment."[272]

CHAPTER 10
DEATH ON JORDAN'S
STORMY BANKS

"Cheat River ran red with their blood."
—James E. Hall, Thirty-first Virginia Infantry

While battle raged at Rich Mountain on the afternoon of July 11, 1861, Confederate General Robert Garnett took supper in front of his tent, sixteen miles north at Laurel Hill. Garnett's camp was under a desultory bombardment, yet he seemed oblivious to the bursting shells. The Confederates at Laurel Hill marveled at his "cool and undisturbed manner." When an exploding round showered Garnett with dirt, he calmly emptied his cup, beckoned to a servant for more coffee, and went on with his meal.[273]

The general soon faced a sterner test. Later that night, word arrived of Pegram's defeat. Now the Federal troops at Rich Mountain could march unimpeded into Beverly—square across Garnett's line of retreat. With General Morris testing his front, and McClellan threatening his rear, Garnett had no choice but to evacuate. Leaving tents in place and campfires burning to deceive Morris, Garnett's army slipped away under cover of darkness.[274]

Heavily laden Confederate wagons creaked over Laurel Mountain, bearing south. As the column neared Beverly at daybreak on July 12, Garnett received more bad news. His scouts—

mistaking Confederate soldiers in town for the enemy—reported that the road ahead was blocked. It was almost a death-knell. Garnett's last avenue of escape was a rough wagon grade leading northeast through the mountains. Backtracking a few miles, the general led his army along the Leading Creek road toward the Cheat River valley, bound for the Northwestern Turnpike at Red House, Maryland. From there, he hoped to cross the Alleghenies by a circuitous route, regaining the Staunton-Parkersburg pike near Monterey, Virginia—a rugged detour of nearly one hundred fifty miles. The alternative was surrender.[275]

The sun was high at Laurel Hill on July 12 before General Morris learned of Garnett's departure. Morris patched together a strike force to give chase, placing a forty-eight-year-old Connecticut Yankee named Henry Washington Benham in command. Benham was an officer of experience. Stout, red-faced, blustering, and dictatorial, he was a veteran of the Mexican War and a crack engineer—having graduated first in his 1837 West Point class. A captain in the regular army, he outranked the militia colonels of Morris's command.[276]

Captain Benham's troops, 1,840 in number, were eager "as bloodhounds for the chase." The Confederates held a twelve-hour lead when they took up the trail. Garnett's army was easily tracked. Deep mud, worked into a jelly by the active feet of men and horses, marked the line of retreat. The route was littered with abandoned equipment, cast off to lighten the wagons. At one place, discarded playing cards shingled the road, prompting a wag to remark that the Rebels must be trumped—they had "thrown down their hands."

Slowed by barricades, intense darkness, and a pelting rain, Benham's bloodhounds halted on the Leading Creek road late that evening. Billy Davis of the Seventh Indiana wrote that "fires were built and we stood around them trying to warm our chilled bodies, looking and longing for the first peep of day." Early on July 13, Colonel Steedman's Fourteenth Ohio Infantry picked up the trail, followed by two guns of Barnett's Cleveland Artillery, Colonel

Dumont's Seventh Indiana, and Colonel Milroy's Ninth Indiana Infantry regiments. The main column under General Morris followed at some distance. Although drenched by mountain storms, these bloodhounds set a furious pace.[277]

At the village of New Interest (present-day Kerens), the track of fleeing Rebels turned east on a rude mountain trace. "That road defies description," reported Cincinnati newsman Whitelaw Reid, hot in pursuit. "Part of the time it ran through lanes so narrow that a horseman could not pass on either side of the wagon train; then it wound through mountain gullies where the wheels of the wagon would be on the sides of the opposite hills, while beneath rushed a stream of water." At every step, the mud grew deeper. Benhams's men slipped and staggered, plunging into knee-deep pools, then "reeling like drunken men in the mire." Kneaded by the feet of thousands, liquid mud "flowed down the mountain road like thick tar."

Discarded equipment again cluttered the way. Roadside thickets were strewn with Confederate officers' baggage; fine campstools with General Garnett's mark lay in the muck. Wrecked wagons hung upside-down in the trees over dizzying precipices. "It was no longer the retreat of an army," thought Reid. "It appeared the pell mell rout of a mob. The destruction of property was enormous. Fine, heavy duck tents, and elegant blankets, far better than the best of ours lay in the road and were trampled by the infantry and ground into the mud by the wagons....Pouring rain soaked elegant clothing till it was almost utterly destroyed. And everytime one of their wagons was upset, the crash of its contents in rolling down the hillside ruined the whole."[278]

The road grew worse by the mile. Benham's pioneers chopped their way through barricades of timber, sometimes with the very axes left in the trees by fleeing Confederates. The race became a test of endurance. "And still it rained!" marveled Whitelaw Reid. "Weary and hungry, our soldiers could hardly have pushed along, but every fresh sight of deserted baggage seemed to convince them that they must be on the very heels of the rebels."[279]

By noon of July 13, Benham's force neared the rocky banks of Shavers Fork, a tributary of Cheat River. The river's name was said to come from the deceptive depth of its waters—a trait that had "cheated" many lives. Dark and turbulent from the rains, this river of death slowed the Confederate retreat. General Garnett's two-mile-long column of wagons and infantry had taken most of the morning to cross the swollen stream at Kalars Ford.

As he reached that crossing, Captain Benham spied the Confederate baggage train at rest in a long meadow on the opposite bank. A straggler's musket shot put the train to flight. Benham's Federals plunged into the river. Grateful as the cold waters purged them of mud, they broke into a chorus of the hymn "On Jordan's Stormy Banks I Stand."[280]

At the second ford, three quarters of a mile downstream, the First Georgia Infantry crouched in ambush. That regiment, the Twenty-third Virginia Infantry, and a section of the Danville Artillery had been detached as a rearguard to delay pursuit. Meanwhile, the remainder of Garnett's 3,500-man force—the Thirty-seventh and Thirty-first Virginia Regiments, Hansbrough's battalion, a section of the Danville Artillery, and a cavalry squadron, followed by the wagons—continued downstream. The delaying strategy might have worked, had not several companies of the Georgians failed to hear an order to retreat and been cut off at the second ford.

The chase now became a running fight. Garnett's Confederates clipped downstream with Benham's bloodhounds at their heels. The Federals pulled a beautiful Georgia banner from a jettisoned wagon and waved it to speed their weary, mud-spattered comrades. Stragglers filled the roadside. General Morris sent orders for Captain Benham to "stop at once," unless he was ready to strike. Now almost three miles below Kalars Ford, Benham replied, "Wait five minutes!"[281]

He approached a dismal crossing, known as Corricks Ford. The current ran deep there, and Garnett's wagons had stalled in the rocky riverbed. The scene was chaotic. Frantic drivers whipped and cursed their teams. Drowning horses thrashed in the swollen stream. The rain hammered down.[282]

Here the Confederates made a stand. Colonel Taliaferro's Twenty-third Virginia Regiment and three guns of the Danville Artillery occupied a steep, eighty-foot bluff on the far bank. Fringed by laurel thickets with a clearing on the crest, that bluff perfectly commanded the ford. Captain Benham, the crack engineer, called it "one of the best natural defensive sites I ever saw."[283]

Dressed in captured gray Confederate coats, skirmishers of the Fourteenth Ohio Infantry charged the riverbank. "Don't shoot!" cried teamsters trying to free wagons in the stream. "We are going to surrender." A mighty "rebel yell"—perhaps the first of the war—rolled across the ford. In that instant a deadly blaze of light flashed from the bluff as Colonel Taliaferro's men opened fire on the Federals below.[284]

On the opposite bank, members of the Fourteenth Ohio leapt behind a rail fence. The Seventh Indiana filed in on their right; the Ninth Indiana crowded on the left, their ranks more than thirty deep as men jostled to get a shot. Barnett's Cleveland Artillery snapped into action. "A terrible fire ensued," wrote James Hall. Cannonballs shrieked across the swollen river. Bullets filled the air, "hissing like venomous serpents."

Most shot high, showering each other with tree boughs. On the riverbank stood Sergeant Copp, "fighting parson" of the Ninth Indiana Infantry. "He fired carefully," Whitelaw Reid reported, "with perfect coolness, and always after a steady aim, and the boys declare that every time, as he took down his gun, after firing, he added, 'And may the Lord have mercy on your soul!'"

The angry skirmish lasted nearly thirty minutes. Colonel Dumont's Seventh Indiana Infantry crossed upstream to take the Rebels in flank, but found a brush-choked ravine impractical to scale. The Seventh was soon back in the river, wading downstream beneath the Confederates, guns and cartridge boxes held high above the current as shot and shell roared overhead. Not a man was lost as they neared Colonel Taliaferro's right flank. Nearly out of ammunition, Taliaferro was forced to retreat. A fine rifled cannon remained on the bluff, its gun carriage shattered by the fall of wounded battery horses. Most of the Confederate wagon train lay abandoned in the road below.[285]

At the sound of battle, General Garnett rode back toward Corricks Ford, finding chaos at every turn. Unable to locate his rearguard, Garnett confronted Colonel Ramsey of the First Georgia Infantry and demanded, "Where is your regiment?" Ramsey's forlorn reply was, "I don't know."

Corricks Ford was actually two river crossings, one at each end of a large island, a half mile apart. The log home of William Corrick overlooked the lower ford. Here General Garnett met Colonel Taliaferro, pointed to a large pile of driftwood on the far bank, and remarked that it would "form capital shelter for skirmishers." Garnett picked ten good riflemen from the Twenty-third Virginia's "Richmond Sharpshooters" and placed them behind the driftwood.

Shots rang out nearby. Colonel Taliaferro urged the general to fall back. "The post of danger is now my post of duty," was Garnett's stiff reply. Taliaferro was ordered to join the retreat. Garnett lingered at the river's edge on horseback, prominently exposed. A young aide named Sam Gaines remained by his side. Federal skirmishers raced toward the crossing. From the driftwood, Garnett's riflemen opened fire. The fragrant cologne of wildflowers along Shavers Fork mixed with the acrid smell of gunpowder.

Bullets hissed across the ford. Gaines ducked as he felt the wind of a ball pass his face. In fatherly tones, Garnett lectured him on the proper bearing for a soldier. The general showed no fear of death.[286]

From the opposite bank, Major Jonathan Gordon of General Morris's staff pointed out a Confederate officer silhouetted above the driftwood. A small party of the Seventh Indiana prepared to give him a volley. Sergeant R.F. Burlingame drew a bead and commanded those Hoosiers to "ready, aim, fire."

Garnett turned in the saddle and ordered his skirmishers to withdraw. In that instant, a ball struck him squarely in the back. He toppled to the riverbank. Federal riflemen splashed across the ford and found him among the wildflowers a few paces from the stream. He lay headfirst, on his back, uttering not a groan. Major Gordon reached Garnett scarcely a moment later, just as his muscles made "their last convulsive twitch."[287]

The fallen general was dressed in a black overcoat and a uniform of handsome blue broadcloth. His identity was unknown— word was sent to the rear that an officer had been killed with "stars on his shoulders." In one of the Civil War's many ironies, a Federal aide, Major John Love, arrived on the scene and grimly identified the dead man as Robert Garnett, his old West Point roommate.

Even in death, Garnett's features "bore a look of calm dignity." Major Gordon gently closed the eyes, straightened the limbs, and bound the jaw with a handkerchief. The general's remains, a dress sword, gold watch, and pocket book, were placed under guard. Beside him was a dead Confederate rifleman, the figure slight and boyish, with "girlish" locks of golden blonde. "There they lay," wrote Whitelaw Reid, "in that wild region, on the banks of the Cheat, with 'back to the field and face to the foe.'" Northern soldiers filed past in silence. Their deference was no conventional thing—Robert Garnett was the first general officer killed in the Civil War.[288]

Garnett's death signaled the end of Captain Benham's pursuit. Federal troops of General Charles W. Hill's railroad detachment were ordered to cut off the fleeing Rebels in western Maryland. Billy Davis and rest of Benham's bloodhounds dropped out for a well-deserved rest, "wet to the skin and mud to our ears." They had slogged over almost thirty miserable miles of road in a twenty-four-hour span, with scarcely a mouthful to eat, fought a lively engagement, routed the enemy, and killed his commander.

They had captured more than fifty Confederate wagons, one hundred fifty horses, three regimental flags, a rifled cannon, medical stores, fine tents, camp equipment, and military chests. "I confess I scarcely see how they can be equipped again," exclaimed Whitelaw Reid. "Their losses along the road, at Cheat River, and beyond are almost incalculable." The quality of Confederate gear— particularly medical supplies—was startling. "It is a fact," Reid observed, "that this army at Laurel Hill was in every respect far better equipped than ours." The temptation proved too great. Federal ninety-day men, nearing the end of their enlistments, shamelessly looted the wagons.[289]

Whitelaw Reid captured the drama of war for readers of the *Cincinnati Daily Gazette*. Leaving General Garnett's body, he returned to the bluff held by Taliaferro's Confederates. Scribed Reid:

> *The first object that caught the eye was a large iron rifled cannon (a 6-pounder) which they had left in their precipitate flight. The star spangled banner of one of our regiments floated over. Around was a sickening sight. Along the brink of that bluff lay ten bodies, stiffening in their own gore, in every contortion which their death anguish had produced. Others were gasping in the last agonies, and still others were writhing with horrible but not mortal wounds, surrounded by the soldiers whom they really believed to be about to plunge the bayonets to their hearts. Never before had I so ghastly a realization of the horrid nature of this fraternal struggle.*
>
> *These men were all Americans—men whom we had once been proud to claim as countrymen—some of them natives of our own Northern States. One poor fellow was shot through the bowels. The ground was soaked with his blood. I stopped and asked him if any thing could be done to make him more comfortable; he only whispered 'I'm so cold!' He lingered for nearly an hour, in terrible agony. Another—young, and just developing into vigorous manhood—had been shot through the head by a large Miniè ball. The skull was shockingly fractured; his brains were protruding from the bullet hole, and lay spread on the grass by his head. And he was still living! I knelt by his side and moistened his lips with water from my*

canteen, and an officer who came up a moment afterward poured a few drops of brandy from his pocket-flask into his mouth. God help us! What more could we do?[290]

Among the wounded was a visiting Massachusetts boy who had been impressed into the Confederate army. While trying to escape as the fighting broke out, he had been shot in the leg by a Rebel officer. The casualties at Corricks Ford fell mostly upon the Twenty-third Virginia and Fourteenth Ohio Regiments. Despite their commanding position, Taliaferro's Confederates suffered more than twice the casualties of Captain Benham's force. Confederate losses totaled at least twenty-nine, but the Federals had only twelve killed and wounded.[291]

Eleven Confederates were buried on the battlefield. The young man killed beside General Garnett was honored with a special plot behind the Corrick house. Captain George Latham's Grafton Guards inscribed a board to mark his grave: "Here lies the body of a youth (name unknown) who fell defending his general while his comrades ran away."[292]

As word of General Garnett's death spread through the Southern ranks, his army fled in disarray. Reports that Yankees awaited to the east on the Northwestern Turnpike near Red House, Maryland, only increased the panic. "The doors of Northern prisons seemed to be standing wide open for us," recalled one demoralized Confederate. The rabble extended for miles. Citizens told of ravenous soldiers who caught poultry from barnyards as they passed, and, tearing off the feathers, devoured them raw.[293]

Nearly four hundred members of the First Georgia Infantry, cut off near Kalars Ford, became lost in a "perfect wilderness." The uninhabited country was terrifying. In crossing McGowan Mountain, the frazzled Georgians hacked their way through immense laurel thickets with Bowie knives. Famished, they peeled the bark of birch trees for sustenance. "Many pathetic instances came to my observation," wrote Georgian Isaac Hermann, "some reading testaments, others taking from their breast-pocket, next to their heart, pictures of loved ones, dropping tears of despair." One captain dug a tiny piece of tallow candle from his haversack and presented it to his son. "Eat that," he said. "It will sustain life."

"No father, you eat it," came the reply. "I am younger than you, and stronger, and therefore can hold out longer." The two looked affectionately at each other as Hermann asked for the candle. "Having my knife in hand," he recalled, "I cut it lengthwise, following the wick, giving each half, and passing the blade between my lips." It was Hermann's first taste of nourishment in four days.[294]

An old trapper, "Tanner Jim" Parsons, discovered the Georgians along the banks of Otter Creek. "Gentlemen," Parsons declared, "I have been raised in these regions, and there is not a living soul within forty miles in the direction you propose to go, and at the rate you are compelled to advance, you would all perish to death, and your carcasses left for food to the wild beasts of the forest." He led the starving Confederates east to settlements on Dry Fork, where a large pone of cornbread was served. "I received about an inch square as my share," Isaac Hermann recalled, "the sweetest morsel that ever passed my lips." Thus ended a four-day wilderness ordeal.[295]

Efforts by General Hill and his railroad detachment to snare the fleeing Confederates near Red House fizzled. Confusion and train delays slowed Hill's pursuit. Federal troops did not reach the Northwestern Turnpike in force until July 14—more than two days after the retreat began and two hours after most of the Confederates had safely passed. Only a few dozen stragglers were rounded up. A chagrined George McClellan could only grumble at the news: "If my generals had obeyed my orders, I should...have captured every rebel in this region."[296]

General Garnett's body was removed to the Corrick house, laid out in fresh clothing, and placed in a rough, salt-lined coffin. Escorted by Major Gordon and a heavy guard, it was conveyed to the railroad at Rowlesburg in the general's captured ambulance wagon for eventual disposition to his family. A crowd gathered as the morbid procession rolled into Wheeling on July 16. Curious onlookers jostled to view the fine metal casket that now contained Robert Garnett's remains. They were captivated by the pathos of his life. Born of Virginia aristocracy, educated at the finest schools, and wed in the glamour of New York society, this promising soldier met tragedy in the mountains of his native state. He had fallen strangely, in the rear of a flying army, deserted by his own troops.[297]

Some believed that Garnett had willed his fate at Corricks Ford. He was deeply humiliated, the story went, and welcomed death to escape dishonor. "I have myself but little doubt," Captain Benham avowed, that Garnett posted himself at the riverbank "in the expectation or hope of losing his life in mortification at this disastrous rout."[298]

"[H]ow bravely he struggled against adverse fortune," eulogized President Jefferson Davis of the fallen Garnett, "and how gallantly he died in the discharge of his duty…the manner of his death was worthy of the way in which he lived." The forlorn remnant of Garnett's command limped back across the mountains. "We have suffered awfully," wrote Colonel Ramsey of the Georgia regiment. "Not many men were killed by the enemy, but there are hundreds missing….What is left of this army will not be fit for service in a month."[299]

CHAPTER 11
VICTORY ON THE WIRES

*"I have made a very clean sweep of it—never was more
complete success gained with smaller sacrifice of life."*

—George B. McClellan

The bustle at headquarters was in sharp contrast to General
McClellan's earlier cautious style. Telegraph man T.B.A. David
strung wire into the deserted Camp Garnett at a frenetic pace.
Within the hour, a fully operational telegraph office was up and
running.

McClellan wasted no time in putting that technology to work.
He ordered David to make contact with the War Department in
Washington. There was no hesitation by the young general now.
Many were taken aback by the novelty of his field telegraph and
the speed at which it appeared. "My God," exclaimed a
Confederate prisoner as he saw David working the keys, "here's
the telegraph!"

Nearly as astonished was General-in-Chief Winfield Scott at
Washington. McClellan's wire carried breathtaking news:

*Rich Mountain, Va.—9 A.M., 12th. We are in possession of
all the enemy's works up to a point in sight of Beverly. Have*

taken all his guns, a very large amount of wagons, tents
&c.—everything he had....A large number of prison-
ers...many killed...Mass of enemy escaped through the
woods entirely disorganized....Our success complete and
almost bloodless.

McClellan's army entered the town of Beverly with banners flying. The finely outfitted Ninth Ohio Germans led the advance, while regimental bands played a beautiful march from the opera *Norma*. Rolls of telegraph line uncoiled at their heels.[300]

In Beverly, McClellan set up a telegraph office hot linked to the War Department. A flurry of messages crackled over the wires: "I have the honor to inform you that the army under my command has gained a decisive victory," cabled McClellan. "They lost many killed....Our success complete and almost bloodless....I shall move on Huttonsville to-morrow morning, and endeavor to seize the Cheat Mountain pass before the enemy can occupy it in strength....We are constantly picking up more prisoners."

He wrote again on the morning of July 13. "Success of today is all that I could desire," McClellan announced. "Their killed and wounded will amount to fully one hundred and fifty...their retreat complete....Garnett abandoned his camp early this morning, leaving much of his equipage. He came within a few miles of Beverly, but our rapid march turned him back in great confusion....I may say that we have driven out some ten thousand troops strongly entrenched."

As McClellan's cables reached General Scott in Washington, tongues wagged. The first great clash of the war at Manassas was more than a week away. This news from Western Virginia was bedazzling. George McClellan was suddenly the talk of the town.

Scott keyed a reply to his young protégé. "The General-in-Chief, and what is more, the Cabinet, including the President, are charmed with your activity, valor, and consequent successes of Rich Mountain the 11th, and of Beverly this morning. We do not doubt that you will in due time sweep the rebels from Western

Virginia, but we do not mean to precipitate you, as you are fast enough." It might have been the last time a military superior praised General McClellan for speed.[301]

—————— ▲ ——————

While cables skipped over the wires on Rich Mountain, Confederate refugees fled for their lives. Parties led by Jed Hotchkiss, Major Nat Tyler, and Colonel Scott reached Beverly ahead of McClellan's troops, filled wagons with quartermaster stores, and took a score of "home-made Yankees" and "Carlile men" from the jail for good measure as they scampered south. One wounded Virginian, however, was left behind. Charles "Lab" Cox grew so weak during the retreat that comrades were forced to abandon him in the forest on Rich Mountain. "He sat himself up against a tree," recalled a Confederate, "those who had a biscuit, or a piece of meat...or a canteen of water, gave it freely to him. All bade him 'Goodbye.' Thus was Charles Cox left alone in the wild mountains of Randolph County." His fate would remain a mystery.[302]

The Confederates with Lt. Colonel Pegram fared little better. On the morning of July 12, Pegram trained a telescope on Beverly from the crest of Rich Mountain, observed Confederate soldiers in the town and—like Garnett's scouts—mistook them for the enemy. So he turned the large column north toward Laurel Hill, stumbling across murky swamps and the meandering Tygart Valley River. Riding ahead to Leadsville Church, Pegram learned of Garnett's retreat, the passing of Federal troops, and the impossibility of escape. Returning to the riverbank, he found his frightened troops firing wildly into the darkness.[303]

Near the river, at the Kittle house, Pegram called a conference of his officers. Captain J.B. Moomau of the Franklin Guards offered to guide them to safety by a route used after the Philippi defeat, but was overruled. Convinced there was no escape, the tired, hungry Confederates voted to surrender. A messenger was sent to find McClellan. On the morning of July 13, nearly six hundred fully armed Confederates under Pegram surrendered to a party of less than two dozen Federals and marched into Beverly. It would later be discovered that members of the Franklin Guards had slipped away by the route offered to all.[304]

General McClellan offered gracious terms of surrender. Tents and rations were provided to enlisted men; Confederate officers were lodged in a Beverly hotel and given the liberty of the town. The ailing Pegram convalesced in a private home, under care of the sister of McClellan's West Point classmate Thomas Jackson.[305]

"I find that the prisoners are beyond measure astonished at my humanity towards them," McClellan informed Nelly. Taken aghast by the tender ages of Reverend Dr. Atkinson's "Hampden-Sydney Boys," McClellan sent the youths home to their mothers. "Boys," he lectured them in a fatherly tone, "secession is dead in this region,—Go back to your college; Take your books and *become wise men*."

There were few guidelines for handling prisoners of war; therefore, McClellan released the Confederates on parole of honor. Each took a pledge not to "bear arms or serve in any military capacity against the United States until released from this obligation according to the ordinary usages of war." Only those who had left United States service to join the Confederacy were sent to prison, an exclusive club that included Dr. Archibald Taylor and Lt. Colonel John Pegram.[306]

The captured slaves of Confederate officers were given a choice—to go north to freedom, remain with the Federal army, or return to their masters. "Nearly all chose the latter alternative," McClellan noted with interest, for while he was no admirer of slavery, he fancied the abolitionists even less. "While I am determined to play my part in this unhappy contest," McClellan informed Confederate authorities, "permit me to assure you of my desire to do all in my power to alleviate its miseries." His benevolent treatment of Confederates at Beverly was in stark contrast to the handling of prisoners there in 1865, when captured Federals were led through mountain snows in bare feet.[307]

Anxious to clear the pass leading over Cheat Mountain, McClellan proceeded south on the Staunton-Parkersburg Turnpike. Many houses along the route were deserted. The reason, John Beatty surmised, was that citizens were told the Yankees "shot men, ravished women and destroyed property." As for Rebels on Cheat, McClellan found none. "Our ride today was truly magnificent," he wrote Nelly on July 14, "some of the most splendid Mt. views I ever beheld....At the Mt. top was a pretty little farm, neat as neat could be. A very old couple lived there, the old lady as rosy & cheerful as a cricket. It is sad that war should visit even such sequestered spots as that."

"After closing my letter last night," he continued, "a courier arrived with the news that the troops I had sent in pursuit of Garnett had caught him, routed his army, captured his baggage...& that Garnett himself lay dead on the field of battle!!! Such is the fate of traitors—one of their comdrs a prisoner, the other killed!" A delighted Nelly urged him to "come home and receive my congratulations."[308]

Sweet news it was, and McClellan sent the telegraph wires dancing with another sensational dispatch:

> *Garnett's forces routed—his baggage & one gun taken, his army demoralized—Garnett killed. We have annihilated the enemy in Western Virginia....We have in all killed at least 200 of the enemy & their prisoners will amount to at least one thousand—have taken 7 guns in all....The troops defeated are the crack regiments of Eastern Virginia....Our success is complete & secession is killed in this country.*[309]

McClellan's magic key tapped out headline-grabbing news. No matter that it was a trifle exaggerated, that he had inflated Confederate strength and casualties, that the "crack regiments" vanquished were a raw gaggle of volunteers, or that mistaken identity—not any "rapid march" by McClellan—had turned back Garnett's column. His florid dispatches created a sensation.

Headlines in the July 13 *New York Herald* screamed, HIGHLY IMPORTANT NEWS FROM WESTERN VIRGINIA. DECISIVE BATTLE OF RICH MOUNTAIN. BRILLIANT UNION TRIUMPHS...MAJOR GENERAL MCCLELLAN HAS MADE EVERY HEART LEAP WITH JOY.

10,000 REBELS DEFEATED. THEY LOSE EVERYTHING. DEATH OF GENERAL GARNETT. THE REBELS ANNIHILATED, echoed the *New York Tribune.*

The *Louisville Journal* called McClellan's campaign "a piece of finished military workmanship by a master hand." The Rebels in Western Virginia hadn't a chance—they had been "McClellanized."

"We like the works and ways of Gen. McClellan," wrote Horace Greeley. "May his shadow never be less!" "Glorious isn't it!" exalted the *New York Times;* "We feel very proud of our wise and brave young Major-General. There is a future before him, if his life be spared, which he will make illustrious." Banner columns hailed "Gen. McClellan, the Napoleon of the Present War."

News of McClellan's deeds sparked "the wildest enthusiasm" in army camps around Washington. Congress passed a joint resolution praising the young major general for his "brilliant" victories. "You have the applause of all who are high in authority here," confirmed Winfield Scott. Almost overnight, George McClellan became the North's first battlefield hero.[310]

Taking the home of a Beverly secessionist as headquarters, the "Young Napoleon" surveyed his domain. "Beverly is a quiet, old fashioned town in a lovely valley," he informed Nelly, "a beautiful stream running by it. A perfectly pastoral scene such as the old painters dreamed of, but never realized. I half think I should be King of it."[311]

A congratulatory address was published for the troops. It was vintage McClellan, straight from the master's gilded pen:

> *Soldiers of the Army of the West! I am more than satisfied with you. You have annihilated two armies, commanded by educated and experienced soldiers, intrenched in mountain fastness fortified at their leisure. You have taken five guns,*

twelve colors, fifteen hundred stand of arms, one thousand prisoners, including more than forty officers—one of the two commanders of the rebels is a prisoner, the other lost his life on the field of battle....You have proved that Union men, fighting for the preservation of our Government, are more than a match for our misguided and erring brethren; more than this, you have shown mercy to the vanquished....

Soldiers! I have confidence in you, and I trust you have learned to confide in me....I am proud to say that you have gained the highest reward that American troops can receive—the thanks of Congress and the applause of your fellow citizens.[312]

The troops were jubilant. "[W]e felt ready to meet all Secessia," boasted an Ohio infantryman. "We have met the enemy and they are ours, except those that ran." But the ninety-day volunteers, nearing the end of their enlistments, were determined to go home. Instructed to fill in Garnett's Laurel Hill earthworks before marching for the railroad, they leveled them like molehills. McClellan could not hide his disappointment. "I lose about 14 rgts now whose term of service is about expiring," he wrote Nelly. The young general assured his wife that he was out of danger. "No possible chance of further fighting here at present," he told her, "no one left to fight with."[313]

───── ▲ ─────

The only action left in McClellan's department was on the Kanawha Valley front, more than 150 miles southwest. There, on July 11, Union General Jacob Cox had crossed the Ohio River at Point Pleasant and launched an invasion with three thousand troops. Stern-wheel steamers ferried much of Cox's army up the Kanawha River toward Charleston, sixty miles southeast. Bands struck up patriotic tunes as the paddle boats chugged upstream. Each new bend of the river opened a picturesque vista. Cox, perched atop the pilothouse of his lead boat, called it "the very romance of campaigning."

But the romance was short-lived. On July 17, outgunned Confederates under ex-Virginia governor Henry Wise battled Cox to a standoff at the mouth of Scary Creek. In the confusion, four high-ranking Federal officers fell into enemy hands. McClellan was infuriated at the news. "Cox checked on the Kanawha," he wired the general-in-chief on July 19. "Has fought something between a victory & a defeat....In heaven's name give me some General Officers who understand their profession....Unless I command every picket & lead every column I cannot be sure of success."[314]

"Cox lost more men in getting a detachment thrashed than I did in routing two armies," McClellan informed Nelly. "The consequence is I shall move down with a heavy column to take Mr. Wise in rear & hope either to drive him out without a battle or to catch him with his whole force. It is absolutely necessary for me to go in person....I don't feel sure that the men will fight very well under anyone but myself."[315]

But developments back east intervened. A large Confederate army under General P.G.T. Beauregard had gathered at Manassas Junction, Virginia, just twenty-five miles southwest of Washington. That army now taunted the capital itself.

Northern politicians clamored for action, and the dramatic news from Western Virginia only increased their fervor. The daily masthead of Horace Greeley's influential *New York Tribune* screamed, FORWARD TO RICHMOND! FORWARD TO RICHMOND!

Facing pressure from President Lincoln and his own deadline of ninety-day enlistments, General Irvin McDowell led thirty-five thousand Federal troops toward the plains of Manassas. A throng of politicians and prominent citizens followed in carriages, loaded for a monster picnic. Everyone anticipated a grand spectacle—the battle to end the war.

McDowell's snail-like pace allowed General Joseph Johnston to rush nine thousand Confederate reinforcements from the Shenandoah Valley, swelling the Southern ranks to more than thirty thousand. McDowell finally struck on July 21, and the two great armies dueled along a torpid little stream known as Bull Run. Just when Union victory appeared certain, a gallant stand on Henry Hill by McClellan's old classmate Tom Jackson turned the tide of battle. The Confederates won a great victory, and Jackson earned a nickname—"Stonewall." By nightfall, panic-stricken Federal troops and picnickers scurried to the rear. Washington was in an uproar.[316]

The events at Manassas dashed expectations of a short, bloodless conflict. President Lincoln spent a nervous night at the White House listening to accounts of the disaster. At 1 A.M. on July 22, General-in-Chief Scott wired McClellan that McDowell's army was in full retreat. "A most unaccountable transformation into a mob of a finely-appointed and admirably-led army," the elderly general reported grimly.

Washington seemed to be in peril. President Lincoln and his Cabinet members sought a new commander. At once, their heads cast to the Alleghenies and that "very God of war," George Brinton McClellan. Who else could save the country now?

It was he who had rescued Western Virginia—bursting over the mountains like a comet, dazzling all with his brilliance. George McClellan had won the first Union victories of the war! True, those victories were small affairs, but embraced by the fates and McClellan's magic telegraph key, they would prove momentous. It was McClellan's destiny, after all—great deeds were expected of him.

On July 22, a message from Washington tapped over the telegraph receiver at McClellan's Beverly headquarters: "Circumstances make your presence here necessary. Charge Rosecrans or some other general with your present department and come hither without delay."[317]

George McClellan was called to save the Union.

PART III

▲

TEMPEST
ON THE
MOUNTAINTOPS

▼

Chapter 12
A Fortress
in the Clouds

"Fine place for an observatory, this Cheat Mountain summit."
—"Prock," Fourteenth Indiana Infantry

General McClellan's train to Washington became the chariot of a conquering hero. At Wheeling, he was reunited with Nelly and fêted by the Restored Government. A huge crowd serenaded him and cheered his every word. More than twenty thousand admirers hailed McClellan at Pittsburgh in "one of the grandest receptions ever given in the city." Stops at Philadelphia and Baltimore brought more of the same—too much for the pregnant Nelly, who returned to Cincinnati.

On July 27, President Lincoln cheerfully received McClellan in Washington. "I find myself in a new & strange position here," McClellan wrote Nelly that evening, "Presdt, Cabinet, Genl Scott & all deferring to me—by some strange operation of magic I seem to have become the power of the land." Noted Whitelaw Reid of all the fuss: "Never was a General more completely master of the situation."³¹⁸

▲

McClellan left General William Rosecrans in charge of Western Virginia, with headquarters on the railroad at Clarksburg. Rosecrans had no easy task. The three-month volunteers were on their way home. Most of the veteran staff officers had followed their victorious chief to Washington. Only about half of McClellan's original force remained, some eleven thousand men.

Rumors abounded that the Rebels intended to reclaim Western Virginia. McClellan and General-in-Chief Scott cautioned Rosecrans that the threat was real. The Federals went on defense. Rosecrans was directed to fortify the turnpikes leading east.

Key to his defense was the important pass over Cheat Mountain, on the Staunton-Parkersburg Turnpike. From that pass, the turnpike wound across the Alleghenies more than eighty miles southeast to Staunton and the Virginia Central Railroad, a main line to Richmond. Cheat Mountain Pass was, in effect, a gateway to the Shenandoah Valley, its agricultural bounty and railroads leading to the capital of the Confederacy. But the pass was also a gateway for the enemy. An incursion by the Rebels could be expected there. Rosecrans ordered General Joseph Reynolds, new commander of the First Brigade, "Army of Occupation," to guard that vital crossing.[319]

Joseph Jones Reynolds was a thirty-nine-year-old Hoosier, lanky, pale, and unassuming. A sworn teetotaler, he had curiously befriended U.S. Grant at West Point. Graduating from the academy in 1843, he returned to teach there under Robert E. Lee. Reynolds quit the army in 1857 to join his brother in the grocery business, but impending war brought him back as a brigadier general of U.S. volunteers. John Beatty fairly described the soft-spoken Reynolds as "an untried quantity."[320]

General Reynolds made headquarters under canvas about two miles south of Huttonsville, on a rocky little stream at the foot of Cheat Mountain. "Cheat Pass" was the name given his camp, often confused with the strategic gap in the mountain above. Indiana and Ohio regiments pitched rows of white tents at Reynolds's encampment. A steep wooded ridge fronted headquarters; from its crest waved a large American flag, visible for miles in every direction. Federal troops and supplies moved from this camp to the front.[321]

Meanwhile, loyal Virginia troops patrolled the countryside. Guards or pickets occupied every road and bridle path, for it was impossible to maintain a chain of sentinels in that rugged terrain. Day and night the pickets paced their lonely beat. Large squads might remain on watch at distant outposts for days without relief, but the camp guard was changed six times nightly.

"Halt! Who comes there?" rang the sentinel as an intruder approached. The ominous click of a musket lock punctuated the call.

"Sergeant of the Guard," was the prompt reply.

"Advance, Sergeant of the Guard, and give the counter sign."

The watchful sentinel received his visitor with bayonet at the ready. Failure of either party to strictly follow this procedure could mean death. "A cowardly sentinel is more likely to shoot at you than a brave one," wrote Lt. Colonel John Beatty from hard experience.[322]

Pickets fired their guns to warn of danger—an act repeated by every sentinel along the line. Shots in the night jolted slumbering camps to life. "Many men, half asleep, rushed from their tents and fired off their guns in their company grounds," recalled John Beatty of the first night alarm at Cheat Pass. "Others, supposing the enemy near, became excited and discharged theirs also. The tents were struck, Loomis' First Michigan Battery manned, and we awaited the attack, but none was made. It was a false alarm. Some sentinel probably halted a stump and fired, thus rousing a thousand men from their warm beds."[323]

Leaving the pass, the Staunton-Parkersburg Turnpike climbed the western slope of Cheat Mountain. There was an air of mystery to the ascent. Enormous moss-covered rocks and huge overhanging trees cast dark shadows on the roadway. Boundless springs gushed forth and plunged across the grade into deep ravines. For nine interminable miles, the turnpike spiraled upward. "So tortuous is its course," recalled a soldier, "that you may travel for miles without gaining in actual distance more than a few hundred yards, and sometimes the extremes of our column, stretching out a mile or nearly so in length, would be within a stone's throw of each other." The steep march tended to dampen military ardor, but "like the man who carried the calf until it grew to be an ox," the troops got accustomed to it.

As the turnpike climbed, its surroundings began to change. Towering spruces lined the roadway. Gnarled thickets of "laurel" or rhododendron blanketed the slopes. At the mountain crest, weary soldiers fell out to catch their breath and marvel.[324]

Cheat Mountain was an authentic wilderness. A traveler in 1861 regarded it "as savage as the unexplored [wilds] of Oregon." The "growl of the bear, the cry of the panther, and the bark of the wolf are sometimes still heard....Laurel-brakes stretch out like inland seas, and with never-fading leaves and snake-like branches interlaced, forbid a passage to even the light-footed deer; black-berry bushes extend miles in compact masses; superb firs lift up their crowned heads to the height of a hundred and fifty feet; and silvery cascades never cease their solitary murmur."[325]

Few had ventured into that wilderness until the turnpike crossed Cheat Mountain in the 1840s. Famed Harvard botanist Asa Gray used the new road to explore, and was rewarded with some of "the choicest botanical treasures which the country affords." Gray found Cheat Mountain to be a most remarkable place. Along its lonely crest he discovered plants unknown to science. Another curiosity was the Shavers Fork of Cheat River, a stream of consid-erable size that glides on *top* of the mountain. One amazed visitor insisted it had been "placed there by a mistake of nature."[326]

The weather on Cheat Mountain was also quite remarkable. Rain and snow fell in prodigious quantities. During the winter of 1855, the Trotter brothers had a contract to carry mail over the turnpike between Staunton and Huttonsville, a distance of more than ninety miles. At one point, a severe snowstorm brought deliv-ery to a halt. When complaints reached authorities in Washington, the brothers dispatched a terse letter to the postmaster general. "Sir," it read, "If you knock the gable end out of Hell and back it up against Cheat Mountain and rain fire and brimstone on it for forty days and forty nights, it won't melt the snow enough to get your d___ mail through on time."[327]

Military strategists eyed Cheat Mountain's defensive qualities. The mountain was a formidable barrier. The Staunton-Parkersburg Turnpike crossed its summit in a gap nearly four thousand feet high. On the afternoon of July 16, 1861, six companies of the Fourteenth Indiana Infantry under Colonel Nathan Kimball commandeered that gap. Kimball, a robust, curly-haired, thirty-nine-year-old medical doctor and Mexican War veteran from Loogootee, Indiana, was the only member of his regiment with military experience. "Our tents were pitched on a rocky point," wrote a member of the Fourteenth in his diary that first night, "with a fine forest on every side and a magnificent view of the Alleghenies in front of us, a beautiful romantic, though desolate looking spot."[328]

One of the few signs of habitation on Cheat Mountain was here—a hardscrabble farmstead scratched out twenty-two years earlier by an old mountaineer named Mathias White. Regimental historian J.T. Pool called it a "splendid farm of twenty acres on which were about ten rocks to one blade of grass." Pool described White as a "gaunt, lean, half starved devil," who "looked as though he had sucked his last meal from the spout of a bellows, and was none the better for it." He had never been inside a schoolhouse or heard a sermon; his piety was said to consist of "playing *jigs* and *hoe downs* on an old fiddle, and shooting mountain hawks on Sunday."

White was a crude blacksmith, and when unfinished Bowie knife blades were found in his shop, the "old sinner" was placed under arrest—suspected of making cutlery for the Rebels. His home was converted to a hospital, his barn into quartermaster and commissary quarters, and his forge put to shoeing Union horses. Any lingering doubt as to the loyalty of his clan was dispelled when a daughter, known by soldiers as the "Maid of the Mist," made it clear that bestowal of her heart and hand should only be in exchange for "Linken's Skaalp."[329]

Colonel Kimball seized a covered bridge over Shavers Fork, one half mile beyond the gap, and sent out patrols to display a bold front. The Hoosiers delighted in their novel assignment. "To one who loves the wildly picturesque in nature," wrote a member of the Fourteenth, "this region could not fail to awe, to please, to fascinate." They scaled the mountain peaks and mailed fragrant spruce-gum to their sweethearts in letters. Cheat Mountain "was an enchanted land," declared Ambrose Bierce. "How we reveled in its savage beauties!"[330]

A typical Federal soldier's day on the summit followed this schedule:

> *Reveille*—5:30 A.M.
> *Wood and water call*—6:00
> *Sick call*—6:30
> *Breakfast*—7:00
> *Guard-mounting*—8:30
> *Company drill*—9:00
> *Recall*—11:00
> *Wood and water call*—11:30
> *Dinner*—12:00
> *Battalion drill*—2:00 P.M.
> *Recall*—4:00
> *Dress parade (inspection of arms)*—5:00
> *Supper*—6:00
> *Tattoo*—8:30
> *Taps*—9:00 P.M.[331]

The troops breakfasted on huge stacks of well-greased flapjacks. Hardtack or "sheet iron crackers," pork, beef, beans, or rice made up the daily ration. Blackberries were ripening, and the boys spent hours picking them for pies and cobbler. At night, they gathered around campfires on the mountaintop, singing "Yankee Doodle," "Hail Columbia," and even "Dixie Land" with a roar that seemed to shake old Cheat to its very foundation.

When Colonel Kimball decided their amusement made too much noise, prayer meetings and debating societies filled the void. "How is the United States bounded?" might be the question posed to a geography class. A swaggering private would answer: "It is bounded on the South-East by Cheat Mountain and the Fourteenth Regiment of Indiana Volunteers; on the South and West by several regiments from the same State, and we defy all creation to get into them."[332]

To keep all creation out, Kimball's Hoosiers cut down the trees around their encampment to give cannons fair play on the turnpike. Tall spruces were felled and lobbed with the tops outward, presenting an "abatis" of sharp points. Then began the construction of an "immense" fort. Logs were stacked in crib fashion above the road and covered with rocks and dirt to form an embankment. "The walls were fourteen feet high," reckoned one soldier, "eight feet through at the base, narrowing to four feet at the top."

Breastworks of great strength were laid out across the road, and a blockhouse was erected. After weeks of toil, a massive fortress glowered from the gap. To the soldiers who built it, Cheat Summit Fort seemed impregnable. That fort "surpassed anything of the kind I have since seen," gloated a veteran of the Fourteenth Indiana, "and with our regiment to garrison it, we felt entirely secure."[333]

On July 30, a second fortification was begun along the Tygart Valley River, eight miles south of Huttonsville. Here defensive works were erected across the narrow valley floor to block the Huntersville Turnpike, at a place known as Elkwater. Colonel George D. Wagner of the Fifteenth Indiana Infantry led more than one thousand Federals in plying axe and spade. "Our fortifications are progressing slowly," John Beatty jotted from his tent at Elkwater on August 8. "If the enemy intends to attack at all he will probably do so before they are complete; and if he does not, the fortifications will be of no use to us."[334]

The Federal defenses formed the points of a triangle. At least one thousand men occupied each point. The supply depot at Cheat Pass was the triangle's apex, fourteen miles south of Beverly.

Cheat Summit Fort was nine miles southeast of the pass on the Staunton-Parkersburg pike; Camp Elkwater was nearly as far south on the Huntersville Turnpike. These fortifications blocked the two major roads leading across the mountains to railroads in Virginia's Shenandoah Valley. No road traversed the seven miles of ground between them.

From the B&O Railroad, seventy miles north, supplies for the Federals came along the turnpikes. Their grades had been designed for civilian traffic, not the tread of armies. The roads were soon cut up by heavy army wagons until routine travel became difficult. It was necessary to lay out bridle paths between the camps for infantry. These rough paths wound up steep slopes and twisted over narrow mountain crags. Squads might be seen on them at any time of day, guiding mounts along precipices more suited to billy goats.

Telegraph lines also connected the Federal camps. On Cheat Mountain, telegrapher E.B. Bryant found old Mathias White taking an interest in his new-fangled device. The rustic mountaineer figured that a paper message could be strung along the wire, but was puzzled how it got past each pole without being ripped to shreds. When Bryant sent a query to Huttonsville and received his answer in fifteen minutes, White was dumbfounded. He looked upon the whole contraption as witchcraft, and on Bryant as one who colluded with the devil.[335]

═══ ▲ ═══

The legendary Cheat Mountain weather also took a devilish turn. Nights on the summit were surprisingly cool. Soldiers slept under two or more blankets, requiring large fires and overcoats even on July mornings. By early August, sunny skies that had enamored the Hoosiers to their camp gave way to dark, angry clouds. Cold rains fell, and fog settled in. The slightest breeze caused the tall spruces to give forth "a most melancholy dirge." When it stormed they howled "as if all the demons of the mountains had congregated to frighten off the intruders who had dared to set foot on their domain."[336]

More unpleasantries were revealed in the valley below. Directly behind General Reynolds' camp at Cheat Pass was an immense blackberry patch that proved to be thick with rattlesnakes. There was no escaping the venomous vipers; they seemed particularly fond of crawling inside the tents and bedding. Snakes were also troublesome at Camp Elkwater. "To-day one of the choppers made a sudden grab for his trouser leg;" recorded John Beatty, "a snake was crawling up. He held the loathsome creature tightly by the head and body, and was fearfully agitated. A comrade slit down the leg of the pantaloon with a knife, when lo! An innocent little roll of red flannel was discovered." "[I]n short," declared Beatty, "the boys have snake on the brain."[337]

$$\text{▲}$$

Confederate authorities found the developments in those mountains to be equally repugnant. Virginia Governor John Letcher had crossed the Alleghenies in haste, directing Southern soldiers to rendezvous at Monterey, a Highland County village forty-seven miles west of the Shenandoah Valley railroad town of Staunton. General Henry Rootes Jackson temporarily took command of the Army of the Northwest at Monterey. Jackson must have seemed out of place in those mountains. A Georgian by birth, he was forty-one years old, gifted and refined, a distinguished graduate of Yale, and a lover of fine art and poetry. Jackson had already been a Superior Court judge and U.S. Minister to Austria. He had also been elected to the Confederate Congress, but experience as a colonel of volunteers in the Mexican War prompted him to enter the service with a brigadier's commission.[338]

Even the diplomatic Jackson was stunned by the wreck of Garnett's army limping into Monterey. The once finely adorned First Georgia Infantry appeared without their drums and fifes, without their fancy regalia, without their guns or even their shoes. "[T]he annals of warfare might be searched in vain to find a more pitiable picture of suffering, destitution, and demoralization than they presented at the close of their memorable retreat," Jackson reported sadly.

General Jackson's command could hardly fight. Ammunition and supplies intended for him had been sent to "Stonewall" Jackson by mistake. But General Henry Jackson did not panic. He sent troops to Huntersville to block the unguarded road that led across the mountains from the enemy camp at Elkwater to Millboro station on the Virginia Central Railroad. With the remainder of his depleted command, Jackson held the Staunton-Parkersburg Turnpike near Monterey. A detachment on Allegheny Mountain, fifteen miles west, constituted his front. Thus positioned, he awaited reinforcements.[339]

The weakened condition of Jackson's force conspired against him. Measles and typhoid fever swept the Confederate camps. Of Garnett's old command, only the Thirty-first and Thirty-seventh Virginia regiments were fit for duty. Nearly half of the newly arrived Third Arkansas Infantry reported sick. "Monterey! What sad recollections cluster around the name!" recalled a Virginian. "For a time the entire town was a hospital."[340]

Still, there was hope. On the afternoon of July 21, Confederate outposts on the heights above Monterey reported strange sounds emanating from the east. Puzzled pickets listened for hours to the faint, protracted "rumble." A veteran officer was finally summoned who recognized that noise. It was the muffled din of cannon fire—more than one hundred twenty miles distant as the crow flies—at the great Battle of Manassas.

"Everyone was wild, nay, frenzied with the excitement of victory," recalled Sam Watkins of the First Tennessee Infantry upon learning the results. "We felt that the war was over, and we would have to return home without even seeing a Yankee soldier. Ah, how we envied those that were wounded. We thought at that time that we would have given a thousand dollars to have been in the battle, and to have had our arm shot off, so we could have returned home with an empty sleeve."[341]

Private Watkins and the First Tennessee Infantry were bound for Jackson's camps, among reinforcements sent by General Lee to "drive back the invaders." Leaving the train at Millboro Station, they began to climb the mountains under a sweltering sun. Sam Watkins called it the hardest march of the war. "It seemed that mountain was piled upon mountain. No sooner would we arrive at a place that seemed to be the top than another view of a higher, and yet higher mountain would rise before us." Most were over-burdened for the march. "First one blanket was thrown away, and then another," recalled Watkins, "now and then a good pair of pants, old boots and shoes, Sunday hats, pistols and Bowie knives strewed the road." Panting Confederates fell by the wayside in droves. Some pitched into healing mineral springs, only to come out "limp as dishrags," unable to march.[342]

Yet these Southerners were unlike the earliest recruits. They had drilled for many weeks in camps of instruction. They hailed from states like Tennessee, Georgia, Arkansas, North Carolina, and Virginia. They were tolerably armed and equipped—ready and able to fight. And they came in high spirits. "We may be killed," pledged one to his gal, "but never will be whipped."[343]

Their new commander was also a fighter. General William Wing Loring, age forty-two, was entering upon his third war. A brusque, goateed, sleepy-eyed bachelor, Loring had first battled Seminole Indians as a boy soldier of sixteen. He had fought in Mexico as a captain of mounted riflemen, won two brevets, and then was struck down at the Battle of Chapultepec. When told that his mangled left arm needed amputation, Loring coolly laid aside a cigar and sat quietly while the arm was cut off—without anes-thetic relief. His men buried that limb on the battlefield with the hand pointed toward their goal, Mexico City. Loring called it the proudest moment of his life.

Loring had been the youngest line colonel in the U.S. Army prior to his resignation. Now he rode into the Alleghenies as a

Confederate brigadier general, stunned to find members of the Army of the Northwest—his soldiers—filling every farmhouse and outbuilding on the road from Staunton. It would not do. Loring gruffly cancelled all furloughs and dispatched officers to round up the men.

He reached Monterey on July 24 and assumed command from General Jackson. Upon reviewing the smartly dressed Twenty-first Virginia Infantry, Loring remarked that they were fine-looking men, but "Until they are able to sleep in winter amidst the snow and ice without tents, they are not soldiers!" John Worsham and his comrades angrily put their one-armed general down as "an officer who knew nothing." Worsham wrote in retrospect: "Alas for our judgment! It was not many months before we were of the same opinion as General Loring."[344]

Loring saw that the best hope for an offensive lay on the Huntersville Road—a dash to Huttonsville that would cut off the Cheat Mountain fortress, turning it completely. Directing Jackson to seize a point on the Staunton-Parkersburg pike at Greenbrier River, twelve miles from the Federals on Cheat Mountain, Loring left him with about five thousand men on the Monterey line and departed for Huntersville.

Huntersville was a tiny crossroads hamlet about fifty miles south of Huttonsville. Originally a wilderness outpost where eastern merchants bartered with trappers and hunters, it was the seat of Pocahontas County and General Loring's new headquarters. The general's talented staff converted Huntersville into a large army depot. Columns of infantry, cavalry, and artillery rolled into the town. Tents steadily filled the fields and slopes. General Loring would soon have nearly eighty-five hundred men on the Huntersville line.[345]

North Carolina Confederates recalled their campground at Huntersville as "one of the most eligible" of the war. A beautiful maple grove shaded tents along the banks of a cool mountain stream. Pointing to the spearmint-fringed margin, one impish company officer declared, "[H]ere [is] the water, here is the mint;

if anyone can furnish the sugar and some one the spirits, we'll have the best mint julep you ever tasted." The ingredients were discreetly secured, and soldiers huddled behind a fence to enjoy their "jolly, jolly grog."[346]

There was more reason for good cheer. Even as Washington, D.C., hailed McClellan as the "Young Napoleon," General Robert E. Lee was riding west into the mountains.

CHAPTER 13
SCOUTS, SPIES, AND
BUSHWHACKERS

*"Like the country, may we not find the people, unpolished,
rugged and uneven, capable of noble heroism or villainy?"*
—Lt. Colonel John Beatty

Only the hoofbeats of horses and creaking saddle leather were discernable as eight finely mounted troopers of Burdsall's First Ohio Cavalry wound cautiously down the mountainside. Their orders were to scout east on the Staunton-Parkersburg Turnpike. It was a dangerous task. Many points between the friendly outposts on Cheat Mountain and the Greenbrier Valley below offered ground where horsemen might be attacked and left powerless to resist.

On this pleasant morning in July 1861, the scouts expected trouble. Each man scanned the roadside for signs of the enemy as their mounts trod down the grade. Near the base of the mountain, the turnpike descended precipitously to the West Fork of Greenbrier River. A small bridge and an old ford crossed the river there. Directly above that crossing was a sinister, laurel-crowned precipice known as the "hanging rock."

It was a prime spot for ambush. As those silent Federal horsemen neared the bridge, they paused to scrutinize the ground.

There was not a hint of danger; in fact, the atmosphere was disarming. Soft rays of sunlight danced across the fern-covered banks of the stream. A gentle, rippling current soothed jittery nerves. Satisfied, the horsemen rode on.

Late that afternoon, the merry riders returned, wheeled directly into the ford, and began to water their mounts. But this time, they were not alone.

A band of mountaineers had gathered at the home of a Mr. Gum on Back Allegheny to go hunting that day. Headed by a local gunsmith, each of the nine men was a practiced slayer of deer and bear. Armed with trusty rifles, they had stalked through dark woods to the hanging rock. The hunters were after big game, but today their quarry would be different.

The stealthy woodsmen chose positions overlooking the crossing and settled in. They were aware that a squad of Yankee cavalry was on the prowl; their plan was to reserve fire until assured of numbers, and then to "let them have it in the back."

The eight riders soon galloped into view. By crossing at the ford rather than the bridge, they might discover the nimrods' hideout if allowed to continue. Hunting rifles slowly came to bear as the cavalry reined in at midstream. The riders conversed in soft tones as their horses drank. Overhead, the hidden marksmen each selected a man. One of the troopers finally drew his reins to start across—the signal those woodsmen had been awaiting.

Rifles cracked. Helpless Federals toppled from their saddles into the cool stream. The mountaineers watched them thrash in mortal agony. One dying trooper grasped a horse's mane to stay above the water. Another reeled forward when shot, desperately hugging his mount. A comrade reached for him just as a fatal bullet likewise struck him. The two handsome cavaliers died arm in arm, their blood mingling in the current. A lone survivor frantically whipped his horse across the river and dashed away.

The woodsmen had already vanished, disbanding by mutual consent. There would be more hunting in the days ahead. Guerrilla warfare had come to the Alleghenies.[347]

═══ ▲ ═══

Despite the danger, scouting was a passion for the Federals. Many an outpost picket was infatuated with the idea of scaling the rugged peaks on every side, of exploring deep and mysterious valleys and ravines. The regular scouts were looked on in reverence. It was little wonder that rumors of an expedition would crowd headquarters with anxious volunteers.

A few hard crackers and a slice of ham or bacon were all the provision needed for these details. Receiving their instructions, scouts plunged into the wilderness, singly or in small groups. Their orders were usually to avoid human contact. Some doubtlessly sought a cozy retreat to pass the time, but the majority were anxious to win distinction. They scaled moss-covered peaks by day and slept under the stars at night, enduring great privation in hope of a simple reward—the sight of an enemy camp, or the discovery of an unguarded path. Nothing would be heard of them for days, until, one by one, they emerged from the thickets to relate their discoveries to the commandant.

Federal soldiers were not alone in their wanderings. Both armies played a deadly game of hide and seek in those mountains. Confederate General Henry Jackson hand picked a rifle corps of eighty men from the local militia as scouts. This band was ordered to watch the turnpikes and to "annoy the enemy from the hills and bushes." Jackson informed the Confederate War Department of his plan: "To me, it is altogether obvious that the only way to hold this country at all is by adopting the guerrilla system." It was strange candor from a diplomat. No reply was forthcoming from General Lee, a man known to have a "pious horror of guerrillas." Jackson would regret the decision.[348]

The mountains were soon infested with guerrillas. Hardy mountaineers, long accustomed to unfettered freedom, cursed the intrusion of armies. Protected by a conspiracy of silence among those who gave them food and shelter, angry natives struck back.

Soldiers were an easy mark for these cold-blooded killers—known derisively as "bushwhackers."

Adjutant Charles Ross of the Thirteenth Indiana described them as "bloodthirsty, moccasin-wearing cut throats (expert woodsmen and mountaineers), crack shots with the rifle...too cowardly to fight in the open." Bushwhackers concealed themselves behind rocks or laurel thickets and picked off soldiers at will. Recalled Ross, "It was no uncommon thing to find a dead picket, or a soldier lying by the roadside, shot through the back, his pockets turned inside out, and invariably some part of his clothing gone."

Regular troops looked upon the bushwhackers with unbridled horror. "Imagine a stolid, vicious-looking countenance, an ungainly figure, and an awkward if not ungraceful, spinal curve in the dorsal region, acquired by laziness and indifference to posture," wrote one Federal, "a garb of the coarsest texture of homespun linen or linsey-woolsey, tattered and torn, and so covered with dirt as not to enable one to guess its original color; dilapidated, rimless hat or cap of some wild animal covering his head, which had not been combed for months; his feet covered with moccasins, and a rifle by his side, a powder-horn and shot-pouch slung around his neck, and you have the beau ideal of a Western Virginia bushwhacker."

Thus equipped, the bushwhacker sallied forth with the stealth of a panther to lay in wait for his victim. He killed "for the sake of killing," and plundered "for the sake of gain." Avowed Charles Ross, "Bushwhackers and rattlesnakes! Of the two I prefer the latter for they at least give notice of attack."[349]

Guerrilla bands inaugurated a rein of terror. "Every man's hand was raised against his neighbor," recalled one observer, "until a spirit of armed resistance to all law largely prevailed." It was a time to settle old scores, often more personal than political. "Persecutions are common, killings not rare, robberies an everyday occurrence," reported Major Rutherford B. Hayes of the Twenty-third Ohio Infantry from the mountains of Western Virginia.

Homes were sacked and burned. Citizens dangled limply from ropes in the woods. John Beatty wrote of a man found "with his head cut off and entrails ripped out, probably a Union man who had been hounded down and killed." One ferocious guerrilla leader stuck the head of a Federal soldier on a pole by the roadside as fair warning to all. "Some bloody deeds are done in these hills," observed Major Hayes, "but not all on one side."[350]

The soldiers adapted to this strange mode of warfare with a reckless, devil-may-care contempt of danger. "Went out a Skouting yesterday," wrote one Hoosier lad to his father. "We got To one House where there was Five Secessionest And they broke and Run and Arch…holoed out to Shoot the ornery Suns of Bitches…[and we] all let go…at them.…Thay may Say what they please, but godamit pa It is Fun."[351]

When guerrillas gunned down Federal scouts near Cheat Mountain on consecutive days in early August, Colonel Nathan Kimball garnered reinforcements and rushed to the scene. Two prisoners were taken into custody, a sulky, dull-looking pair who called themselves "Mountain Rangers." The angry colonel questioned them, demanding the number and whereabouts of their gang. But they said nothing, a right given to all prisoners of war except bushwhackers. These men were looked upon as outlaws—assassins caught in the act of murder.

Colonel Kimball became increasingly animated as he tried to loosen their tongues. Finally—exasperated beyond control—Kimball drew his pistol and shot one of the bushwhackers. The horrified prisoner began to speak freely, after which his wound was attended to. Such captives were routinely sent to Ohio prisons to await trial until the Virginia courts were reorganized.[352]

Guerrilla warfare hardened regular soldiers to the plight of civilians. Despite rules to the contrary, Federal troops routinely looted farms. Many a mess on Cheat Mountain had veal, new potatoes, and maple syrup after a scouting foray. Entire harvests were stolen or destroyed. A sympathetic Confederate wrote of dwellings "that had Bin Rob & plunderd Killing hogs Cattle sheep poltery of all Kinds [besides] Taking out the huney & Busting them all to peaces [and] Tearing Down fences." The Confederates were no less active. "We foraged rather extensively," admitted a Tennessean near Huntersville, "and fat mountain pigs, young chickens, and potatoes and green corn, all made up a pretty good living for soldiers, as long as they lasted."[353]

There was little compassion for the natives. An Indiana soldier declared, "The people out here are very ignorant and the farther we go the more ignorant they are. You scarcely ever find one that was ever out of the state.…They are ignorant beyond…imagination." A mountaineer who had lived thirty years on one farm was asked the name of his county by some scouts. "Virginny!" he answered, positively unaware of any subdivisions of the state. He seemed as informed as his neighbors, one of whom admonished that her family was neither Unionists nor Secessionists—they were Baptists.

As viewed through the eyes of civilized soldiers, these isolated mountain folk lived in log dwellings that more resembled woodpiles. Newspapers were a curiosity to them, books a sealed mystery, the locomotive an "unimaginable monster." Fair-minded observers noted a "sprinkling of loyal, intelligent people," but adventures like that of a Federal scout near Elkwater were more amusing to relate.

Spying a little log hut tucked in a dark ravine, the scout rode to the front door—no doubt anticipating a hearty meal. Greeting an old woman "with a face like a pig's," he dismounted and asked for some dinner. "What! Wittles?" exclaimed the horrible-looking creature. "Whar did you come from, and what be a sojer doin' here?"

"Well, I came from Indianapolis, and be after something to eat," he replied. "Are there any secesh in these parts?"

"Any what?"

"Secesh."

"Why, gracious, what's them?"

"Are you and your folks for the Union?"

"Why sartin. That's the old man, neow."

Just then appeared a "gaunt-eyed, slim-livered, carnivorous, yellow-skinned, mountain Virginian—no doubt one of the first families."

"Look heah," the old woman said, "This 'ere sojer wants to know if you be Union."

The old fellow looked more astonished than the woman. As their parley continued, the soldier inquired what the old man thought of the war.

"What war?" exclaimed the mountaineer. "The Revolution?"

"Yes, the rebellion, we call it."

"Oh, why, we gin the Britishers fits, didn't we?"

That old couple knew nothing of the conflict in their mountains.[354]

━━━ ▲ ━━━

During one scouting foray, Federals halted a wagon bearing a lone Confederate under flag of truce. He proved to be Lt. James Dorset of the Twentieth Virginia Infantry, captured during the Battle of Rich Mountain. Dorset had escorted the body of Captain William Skipwith home to Richmond for burial, pledging to return as a prisoner of war. The chivalrous lieutenant made the long journey back to honor his word. Adjutant Charles Ross claimed this incident was the only one of its kind during the war.[355]

Another remarkable figure was nabbed by Federal pickets in the woods near Elkwater on August 14. His clothing was badly ripped by briers; his hands and face were bleeding. Toting a shoulder bag and walking staff, he professed to be a farmhand out looking for a strayed steer. He had removed his boots to relieve swollen feet and was carrying them when apprehended.

Imitating the rough language and manner of a mountaineer, he asked if the sentinel "had seed anything of a red steer."

The sentinel had not.

"Well, I must be a goin'," the herder said. "It is a gettin' late, and I am durned feared I won't git back to the farm afore night. Good day."

"Hold on," barked the sentinel. "Better go and see the Captain."

"Oh, no, don't want to trouble him, it is not likely he has seed the steer, and it's a gettin' late."

"Come right along," replied the guard as he leveled his musket. "The Captain will not mind being troubled; in fact, I am instructed to take men such as you to him."

Captain Henry Cunard of the Third Ohio Infantry questioned the herder closely about his work. Pointing to the pair of long-legged military boots in his hand, Cunard asked how much they cost.

"Fifteen dollars," replied the herder.

"Fifteen dollars!" the captain exclaimed. "Is that rather more than a farmhand who gets but twelve dollars a month can afford to pay for boots?"

"Well, the fact is, boots is a gettin' high since the war, as well as every thing else."

This herder was not up to the character he played. Cunard informed him he would be sent to headquarters. Betrayed by his footgear, the herder confessed his true identity—he was Confederate Captain Julius DeLagnel, thought to have been killed at Rich Mountain.

DeLagnel related how, wounded and bleeding, he had crawled from the battlefield to a farmhouse near Beverly. Secreted there, he had been nursed back to health. DeLagnel's hosts had dressed him in herder's garb in order to sneak through the Federal lines. He had been in the mountains for five days, presumably beyond danger, when caught at the last Union outpost. General Reynolds, an old army friend, received him warmly at Camp Elkwater, but as a former U.S. Army officer in Confederate service, DeLagnel would go to prison.[356]

━━━━ ▲ ━━━━

Spies roamed the countryside. Citizens swept dusty roads to count the number of passing horsemen. Deserters and paroled prisoners offered details of enemy troop strength. Elderly gentlemen were caught with sketches of the Federal camps hidden inside their shoes. "A spy is on every hill top, at every cabin," complained one general in Western Virginia.[357]

Two Pinkerton operatives, Pryce Lewis and Samuel Bridgeman, managed to infiltrate Confederate camps on the Kanawha River near Charleston. Lewis posed as an English tourist, dapper in a tall silk hat and new suit of baggy tweeds. Bridgeman played his servant, driving a carriage stocked with fine cigars, port, and champagne. The pair even duped Captain George S. Patton (grandfather of the famous World War II general) into dinner and an offer to tour the Southern defenses.[358]

Slaves also took a turn. Spying for the Confederates was a Randolph County slave named Richard Green. When the soldiers needed a guide, he piloted them through the mountains; when food was sought, he brought it through the lines. He was known to recover horses and cows stolen by the Yankees and bring them back to the rightful owners. The citizens near Huttonsville long remembered the goodwill of "Old Dick" Green.[359]

Women proved to be the most formidable spies. The daring duo Abbie Kerr and Mollie McLeod continued to aide the Southern cause after their exploit at Philippi. Far less subtle was Mary Jane Green, an illiterate and perfectly fearless Braxton County teen. She was an unabashed Confederate partisan, fond of cutting the telegraph wires. Her hatred of the "Yankee vagabonds" knew no limits.

When Federal troops arrested Mary Jane for carrying Rebel correspondence, she cursed them like a teamster. The brazen creature declared she would have the "heart's blood of every 'Lincoln pup' in Western Virginia." Upon learning that her brother had taken the loyalty oath, Mary Jane denounced him as a coward, swearing that they could not "make a d___d Abolitionist of her."

Packed off to the Clarksburg jail, she dreadfully abused passers by. Mary Jane shouted lustily for "Jeff. Davis and the Southern Confederacy;" she pledged to "have the heart of General Rosecrans" himself. A move to Wheeling's Atheneum Prison only increased her tantrums. In short order, she had the entire prison roiled. Guards delighted in teasing her, and Mary Jane retaliated with unprintable language about their ancestors.

Federal authorities called her a "perfect she-devil," the meanest Rebel in Wheeling. They bound her with rope to protect the guards; when a sympathetic bailiff foolishly cut those bonds, she clobbered him with a brick. General Rosecrans finally ordered that Mary Jane be taken home—fervently praying that an exasperated soldier would shoot her along the way![360]

If any woman could rival Mary Jane Green, it was Nancy Hart, a Rebel spy and bushwhacker of legendary proportions. Deadly as a rattlesnake, this mountain spitfire rode with a guerrilla band known as the Moccasin Rangers. Nancy was a pert, vivacious lass in her early twenties—not prone to give quarter as she terrorized Virginia counties west of the Alleghenies. When not marauding, Nancy posed as an innocent mountain girl, traveling the country-side with two adorable pet fawns. Who would have guessed she was a Confederate spy?[361]

═══ ▲ ═══

The Hoosier fife major Dr. William Fletcher also sleuthed. On July 30, Fletcher was called to General Reynolds's tent and given orders to search out Confederates lines on the Huntersville road. Fletcher's companion on this two-day mission was Leonard Clark, a native of Western Virginia. Clark was a spy of repute, cool and sharp-witted, but quieter than the debonair doctor. Wearing a mixture of civilian and Confederate clothing for their assignment, the two agents procured horses and stuffed revolvers into their belts. Riding to the outer picket line about fourteen miles south of Huttonsville, they continued on foot.

Lighthearted banter gave way to silence. Only a few dwellings, mostly vacant, were observed as Fletcher and Clark followed the Huntersville road to Mingo Flats. Some women there informed them that lodging could be had at a place called Big Spring, four miles south. A sinking sun cast long shadows as the roadway climbed mountain spurs. Although the citizens had claimed no soldiers were about, fresh horse tracks were observed. The route began a gentle descent. Each man squinted into the growing darkness. A death-like stillness pervaded the scene. Only the plaintive call of a whippoorwill could be heard.

Clark froze. "I saw a man move behind that tree," he warned, pointing toward a large oak about a hundred yards ahead. "Let us take to the woods and go around."

"No, I think you are mistaken," Fletcher replied, "I can make out any form I wish on dark and shadowy evenings. I think it's imagination."

Clark trailed Fletcher at a cautious pace. "Halt! Halt! Halt!" rang out from every direction—the two had blundered into a trap.

Fighting the urge to run, Fletcher put on a bold face. "What are you stopping citizens here for, in the public highway?"

"Surrender!" barked a tall soldier as he leveled a deer rifle on Fletcher's chest.

"Run, Clark, run!" Fletcher hissed to his companion, a few paces behind.

"Just you stand still," commanded the Rebel, "If your friend moves, I'll blow you to h__l!"

Fletcher threw down his revolver as bayonets closed around. Clark was still outside the circle of pickets and might have escaped, but surrendered to preserve his friend's life.

"What shall we tell them?" whispered Clark.

"Truth only, and as little as possible," Fletcher muttered.

The pair was taken to Confederate headquarters, a log house at Big Spring. Fletcher gave his real name and rank to the commanding officer, adding that they were scouting under orders and had walked into the ambuscade. Clark identified himself as a native

Virginian serving in the Union army. At that, a crimson-faced officer drew his sword and lunged forward. "Don't you know, sir," he
yelled at Clark, "you are guilty of the most damnable treason, taking up arms against your native State....I'll cut your damned heart
out!"

Fletcher and Clark had been captured under "very suspicious
circumstances." Their future looked grim—the penalty for spying
was death.[362]

CHAPTER 14
MUD, MEASLES,
AND MUTINY

*"Since the days of the deluge, I do not
think it has stormed so hard and long."*
—William B. Fletcher

On July 29, 1861, a small party of Confederates rode west into the mountains from Staunton, Virginia. At the head of that party was General Robert E. Lee. The general had no bodyguard. Only staff members John A. Washington and Walter Taylor, a cook named Meredith, and a servant named Perry accompanied him. All of the headquarters baggage was in a single wagon.[363]

If the procession was plain, the general himself commanded attention. Only days before he took leave for Western Virginia, Lee had encountered three prominent ladies on a Richmond street.

"He sat his horse gracefully," Mary Chesnut recalled, "and he was so distinguished at all points that I very much regretted not catching the name....We chatted lightly and I enjoyed it, since the man and horse and everything about them was perfection."

As Lee rode off, Mrs. Chesnut asked eagerly, "Who is he?"

"You did not know?" one of her companions exclaimed. "Why that was Robert E. Lee, the first gentleman of Virginia."

"He looks so cold, quiet, and grand," concluded Mrs. Chesnut.[364]

The gentleman who had impressed those ladies was anxious to reach the Alleghenies. As military advisor to President Jefferson Davis, Lee had been "mortified" by his absence from the field of battle at Manassas. Now he hoped to make amends.

President Davis must have been loath to detach the general from his side, for Lee entered the mountains without formal orders. "General Lee has gone to Western Virginia, and I hope may be able to strike a decisive blow at the enemy," wrote the president on August 1. "Or, failing in that, will be able to organize and post our troops so as to check the enemy, after which he will return to this place." Lee was to coordinate the effort of Generals William Loring, Henry Wise, and John Floyd. President Davis concluded that his skill and diplomacy would best serve their independent commands.

Robert E. Lee did not formally take charge of the Confederate Army of the Northwest, but he would endorse orders as the "General Commanding." Lee's mission was not well understood by the southern public. Nonetheless, high expectations followed him into the mountains.[365]

As his tiny escort followed the Staunton-Parkersburg Turnpike, Lee was reminded of happier days. "A part of the road, as far as Buffalo Gap, I passed over in the summer of 1840, on my return to St. Louis, after bringing you home," he wrote his wife, Mary. "If any one had then told me that the next time I traveled that road would have been on my present errand, I should have supposed him insane." Lee found the mountains too "peaceful" and "magnificent" for war. Rain fell on that first day, but he failed to regard it as an omen.[366]

Upon reaching Monterey, Lee conferred with General Jackson and inspected the troops. He gracefully consented when asked to present a flag made by the ladies of Augusta County, but turned to the company officer after the formalities. "Now Captain," Lee spoke gently, "I would advise you to roll up that beautiful banner, and return it to the ladies for safe keeping. You are now in for a number of years of hard military service, and you will not need your beautiful flag."[367]

Arriving in Huntersville on August 3, Lee found General Loring stocking his depot and organizing a supply train. The one-armed general did not welcome Lee's visit. Loring's orders were less than two weeks old—yet here was Lee already looking over his shoulder. Loring had outranked Lee in the old army. He was fighting Indians when Lee was a mere staff lieutenant! He had marched troops across the continent and won battles in more rugged country than this. Why was Lee meddling? Loring's hackles were up; jealousy oozed from his pores.[368]

While Loring saw red, Lee saw opportunity. The enemy was known to be fortifying only forty miles north at Elkwater, a two-day march. If Loring moved promptly, the bluecoats might be driven back before their defenses were complete. Beef cattle were abundant on that line. The army could live off the land for a few days if needed until the pass over Cheat Mountain was cleared, opening the turnpike to Staunton. Yet Loring seemed fixated on the gathering of supplies, unwilling to be hurried along.

Lee discreetly urged Loring to advance. By power of suggestion rather than command, he tried to smooth Loring's ruffled feathers, to gently coax him forward. Lee's honor as a gentleman clouded his judgment as a soldier. On August 6, tired of watching supply wagons roll through Huntersville, he said good-bye to General Loring, gathered his small escort, and rode twenty-eight miles north to Valley Mountain.

Here was the Confederate front. The coveted B&O Railroad at Grafton lay eighty-five miles north, while Lee's back was to Richmond, about one hundred ninety miles southeast. From this staging area, he would try to reclaim Western Virginia. At Valley Mountain, Lee found magnificent grazing country. Lush fields of bluegrass and clover rippled on the 3,600-foot heights. Tents of the Twenty-first Virginia and the Sixth North Carolina Infantry regiments dotted the crest of Valley Mountain. "We are on the dividing ridge," Lee wrote Mary from his new camp. "Looking north down the Tygart's river valley, whose waters flow into the Monongahela & south towards the Elk River & Greenbrier, flowing into the Kanawha. In the valley north of us lies Huttonsville & Beverly, occupied by our invaders, & the Rich Mountains west, the scene of our former disaster, & the Cheat Mountains east, their present stronghold, are in full view."[369]

Lee's headquarters consisted of a solitary tent shared with Colonel Washington and Captain Taylor. The three officers ate from simple tin plates and drank from tin cups. A small table was their only furniture. Rough logs served as benches.[370]

Lee's son William Henry Fitzhugh, or "Rooney" Lee, a twenty-four-year-old major of Virginia cavalry, served on outpost duty at Valley Mountain. Rooney was a figure of grand proportions— "too big to be a man and not big enough to be a horse," thought one observer. He had been a noted oarsman at Harvard, was spirited, hearty, and intensely proud of his birthright.[371]

General Lee now directed his son to carry a message to the enemy. In it, Lee proposed an exchange of prisoners—the Confederates paroled at Rich Mountain for Union soldiers taken at Manassas. It would be the first large-scale prisoner exchange of the war. Under a flag of truce, Rooney rode north to the Federal outposts near Camp Elkwater. The proposal was rejected, but Lee's effort confirmed Federal troop locations and revealed that an old friend, Joseph Reynolds, was in command. The affair served Reynolds as well, for he took the opportunity to inquire about two missing "citizens"—the Union spies Fletcher and Clark.[372]

▲

While in custody, Fletcher had burned some incriminating papers in his corncob pipe, but he and Clark remained in deep trouble. A party of heavily armed cavalrymen led them from Big Spring to Edray, eighteen miles south, where they were locked in irons and confined in a brick house. Presently, a commotion erupted outside, and then a tall, well-dressed Virginian was thrown into their room. He too was in chains. The three stared at each other in silence. "Don't give it up, men!" the stranger began. "I was captured at the same place you were, last night. I'm not going to back out for these d____d traitors; it a'n't my way. I've been leading Rosecrans and General McClellan and I am not done yet! Where are you from boys? Don't look down. We'll be even by God. Come, be social. You don't say a word; you're scared, I suppose."

"We are not very badly scared," replied Fletcher. "And as I have seen first-class players, real stars on the boards, I can't compliment your acting; you overdo it; and, besides, we are not trying to make many new acquaintances down here." The Virginian clammed up. An officer who had been listening at the door then burst in, abused the new prisoner as a "Union man," and carried him roughly away—as if to an execution.

"Clark," smiled Fletcher, "we won't be caught by stool-pigeons."

The two were taken to Huntersville and placed in separate quarters. Guards led Fletcher past curious soldiers to a hotel in the heart of town, and up an old staircase.

"That Yankee spy is here, General," spoke an orderly.

"Send him in, send him in," came a rough voice from the next room. "Put a strong guard at the door, also at the windows outside. Take off his irons, too, and let no one in till I call."

Fletcher was ushered to a long table covered with maps. Behind it sat a small, demonic-looking man with black hair, piercing eyes, and an empty sleeve—General Loring himself.

Loring placed a large revolver on the table and motioned for Fletcher to sit opposite. The general began rattling off questions, trying to catch Fletcher in a lie. Loring was alternately persuading, insulting, and threatening. Some two tedious hours later, he threw up his hands. "Before to-morrow's sun goes down," he warned Fletcher, "I'll hang you both. Your only hope for mercy is in confessing *all, all* you know."

"General, you have the hanging power," Fletcher replied, "but wouldn't it set a bad example to our army to begin hanging soldiers who fall into your hands?"

Loring sent him away in a huff.

Fletcher was taken back to Loring's office the next day for more questioning. This time, General Lee was present.

"Young man, how long have you been soldiering?" Lee inquired.

"Three months, General."

"Were you persuaded to go into the army, or did you choose it?"

"I went in *because of the cause.*"

"How many men from Indiana are in the field?"

"As I said before, General, I was a three-months' man. I do not know how many are in the field now; but if the men of Indiana were to see me here in irons, and then remember the treatment of prisoners at Cheat River, Laurel Hill and Rich Mountain, a hundred thousand men would be in arms to-morrow...."

"I shall not let you talk so," General Loring angrily broke in.

"Remember, you were not taken in battle," Lee interjected. "If you were, you would not be in irons." Intently, he questioned Fletcher on the Federal commanders in Western Virginia, his impression of General Reynolds, and other topics. Finally, Lee said, "Young man, we will have to keep you very close, very safe, until we can get the evidence of those who captured you."[373]

General Lee prepared to gather intelligence in a more familiar way.

═══ ▲ ═══

During the Mexican War, Captain Robert E. Lee had distinguished himself as a master of reconnaissance. His bold forays around enemy lines and uncanny ability to read terrain were instrumental in Winfield Scott's success. That had been fourteen years ago. Now the fit and athletic fifty-four-year-old general saw need for careful reconnaissance of the enemy in Western Virginia.

Rank and age had not diminished Lee's talent, and with scarcely anyone present experienced in that work, he began to scout the Federal defenses.

Nearly every day at Valley Mountain, Lee and his aides rode off to reconnoiter. He was constantly in the saddle, a large opera glass slung over his shoulder, guiding his mount over rocks and mountain crags. It became apparent that the opportunity for a surprise rush down the Tygart Valley was lost. Lee traced countless bridle paths, hoping to find a route by which the enemy might be flanked to avoid needless loss of life. He seemed to be everywhere. One day, a Confederate captain on outpost duty spotted three men well in advance of the picket line. Believing them to be Federal scouts, the captain and his party slipped forward and burst upon the unsuspecting trio. To the captain's amazement, General Lee stood before him![374]

The general made quite an impression. "He looked every inch a soldier," thought Isaac Hermann as Lee inspected his regiment. "He was clean shaven, with the exception of a heavy iron gray mustache. He complimented us for our soldierly bearing." Sam Watkins remarked that Lee "had a calm and collected air about him, his voice was kind and tender, and his eye was gentle as a dove's. His whole make-up of form and person, looks and manner had a kind of gentle and soothing magnetism about it that drew every one to him and made them love, respect and honor him."

Marcus Toney knelt to take a drink of water on Valley Mountain when he first encountered Lee. "Don't drink out of that spring," the general called out. "My horse uses it. Come and drink out of this spring near my tent." Toney did so, and when he passed, the seated commander threw his hand to musket, palm extended, as a private's salute. Lee returned it with a salute from his brow.[375]

Enlisted men noted with approval that Lee ate the same rough rations they did. It became known that when visitors brought gifts of food to the general, he always sent the articles to a sick soldier as soon as the messenger was out of sight. Once, a private was charged with falling asleep at his post. The young man insisted he had only taken a seat out of the rain and was unable to hear the approach of the corporal of the guard. The offense was punishable by death—the private's regimental officers thought he must be shot as an example for the rest. His case was brought to General Lee. "Captain," Lee replied after hearing the facts, "you know the arduous duties these men have to do daily. Suppose the man who was found on his post asleep had been you, or me. What do you think should be done to him?" The captain replied that he had not thought of it in that way. Lee then turned to the frightened private. "My man," he said firmly, "go back to your quarters, and never let it be said you were found asleep on your post."[376]

The kind-hearted general could also make a point with humor. While examining the ridges near an outpost with his field glass, Lee found soldiers crowding around. He turned mildly on the most inquisitive.

"What regiment do you belong to?" Lee asked the man.

"First Tennessee, Maury Grays," was the reply.

"Are you well drilled?"

"Yes, indeed," answered the proud private.

"Take the position of a soldier."

The young man did so. "Forward march," commanded the general. "By the right flank, march." When the soldier's movements pointed him toward camp, Lee added; "Double-quick, march."

Lee was bothered no more.[377]

—————— ▲ ——————

Federal authorities were troubled by Lee's activity. The defensive posture of Confederate troops less than twenty-five miles from Washington fueled suspicion of an impending assault by Lee in Western Virginia. Generals Scott and McClellan encouraged General Rosecrans to complete his fortifications—they could not be "too strong" in McClellan's view—and to be certain he had an escape plan in case of disaster. But a deaf ear was turned when Rosecrans sought reinforcements. Again, it was McClellan who urgently needed troops. Greatly overestimating the number of Confederates near Washington, he declared a state of emergency.[378]

On August 4, McClellan had offered President Lincoln a plan to "crush the rebellion at one blow." To pull it off he required a massive army—no fewer than 273,000 men and six hundred guns. With this juggernaut, McClellan would march on Richmond to smash the Southern Confederacy. He furnished no timetable for the grand offensive, but did not expect to move before spring.

In the meantime, McClellan restored order around Washington. He took headquarters in a spacious house on Pennsylvania Avenue. When not dining with the president, royalty, or other heads of state, he inspected the camps and forts. The soldiers roared whenever McClellan appeared. He posed for photographers with folded arms, in fine Napoleonic style. A New York editor asserted, "Genl McClellan has done more in ten days towards organizing the advance than Scott did in ten weeks."[379]

━━━━ ▲ ━━━━

Another threat loomed in the Alleghenies. By August 12, General Loring joined Lee at Valley Mountain. On the Monterey line, General Henry Jackson established Camp Bartow, twelve miles east of the Federals at Cheat Mountain. The Confederates amassed a force of more than ten thousand—actually outnumbering their foe. They might now reclaim Western Virginia.

Lee would soon be confirmed as a full general—the third-highest-ranking officer in the Confederacy. His rank and diplomacy seemed to make Loring more amenable. But as the two generals readied for battle, a trio of foes intervened.[380]

First came the rain. The very heavens had opened since Lee reached Western Virginia. "It rains here all the time, literally," he wrote Mary. "There has not been sunshine enough since my arrival to dry my clothes."

"Rain, rain, rain! Mud, mud, mud!" groused a Tennessee foot soldier at Valley Mountain. "In all my experience of the war I never saw as much mud," recalled Virginian John Worsham. "It seemed to rain every day. It got to be a saying in our company that you must not halloo loud; for if you should, we would immediately have a hard shower. When some of the men on their return from picket had to shoot off their guns to get the load out, it brought on a regular flood."[381]

"We were camped on Valley Mountain 43 days," added George Peterkin of the Twenty-first Virginia, "and it rained 37 days out of the number." Springs bubbled up everywhere, flooding the tents. One disgusted colonel likened his regimental camp to a "Tennessee hog pen."[382]

Endless showers turned the roads into bottomless quagmires. All efforts to advance were paralyzed. "Time and again could be seen double teams of horses struggling with six or eight barrels of flour, and the axle of the wagon scraping and leveling the roadbed," recalled Lee's aide Walter Taylor. Wagoners complained it was difficult to haul more than feed for their teams from the rail depot at Millboro, sixty miles away. John Worsham swore he saw dead mules lying in the road "with nothing but their ears showing above the mud."[383]

Unable to bring up supplies, the Confederates were placed on short rations. "Mud and water were the prevailing commodities," recalled a Tennessean. Lee and Loring seriously debated whether the army might be forced to retire to a point nearer the railroad.[384]

Next came sickness. Poor sanitation, rain, and toil spread the epidemic of measles, dysentery, and typhoid fever that had ravaged the Confederates at Monterey. Illness reduced entire regiments to token strength. "There is nearly half the regiment sick," wrote Shepherd Pryor of the Twelfth Georgia Infantry, "some getting well, some getting sick every day...we are more subject to die by disease than the bullet. Our regiment has lost more men than they would in a Battle of Manassas." General Lee confessed that the sick list at Valley Mountain "would form an army."[385]

Then came the cold. "The wind blows like winter," grumbled a Tennessean at Valley Mountain on August 16. "Ice was abundant yesterday morning, a large frost covering the ground." Shivering men huddled around huge bonfires to keep warm. Even General Lee was stunned by this latest trick of nature. "The cold," he wrote, "has been greater than I could have conceived. In my winter clothing and buttoned up in my overcoat, I have still been cold."[386]

The weather aggravated sickness, resulting in many deaths. Row upon row of freshly dug graves sprung up behind the regimental camps. "To die, away from all the comforts and endearments of home, on the ground, in a wilderness, and be buried alone, without a stone to mark our resting-place, is pitiable," mourned a Tennessee officer.[387]

The Confederates were stymied—mired in the mud—unable to move until the heavens relented and the roads dried up. Yet there was no let-up in sight. Lee wrote to his daughters in late August, "It is raining now. Has been all day, last night, day before & day before that, &c. But we must be patient."[388]

▲

It was little consolation that the Federals were also suffering. "The angels in Heaven seem to be weeping constantly over the unhappy condition of this once most peaceful and prosperous Republic," wrote an Indiana soldier of the rain. Downpours swelled the Tygart Valley River, inundating Camp Elkwater. The hospital tent had been imprudently placed on a small island. As rising waters threatened the sick, John Beatty led a rescue effort that left him stranded in a tree above the raging torrent. Men and horses were drowned in the flood.[389]

Cold, chiseling rains wore on the constitutions of the volunteers. Even in the "dog days" of August, brisk temperatures on Cheat Mountain compelled the men to heat flat rocks by campfires and place them at their feet each night for any hope of comfortable rest. "Very wet, cold and disagreeable. Almost as cold as December," scrawled a member of the Fourteenth Indiana upon his diary in mid-August. "We are shivering in an almost winter atmosphere. The scarcity of overcoats render it still more disagreeable."[390]

Frigid it was on the summit of Cheat Mountain. To the Hoosiers' disbelief, snow fell on the afternoon of August 13! "What do you say to that, ye drinkers of Patrick's soda water, and eaters of Scudder's ice creams?" howled J.T. Pool in a report to the folks at home. Huffed an astonished Federal, "While our friends in the States are basking in the sunshine, eating peaches and watermelons, we poor devils are nearly freezing to death upon the top of Cheat Mountain."[391]

To make matters worse, their flimsy wedge tents were attacked by mildew and began to rot. The crumbling shelters offered little protection against fierce mountain storms that drove rain through "as though they had been mosquito bars." The Hoosiers' state-issued uniforms fared no better. "Our regiment is sadly in want of clothing," wrote an officer of the Fourteenth Indiana on August 23. "The worse than second rate clothing which was issued to us at Camp Vigo is in rags."

Scouts returned to camp with only the waistband of what had been a pair of pantaloons—having left the remainder shredded in the laurel thickets. It was said that a man's rank could be determined by the amount of his backside exposed. If the view proved too offensive, *dab!* would come a pound of black mud from snickering comrades. To hide their nakedness, many strolled around camp wrapped in blankets—like "Scotch Highlanders" in their kilts.[392]

As the rain and temperatures plummeted, so did morale. "[W]e are still stationed on the summit of this infernal mountain which is the meanest camping ground that I have ever seen," growled a soldier on Cheat Mountain. "The mud is not less than shoe top deep any place and if [it] continues to rain there is no telling how deep it will be...." Tents were pitched on the slopes, and men had to brace their feet against rocks or stumps at night to keep from sliding down the mountainside. Speaking for all, a Hoosier declared: "The name of this mountain certainly could not have been more appropriate...For we have been *cheated* in various ways...since our arrival."[393]

The mood blackened. Shivering men watched their comrades fall to disease, then laid them to rest in shallow, rocky graves. Tall spruces around the dreary, windswept fortress on Cheat Mountain seemed to wail a constant "funeral dirge."[394]

Political intrigue grew thick as the billowing fog. The Ohio Twenty-fourth and Twenty-fifth Infantry regiments appeared on Cheat Mountain with new uniforms, overcoats, and money from the paymaster. Kimball's suffering Fourteenth Indiana boys had none of those luxuries. Bitterness turned to mutiny. Homesick Hoosiers were determined to leave that wretched mountain. Their leaders were openly denounced. "I know that there is not a man in our company but what would be pleased to get rid of our captain," swore one, "and many are the curses not loud but deep that he gets." When officers began to resign, the men refused to elect replacements. Resistance grew so impassioned that General Reynolds was called up to force the issue. Malcontents were tossed in the guardhouse; everyone was ordered not to write home of the incident.[395]

Reynolds placed the troops under tighter discipline. Haphazardly pitched regimental camps were lined up in the strictest military order. Company streets were paved with stone to combat the mud. All the ditching, paving, and cleaning brought a remarkable transformation to the camp on Cheat Mountain. The hum of camp life became more animated. The stroke of axes, the roar and crash of towering spruces, the clash of shovels and picks in the trenches, and the ringing of blacksmith hammers all had a sound of renewed purpose.[396]

Discord seemed to melt away with the August snow. "I for one say we will neve[r] give up the ship," vowed a member of the Fourteenth Indiana. "We have been looking so long for a battle," wrote another, "that the men are really anxious to be attacked."[397]

CHAPTER 15
FEUDING GENERALS AND
DICKERING DELEGATES

"Old Governor Wise, with his goggle eyes."
—A popular Federal tune

His face was deeply chiseled. His hair was long, thick, and nearly white. His eyes bulged with fierce intensity. His form was trim and active. His style was charismatic, rash, and independent. His name was Henry Alexander Wise.

Wise was born a Virginian in 1806, native of Accomac County. He could swagger; he could bully; he was not averse to a duel. He had been a lawyer, Congressman, foreign minister and governor of Virginia (1856–60). He was a champion of Southern rights—he had sent John Brown to the gallows and been the linchpin of Virginia secession.

Governor Henry Wise had earned the respect of Virginia's western counties, and President Davis commissioned him a brigadier general in the hope that his influence could rally wavering secessionists in the Kanawha Valley. During June–July 1861, he patched together an independent body of Confederate infantry, cavalry, and artillery known as the "Wise Legion." His force, coupled with local militia, totaled about 3,500 men.

With a few notable exceptions, the Wise Legion was poorly armed and equipped. The ex-governor, however, was not troubled in the least. A recruiting advertisement in the *Richmond Enquirer* boasted that no long-range arms (rifles) would be needed, as "Gov. Wise is not the man to stand at long range."[398]

On July 17, General Wise backed up his bluster at Scary Creek with a victory of sorts. But he was soon overwhelmed by Federal troops under General Jacob Cox and fled the Kanawha Valley by the end of the month. The ex-governor justified his move in a letter to General Lee: "The Kanawha Valley is wholly disaffected and traitorous. It was gone from Charleston down to Point Pleasant before I got there.…I have fallen back not a minute too soon." It was not a retreat, Wise informed his troops, only a "retrograde movement."[399]

Wise and his legion regrouped at White Sulphur Springs on the James River and Kanawha Turnpike, more than sixty miles east of the enemy at Gauley Bridge—minus several hundred volunteers who had disappeared along the way. There he awaited the arrival of a rifle brigade from Covington led by John B. Floyd. Generals Wise and Floyd had orders to "cordially co-operate" in an effort to check Union General Cox's advance up the Kanawha River. Unfortunately for the Confederates, their union would be anything but cordial.[400]

Wise and Floyd seemed to have much in common. John Buchanan Floyd was, like Henry Wise, in his fifty-fifth year of life. He too was a lawyer, former legislator, and Virginia governor (1849–1852). President James Buchanan had appointed him secretary of war in 1857, but Floyd resigned his post in December 1860 upon Buchanan's refusal to withdraw Federal troops from Fort Sumter. Floyd had been accused of stockpiling weapons in southern arsenals before his resignation. He was further sullied in a government bond scandal. As a result, he became known in the north as "Thieving Floyd."

General Floyd hoped to extract a measure of revenge for the Northern charges, and carried no fewer than three newspaper reporters on his staff. Like General Wise, he had been awarded a brigadier's star by President Davis for political, rather than military, prowess. Despite his former role as secretary of war, Floyd knew little of the art. His own inspector-general, the West Point–trained Henry Heth, claimed that Floyd "was as incapacitated for the work he had undertaken as I would have been to lead an Italian opera."

General Floyd was headstrong and impetuous, much like General Wise. Worst of all, the two were ancient political rivals. Floyd, a native of southwestern Virginia, was said to be furious when he learned of Wise's mission. He began to curse his old nemesis: "G__d___ him, why does he come to *my country*? Why does he not stay in the east and defend *his own country*, Accomac and Southampton; there is where he belongs. I don't want the d_____ rascal here, I will not stand it."[401]

The two iron-willed ex-governors met at White Sulphur Springs on August 6 in a council of war. A few polite formalities were observed. And then General Wise grasped the back of a chair and began one of his famous "windbag" speeches. Wise reviewed the history of the country from its discovery, spanning the Revolution, the Mexican War, the cause of the present conflict, his march down the Kanawha, the affair at Scary Creek, and his so-called retrograde movement. The valedictory went on for nearly two hours.

General Floyd sat patiently, not uttering a word.

General Wise finally took a seat, and asked Floyd of his destination.

"Down that road," Floyd replied, pointing to the route upon which Wise had retreated.

"What are you going to do, Floyd?"

"Fight," snapped Floyd, intimating that Wise had failed to do just that.

General Wise began to quake with anger. "If a look could kill," recalled Henry Heth, "Floyd would have been annihilated."

Floyd's commission predated that of Wise by only a few days, yet as the senior officer he was dead set on asserting his authority.

But Wise was just as determined to retain the independent command given him by President Davis. A bitter feud was brewing in those mountains.[402]

The relationship between these old rivals grew worse by the day. Even their military strategies clashed. Despite limited resources, Floyd sought to carry the war down the Kanawha Valley and into Ohio. Wise, in contrast, hoped to lure the Federals east, away from their supply line and into a trap deep within the Alleghenies.

On August 11, Floyd assumed command of the Confederate Army of Kanawha and prepared to move on General Cox's position at Gauley Bridge without delay. Wise, however, needed time to refit his worn-out legion. Sparks flew as the hotheaded generals parted without agreement. Wise petitioned General Lee to detach his command from Floyd's. Lee rejected the appeal, hoping to unite their forces for an offensive. Although rebuffed, Wise looked to Lee as his defender. Floyd, in turn, sought out President Davis for his own counsel. By the time Lee reached Western Virginia as a "coordinator," his two generals had already drawn a line in the sand.

They refused to occupy the same camp. Wise and his tattered command remained at White Sulphur Springs, while Floyd marched fourteen miles west to Lewisburg. Their combined force was reportedly 5,500 men, but Floyd couldn't be sure of that—Wise refused to forward returns of his effective strength.[403]

The two generals squared off like old gamecocks. When Floyd called for artillery, Wise sent a squad of demoralized gunners. Floyd retaliated by informing President Davis of the "great disorganization" in Wise's command. General Lee, preoccupied with the enemy seventy-five miles north at Valley Mountain, could only grit his teeth.

As Wise and Floyd quarreled, Federal troops began to move against them. Under orders from General Rosecrans, Colonel Erastus B. Tyler's Seventh Ohio Infantry marched south on the Weston-Gauley Bridge Turnpike to open a line of communication with General Cox's Kanawha Brigade, then fortifying at Gauley Bridge. By August 15, Tyler reached a point near Summersville named (Kesslers) Cross Lanes, twenty miles northeast of Cox's position. The Weston-Gauley Bridge Turnpike intersected a road leading to the James River and Kanawha Turnpike at Cross Lanes, near an important Gauley River passage known as Carnifex Ferry.[404]

Floyd's army was threatened by that move. Again he called on Wise for artillery. Wise dismissed the alarm. Floyd countered by ordering a regiment to join him at Meadow Bluff on the James River and Kanawha pike, but Wise argued the regiment could not move—had not Floyd himself criticized its state of "great dilapidation and destitution(!)"? In a third letter to his antagonist on August 13, Floyd instructed Wise to bring up his entire legion. Time was of the essence—the enemy was said to be only eighteen miles ahead. "I hope to see you early," Floyd added in a bit of wishful thinking.

Instead, Wise took his case to General Lee, arguing that Floyd had no grounds to interfere. Lee made clear that Floyd was in command, but he also reminded Floyd of President Davis's intention that the Wise Legion be independent. The divided Confederate command structure in Western Virginia was becoming a nightmare.[405]

General Wise ignored another direct order to come to Floyd's aid. Grudgingly, Wise forwarded a troop of cavalry. General Floyd's temper must have reached the boiling point when he discovered that the horsemen sent by his rival lacked one important detail: Wise had neglected to issue any ammunition.[406]

Despite Lee's best long-distance effort, this spat was beyond mending. Wise groused to the secretary of war that Floyd was out to "destroy" his command. He refused to stand by and watch the Wise Legion being "torn to pieces by maladministration." He alleged that Floyd plotted to sink him—the second in command—"even below his majors and captains."[407]

On August 15, General Wise ended his filibuster and marched west toward General Floyd's camp on Big Sewell Mountain. But the petty bickering continued. Wise accused Floyd of meddling with his command; Floyd responded with less than the tact Lee had begged of him. In a scathing letter to President Davis, Floyd charged that Wise's "unwillingness to co-operate...is so great that it amounts...almost to open opposition." Yet he admitted to no problem in handling his irascible second in command. "I know perfectly well how to enforce obedience," Floyd avowed to the president, "and will, without the least hesitation, do it."[408]

Wise now began to harass the "other" foe. On August 20, his scouts dueled with Federal troops along the James River and Kanawha pike near Hawk's Nest. The commands of Wise and Floyd were "united," more or less, at Dogwood Gap, just ten miles east of General Cox's position near Gauley Bridge. Yet even in the shadow of the enemy, those two rivals kept separate camps.

Learning of the retreat of Colonel Tyler from Cross Lanes, Floyd crossed the Gauley River at Carnifex Ferry on the night of August 21, seized high bluffs north of the stream, and began to fortify Camp Gauley. By occupying that strategic point, about eight miles below Summersville, he threatened either General Cox or Colonel Tyler on the Weston and Gauley Bridge road. Floyd began to smell blood, but could accomplish little without help from General Wise. Frustrated beyond measure at his rival's obstinacy, Floyd wrote to the Confederate secretary of war, offering to trade the Wise Legion for any "three good regiments."[409]

Wise complained to Lee of vacillating orders from Floyd, asserting that his nemesis was in danger of being trapped. "I am willing, anxious, to do and suffer anything for the cause I serve," Wise pleaded, "but...I have not been treated with respect by General Floyd, and cooperation with him will be difficult and disagreeable, if not impossible."

By this time, even Lee's proverbial patience must have neared the breaking point. "The Army of Kanawha is too small...to be divided," he replied on August 27. "I beg, therefore, for the sake of the cause you have so much at heart, you will permit no division of sentiment or action to disturb its harmony or arrest its efficiency."[410]

General Floyd, entrenched at Camp Gauley, was distracted by the Federals. Colonel Tyler's Seventh Ohio Infantry had reappeared at Cross Lanes, only three miles in Floyd's front. Tyler, an old Virginia fur trader who had earlier seized the gold from Weston's Exchange Bank, announced he was back to deal in "rebel skins." He nearly lost his own hide, instead.

As the sun rose on August 26, Floyd surprised Tyler's men at breakfast. Driving the Buckeyes from hot meals, he routed them, killing or wounding about thirty and capturing more than one hundred. Floyd jubilantly notified Lee of his success. The envious General Wise informed the secretary of war that Floyd was recklessly exposed. Wise cautioned that his fellow general was too "elated" by victory to see the danger. He blamed it on Floyd's little success—that "battle of knives and forks at Cross Lanes."[411]

Wise could suffer his rival no longer. If forced to remain with Floyd's brigade, he warned Lee in dark tones, "we will unite in more wars than one."[412]

▲

The feuding of Generals Wise and Floyd was nearly matched by the political wrangling of Virginia's new "Restored Government." That body had received a boost when President Lincoln extended official recognition in his July 4 message to Congress: "These loyal citizens," Lincoln pledged, "this government is bound to recognize, and protect, as being Virginia."[413]

A rump legislature, made up of loyal Unionists from the General Assembly, met in Wheeling on July 1 and elected new United States Senators—the statehood firebrand John Carlile and his law-and-order foe Waitman Willey. Virginia's "disloyal" senators, R.M.T. Hunter and James M. Mason, had vacated their seats in Washington by the time Carlile and Willey were confirmed. Three new Congressmen, William G. Brown, Kellian V. Whaley, and Jacob B. Blair, were elected to the House of Representatives.[414]

The Restored Government offered a platform upon which Virginia Unionists could rally, but unqualified support came only from strongholds in the panhandle and a few Potomac River counties near Washington. Many county officials refused to swear an oath of loyalty. Local governments were thrown into chaos as "bogus" representatives clung to office by force. In fact, without the presence of Federal soldiers, the new government could hardly have existed. The *Wheeling Intelligencer* proclaimed on August 6, "The news comes in constantly that people by counties and by communities, wherever our victorious arms have spread, are gladly rallying to its support and defense."[415]

Virginia's Restored Government now became the catalyst for a new state. On August 6, the Second Wheeling Convention reassembled at the Custom House. "The members of this Convention are satisfied that a large majority of the good and loyal citizens of Western Virginia are in favor of a division of the State," read its opening preamble. "Yet there seems to exist a difference of opinion as to the proper time, as well as the proper means to be used to effect the object."

Progress was stymied for three days until John Carlile, "loyal" Virginia's dapper new senator, arrived from Washington to energize the fight. Independent statehood was the only salvation for Western Virginia; Carlile termed it the "cherished object" of his life. He warned that procrastination might be "death." Virginia must be cleft in two. "Cut the knot now!" he bellowed to loud applause. "Cut it now! Apply the knife!"[416]

Opponents made strong arguments for delay. Their trump card was a letter from Edward Bates, venerable attorney general of the United States. "The formation of a new State out of Western Virginia is an original, independent act of Revolution," Bates had written on August 12. "Any attempt to carry it out involves a plain breach of...the Constitution—of Virginia and the Nation. And hence it is plain that you cannot take that course without weakening, if not destroying, your claims upon the sympathy and support of the General Government."

Bates praised the Restored Government as a "legal, constitutional and safe refuge from revolution and anarchy," a model for restoring other seceded states to the Union. "Must all this be undone," the attorney general concluded, "and a new and hazardous experiment be ventured upon, at the moment when danger and difficulties are thickening around us? I hope not—for the sake of the nation and the State, I hope not."[417]

Critics viewed the statehood advocates as zealots, and their position as nothing more than "legal fiction." Many vexing questions had been ignored: What would become of Virginia's debt? What would become of loyal Unionists in the *eastern* part of the state? And what would be done about the ticklish question of slavery? The treatment of slaves was certain to ignite controversy. It could hardly be ignored in the adoption of a state constitution. Abolition was not then an aim of the Union war effort. President Lincoln had pledged not "to interfere with slavery in the States where it exists."[418]

But statehood advocates would not be silenced. Floor debate grew heated as John Carlile lurched up on the convention's tenth day: "Yes Sir, and you may say 'down!' 'down!' But, gentlemen, it will not go down. It will be agitated. It is a question...that has been looked to and expected from the foundation of our government....Why, take the map of Virginia and look at it, and you will see at once, that this is an unnatural connection."

A committee of three statehood advocates and three opponents met on Monday, August 19, to break the deadlock. One day later they presented a dismemberment ordinance. The new "State of Kanawha" would consist of thirty-nine Virginia counties, with provision for the inclusion of Greenbrier, Pocahontas, Hampshire, Hardy, Morgan, Berkeley, and Jefferson if a majority of voters in each of those counties approved. This new state would assume a fair share of Virginia's debt and safeguard property rights. Any Virginia counties not included in the new state boundary would remain under jurisdiction of the Restored Government.[419]

On August 20, Wheeling delegates passed the dismemberment ordinance by a vote of fifty to twenty-eight. Residents of "Kanawha" would put the ordinance to a vote in October. In a bold stroke, Western Virginia had nearly severed her ties to the Old Dominion—and to the Confederacy. The war for her borders was about to take on a new urgency.[420]

CHAPTER 16
THE PERFECT ROLL DOWN

"Now we are sure of a fight, the result of
which we little doubt will favor us."
—George P. Morgan, Thirty-first Virginia Infantry

September greeted the Confederates on Valley Mountain with blue skies, the first in nearly a month. The army's mood seemed to lift with the storm clouds. Sugar maples began to turn; fall warblers sang from their branches with robust cheer. General Lee marveled at the transformation. "The glorious sun has been shining these four days," he wrote on September 3. "The drowned earth is warming. The sick are improving, and the spirits of all are rising....I feel stronger, we are stronger....Now...a battle must come off, and I am anxious to begin it."

The roads dried out, allowing wagons to bring up supplies. Upon Lee's urging, General Loring organized the Army of the Northwest into six brigades of Virginia, Tennessee, Georgia, Arkansas, and North Carolina troops. The Huntersville Division, commanded by General Loring and the Monterey Division, under General Henry Jackson, gave the Confederates a total force of nearly eleven thousand, but their effective strength was much reduced by sickness. Union General Reynolds, commanding the Cheat Mountain District, had fewer than nine thousand defenders.[421]

The Confederates girded for battle. Soldiers filled cartridge boxes and burnished steel. They eyed the Union defenses on Cheat Mountain, blocking the vital Staunton-Parkersburg Turnpike pass. To Federals, the Staunton-Parkersburg Turnpike was a portal to the Shenandoah Valley and railroads leading to Richmond. For Confederates, the turnpike led northwest to the B&O Railroad and Parkersburg, on the Ohio River. "The enemy holds Cheat Mountain," wrote a Georgian to his mother, "and to undertake to drive them off...by attacking them in front, we might as well try to take Gibraltar."[422]

To get around that fortress, the Confederates needed maps. No detailed chart of the region was at hand; therefore, engineer Jed Hotchkiss set to work once again. As he drew maps upon a barrelhead at Valley Mountain, Hotchkiss noted with approval Lee's energy and persistence. The general had refused to allow the weather to be a deterrent, in marked contrast to General Loring, whom Hotchkiss found unduly negative and too often "filling himself with brandy."[423]

While General Lee studied routes for infantry, couriers reported the discovery of an unguarded path to the crest of Cheat Mountain. A civilian surveyor named John Yeager had clambered through the wilderness to gain an unobstructed view of the Federal fortress on the summit. To prove his story, Yeager made a second reconnaissance with Colonel Albert Rust of the Third Arkansas Infantry. Rust inspected the enemy fortifications with a spyglass, then spurred his horse for Lee's camp.[424]

Albert Rust was a towering, black-bearded giant, well over six feet tall and broad of physique. Virginia-born in 1818, he had immigrated to Arkansas as a youth, studied law, and served in the Congress. He was bold, energetic, and domineering. When newsman Horace Greeley criticized the fiery Razorback Congressman for his pro-slavery acts in 1855, Rust brutally skulled with a cane.

View of the Allegheny Mountain region of Western Virginia. (*Harper's Weekly,* November 23, 1861)

General George McClellan and his "charming Nelly." He pledged to write her a letter every day while at war.

Robert E. Lee as Americans saw him in 1861, with the uniform painted on. He would leave the Alleghenies with a humiliating nickname—"Granny."

The "Philippi Races," first land battle of the Civil War. (*Frank Leslie's Illustrated,* June 22, 1861)

Benjamin Kelley—commander of a regiment of Virginia soldiers fighting for the Union.

Frederick W. Lander, U.S.A., a fearless warrior and poet.

Firebrand John Carlile led the West Virginia statehood movement—then abruptly became its "Judas."

Francis H. Pierpont—as governor of "loyal" Virginia in Wheeling, he defied the Confederates in Richmond.

Wheeling's Custom House, seat of the Restored Government of Virginia. (*Frank Leslie's Illustrated*, August 10, 1861)

Yankee foragers with their plunder at Philippi. (*Harper's Weekly*, August 17, 1861)

Tray Run Viaduct near Rowlesburg. General Lee thought the destruction of this vital crossing of the Baltimore and Ohio Railroad was "worth…an army." (*Frank Leslie's Illustrated*, August 3, 1861)

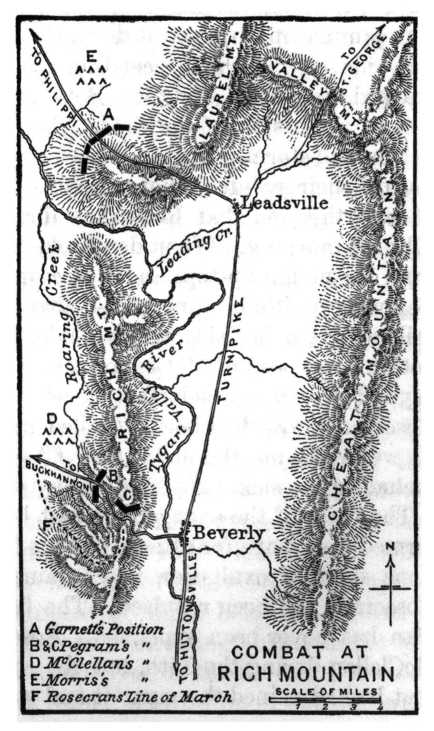

A *Garnett's Position*
B & C *Pegram's "*
D *McClellan's "*
E *Morris's "*
F *Rosecrans' Line of March*

COMBAT AT
RICH MOUNTAIN

SCALE OF MILES

Confederate positions at Laurel Hill (A) and Rich Mountain (B). These turnpike passes were General Garnett's "gateways to the northwestern country." *(Battles and Leaders of the Civil War)*

Virginia Unionist Waitman Willey—dazzling orator and a senator from the Restored Government. (WVSA)

Robert S. Garnett, a dreary-hearted Confederate—the first general killed in the Civil War. (Library of Congress)

Union General William S. Rosecrans—McClellan's "silly fussy goose." He planned and won the battle of Rich Mountain.

John Pegram, dashing commander of Confederate forces at Rich Mountain.

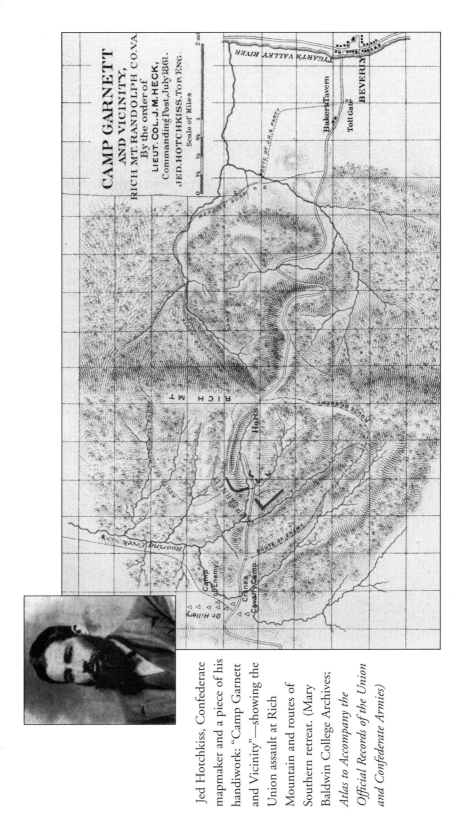

Jed Hotchkiss, Confederate mapmaker and a piece of his handiwork: "Camp Garnett and Vicinity"—showing the Union assault at Rich Mountain and routes of Southern retreat. (Mary Baldwin College Archives; *Atlas to Accompany the Official Records of the Union and Confederate Armies*)

Battle of Rich Mountain, July 11, 1861—a small Union victory with huge repercussions. (*Frank Leslie's Illustrated*, July 27, 1861)

Indiana volunteers bury their dead on the battlefield of Rich Mountain. (*Frank Leslie's Illustrated*, August 10, 1861)

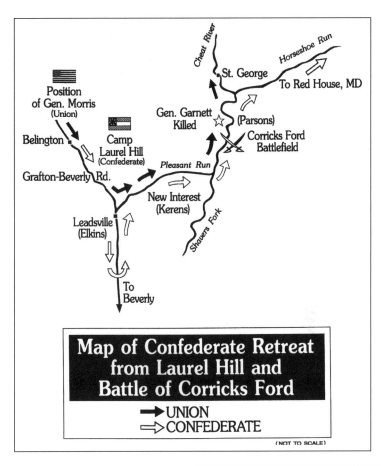

Map of Confederate Retreat from Laurel Hill and Battle of Corricks Ford

➡ UNION
⇨ CONFEDERATE

(NOT TO SCALE)

Whitelaw Reid—this talented young reporter was one of the first to bring the grim reality of war to Northern doorsteps.

George B. McClellan, the "Young Napoleon." His victories and clever use of the telegraph in Western Virginia made him the North's first battlefield hero.

Battle of Corricks Ford, July 13, 1861—Union troops in the foreground strike General Garnett's rearguard. Like much of the first campaign, it was fought in a rainstorm. (Below): Indiana soldiers discover the body of General Garnett. (*Frank Leslie's Illustrated,* August 3, 1861)

Union General Joseph J. Reynolds—a modest teetotaler in command of the Cheat Mountain District.

William W. Loring. This one-armed Confederate general did not welcome the aid of Robert E. Lee.

The Union fortress on Cheat Mountain. Soldiers of both armies declared it impregnable. (*History of the Fifth West Virginia Cavalry*)

Secessionist riflemen of the Alleghenies—the dreaded "bushwhackers." (*Harper's Weekly*, July 20, 1861)

Nancy Hart, the lady guerrilla—"deadly as a copperhead snake." (WVSA)

Dr. William B. Fletcher, dapper spy for the Union. (*Indiana Magazine of History and Biography*)

Confederate generals Henry Wise (left) and John Floyd (right), old political rivals who hated each other worse than the Federals.

Lt. Colonel John Augustine Washington, killed at Elkwater—General Lee's tent mate and great-grandnephew of the first president. (*Mount Vernon: Washington's Home and the Nation's Shrine*)

Albert Rust, the domineering Arkansas colonel who failed General Lee. (Library of Congress)

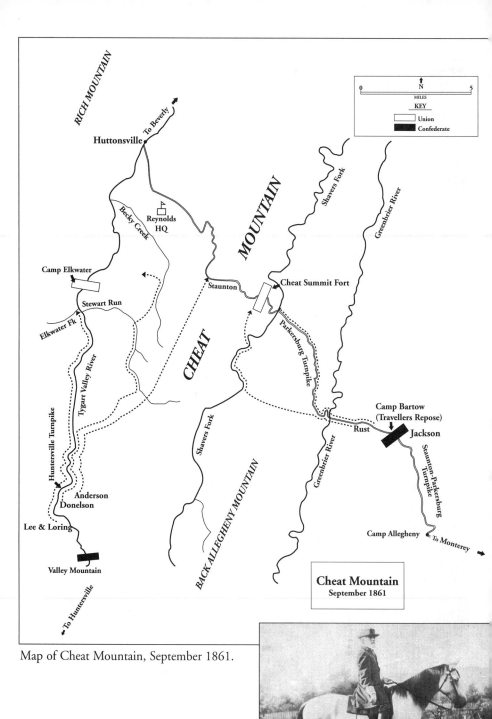

Map of Cheat Mountain, September 1861.

Robert E. Lee on his warhorse Traveller—the horse and Lee's beard were legacies of the first campaign.

Union General Robert H. Milroy, with his quills up.

Confederate General Edward "Allegheny" Johnson—a profane bulldog in combat.

Little Josie Gordon, Ninth Indiana Volunteers—a bloodstained letter broke his father's heart.

A cartoon from *Harper's Weekly* (January 4, 1862) mocks suffering Confederates in the frigid mountains of Western Virginia.

Thomas J. "Stonewall" Jackson sought to drive the Yankees from his boyhood home. (*War Songs and Poems of the Southern Confederacy, 1861–1865*)

Laura Jackson Arnold nursed Federal soldiers as fast as her brother Stonewall wounded them. (WVU)

Veteran Ambrose Bierce (wrapped in the flag at far right) and friends on a return to the battlefields, ca. 1913. (Stanford University Libraries)

Now the impetuous colonel glowered over General Lee. Rust was emphatic. The Yankee right flank on Cheat Mountain was exposed; a force slipping around that flank could take the fort. Rust was certain of it—he had seen the vulnerable flank with his own eyes. If Lee was to seize this opportunity, Rust requested the honor to lead the attack.[425]

It was an awkward petition. Rust had scant military experience. Had he not led an aborted reconnaissance of Cheat Mountain just two weeks prior—a strange effort in which his command got lost and wandered about in "reckless folly"? Yet Lee admired Rust's initiative. He also knew that the big Arkansas colonel was a friend of President Davis. Rust's zeal and commanding presence won out; he was directed to lead the assault.[426]

For the first time as a commanding general, Lee prepared to give battle. On September 8, a crisply worded "Special Order No. 28" directed five independent columns through the mountains to surround Cheat Fort. The plan, issued in General Loring's name, was crafted by Lee. It called for Colonel Rust to lead a brigade to the unguarded ridge behind the Federal fortress, while General Henry Jackson's column marched up the Staunton-Parkersburg Turnpike to create a diversion in front. From Valley Mountain, two brigades of Tennessee Confederates would move by footpaths to support Rust. The first, General Samuel Anderson's brigade, was to gain the Staunton-Parkersburg pike west of the fort. The second, General Daniel Donelson's brigade, would seize bridle paths east of Tygart Valley River to protect General Loring's column as it advanced down the Huttonsville road on Camp Elkwater.

Rust would launch the attack—surprising the entrenched Federals on Cheat Mountain at dawn on September 12. Upon carrying the works, Confederates would sweep down the turnpike to Huttonsville, trapping the enemy at Camp Elkwater. Federal defenses in the Alleghenies would drop like a house of cards. The victorious Confederates might then reclaim Western Virginia.

It was daring strategy, requiring secrecy and coordination. Artillery and supply wagons could follow Generals Loring and

Jackson along the turnpikes, but the other Confederate brigades had to traverse miles of rugged wilderness without support. All would slip into position, awaiting Colonel Rust's assault.[427]

In a supplementary order, General Lee urged the troops to "keep steadily in view the great principles" they fought for. "The eyes of the country are upon you," he admonished. "The safety of your homes, and the lives of all you hold dear, depend upon your courage and exertions. Let each man resolve to be victorious, and that the right of self-government, liberty and peace, shall in him find a defender. The progress of this army must be forward."[428]

Each Confederate wore a "badge" of white cloth on his cap to distinguish the various columns from Federal troops. Nervous soldiers affixed the cloth patches, a grim reminder of what lay ahead. James Hall of the Thirty-first Virginia dreaded the assault of Cheat Mountain, "where there are Yankees, rattlesnakes and bears. *A onme id genus*" (All of a kind).[429]

Confederate preparations at Valley Mountain did not escape the notice of the enemy at Elkwater, fifteen miles north. Federal scouts probed eleven miles south along the Huntersville pike on September 9, stumbling upon the foe near Marshall's store before falling back. On Cheat Mountain, Colonel Nathan Kimball strengthened his guard, removed the planking of the bridge over Shavers Fork, and built wings of logs on each side for sharpshooters. His sentinels literally danced at their posts in anticipation of a Confederate *sortie*. They had not long to wait.[430]

═══ ▲ ═══

On September 9, Colonel Rust's sixteen-hundred-man brigade, consisting of the Third Arkansas, Twenty-third, Thirty-first, and Thirty-seventh Virginia Regiments, and Hansbrough's battalion, began the march to Kimball's fort. The Confederates left Camp Bartow on the Greenbrier River with four days' rations, followed the Staunton-Parkersburg pike for several miles, and then began a rugged ascent of Cheat Mountain, 4,600 feet high. Their route lay through an unbroken wilderness.

A chilling rain set in as Rust's soldiers labored to the summit and descended upon Shavers Fork. Forced into the rocky riverbed by laurel thickets, they waded the ice-cold waters for miles. Each man clung to the jacket or belt of his file leader on the final leg of the journey in darkness. "Many slipped and fell and some were right much hurt," wrote John Cammack of the miserable march. Despite great hardship, Rust's brigade reached the designated ridge on the evening of September 11, little more than a mile from Cheat Fort. "[W]e lay there all night, without fire, in a drenching rain," recalled a member of the Thirty-seventh Virginia, "many of our men chilled almost to insensibility."[431]

Two Confederate brigades marched from the vicinity of Valley Mountain on the morning of September 10. A dense fog enveloped the Tygart Valley below, swirling uniformly along the slopes and circumscribing ridge tops to give the appearance of tiny islands on a vast inland sea. Beyond that surreal landscape laid the enemy to be dislodged.

General Daniel Smith Donelson's brigade was made up of the Eighth and Sixteenth Tennessee Regiments, more than sixteen hundred strong. Donelson was something of an antique: gray, sixty years of age, a West Pointer, former speaker of the Tennessee House of Representatives, and a nephew of Andrew Jackson. Each member of his brigade carried antiques as well—flintlock or percussion smoothbore muskets weighing close to ten pounds, old-fashioned cartridge boxes stuffed with forty rounds, a bayonet and scabbard, a blanket or quilt rolled up and tied over the shoulder, a canteen filled with water, and an empty haversack—thanks to a cooking detail that failed to show up with rations.[432]

General Donelson's route led more than twenty miles across rugged mountain spurs. There was no road, often not even a path. Fortunately, the general had local guides, including a mysterious old character known by his surname, Samuel. One member of the Eighth Tennessee thought Samuel looked "just out of some dark cavern or hollow tree, and was a second cousin to the ground squirrel family. He wore an old-fashioned bee-gum hat, and there was fully as much of the hat as there was of the guide, and each was about the same age, both relics of the Revolutionary war....Around this old hat was tied a white rag, which could be seen through the dense timber and huge mountain cliffs, bobbing along like an old crippled ghost...bell-wether of the flock."[433]

A detail of pioneers roughed out the trail. The soldiers joined hands to climb perpendicular ridges and descend into frightful chasms. Field officers weaved their horses tediously along the slopes as if following an imaginary worm fence. One sheer precipice caused many to speculate how the animals could follow at all. It was said the old guide Samuel possessed mystical powers— that he took the horses apart and carried them piece by piece up the slope, laid them in a heap, and commanded "Horses come forth" to reassemble the parts. No one was inclined to question the old guide's magic.

On the morning of September 11, the hungry brigade descended a gorge into Stewart Run. Confederates bowed under a steady rain as the little watercourse was followed downstream. A meager ration of bread or hardtack was shared among the troops. One swore that a pickaxe or bayonet was needed to work it into fragments, for no man in the army could chew it.

Musket blasts snapped every head to attention. Four "well dressed fat looking Yankees" were soon paraded to the rear. Quite a curiosity, they were the first enemy soldiers the Confederates had ever seen.[434]

Leading Donelson's brigade were two companies of the Sixteenth Tennessee Infantry, commanded by Colonel John Savage, a Tennessee Congressman and Mexican War veteran. As the column marched down Stewart Run, more Yankee pickets were encountered. All were captured or shot down before they could escape. Most had been lounging or blissfully fishing, astonished to find an entire Confederate brigade in their midst.[435]

From the prisoners, Colonel Savage learned that a company of Federals occupied the Simmons house, masked by an angle of woods just below. Ordering his men forward at "double-quick" time, Savage spurred his mount over a fence and landed in the midst of the startled Yankees. "Down with your arms or you die!" he cried, flourishing a huge pistol. Confederate troops swarmed into the yard to confirm his threat. The entire Federal company—fifty members of the Sixth Ohio Infantry—surrendered without a shot.

With the captured Yankees in tow, Donelson's Confederates followed a rough path from the Simmons house over the ridge to Becky Creek. As troops filed over that ridge, a bundle of Union dispatches were uncovered in the leaves. Addressed to the commander of the pickets, they warned of the danger of surprise—a bit too late.[436]

Donelson's brigade continued down Becky Creek. As darkness fell, the men bivouacked on a high ridge overlooking the Federals at Elkwater. Hundreds of enemy campfires flickered below. The night was one of "Egyptian" darkness—so thick that some Tennesseans swore they cut it into pieces and others, equally as serious, claimed they tried to eat it. Rain descended in "perfect torrents." Not a gun would have fired in the downpour. The Confederates hunkered against trees, punished by the howling storm. Adding to their misery, a bear wandered through camp near midnight, throwing the brigade into terror. During that fracas, the prisoners made an aborted effort to escape. Donelson's men endured a horrible night, christening the place "Flood Mountain."[437]

▲

Confederate General Samuel R. Anderson's brigade also left camp near Valley Mountain on the morning of September 10. Anderson, a Mexican War veteran, directed the First, Seventh, and Fourteenth Tennessee Regiments along a path that led to the Staunton-Parkersburg Turnpike, two miles west of Cheat Fort.

Commencing the march from Mingo Flats, members of the First Tennessee spied a "comely Virginia lass" at her cabin window. As admiring regiments filed past, each gave her a tremendous Rebel yell. The boys hoped it was an omen of success.

General Anderson's route led for twenty miles over winding farm lanes, stock trails, and untrodden wilderness along the western slope of Cheat Mountain. Guides blazed the trees with hatchets to mark the way. Marcus Toney of the First Tennessee called it "the roughest and wildest country that I ever beheld." The troops marched in single file, strung out for miles. "It was no uncommon thing for a mule to slide twenty feet down a slope," wrote a surgeon of that march, "and I could see strong men sink exhausted trying to get up the mountain side." Confederates tumbled into steep ravines, rising painfully only to fall again—a tortuous advance that one Tennessean styled the "perfect roll down."[438]

Anderson's Confederates neared the Staunton-Parkersburg Turnpike by nightfall on September 11. "It was the most awful night I ever spent," recalled a soldier of the Fourteenth Tennessee of his bivouac on the slopes of Cheat Mountain. "Here we tried to sleep," wrote another, "but the rain poured so, and the torrents ran down the mountain such a flood of water that we would have been drowned had we lain on the ground." Nervous soldiers tried to keep their powder dry, for the ominous sound of drumbeats had been heard in the distance.[439]

═══ ▲ ═══

On September 11, General Loring's column marched north toward Elkwater, overwhelming Federal outposts along the Huttonsville road. Near Conrad's Mill, members of John Worsham's Twenty-first Virginia Infantry passed their first dead Yankee. "He made a lasting impression," Worsham noted, "for he lay on the side of the road, his face upturned and a fresh pool of blood at his side, showing that his life had just passed away." By nightfall, Loring was before Camp Elkwater, and General Henry

Jackson's brigade was on the Staunton–Parkersburg pike in front of Cheat Fort.[440]

That night, the dreadful tempest lashed Cheat Mountain with a fury. The Federals were confident that no humans lurked about. They had not considered the will of Lee's men. When Anderson's waterlogged Confederates cut the telegraph wire, the operator assumed that a tree had fallen across it in the storm.

"There lay the camp on Cheat Mountain summit," wrote correspondent J.T. Pool, "and spread out on the slopes were the tents of full three thousand Union soldiers who were that moment under their shelter, snoring away in all the fancied security of men who expected to wake up in the morning with a whole skin and an appetite that would astonish the commissary department."

Few would have dreamed that five thousand enemy troops surrounded their mountain fortress, waiting for dawn to spring the trap.[441]

CHAPTER 17
ROBERT E. LEE'S
FORLORN HOPE

"The fort on Cheat Mountain is said to
be a defense almost impregnable."
—*Richmond Daily Dispatch*

September 12, 1861, opened with great promise for General Lee's Confederates. The brigades of Rust, Anderson, and Jackson surrounded the Union fortress on Cheat Mountain. Despite numbing cold and billowing fog, the Confederates were ready to strike. Union defenders were blissfully unaware of their presence. Lee's aide Walter Taylor relished the dawn, for everything was "just as the most confident could have hoped."

Matters rested on the broad shoulders of Colonel Albert Rust. "Day at length dawned upon the most forlorn and wretched set of human beings that ever existed," wrote a member of Rust's mountaintop bivouac. The big colonel seemed indefatigable, but found his wet, shivering Confederates barely able to rise. With almost superhuman effort, Rust prodded his soldiers into line. Down the ridge he led them in single file, to the Staunton-Parkersburg pike, about one half-mile behind the enemy fort.

The Confederates burst upon a pair of Federal pickets, who went screaming up the road and were shot down. Three supply wagons appeared from the fort; Rust's men captured the teams and drivers. The prisoners told Colonel Rust that their fort held nearly five thousand defenders (the true number was no more than three thousand) and boasted of its great strength. Rust entered a clearing to view the redoubt. A blockhouse and "heavy guns" could be seen, with infantry in the trenches. The Cheat Mountain fortress *was* stronger than he had supposed. It not only looked impregnable in a military sense; it was literally unapproachable, due to the "abatis" of wooden spikes on the perimeter. Summoning his officers, Rust concluded that it would be "madness" to storm those works.[442]

Now the Federals were aroused. Colonel Nathan Kimball led a detachment to the point of attack. Supposing Rust's brigade was only a scouting party of the enemy, he deployed two companies of the Fourteenth Indiana Infantry as skirmishers. Turning up their slouch hats, Kimball's men plunged into the thick woods and opened fire. Rust's sixteen hundred Confederates broke for the rear, casting aside guns, clothing, blankets—anything that impeded their flight. Colonel Kimball rushed into the fray, swinging his hat in the air. "Hurrah for Indiana!" he roared. "Trail them boys! Trail them!"

Rebel baggage littered the woods in quantity, revealing the stakes to Kimball's men. Inside the fort, bandsmen, teamsters, and sutlers gathered up spare guns and joined defenders in the trenches. Colonel Kimball returned from the action, his face red with excitement. "Our boys are peppering them good out there," he told the cheering garrison.[443]

═════ ▲ ═════

Over on "Flood Mountain," a cold, gray dawn found General Donelson's brigade glaring down on the unsuspecting Federals at Camp Elkwater. Fearful that the storm had dampened their powder enough to cause a "flash in the pan," Donelson's Confederates attended to their weapons. "Of all the picking, hammering, rattling of ramrods, rubbing, twisting out bullets and wet powder from old muskets ever witnessed," reflected a member of the Eighth

Tennessee, "perhaps the occasion here presented was never surpassed. The wet loads had to be drawn from the guns and the guns
thoroughly dried before they could be reloaded. To do this much
noise and confusion existed. The popping of caps, the shooting of
blank cartridges, intermingled with the Babel-like confusion existing at the time, all contributed to a general 'hoodlum' on the
mountain."[444]

Their clamor drew the attention of General Lee. He had followed Donelson's brigade on the evening of September 11, believing they had advanced too far. Darkness and the terrible storm had
forced Lee and his small escort to bivouac against some haystacks
near Becky Creek, less than a mile from Flood Mountain—well
behind enemy lines.

Lee was back in the saddle at dawn. He had scarcely emerged
from the woods when a large troop of Federal cavalry thundered
along the Becky Creek road in his front. Those horsemen spotted
Donelson's infantry and galloped away, but aide Walter Taylor
shuddered at the close call. General Lee "came very near" being
captured![445]

"Just as the scattering rays of the morning sun began to make
their appearance over the eastern hills," recalled one of Donelson's
men, "to the great surprise of the whole command, Gen. Lee and
staff rode to the head of the brigade." Soldiers rose to present arms,
but Lee waved off the tribute, offering sympathy to those "who
had lain out all night in such a drenching storm." Confederates jostled to get a glimpse of their leader. "He looked like a hero,"
thought one as Lee sat erect "on his fine white horse, half hid in
the bushes....Grand and dignified he sat there...seeming to grasp
the situation and to hold it in the hollow of his hand."[446]

Lee climbed to a point on the ridge overlooking Camp
Elkwater. "I could see the enemy's tents on Valley River, at the
point on the Huttonsville road just below me," he wrote. "It was a
tempting sight. We waited for the attack on Cheat Mountain,
which was to be the signal, till 10 A.M.; the men were cleaning
their unserviceable arms. But the signal did not come."

Lee found the men of Donelson's brigade in no condition to fall upon the Federals at Elkwater. The storm had destroyed their scant provisions and sapped their will. The enemy had been alerted. The chance for surprise was lost. Reluctantly, Lee ordered Donelson to withdraw.[447]

As the Tennesseans followed a narrow path down the ridge to Becky Creek, they came upon sixty Federal scouts from Cheat Fort under Captain John Coons of the Fourteenth Indiana Infantry. Coons had been sent to picket the important bridle path to Elkwater. Here a sharp skirmish broke out. Hidden by dense undergrowth, both sides fired wildly at the smoke of enemy guns. Confederate regiments swarmed down the slope, forming lines of battle near the creek. Captain Coons's little band was nearly overwhelmed by a bayonet charge before he broke off the fight and retreated.[448]

═══ ▲ ═══

Nearly two miles west of Cheat Fort, Confederate General Anderson's brigade held the Staunton-Parkersburg Turnpike in dense fog. "I was well soaked," recollected Dr. Charles Quintard, chaplain of the First Tennessee Infantry, "my fingers were corrugated and my whole body chilled through. I was very hungry also, but all I could get to eat was one tough biscuit that almost defied my most vigorous assaults." So quiet had been their approach that at least two well-mounted Federals rode unwarily into the line and were taken. One of them, Lieutenant William Merrill—a member of General Reynolds's staff—was so astonished to see Confederate soldiers that he muttered, "Did you men come from the clouds?"

The First Tennessee Infantry moved cautiously up the turnpike. "Pop, pop, pop, pop, went several guns and then a tremendous volley shook the mountain sides," recalled a Tennessean. They had met a detachment of ninety Federals sent from the fort to aid Captain Coons. "The balls whistled in a way that can never be appreciated by one who has not heard them," asserted Dr. Quintard. Pouring on the musketry, the Federals, led by Captain David Higgins of the

Twenty-fourth Ohio, soon realized they were badly outnumbered and fell back.[449]

Captain Coons's little band of Federals now rejoined the fray. Emerging from the fog, Coons's skirmishers poured three quick volleys into General Anderson's rear guard, mostly slaves and quartermasters, causing the Tennesseans to scatter. Coons found the mountaintop swarming with Rebels. Vowing to cut his way through or die, the beleaguered captain barked "right face" and led his band in single file through the woods, finally reaching the fort at sunset.[450]

"After the fighting was over, where, O where, was all the fine rigging heretofore on our officers?" reflected Sam Watkins of the First Tennessee. "They could not be seen. Corporals, sergeants, lieutenants, captains, all had torn all the fine lace off their clothing. I noticed that at the time and was surprised and hurt. I asked several of them why they had torn off the insignia of their rank, and they always answered, 'Humph, you think that I was going to be a target for the Yankees to shoot at?'

"You see, this was our first battle, and the officers had not found out that minnie as well as cannon balls were blind; that they had no eyes and could not see. They thought that the balls would hunt for them and not hurt the privates. I always shot at privates. It was they that did the shooting and killing, and if I could kill or wound a private, why, my chances were so much the better."[451]

The Confederates had no swagger. Meeting the enemy at every turn, their courage melted away. "I had expected an open field and a fair fight," complained Dr. Quintard, "but this bushwhacking was entirely out of my line." In the dense forest, small roving bands of bluecoats looked like whole regiments. Anticipating mere scouting parties of the enemy, the Federals pitched in with vigor. Success against overwhelming numbers only made them bolder. "By this time, we felt that we could whip the whole rebel army," declared one of Captain Coons's men.[452]

━━━ ▲ ━━━

On the turnpike east of Cheat Fort, Confederate General Henry Jackson's brigade also grew nervous. Peering through the fog, Jackson's men shot into their advance guard by mistake—killing and wounding a number of fellow Georgians. Those disheartened Confederates remained in front of the enemy fort, listening for the sound of Colonel Rust's guns. But no signal came from the big Arkansas colonel. The few shots that morning from Rust's quarter had been muffled by the dense forest and the fog.

As the day wore on, from every position could be heard, "What has become of Rust? Why doesn't he attack? Rust must have lost his way." General Jackson's men wondered why more Federal soldiers weren't visible in the fort. "We thought Reynolds had given us the slip," fretted Isaac Hermann, "and that we would find him in our rear and in our camp before we could get back." Morale plummeted as General Lee's plan unraveled. "Would Rust *never* attack?" agonized Walter Taylor. "Alas! he never did!"[453]

▲

Union General Reynolds was distracted by events in the Tygart Valley. On the afternoon of September 12, skirmishers in front of Camp Elkwater kept up a bickering fire. Reynolds watched the drama from an outpost one mile in front of the fortifications. General Loring's Confederate infantry rested on their arms, clearly awaiting a signal. General Reynolds rode forward and swept the enemy position with a telescope. Rebel gunners lobbed a twelve-pound shot in his direction. Reynolds ordered up a cannon to hurl a few shots in reply. Darkness settled in, and with it a conviction that Loring would not attack. The Confederates were on their heels. "Detached, discovered, without knowledge of the cause of Rust's silence," wrote Walter Taylor, "the other commands were powerless for good."[454]

While Reynolds faced down Loring in the Tygart Valley, General Lee spent much of September 12 extricating Donelson's brigade from Federal pursuit on Becky Creek. Late that afternoon, the Confederates reached the safety of an isolated mountain farm and collapsed in a meadow, famished and utterly exhausted. Lee followed them up the trail on horseback. Word passed among the troops of how he learned of their critical position, how he had ridden for miles and placed himself in great peril to rescue them from the "jaws of death." As Lee's horse ambled through the reposing brigade, someone raised a yell. Every man picked up the cheer, and for a few moments, the mountaintops echoed with wild cries in honor of the general.

"Yes, shout after shout rang out on the mountain wilderness," recalled a Tennessean of Lee's appearance. "With a grand and noble heart, he lifted his hat, and with a smile on his face, and bowing to the men on the left and on the right, he rode off and by many of us was never seen again."[455]

Donelson's Confederates soon discovered a browsing herd of cattle, making their deliverance complete. Hungry Tennesseans dispatched the entire herd. Huge chunks of raw meat soon dangled from ramrods over sputtering fires. Every man ate his fill—one swore the meal was savored "as no king or potentate ever relished his most sumptuous banquets or feast." Confederates fondly remembered the spot as "Jubilee" or "Beef" Mountain.[456]

---- ▲ ----

On September 13, Generals Lee and Loring conferred in front of Camp Elkwater. Loring wished to storm the works, but Lee ruled out a frontal assault as too costly. Now that the enemy was fully aroused, Lee would probe his right flank—hoping to coax Reynolds out of his trenches.[457]

The mounted general cut a prominent figure at the head of his troops. Aides urged him to withdraw as Federal artillery opened fire. A shell howled across the contested valley and struck the ground nearly at his feet. Miraculously, it did not explode. Was the lucky horseman Lee? Federal gunners claimed so. Regardless, it was a strange twist on a day known for misfortune—Friday the thirteenth.[458]

Fate would not be so kind to Lee's *aide-de-camp*, Lt. Colonel John Augustine Washington. Forty years of age, trim and courtly, he was the great-grandnephew of America's first president. Washington had inherited Mt. Vernon, the ancestral estate. Yet he lacked financial means for its upkeep or to entertain the influx of visitors and curiosity seekers. Facing bankruptcy, he had sold out to the Mt. Vernon Ladies Association of the Union in 1859 and moved to Waveland in Fauquier County, Virginia. Washington's wife died not long after, leaving seven young children.

Critics decried the sale of Mt. Vernon and blasted Washington as a vile speculator in his ancestor's legacy. His decision to take up arms for Virginia proved equally unpopular. The chestnut-haired Washington became "Chief of Staff" to his kinsman, Robert E. Lee. Morning and evening found him at prayer in the tent shared with Lee and Walter Taylor at Valley Mountain. He read the Bible in spare moments or used it to press wildflowers for his beloved daughters.[459]

On that Friday the thirteenth of September 1861, Colonel Washington joined Rooney Lee's cavalry battalion on a reconnaissance. From a tall hill overlooking the enemy right flank, they spied a vidette, or mounted rifleman, near the mouth of Elkwater Fork. Rooney Lee studied the ground for some minutes before declaring the mission complete. But Colonel Washington dared him on. "Let us ride down and capture that fellow on the gray horse," he urged. Young Lee consented. Joined by a pair of escorts, he and Washington spurred their mounts down the little valley toward their quarry.

Federal scouts were at that moment prowling a wooded hillside just above the mouth of Elkwater Fork. Led by Sergeant John Weiler of the Seventeenth Indiana Infantry, the small party heard galloping horses below, spotting the riders as they wheeled past a fallen tree. Weiler's men recognized the white badge on Colonel Washington's cap as that of the enemy, raised their guns, and fired.

Colonel Washington toppled from his bay charger, struck in the back by three balls. Rooney Lee's horse crumpled to the ground. Unscathed, young Lee sprang to his feet and raced up Elkwater Fork, using the bank as cover until he leaped onto Washington's mount and made his escape.[460]

Federal scouts rushed to the fallen Washington. He muttered for water, but died before it reached his lips. Fashioning a litter of guns and accoutrements, the scouts carried him to a nearby outpost. The strong features, fine dress, and accoutrements sparked curiosity. Initials found on gauntlet cuffs and a napkin in his haversack suggested they had killed "the veritable John A. Washington of Mt. Vernon." An acquaintance, Captain Loomis of the Michigan artillery, soon confirmed the deed.

Washington's demise drew macabre attention. The Federals treated his remains with dignity, but doled out his military effects as spoils of war. General Reynolds claimed Washington's field glass. A revolver was forwarded to Secretary of War Simon Cameron, who dictated that Sergeant Weiler retain its twin. The gauntlets, a large knife, spurs, and powder flask went to soldiers of the Seventeenth Indiana. A member of General Reynolds's staff kept several letters, one pierced by a fatal bullet. There seemed to be general regret that Washington's sword escaped with his horse.[461]

This scion of the Washington clan was viewed as a traitor. Soldiers rough in speech were taken by the irony of his name. "The boys wonder what George said to John when he 'went up,'" wrote one Federal. "I don't think John went *up*." Upon a smooth-barked beech on Elkwater Fork, they carved his memorial: "Under this tree, on the 13ᵗʰ of Sept., 1861, fell Col. John A. Washington, the degenerate descendant of the Father of his Country."

The body was handed over to Confederate forces the next day. Chaplain Quintard met General Lee just as he received confirmation of Washington's death. "He was standing with his right arm, thrown over the neck of his horse," recalled Quintard of Lee, "and I was impressed first of all by the man's splendid physique, and then by the look of extreme sadness that pervaded his countenance. He felt the death of his relative very keenly..."[462]

"I am much grieved," Lee wrote Mary of the loss. "He was always anxious to go on these expeditions. This was the first day I assented....May God have mercy on us all!" Lee forwarded Washington's belongings to the colonel's eldest daughter with a letter of condolence. "My Dear Miss Louisa," he began, "with a heart filled with grief, I have to communicate the saddest tidings which you have ever heard." The deaths of General Garnett and Lt. Colonel Washington in Western Virginia had claimed half of Lee's original staff.[463]

On September 14, Lee ordered the Confederates back to their camps. Colonel Albert Rust finally returned from the wilderness. His inaction was summarized in a terse sentence: "The expedition against Cheat Mountain failed." Perhaps to lessen its demoralizing effect, Lee called the effort a "forced reconnaissance" rather than a battle unfought. He praised the troops for "cheerfulness and alacrity," traits certain to bring victory at the next "fit opportunity."[464]

General Loring cursed the order, as stubborn in retreat as he had been in advance. He wore a black corduroy suit and a broad-brimmed hat topped with a cockade plume for the occasion. As Donelson's brigade passed headquarters, Loring popped up on a stump, "erect as a cock partridge in August," to give the soldiers a military review. "Our men had been instructed to salute the General as they passed," recalled a Tennessean, "but if a single man in the ranks did any such thing we did not see or hear of it...Not a voice was raised nor an old cap or hat lifted as we sullenly passed by." The admiration of the troops for Loring fell short of that won by Lee.[465]

The Confederates had suffered awfully. Many were barefoot from the trials, their feet swollen and bloodied. "We have had the hardest time that ever any soldiers in the world had," wrote a member of Anderson's brigade upon returning to Valley Mountain. Weakened by exposure, large numbers fell victim to disease. A veteran would later remark that he never understood the word "Hell" until the Cheat Mountain affair.[466]

Meanwhile, the Federals reveled in victory. "It is glorious to meet the bloodthirsty enemies of our country and crush them!" exulted a defender of Cheat Fort. "General, I think my men have done wonders," a proud Colonel Kimball wrote General Reynolds. "How it happened that with less than 250 men we dispersed 5,800 of the rebels I can't say but such is the fact, incredible as it may seem."

The Federals lost only ten killed, fourteen wounded, and sixty-four prisoners. Confederate losses were never officially reported, but Reynolds and Kimball inflated them to "near 100" killed with a score of prisoners. "Their bodies can be seen laying at the roadsides by anyone passing by," boasted a Hoosier on the summit. Some crawled away to die in the laurel thickets, marked only by the stench and hovering of vultures and crows.[467]

▲

General Lee was humiliated by the debacle at Cheat Mountain. Seldom in military annals had a strategic design, so well conceived and boldly carried to the point of attack, failed so miserably. "I cannot tell you my regret & mortification at the untoward events that caused the failure of the plan," Lee wrote Mary from Valley Mountain on September 17. "I had taken every precaution to ensure success & counted on it. But the Ruler of the Universe willed otherwise..." To Governor Letcher he expressed "grievous disappointment....But for the rain-storm, I have no doubt it would have succeeded. This, Governor, is for your own eye. Please do not speak of it; we must try again."[468]

Lee was "Cheated" out of victory on that mountain—by rain, mud, and temerity. Yet he refused to point a finger of blame at Albert Rust, the gargantuan colonel who had awed nearly everyone but the Yankees. Jefferson Davis spoke of Lee after the failure: "[W]ith a magnanimity rarely equaled, he stood in silence...unwilling to offend any one who was wearing a sword and striking blows for the Confederacy." Lee never filed an official report. Privately, he dubbed the affair a "forlorn hope expedition."[469]

Critics styled Lee overcautious and too much a theorist—his plan of attack too complicated for the tools at hand. Southern editors chided that "in mountain warfare, the learning of the books and of the strategists is of little value." While pundits prattled, matters grew ominous in the Kanawha Valley. The feuding of Confederate Generals Wise and Floyd in that region portended disaster. Leaving a sufficient force behind to watch Reynolds, Lee reined his tiny escort south to try again.[470]

CHAPTER 18
MIXING OIL AND WATER

"As well might peace and harmony and concert of action have been expected if you threw a game cock into another game cock's yard."
—Henry Heth, C.S.A.

Robert E. Lee rode seventy-five miles south of Valley Mountain to the Kanawha theater of operations. He was anxious to "restore harmony" between Generals Wise and Floyd. It was an urgent mission, for the bickering ex-governors were threatened with annihilation.

During the first week of September 1861, Union General William Rosecrans led three brigades south from Clarksburg toward those feuding Confederates. Rosecrans's march covered one hundred and twenty miles, by way of Weston, Bulltown, and Sutton on the Weston and Gauley Bridge Turnpike. His plan was to join forces with General Jacob Cox near the terminus of that road, driving the Confederates under Wise and Floyd out of Western Virginia for good.[471]

General Lee had learned of Rosecrans's advance. Lee urged General Floyd to withdraw from his entrenched position at Carnifex Ferry on the Gauley River, between the Federal commands. But Floyd chose to remain in the formidable works of Camp Gauley, with the river at his back. There he dug in furiously, threatening to defy "the world, the flesh, and the devil." Floyd's arch rival Henry Wise presumably fell into the last category.

Confederate General Wise held the James River and Kanawha Turnpike on the New River at Hawks Nest, six miles east of Federals under General Cox. Wise was positioned there ostensibly to protect Floyd's left flank. On September 9, Floyd called on his nemesis for reinforcements. Wise refused. The feuding generals began another "sulphurous exchange." Wise claimed he had already been "twice fooled" into marching to Floyd's aid, only to receive contrary orders. "Under these circumstances," asserted Wise, "I shall, upon my legitimate responsibility, exercise a strong discretion whether to obey your very preemptory orders of to-day or not."[472]

In hindsight, Union General Cox marveled at Wise's talent for keeping a command in hot water. "If he had been half as trouble-some to me as he was to Floyd," Cox wrote, "I should, indeed, have had a hot time of it. But he did me royal service by preventing any-thing approaching unity of action between the principal Confederate columns."[473]

Before Floyd could address Wise's latest act of insubordination, Rosecrans struck him on the afternoon of September 10 at Carnifex Ferry. The action began as a reconnaissance, but newly minted Brigadier General Henry Benham (the eager engineer who had chased down General Garnett) led Federal troops straight into the teeth of Floyd's defenses. The afternoon reconnaissance turned into a bloody assault.

Floyd's defenses were strong, hidden in dense forest with unscalable cliffs on the flanks, but his back was to the Gauley River in a deep canyon below, crossable only at the tenuous Carnifex Ferry. Although outnumbered nearly three to one, his eighteen hundred Confederates put up a spirited defense. They drove back successive Federal thrusts until darkness overtook the battlefield.[474]

By daybreak, Floyd's little Army of the Kanawha had vanished across the Gauley, sinking a footbridge and the ferryboats, leaving Rosecrans mystified but holding the field. Floyd claimed victory nonetheless. He had been shot in the right forearm, however. It was a minor wound with major consequences—Floyd could no longer hold a pen in his war of words with General Wise.

Later that day, Wise found his antagonist prostrate on the roadside east of Hawks Nest. Floyd's wound had left him stunned and bewildered. Wise demanded orders. A dazed Floyd replied that "he did not know what orders to give." Jumping at the opportunity, Wise fired off a scathing letter to General Lee. "Disasters have come, and disasters are coming," he warned, "which you alone, I fear, can repair and prevent....I solemnly protest that my force is not safe under [Floyd's] command, and I ask to be allowed to co-operate with some other superior."[475]

On September 13, the warring generals retreated seventeen miles east on the James River and Kanawha Turnpike to Big Sewell Mountain. As usual, they camped more than a mile apart. Three days later, Floyd amicably sought Wise's council. The Yankees were reportedly approaching in two columns; General Cox from the west on the James River and Kanawha pike, and Rosecrans from the north as he shuttled troops across the river at Carnifex Ferry. General Wise argued that Floyd's camp on Big Sewell Mountain was "indefensible," and urged that his own formidable post, one and one half miles east, should be occupied by the entire army. Wise proposed a counteroffensive. Floyd reportedly "liked the idea" and agreed to examine Wise's position the next morning. At that, General Wise returned to camp, satisfied that he had won the day.

But Wise had barely reached headquarters when General Floyd's wagon train began rolling through his camp—the Army of the Kanawha was in retreat! A dispatch from Floyd announced that he was falling back. Wise was instructed to hold himself in readiness to "bring up the rear." This was too much for the hotheaded Wise. Incensed at Floyd's deception, he snapped at the messenger, "Tell General Floyd I will do no such thing; I propose to stay here and fight until doomsday."[476]

As Floyd's little army filed past, a red-faced General Wise rode among his own troops. Still burning over Floyd's criticism of his Kanawha retreat, he rose in the stirrups and called out in a stentorian voice, "Who is retreating now? Who is retreating now?" Wise repeated the query to another group of soldiers. Presently his entire command had assembled. Wise cried out again, "Men, who is retreating now? John B. Floyd, G__d__ him, the bullet-hit son of a b____, he is retreating now."

True to his word, General Wise did not budge. For nearly a week, he traded barbed missives over his failure to join Floyd at Meadow Bluff, some twelve miles east. "I have not yet been able to discover how you could bring up the rear of a moving column by remaining stationary after this column had passed," scolded Floyd. "Disastrous consequences…may ensue from a divided force," he cautioned Wise on September 19. "If you still have time…to join my force and make a stand against the enemy at this point, I hope you will see the necessity of doing so at once."[477]

The Federals under General Cox reached Floyd's abandoned camp on Big Sewell Mountain the next day. Cox had orders to probe Wise's defenses, postponing a general assault until Rosecrans's troops crossed the Gauley River to join him. Wise and his 2,200-man legion faced the prospect of holding back at least 5,300 Federals, with more on the way. Isolated from Floyd by twelve miles of muddy turnpike, he was in danger of being cut to pieces. But Wise refused to retreat. Fittingly, he named his post "Camp Defiance."[478]

On September 15, Floyd wrote to President Jefferson Davis, "The petty jealousy of General Wise; his utter ignorance of all military rule and discipline; the peculiar contrariness of his character and disposition, are beginning to produce rapidly a disorganization which will prove fatal to the interests of the army if not arrested at once." The cantankerous Wise, he grumbled, "obeys no orders without cavil, and does not hesitate to disregard a positive and peremptory order, upon the most frivolous pretext."

Loath to arrest Wise and demoralize the entire legion, Floyd urged the president to transfer his combative opponent. "It is impossible for me to conduct a campaign with General Wise attached to my command," Floyd informed Davis. "His presence with my force is almost as injurious as if he were in the camp of the enemy with his whole command."[479]

By now, the quarrel between Generals Wise and Floyd had become a public scandal. From Lewisburg, a member of the Richmond legislature warned President Davis of the dangers brought on by their feud. "They are inimical to each other as men can be," he wrote on September 19, "and from their course and actions I am fully satisfied that each of them would be highly gratified to see the other annihilated....It would be just as easy to combine oil and water as to expect a union of action between these gentlemen."[480]

Into this hornet's nest of controversy rode the genteel Lee. As he drew rein at Floyd's Meadow Bluff headquarters on September 21, Lee's role as a "facilitator" was to be sorely tested. He was horrified to find Wise and Floyd separated in the face of the enemy. Lee fired off a dispatch to Wise, pleading for cooperation. "I know nothing of the relative advantages of the points occupied by yourself and General Floyd," he wrote, "but as far as I can judge our united forces are not more than one-half of the strength of the enemy. Together they may not be able to stand his assault. It would be the height of imprudence to submit them separately to his attack....I beg therefore, if not too late, that the troops be united, and that we conquer or die together."[481]

That letter angered Wise. His reply must have stunned Lee. "I consider my force united with that of General Floyd as much as it ever has been," Wise retorted. "The two positions had perhaps better be examined, I respectfully submit, before my judgment is condemned....Just say, then, where we are to unite and 'conquer or die together'...no man consults more the interest of the cause, according to his best ability and means, than I do....Any imputation upon my motives or intentions in that respect by my superior would make me, perhaps, no longer a military subordinate of any man who breathes."[482]

With disaster looming, Lee rode forward on September 22 to examine Big Sewell Mountain. He found the rebellious Wise ensconced on the crest of the mountain at "Camp Defiance." It was a very strong natural position—much stronger, in fact, than Floyd's post at Meadow Bluff. From Camp Defiance, Federal troops could be seen on the heights a little more than one mile west. Between the two armies stood a deep gorge, passable only by the James River and Kanawha Turnpike, which led directly through Wise's camp.

If the Federals launched a frontal assault, General Wise's position was superior to that of Floyd. But there was a threat of attack from the flanks. Rough traces led around Sewell Mountain from the north and south. Union General Rosecrans had already pulled a flank march at Rich Mountain; if he worked that strategy again, General Floyd was best positioned. But no flank movement had been detected. Lee returned to Meadow Bluff without ordering Wise to follow.[483]

General Wise came under heavy fire the next morning. The enemy appeared to be massing on Big Sewell in force. "I am compelled to stand here and fight as long as I can endure," Wise told Lee. "All is at stake with my command, and it shall be sold dearly."

Lee was in a quandary. The demonstration against Wise might be a feint—designed to hold the defiant general in place while Federal troops moved by side roads to surprise Floyd at Meadow Bluff. If Wise was flanked, both commands could be destroyed. Lee did not know whether General Rosecrans had linked up with Cox—the reports from Wise were contradictory. "If you cannot resist [the enemy]," Lee urged his recalcitrant general, "and are able to withdraw your command, you had best do so."[484]

Wise would not retreat. "I tell you emphatically, sir, that the enemy are advancing in strong force on this turnpike," he wrote on the morning of September 24. Lee wearily asked if Wise had sufficient ammunition. If the Confederate forces must remain divided, thought Lee, they could at least be equalized. Taking four of General Floyd's regiments, he rushed to the aid of Wise.[485]

Understandably, Lee arrived at Sewell Mountain in an ill humor. He found Wise's command in wretched condition—the officers nearly as bitter toward Floyd as their general was. Clad in a wide-brimmed black hat, Lee stood by a campfire in the rain, hands clasped behind his back as though in deep thought. A young lieutenant approached, inquiring about ammunition. Lee eyed the intruder with a steely glare. "I think it very strange, Lieutenant," he snapped, "that an officer of this command, which has been here a week, should come to me, who am just arrived, to ask who his ordnance officer is and where to find his ammunition. This is in keeping with everything else I find here—no order, no organization; nobody knows where anything is, no one understands his duty; officers and men alike are equally ignorant. This will not do." [486]

Lee's headquarters wagon had not come up; he bivouacked in the rain, sheltered only by an overcoat. Dawn of September 25 found him reconnoitering the Federal lines with his glass. It now appeared that the entire army of General Rosecrans was before him. There was no movement on the flanks. He reported these developments to General Floyd by dispatch. "I suppose if we fall back the enemy will follow," wrote Lee. "This is a strong point, if they will fight us here. The advantage is, they can get no position for their artillery, and their men I think will not advance without it. If they do not turn it, how would it do to make a stand here?" [487]

The risk in Lee's proposal was as much political as it was military. His suggestion that Floyd return to Sewell Mountain could be viewed as approval of Wise's insubordination. Floyd would regard it as a distinct rebuff. The two ex-governors might refuse to fight side by side. The war was young, the politicians powerful, and Lee unsure. He had been sent to these mountains for diplomacy. How would Floyd respond? A campaign hung in the balance. [488]

Lee's thoughts were interrupted by gunfire on the skirmish lines. General Wise spurred his mount into the action. Bullets sizzled through the trees as a blue-clad line drove Confederate skirmishers into Camp Defiance. Things began to look serious as Wise galloped back to a young artillery officer and ordered him to open fire. The cannoneer protested; a dense forest hid the enemy—his guns could "do no execution."

"D__n the execution, sir," Wise bellowed. "It's the *noise* that we want."[489]

Even as Wise gallantly held the Yankees at bay, the answer to Lee's burning question arrived. It came in a dispatch, not from General Floyd, but from Richmond. Inside were orders to General Wise:

> SIR: *You are instructed to turn over all the troops heretofore immediately under your command to General Floyd, and report yourself in person to the Adjutant-General in this city with the least delay...By order of the President.*[490]

Wise was mortified. Surely President Davis had not meant to order him away just as the fateful battle loomed? The order was humiliating! Wise wanted to ignore it until after the impending fight. "Dare I do so?" he asked Lee. "On the other hand, can I, in honor, leave you at this moment, though the disobedience of the order may subject me to the severest penalties?" Wise had defied General Floyd; he had defied Lee—would he now defy the President himself?

Lee urged Wise to obey. If he had not advised the president's action, he quietly concurred. The good of the service required that one of those rival generals be removed. Wise drafted a farewell to his beloved legion. "[P]rompt obedience is the first duty of military service," he told them, with no little irony.[491]

Privately, Wise claimed he had relinquished command only in deference to Lee's judgment, rather than in compliance with the order. Defiant as ever, he called on President Davis upon arriving in Richmond.

"General Wise, I think I will have to shoot you," said the president, not entirely in jest.

"Mr. President, shoot me," Wise replied. "That is all right, but for God's sake let me see you hang that d___ rascal Floyd first."[492]

CHAPTER 19
TOO TENDER OF BLOOD

"The enemy is in our presence & testing the strength of our position. What may be the result...cannot now be foreseen."
—Robert E. Lee

As September closed, the army of Union General Rosecrans confronted that of Lee. Rosecrans had 5,300 troops at Sewell Mountain, and a total force of 8,500 upon linking up with General Cox. The arrival of General Loring's division swelled Lee's own force to nearly 9,000 men. The armies scowled at each other across a deep canyon as they fortified opposite spurs of Sewell Mountain. "If they would attack us," wrote a Confederate correspondent, "we could whip them without, perhaps, the loss of a man; but, if we have to attack them, the thing will be different."[493]

The commanding generals agreed. "We have been threatened with an attack every day, but it has yet been suspended," wrote Lee. By September 30, he acknowledged, "I begin to fear the enemy will not attack us. We shall therefore have to attack him."

But the army could not move forward. A fierce storm had rendered the James River and Kanawha Turnpike nearly impassable—General Floyd now declared it "the worst road in Virginia." The Confederates were seventy mountainous miles west of Shenandoah

Valley railroads. Staggering teams labored to bring up supplies. "We can only get up provisions from day to day, which paralyses our operations," Lee admitted. Unable to sustain an advance, the Confederates were resigned to wait.[494]

While they waited, rain and bitter winds whipped across the peaks of Sewell Mountain. "One very cold night," recalled aide Walter Taylor, "as we drew close to our camp fire, General Lee suggested that it was advisable to make one bed, put our blankets together in order to have sufficient covering to make us comfortable, and so it happened that it was vouchsafed for me to occupy very close relations with my old commander, and to be able to testify to his self-denial."[495]

Lee watched the Federals as the first days of October slipped by. On October 5, renewed activity could be seen in the enemy camps. An assault seemed imminent. Lee's decision to await Rosecrans was about to be rewarded. Throughout the night, Confederate pickets heard the rumble of wheels and concluded that the enemy was moving up guns in preparation for an attack.

The predawn hours of October 6 found General Lee expectant. Atonement was at hand. His troops were to give battle at last. Rosecrans would assail Lee's strong defenses and be repulsed with fearful loss. But dawn revealed only silence. No movement could be seen across the great chasm on Sewell Mountain. Not a single Federal soldier remained in the trenches. Rosecrans had vanished!

Lee was bitterly disappointed. The rumble of wheels by night had not been those of advancing artillery, but of departing wagons. Rosecrans had arrived at the same conclusion as Lee—it was far better to receive an assault in that rugged terrain than to deliver one. Failing to draw Lee out, Rosecrans had ordered his brigades back to the navigable Kanawha River near Gauley Bridge, prudently shortening his supply line for the approaching winter.[496]

It was Cheat Mountain all over again. After great toil and expectation, Lee had failed to fight. Rosecrans escaped without the loss of a man. The Southern press was not reticent in pointing out that a "more adventurous policy" was needed in Western Virginia. Lee was painfully aware of the criticism. "I am sorry, as you say, that the movements of the armies cannot keep pace with the expectations of the editors of papers," he wrote Mary after the failure. "I know they can regulate matters satisfactorily to themselves on paper. I wish they could do so in the field. No one wishes them more success than I do & would be happy to see them have full swing."[497]

Lee pondered an offensive, but it was little more than a pipe dream. The turnpike remained in miserable shape. The hospitals in the rear were overflowing with sick soldiers. Adding insult, Richmond newspapers were printing details of what Lee had intended as a secret move![498]

The Confederates withdrew from Sewell Mountain. General Loring's division returned to the Huntersville line. Lee's effort to reclaim Western Virginia was over.

Lee announced his impending departure and directed that future operations be governed by General Floyd's own "good judgment." But Floyd's judgment was clouded by politics. Hoping to bolster his reputation, Floyd marched on the Federals at Gauley Bridge with about four thousand men. By the first of November, he had placed light artillery on an eminence known as Cotton Hill and began annoying Rosecrans's camps below. The demonstration proved far "more noisy than dangerous." Learning that Rosecrans had sent detachments to entrap him, Floyd decamped on November 12 and fled back across the Alleghenies.[499]

━━━ ▲ ━━━

General Robert E. Lee left the mountains on October 30, 1861. His failure was complete; six days prior, the people of Western Virginia had approved an ordinance to form a new state, one loyal to the Union. Accompanying Lee on the ride east was Walter Taylor, his lone surviving aide. A new beard framed Lee's tired face. The arduous days of reconnaissance and nights away from headquarters had caused him to give up shaving. Appropriately, his beard came out Confederate gray. To the youthful troops, it gave Lee the look of a patriarch. He would retain it for life, a memento of opportunity lost.[500]

Lee's musings on that lonely ride must have turned to a new warhorse. Neither of the mounts he rode in Western Virginia, "Richmond," a bay stallion, nor another called the "Brown Roan," suited him completely. But on Sewell Mountain, a striking four-year-old thoroughbred had caught Lee's eye. The general, a lover of horses, marveled at its proportions. Sixteen hands high, it was iron gray in color with a black mane and tail. Strong, spirited, and bold of carriage, this horse required neither whip nor spur to maintain a rapid "buck-trot." Lee was instantly taken in. "Such a picture would inspire a poet," he trilled.

The horse, originally named "Jeff Davis," came from a farm near Blue Sulphur Springs and had garnered two first prizes at the Greenbrier County fair. Major Thomas Broun of the Wise Legion had purchased him in the fall of 1861. General Lee encountered Broun's brother Joseph on the horse at Sewell Mountain, often stopping to admire the animal. Lee began to call him "my colt," hinting that he would be needed before the war was over. Four months later, near Pocataligo, South Carolina, he secured Broun's horse for $200. Impressed by the handsome thoroughbred's ability to cover long distances, Lee gave him the name "Traveller."[501]

━━━━━ ▲ ━━━━━

Lee left Western Virginia under a shadow of disgrace, his military reputation badly tarnished. Critics pronounced him outwitted and outgeneraled. They failed to understand the difficulties, the measles and mud, or the recalcitrant commanders. Learned men shook their heads and said that Lee had been overrated as a soldier, that he relied on a showy presence and an historic name, that he was "too tender of blood." Lee erred on the "engineer side of a military question," they feared, "preferring rather to dig entrenchments than to fight."[502]

"Poor Lee!" railed a columnist in the *Charleston Mercury*. "Rosecrans has fooled him again....The people are getting mighty sick of this dilly-dally, dirt digging, scientific warfare; so much so that they will demand that the Great Entrencher be brought back and permitted to pay court to the ladies." They called him "Granny Lee."[503]

Lee did not respond to the critics. Upon his return to Richmond, President Davis received him warmly, one of the few who retained full confidence in his ability. "He came back," Davis recalled, "carrying the heavy weight of defeat, and unappreciated by the people whom he served, for they could not know, as I knew, that, if his plans and orders had been carried out, the result would have been victory rather than defeat."[504]

Before the general could reunite with Mary and the girls, he received a new assignment. A fleet of Federal warships threatened the southeastern states; Lee was to supervise coastal defenses in South Carolina, Georgia, and east Florida. His reputation had suffered so that President Davis was forced to send a letter to the governor of South Carolina on Lee's departure, informing him "what manner of man he was."[505]

━━━ ▲ ━━━

Nature bathed the Allegheny Mountains in a spectacular display of autumn hues in 1861. "The beech and maples...touched by the heavy frosts shone with their gold and scarlet, rendering the landscape a scene of most perfect beauty," wrote a member of the Fourteenth Indiana during the month of October. Another spellbound soldier declared, "The surrounding mountains, always a grand and imposing sight, are now picturesque in the extreme."[506]

That panoply of colors proved bittersweet for the Union spies Fletcher and Clark. The two had offered scant information to their Confederate captors. Imprisoned in a tent at Huntersville, they received little food or water, and no blankets or straw for bedding.

Each night they were tied snugly to prevent escape. Both suffered miserably from "camp diarrhea."

One day, a Confederate chaplain appeared at the tent to inquire on the prisoners' spiritual state. He asked if they were "prepared to die." Fletcher was then led away and grilled by Squire Skeen, a local prosecutor. Two men wrote down his answers. Most of the questions concerned Clark, a native Virginian whom it was feared could do great harm to the Confederate cause.

Night came on before Fletcher returned to the tent. Clark listened anxiously to his description of the examination. The two men stared out as a full moon rolled over the mountains, bathing the valley in a mournful glow.

"They are going to kill us, Fletcher—me, at any rate."

"Oh, no! Don't get gloomy; they will not dare kill us."

While they talked, Confederate General Donelson and staff rode to the tent. The two prisoners were brought out and led to a large field beyond the camp. A crowd of men followed them until restrained by the guards.

Clark and Fletcher were halted in the field. The officers stood fifty paces off, apparently deep in consultation. The tread of boots was heard; a squad of riflemen filed into place, their bayonets glittering in the moonlight.

Fletcher paled. Every sound was so cold and cheerless.

"Prisoners," interrupted a Confederate colonel, "if you have anything to say, you must say it now, as you will never have another opportunity. You must hold all conversation in the presence of these officers."

Fletcher swallowed hard and turned to his friend. "Well, Clark, I am sorry to part with one who became a prisoner to save my life. Your life as a prisoner, under all your trials and fortunes, has shown you to be ever the same brave, unwavering, honorable man. Whatever may be our future, I respect and love you. We shall meet again, but until then good-bye."

Clark responded: "Fletcher, I am not sorry that I gave myself up to save you. I feel that you are a true man. If you ever get home, see my wife and children; tell her to do for them as I intended to do. I am not afraid to die for my country. This is all I wish to say."

Interminable silence followed. The seconds ticked by like hours. The spies stood alone in the darkness. The squad of riflemen were poised for their orders.

"Return these men to separate quarters," rasped General Donelson, "and do not permit them to speak to each other." Fletcher concluded that the whole stunt was "foolery," aimed to get each man to condemn the other.

In the morning, Clark was bound to a horse and led away. A feeling of grim resolve rose within Fletcher's breast. With Clark gone, there was nothing to keep him a prisoner but the guns. Fletcher made up his mind to escape.[507]

One stormy night, Fletcher slipped out of his irons, crawled out of the back of his tent, and struck into the hills. His destination was the Union fortress on Cheat Mountain, and he had saved enough fat pork for a journey of four days. The intense darkness, steep ledges, and tangled laurel brakes hampered his escape.

Signal shots echoed from the distant camp; Fletcher's absence had been discovered. No pains would be spared to retake him. There could be no turning back. He had been warned that a speedy hanging would follow any escape attempt. Losing his way in the darkness time and again, Fletcher scrambled up the mountain as if in a "horrid nightmare." When dawn broke, he crawled into a laurel thicket for sanctuary. Far below could be seen the Confederate camp, where mounted scouts dashed in every direction, some toward the very ridge upon which he hid.

At nightfall, Fletcher began anew. Cresting the ridge top, he descended to a brawling stream and followed its bed for perhaps two miles. "Halt, halt!" rang out from above, followed by two or three shots. Fletcher dashed up the stream like a madman. "Halt!" cried out a strong voice. "Halt!" A sentinel fired—so near that Fletcher could have touched the barrel of his gun. Climbing the rocky streambed like a staircase, Fletcher raced for his life, with the sentinel at his heels. In desperation, he turned and pounced, receiving the point of the sentinel's bayonet in his left hip. Falling to the water in agony, Fletcher was again a prisoner of war.[508]

This time he was taken to the county jail at Huntersville. "Well, you got de Yankee, did you?" exclaimed the wrinkled old jailer as Fletcher was carried into the two-story brick bastion. The jailer inserted his key into a padlock and opened a huge oak door covered with spikes. A second door, forged of iron crossbars, was revealed. "I hardly ever unlock this door, and it's mighty rusty," he added while fumbling with the second lock. The iron door finally swung open, shrieking on its corroded hinges. Fletcher was shoved inside as it slammed shut.

His eyes gradually adjusted to a dank cell about fourteen feet long and twelve feet wide. Two small, double-grated windows allowed sparse light. The air was so foul that Fletcher laid upon the floor at night, his face pushed against a small crack at the bottom of the door.

A runaway slave named Jim and a "poor idiot boy" named Moses were Fletcher's jail-mates. With kindness, he soon won their confidence. Jim waited on Fletcher, brushed his clothes with an old broom, and blackened his weathered shoes with soot. Fletcher, in turn, taught Jim the alphabet by drawing figures on the floor with bits of charcoal. Jim learned quickly, and when citizens came to gawk at Fletcher, he would take a stand by the door and do all the talking "as the keeper of wild animals stands by their cage and explains where they were caught, how trained, and their habits." Jim spun marvelous tales of "the Yankee," embellishing his story with gusto.

But with each passing day, Fletcher grew weaker. He could not sleep in that stifling cell; the foul air was a poison. The weeks passed slowly until one day, a body of Federal prisoners from Cheat Mountain arrived in Huntersville. Fletcher learned he, would accompany them to Richmond.

Jim and Moses shared tearful good-byes. The huge door was thrown open at last. "Oh, how soft and balmy seemed the air," Fletcher marveled. "How quiet and free everything seemed!"

Fletcher hobbled into line with the Yankee prisoners, looked each man in the face, hoping for some sign of recognition. The soldiers glared at his wild, furrowed countenance.

Finally, a young man stepped forward.

"My God," he said, "is this Dr. Fletcher?"

"Yes," came the feeble reply, "it is what remains of him."

Fletcher was introduced to Captain Bense of the Sixth Ohio Infantry, the ranking officer among the prisoners. The long imprisonment left Fletcher unable to march. A comrade shouldered him for a time, then he was laid in a wagon, and finally atop a mule for the journey to the railroad at Millboro.[509]

There the prisoners were loaded into boxcars and taken to Richmond. Citizens and soldiers taunted and jeered as the captives were led through the city to a large tobacco warehouse. "The guards threw up their guns, and we walked in amid the noise and bustle of a soldier-prison," recalled Fletcher. "The rooms were very large, and the gas burning brightly. Here were men from every State, in all sorts of uniforms, laughing, singing, playing cards....Before we had been in half an hour, I heard some two shots fired at the new prisoners who had foolishly gone near a third-story window."

By a stroke of luck, the list of new inmates was unreadable—scrawled by a drunken lieutenant. A perplexed Confederate officer handed it to Captain Bense for translation. Coming to the last name, instead of reading Fletcher's charge as "captured in July as a spy," the clever captain read; "captured in September at Elk Water; belonging to the Sixth Regiment Indiana Volunteers." A scribe copied those words onto the new roll sheet.

"All commissioned officers step two paces to the front," a Confederate sergeant commanded. Captain Bense and two others stepped out. Bense looked back, saw Fletcher in line, and said, "There is Dr. Fletcher, Assistant Surgeon of the Sixth Regiment." Fletcher took the hint and followed them to the officers' quarters. He was ragged and filthy—shunned by the other prisoners—but alive! The fate of Clark now became his obsession.[510]

The date was October 3, 1861. Back in Western Virginia, the crash of artillery echoed from the hills around a little tavern known as Travellers Repose.

CHAPTER 20
A TOUCH OF LOYAL
THUNDER AND LIGHTNING

"To meet those cannonballs & muskets is an awful
thing; a man can see death tolerable plain."
—Shepherd Pryor, Twelfth Georgia Infantry

Travellers Repose was once a renowned wayside inn. It was located astride the Staunton-Parkersburg Turnpike, a vital link between the Shenandoah Valley and the Ohio River. Tucked in a picturesque glen near the eastern base of Cheat Mountain, about seventy miles west of the Virginia Central Railroad and more than one hundred and fifty miles from Richmond, this delightful tavern, mill, and farmstead sprawled along the lonely headwaters of the Greenbrier River. Its pastoral setting offered welcome respite from a bone-jarring stagecoach ride across the Alleghenies.

Guests could expect comfortable lodging at Travellers Repose. The inn exuded tranquility and charm. Feasts of mountain trout and mutton awaited; the breakfast tables overflowed with stacks of pancakes and maple syrup. Meals were offered for the quaint charge of "four pence ha' penny" (six and one quarter cents).

Innkeeper Andrew Yeager must have turned heads in early 1861 with a prophecy that the scourge of war would reach his peaceful little valley. Armies would contend for the turnpike, he had stated, "houses and barns would be put to the torch and families turned out of their homes." It all seemed unthinkable to the cheerful patrons of Travellers Repose.[511]

But Yeager's tranquil tavern soon lay square between the armies, in a coveted "middle ground." By mid-July, Confederates dug in on Allegheny Mountain, only nine miles east of Travellers Repose, while the Federals erected their Cheat Mountain fortress twelve miles west. A wagon road led to the Confederate depot at Huntersville from a turnpike intersection near Yeager's front door. The East Fork of Greenbrier River rollicked through lush meadows in the rear, offering ample water and campgrounds for troops.

On August 13, 1861, Confederate forces under General Henry Jackson seized Travellers Repose. Tents soon covered the lush meadows. Majestic trees were felled and their branches sharpened as abatis. Above the inn, pleasant hills were girdled with rifle pits. The millrace became a defensive moat. Cannons frowned upon that once tranquil land.[512]

The Confederate defenses were named "Camp Bartow" after a brave Georgian killed at the battle of Manassas. General Jackson thought this new post was not so strong as it looked. His flanks were exposed to salient hills. Two Confederate brigades, greatly weakened by sickness and detached service, were barely adequate to cover the mile-long defenses.[513]

▲

By mid-September, a sense of urgency filled the air. Frosty mornings hinted of winter and an end to campaigning. As Union General Rosecrans marched south to test Lee at Sewell Mountain, General Joseph Reynolds, now commanding some ten thousand Federal troops in the Cheat Mountain District, was ordered to "worry and harass" the Rebels in his front. There was talk that Reynolds might "strike a decisive blow." The soldiers on Cheat Mountain dreamed of leaving their cheerless lair for the

Shenandoah Valley, eighty miles southeast, prayed that before snow whitened the ridge tops, they would march to the "garden of Virginia." To reach that garden, they first had to drive the Rebels from Camp Bartow.[514]

But nature had yet to weigh in. On September 27 and 28, "one of the most terrible storms ever known" in that region slammed the Alleghenies. Howling winds flattened shelters and tents. Mountain freshets turned the rivers into raging torrents. Floodwaters drowned men, dashed away some of the works at Elkwater, and washed out entire camps. Temperatures plummeted on Cheat Mountain—more than a dozen horses "chilled to death" from exposure. "[I]t seemed as though the storm-king had become angry with the puny efforts of the contending hosts," wrote J.T. Pool, "and was about to settle the disputes in the wilds of Western Virginia, by annihilating both parties."[515]

As the skies cleared and the waters receded, Union General Reynolds amassed a large force on the summit of Cheat Mountain. There, during the night of October 2, soldiers gathered around bright campfires to speculate on the coming fight. "There was a constant jingle, jingle of iron ram-rods, snapping of caps, and sputtering of hot grease in sundry frying pans," recalled one, "notes of preparation for the morrow." Precisely at midnight, the order was given to advance. Within an hour, nearly five thousand Federal infantry, cavalry, and thirteen pieces of artillery wound down the mountain toward Camp Bartow.[516]

The night was dank and misty. Tall spruces overhanging the Staunton-Parkersburg Turnpike cast intense darkness upon the line of march. The troops were ordered to be silent; only the measured tramp, tramp, tramp of boots filled the night air. Suddenly, the cry of an owl reverberated from the forest: "Hoo! Hoo! Hoo-hoo-hoo!" Another feathered lookout picked up the call. Then another, and another, until the sound gradually died away in the direction of the Rebel camp. Many of the Federals were seized by terror—convinced that "cunning mountaineers" uttered those doleful notes to warn of their approach.[517]

It was the rumble of rolling artillery and caissons, not the hooting of owls, that alerted Confederate pickets to the enemy. Near dawn, at the bridge over West Fork Greenbrier River, they shot down two Federal soldiers before the Ninth Indiana Infantry fired a volley that put them to flight. The pickets retreated to a guard station about one mile in front of Camp Bartow and sounded the alarm.[518]

Here Colonel Edward Johnson of the Twelfth Georgia Infantry chose to make a stand. Virginia-born, forty-five years old, a West Point graduate, and decorated veteran of the Seminole and Mexican Wars, Ed Johnson was a man of "undoubted courage." He was a rigid disciplinarian, irascible and profane, a real "bulldog" in combat. "His manner of fighting was like his speech," thought one Confederate, "no circumvention, no flank movements, no maneuvering for position, no delay—in short, he seemed opposed to taking what might be considered any undue advantage of the enemy."

Despite his brusque demeanor, this ruddy-faced bachelor was something of a ladies' man. Johnson had suffered a wound in the Mexican War that caused an incessant wink and twitch of the lip when aroused. His head was strangely cone-shaped, not unlike an old-fashioned beehive. "There are three tiers to it," bubbled Richmond socialite Mary Chesnut. "It is like the Pope's tiara!"[519]

Colonel Johnson was no holy pontiff. He cursed the frightened pickets as "low grade" cowards and soon had them posted along a wooded mountain spur, part of a force of one hundred Confederates to meet the advancing foe. Around 7 A.M., the colonel began a spirited fight. Johnson stalled the attackers for nearly an hour until finally driven back—getting his horse shot out from under him in the process.[520]

From the parapets of Camp Bartow, Confederates cheered him as they prepared for battle. But Captain Henry Sturm's "Mountain Guards," Thirty-first Virginia Infantry, were slow getting into the trenches—their sixty-seven-year-old captain had misplaced his boots! Finally, the missing footgear was uncovered; the veins of Captain Sturm's neck bulged as he strained to pull them on.

"Where is my gun?" hollered Sturm, a veteran of the War of 1812. One of the boys handed over an ancient, long-barreled mountain rifle.

"By hell I want my tackle," the aged captain barked. Another soldier produced the old-fashioned powder horn and shot pouch.

Captain Sturm commenced to load in a series of jerks. With his rifle charged and primed, the captain dipped a hand into one pants pocket, then the other, patted his vest and coat in vain. A perplexed look came over his face.

"Where's my specks?"

One of his boys produced the glasses. The venerable patriarch led his tribe willy-nilly toward headquarters. "Captain Sturm, get your men in order," yelled a scowling colonel.

"I'm no drill man," Sturm replied, "but I know how to use this feller," giving his old rifle a pat.[521]

That spirit was welcomed—the Confederates were badly outnumbered. General Jackson had only eighteen hundred men to contest the five thousand under Union General Reynolds. Deploying his regiments of Virginia, Georgia, and Arkansas infantry in the trenches, Jackson looked to batteries of Virginia artillery under Captains Pierce Anderson, William Rice, and Lindsey Shumaker to blunt the Federal assault.[522]

The defenders overlooked a broad meadow, framed by wooded ridges in splendid autumn foliage. Birds were singing; a welcome sun had just illuminated the horizon. One witness described the scene as reminiscent of an "immense floral wreath." It was an unlikely setting for what followed.

Federal troops sprinted across the meadow. Behind them, the guns of Captain C.O. Loomis's First Michigan Light Artillery wheeled smartly into line. Loomis, a skilled artillerist, had been awarded six of the first rifled Parrott guns shipped to the U.S. Army. Rifling, or grooves inside the bore, imparted greater accuracy. The Parrott threw a ten-pound projectile—with those new guns Captain Loomis bragged his crews could "hit a hogshead" at more than a mile.[523]

Captain Albion Howe's battery of the Fourth U.S. Artillery and one gun of Captain Philip Daum's First (U.S.) Virginia Light Artillery dashed forward and unlimbered their guns within eight hundred yards of the enemy camp. Captain Loomis placed his long-range guns between them, behind an orchard, and opened fire. One of Captain Shumaker's cannons promptly answered with a roar. A ball whistled over the Federal guns, striking the ground within ten feet of General Reynolds.

By 8 A.M., a lively artillery duel began. Thirteen Federal guns poured a tornado of shot and shell into Camp Bartow. From the hills behind Travellers Repose, six Confederate six-pounders replied. One of those, a rifled gun of Captain Shumaker's battery, was promptly taken out of action by a fouled ball. "They fired an average 4 rounds to our one," noted a Georgian in the trenches.[524]

Huge billows of white smoke rolled from the cannon muzzles as the grim beat of war played out above Greenbrier River. "The ball was now opened," wrote an Indiana soldier, "roar after [roar] in quick succession from the big guns on both sides—the storm of shot and shell traversing mid air not more than fifty feet from our heads, was at once terribly grand and terrific." That noise was likened to "10,000 packs of fire-crackers set off [all] at once."

The guns fired with extraordinary rapidity. "There was no cessation of the infernal roar of the artillery," wrote a Union correspondent. "Sometimes a half-dozen of our pieces would send forth a simultaneous roar, making the earth tremble, and the return fire seemed spiteful as it whizzed the shot mostly over our heads." Reports echoed back and forth against the ridges, making the duel of cannons in that little valley "ever memorable."[525]

Projectiles arched through the sky and exploded in a shower of death, or smacked the earth and bored deep like "iron moles." To escape them, Confederates huddled in the safety of their trenches. Federal soldiers laid flat behind rail fences. "The balls pass directly over us, bursted over us, and the fragments rattled like rain on our backs," wrote a member of the Fourteenth Indiana, "some fell before us, ploughed great furrows in the earth and blinded us with dirt." The shells emitted a wicked hiss or buzzing noise in flight—green troops dodged wildly at the sound of their approach. Wrote a horrified observer: "Of all the infernal inventions of war, it is these shells. They tear men and horses to tatters in an instant, as they fall whizzing among them."[526]

Around 9:30 A.M., the pace of fire slowed. Federal infantry advanced to test the left flank of Camp Bartow. On the wooded heights above, Colonel Albert Rust's Third Arkansas Regiment waited—eager to atone for their failure at Cheat Mountain. A crisp volley by the Razorbacks chased the Yankees back. Federal guns turned spitefully on Rust's position, throwing shot and shell toward the woods in a futile effort to drive him out.[527]

Soldiers gradually became conditioned to the bombardment. Some began to joke at their predicament. In one fence corner, men huddled in a lively game of cards. Elsewhere, tired Federals warmed by the rising sun actually fell asleep as they lay on the battlefield.[528]

But there was little rest when the iron messengers of death arrived. "I laid about 20 feet from one of Howe's men that was struck in the breast and tore all to pieces," wrote a soldier of the Thirteenth Indiana, "2 or 3 minutes after 3 horses attached to one of the 'caissons' was killed. This made the 'Boys' open their eyes." A Union cannoneer, hit beneath the left shoulder by a round shot, used his pocketknife to detach the remaining sliver of flesh connecting his mangled arm. "That is pretty well done," he muttered, then picked up the bloody limb and walked to the rear.[529]

One shell landed in a chicken coop, exploding in a cloud of feathers. Another bounced wildly through Camp Bartow until it struck the end of a Virginian's musket, doubling it into the shape of a hoop. Another sputtering ball rolled into the crowded trenches—only to be thrown out by a heroic Confederate just before it exploded. A small kitten belonging to members of the Twenty-third Virginia Infantry seemed equally brave, scurrying back and forth on the parapet, oblivious to the storm of death. Whenever a ball kicked up the dirt nearby, the little feline gamboled about it in playful glee.[530]

At some point during the bombardment, a white flag appeared over Travellers Repose. Lacking a yellow flag to mark it as a hospital, a harried Confederate surgeon had unfurled it instead. When a messenger from General Reynolds rode forward to inquire if the Rebels meant to surrender, Colonel Ed Johnson dismissed him with the curt reply: "go back and shoot your d__n guns."[531]

Those guns soon got the range of Confederate batteries. The artillerists were badly mauled, forcing Captain Shumaker to move his cannons after every third fire. Confederate gunners disabled Captain Daum's six-pounder—snapping the axle with a well-aimed, solid shot, but many had dropped out of the action with wounds. Federal troops picked up shells with uncut fuses—evidence that green hands were now working the guns. The fire slackened until only a single cannon answered the Union barrage. After nearly three hours of spirited fire, the bloodied Southerners wheeled their pieces behind the crests of hills to cool.[532]

A lull came over the battlefield. Grown tired of watching the artillery, Federal colonels urged General Reynolds to take the works by storm, which he refused to do. Orders were given instead to test the Confederate right flank. The Seventh, Fourteenth, and Fifteenth Indiana and the Twenty-fourth Ohio Infantry regiments crossed the face of a wooded hill and closed upon the enemy.[533]

Watching from the heights of Camp Bartow, Captain Shumaker's grimy cannoneers swabbed and packed their guns. As Colonel Dumont's Seventh Indiana Infantry drew within range, Shumaker's guns punished them with lethal loads of canister. The Federals staggered. "Distinctly could their officers be heard, with words of mingled command, remonstrance, and entreaty, attempting to rally their battalions into line," wrote General Jackson. Shumaker's artillery poured on a "perfect rain" of canister, shot, and shell as the Federals retreated in confusion.[534]

General Reynolds surveyed the battlefield from an eminence. "[W]e distinctly saw heavy re-enforcements of infantry and artillery while we were in front of the works," he claimed. That infantry amounted to elements of a single Confederate regiment (the Fifty-second Virginia Infantry), and the artillery probably one or more guns earlier taken to the rear for repairs. Fearing that he was greatly outnumbered, with his batteries dangerously low on ammunition, Reynolds broke off the engagement. By 1 P.M., the Federals loaded their ambulances with the dead and wounded and marched back to Cheat Mountain. Jackson's Confederates did not pursue them.[535]

The October 3, 1861, "engagement at Greenbrier River" was a severe test for both armies. In an eighteen-hour period, Federal troops had marched at least twenty-four miles and endured a four-and-one-half-hour cannonade. "I marched 30 miles," wrote one exhausted volunteer, "went double quick four miles, fought six hours, was knocked down with a cannon ball, & all this without breakfast or dinner—enough to kill a mule."[536]

Camp Bartow was riddled by the bombardment. "Hundreds of our tents are shot through and through with cannon balls," wrote the Thirty-first Virginia's James Hall. Bursting shells set a number of tents ablaze, consuming the contents. Dead horses lay about. More than eleven hundred rounds of Federal artillery were thrown into Camp Bartow during the fight. Southern cannons also ran hot. "The gun just above me fired 85 times," reckoned John Cammack, "and the reports were deafening....My hearing was badly injured by the noise."[537]

Both commanders imagined their shelling had generated large losses; Generals Reynolds and Jackson each pegged enemy casualties at three hundred or more. Yet the Federals reported a "surprisingly small" loss of eight killed and thirty-five wounded. Reynolds believed that "the proximity of our batteries to the intrenchments caus[ed] many shots to pass over us." Thanks in large part to those earthworks, the Confederate casualties were also light—six killed, thirty-three wounded, and thirteen missing.[538]

The thirteen missing Confederates turned up as prisoners, one of them in amusing style. A member of the Fourteenth Indiana, Brown by name, encountered a man he assumed was from one of the Ohio regiments. The stranger, in turn, presumed that Brown was a Confederate. Each wore the same color uniform; each felt so sure of the other's identity that neither thought of inquiring. As they walked together along the mountain slope, Federal soldiers appeared in the meadow below.

"Here," said Brown's companion. "We can get a good shot."

"Why, those are our own men," replied Brown.

"No they ain't," insisted the other. "If they were, their faces would be turned the other way."

Brown then became suspicious. He slowly brought his gun to bear.

"What company do you belong to?" he asked.

"To Captain Taylor's."

"What regiment?" queried Brown.

"Third Arkansas."

Before the words were fairly uttered, Brown leveled his musket.

"Now," said Brown, "lay down that gun or you are a dead rebel."

"Well, you haven't a great deal the advantage of me any way," huffed the Confederate as he surrendered, "for you were as much mistaken as myself."[539]

═══ ▲ ═══

"The ground is plowed up in every direction by our balls," wrote a Georgian upon touring the battlefield. "The ground around where their cannon were placed is stained with blood; and in every fence corner and behind every bush were left caps, canteens, haversacks filled with provisions &c., showing the haste with which they took their departure." The First Georgia Infantry had a grand time picking up souvenirs—ample revenge for their disastrous flight from Laurel Hill. Members of the regiment honored General Jackson with a large United States flag. That beautiful silk banner was not captured in battle. It had been found resting against a tree—much to the chagrin of members of the Seventh Indiana Infantry, who had forgotten it! The Seventh would redeem themselves on other fields, but this embarrassing incident gave them a nickname—the "Banner Regiment."[540]

A number of dead Federal soldiers were found "mutilated in the most awful kind of way. [G]rape & even the cannon balls had passed through cutting them clean in t[w]o." Among the dead was James Abbott of the Ninth Indiana Infantry. "[T]here was something unusual in the manner of Abbott's taking off," wrote Ambrose Bierce in later years. "He was lying flat upon his stomach and was killed by being struck in the side by a nearly spent cannon-shot that came rolling in among us....It was a solid round-shot, evidently cast in some private foundry, whose proprietor, setting the laws of thrift above those of ballistics, had put his 'imprint' upon it: it bore, in slightly sunken letters, the name 'Abbott.'"[541]

▲

The Battle of Greenbrier River was a rare victory for Confederates in Western Virginia. But Union General Reynolds, declaring the effort an "armed reconnaissance," also claimed success. Many of his troops called it a "farce." A correspondent for the *Cincinnati Times* styled the affair "a touch of loyal thunder and lightning....The idea occurs to me that if Gen. Reynolds deals such heavy blows in a mere reconnaissance, what will he do when he marches out for a full fight?"

"So now both armies occupy the same ground they did before," mused another Union wag, "and with the exception of a good artillery practice, I can see no advantage gained by our forces. They say we would have won the fight but the ammunition gave out. I think the ammunition story about played out, and would respectfully urge the adoption of something new."[542]

General Henry Jackson pointed to "four days' cooked rations" in the haversacks of Yankee dead as evidence that Reynolds had hoped "to prosecute a rapid march either on Staunton or Huntersville." Jackson issued a laudatory address to his troops and penned a lengthy official report. The Confederate War Department joined General Loring in congratulating Jackson and his men for their "brilliant conduct." In fact, the outpouring of praise for this little Confederate victory moved a skeptic at the *Richmond Examiner* to claim that there were "more casualties from overwork and exhaustion in setting up type" for the reports than from the shot and shell of battle.

General Jackson was unapologetic: "What would have been the results of our defeat who can fully estimate? And yet, because it was comparatively bloodless, for the achievement of the victory who will ever give us full credit?" Fate had "decreed a terrible antithesis" for troops in the Alleghenies, he bemoaned, "the misery and obscurity here, the sympathy and the glory elsewhere."[543]

Pity the poor Yeagers of Travellers Repose! Shells had riddled their stately home. Soldiers had ransacked and wrecked their once-bucolic farmstead. All would soon be put to the torch, and the family driven from their ancestral land. Innkeeper Andrew Yeager's chilling prophecy of invading armies, doom, and destruction had been fulfilled.[544]

PART IV

▲

THE RENDING
OF VIRGINIA

CHAPTER 21
THE GREAT QUESTION

"Nature has defeated both sides; these mountain barriers are far more potent than the sand batteries erected by military science."
—Anonymous Confederate volunteer

A statehood referendum was put before the citizens of Western Virginia on October 24, 1861. Archibald W. Campbell, talented editor of the *Wheeling Daily Intelligencer*, played a unique role in the new-state movement. The twenty-eight-year-old Campbell was a pioneer Republican leader in Virginia. Schooled as an attorney, he was a disciple of Secretary of State William Seward, a confidant of President Lincoln, an unflinching Unionist, and an outspoken anti-slavery man.

Campbell's *Intelligencer* was the leading newspaper in Western Virginia. He had gained editorial control of the paper in 1856, and by 1861, his politics made it a relentless "organ of division." Always faithful and authoritative, the *Intelligencer* became an anchor for new-state advocates. Governor Pierpont of the Restored Government called it "the right arm of our movement."[545]

Editor Campbell had predicted that an "overwhelming" majority of Western Virginians would approve statehood. The October 24 referendum mirrored his optimism. By a vote of 18,408 to 781,

Western Virginians desired a new state, but the landslide masked bitter division. No more than a third of the eligible voters in forty-one Virginia counties had spoken. Secessionists avoided the polls. Balloting was by voice at polling places and a vote against the ordinance in areas controlled by Federal soldiers might bring charges of disloyalty and subject dissenters to imprisonment.[546]

Virginia Confederates also held elections. In early November, delegates to the state convention were picked to replace expelled Unionists. Virginia Congressional seats were filled. "The election fever has broken out," wrote a Confederate diarist at Camp Bartow. "Candidates are getting plentiful & very sociable." On November 6, ballots were cast for president and vice president of the Confederate States. "At the close of the day," wrote Virginian John Worsham, "when it was announced the entire regiment had voted for Jefferson Davis and Alexander H. Stephens, there were loud and repeated cheers for them and the Confederacy." It mattered not that Davis and Stephens ran unopposed.[547]

Autumn brought change to the armies. Union General Rosecrans now commanded the Department of Western Virginia, a military district that included all territory west of the Blue Ridge. Troops began to leave for other theaters of war. Few were more grateful than Colonel Kimball's Fourteenth Indiana Infantry. Recalled one of them, "No poor sinner, who having worked out his probation in purgatory, and…turns his back upon the scene of his late sufferings could feel more pleasure than did the boys of the Fourteenth Regiment…in turning their backs on the horrors of Cheat Mountain."[548]

Those remaining settled into a routine. The boredom of camp life was periodically broken by clashes among the outposts and other minor affairs. Scouting parties combed the mountains for troublesome nests of bushwhackers. Western Virginia became a backwater of war.

On the eastern Virginia front, October 21 brought a stunning Federal defeat on the Potomac River at Ball's Bluff. That miscalculation sparked anguish in Washington. The intrepid Frederick

Lander—now a brigadier general in command of the Department of Harpers Ferry and Cumberland (Maryland)—had been wounded in a mop-up of the affair, and his command devolved upon General Ben Kelley of "Philippi Races" fame. Kelley promptly went on the offensive. Leading three thousand Federals south from the B&O Railroad at New Creek, Virginia, on October 26, he drove Confederate forces out of the strategic upper Potomac town of Romney.

By seizing Romney, Kelley controlled a sixty-mile arc of the vital railroad. The move placed him only forty miles west of Confederate forces under Stonewall Jackson at Winchester, a Shenandoah Valley railroad town about seventy-five miles west of Washington. If reinforced, Kelley might also threaten Rebels on the Monterey line, seventy miles south.[549]

▲

Major General George McClellan was relieved to learn of Kelley's success, following so closely the fiasco at Ball's Bluff. From headquarters in Washington, McClellan had built a second Union fighting force—the gargantuan Army of the Potomac. His energy and stellar organizational skills were again on display. With that army he staged reviews, each one grander than the last. Up to seven divisions—nearly sixty-five thousand men—stood in gilded lines that stretched to the horizon. Bands played, artillery boomed, and cavalry rumbled in gaudy display. Thousands of spectators came out to watch, including diplomats, cabinet secretaries, and President Lincoln himself. McClellan would appear on a splendid mount, galloping across the reviewing grounds as the entire army waved their hats and hurrahed, a spectacle that *Harper's Weekly* called "brilliant beyond description."[550]

McClellan's army looked ready to crush the rebellion, but the general showed no inclination to fight. "I will advance & force the rebels to a battle on a field of my own selection," he wrote Nelly in early October. "A long time must yet elapse before I can do this."

In the meantime, he sparred with General-in-Chief Winfield Scott. McClellan believed he was outnumbered. By his latest estimate, some one hundred and fifty thousand Confederates threatened Washington—a number more than three times their actual strength. When General Scott questioned the amazing figure, McClellan swore he could not tell if the old warrior was a "*dotard or a traitor!*" Their dispute—now a raw struggle for power—finally boiled over in a stormy high-level meeting. The cantankerous Scott angrily confronted his young protégé. "I kept cool, looked him square in the face, & *rather* I think got the advantage of him," McClellan boasted of the exchange.[551]

In a letter to Secretary of War Cameron, Scott charged that the brash young general had repeatedly broken the chain of command, going directly to Lincoln and certain Cabinet members without Scott's knowledge. McClellan reportedly withheld sensitive information from Scott, yet shared it with the politicians.

McClellan had allied himself with powerful forces, and Scott was enfeebled by poor health. "I am unable to ride in the saddle or to walk by reason of dropsy in my feet and legs and paralysis in the small of my back," the aged Scott admitted. "I shall definitely retire from the Army." He did so on October 31. One day later, President Lincoln appointed George McClellan as the new general-in-chief. At the tender age of thirty-four, McClellan now commanded *all* United States armies.[552]

That evening, President Lincoln called on McClellan. "I should be perfectly satisfied if I thought that this vast increase of responsibility would not embarrass you," the president said, reflecting some misgivings.

"It is a great relief, Sir," McClellan assured him. "I feel as if several tons were taken from my shoulders today. I am now in contact with you, and the Secretary. I am not embarrassed by intervention."

"Well, draw on me for all the sense I have, and all the information," Lincoln said. "In addition to your present command, the supreme command of the army will entail a vast labor upon you."

McClellan responded quietly, "I can do it all."[553]

He chose to do it alone, uninspired by the president or his staff. "It is perfectly sickening to have to work with such people & to see the fate of the nation in such hands," McClellan informed Nelly on the eve of his appointment. He looked upon the cabinet secretaries as "a set of scamps," vile, cowardly rascals and fools. McClellan viewed Lincoln as honest but "unworthy" to be president, a fancier of quaint anecdotes that were beneath the dignity of his office—traits that moved him to call Lincoln "the *original gorilla*" and "nothing more than a well-meaning baboon."[554]

McClellan was more gracious to the departing Winfield Scott. And even while Congressional Republicans carped over the army's inertia, the troops were endeared to their new general-in-chief. "If McClellan wields the sword as well as he does the pen," editor Archibald Campbell wrote presciently, "the nation may well have confidence in the new commander of our forces." In the meantime, there were grand reviews and bulletins assuring Lincoln that the capital was safe. "All quiet on the Potomac," became McClellan's watchphrase. "I am doing all I can to get ready to move before winter sets in," he informed Nelly, "but it now begins to look as if we are condemned to a winter of inactivity."[555]

═══ ▲ ═══

As campaigning drew to a close, troops in the mountains of Western Virginia sought escape from the drudgery of army life. In the absence of ladies, the boys held stag dances. "Chestnutting and exploring expeditions; trout fishing and bathing; chuck-a-luck, seven-up, and what not modes of gambling besides," recalled an Ohio Federal, "checker-playing, with chess—kingliest of games; these, and the like, commanded general attention, and were practiced daily. But pipe-making was the supreme passion." Soldiers dug up the abundant laurel or rhododendron bushes and from the roots carved handsome smoking pipes, rings, and other objects with their jackknifes. Countless such mementoes of soldier life were mailed to the loved ones at home.[556]

The troops avidly penned and read letters. James Hall, working in the post office at Camp Bartow, claimed that nearly eight hundred letters passed through each day. Although notoriously unreliable, the mails were important for morale. "Your letters are my only comfort," wrote Georgian Shepherd Pryor to his wife, a common theme among the troops.[557]

Hunting became a popular pastime. Soldiers gained passes to chase the abundant game in those mountains, but usually returned to camp empty-handed. "We were the original game-preservers of the Cheat Mountain region," Ambrose Bierce confessed years later, "for although we hunted...over as wide an area as we dared to cover we took less game, probably, than would have been taken by a certain hunter of disloyal views whom we scared away."[558]

There was always the lucrative art of foraging. "Our Indiana friends are providing for the winter by laying in a stock of household furniture at very much less than its original cost, and without even consulting the owners," wrote John Beatty from Camp Elkwater. Enterprising country folk extracted revenge by selling the troops eggs, butter, and other scarce items at greatly inflated prices. "Sometimes we give them a cursing and march them out of camp at double-quick," admitted James Hall from Camp Bartow, "and then half starve for the fun!"[559]

Africans—enslaved and free—served the armies. Body servants like Shepherd Pryor's "Henry" performed domestic chores in the Confederate camps. Free blacks like John Beatty's "Willis" cooked, washed, and played fiddle or banjo music for the Federals. A self-described "gemman ob culler" tried to enter battle with the Fourteenth Indiana more than once during 1861, but nearly two years would pass before men of his race could legally fight for the Union.[560]

In late October, a runaway slave named Ben approached the Federal pickets on Cheat Mountain. Displaying a white flag, he offered information about the enemy in exchange for freedom.

Ben was a powerfully built mulatto of noted bearing and intellect. Newly minted Brigadier General Robert Milroy, a strident abolitionist, readily took him in. Christened "Benjamin Summit" by Milroy, he worked at headquarters and served as a guide for the Federals.[561]

The abolitionists in Federal arms were a distinct minority in 1861, and mostly of the closet variety. "Slavery always has been and always will be a source of strife as long as it exists," penned a member of the Thirteenth Indiana from Beverly that fall, "and although I hope and believe the present war will be the cause of its extinction, I do not believe the time has arrived at which such an opinion should be expressed publicly."

Even Northern newspapers railed "Against a War for Emancipation." An October 1861 editorial in the Boston *Advertiser* claimed "that neither man nor money will be forthcoming for this war if...the people are impressed with the belief that the abolition of slavery and not the defense of the Union is its object." Romantic visions of war were gone. In the Alleghenies, soldiers were jaded and anxious to return home.[562]

Miserable camp conditions fueled dissatisfaction. Body lice were a constant nuisance, infesting the garments of lowly privates and officers alike—literally eating them up. Despondent men scrubbed in frigid streams or buried underclothes to rid themselves of the vermin.[563]

It became increasingly difficult to supply troops in the mountains. "The roads are awful," wrote a member of the Fourteenth Indiana, "and when our train returns from Huttonsville it is hard to tell whether our teams are horses and men or statues of mud." Another noted that "a single cold night will freeze the top of this mud, and then no team can pass at all, unless the freezing should continue till the ice will bear a team; and at the first thaw the road will again be impassable." Shortages of all types ensued, which bred further discontent.[564]

As winter neared, the troops were destitute of blankets and clothing. "I state by personal investigation when I say there is not a regiment in this command that can muster over twenty five pair of pantaloons, twenty shirts or thirty blankets," wrote a correspondent from Cheat Mountain in October. "All the men are without socks, and many barefooted." Governors of the home states responded by sending clothes to the soldiers. The Confederates received badly needed garments from families and soldiers' "relief societies" in the South.[565]

Accidents were commonplace. A shell from Greenbrier River was thoughtlessly tossed into a campfire, where it exploded, killing a man and wounding others. "[F]rom accidental discharges of their guns many have lost their fingers; some have shot themselves in different parts of their bodies. Some have died from these wounds," a member of the Cheat Mountain garrison related. Another soldier confessed, "I am not half as fearful of being shot by the rebels as I am by some of our own men."[566]

Disease was a grim companion. "There is scarcely a man you meet that can speak plainly, in consequence of colds," wrote a Confederate correspondent, "and the frequent barking of nights would remind one of a pack of hounds in full chase." A virulent form of typhoid fever struck the camps. Men died with heart-wrenching suddenness. "Imagine yourself in the midst of more than five hundred sick and dying comrades, with scorching fevers and parched lips, far away from all that is near and dear to them," intoned a sad commentary from Camp Bartow. "The hospital arrangements are insufficient," complained a Georgian. "We are without nurses, and nothing for the sick fit for diet. The rooms are filthy, loathsome, and some actually full of lice."[567]

Spirits reached low ebb. "Nothing going on...Mud knee deep, no news from home, no papers, all we can do is sit in our tents and brood over our gloomy situation," wrote an Indiana soldier. The army was "such a wicked place" to Georgian Shepherd Pryor, "so much profanity in camp life, though there isent a day passes over my head but that I think of death and its consequences." "Western Virginia has no charm for me," declared another. "It is the most God forsaken Country I ever laid eyes upon that is certain."[568]

Arrival of the paymaster jolted the camps to life. He had been long awaited; many of the troops had not received a penny during five months of service. The soldiers took their pay (eleven to thirteen dollars a month for privates of both armies) in silver, gold, or more dubious paper notes. "[I]t was truly diverting to see them seated on the grass, and counting it out in different piles," wrote one observer, "each pile having its particular object, or destination, those of home and the girls being much the largest." Some paid off debts owed to the sutlers. Others went straight to gambling and in search of a bottle of old "tangle-leg."[569]

General Reynolds may have been a teetotaler, but his army imbibed freely. Sutlers smuggled whiskey in boxes of "Palm Soap" and "Pearl Starch." Local mountaineers hawked potent home brew. "They have been forbidden to sell to soldiers but they still do it slyly," wrote a Federal. "The consequence is the Col sends out every day or two and hunts them up, destroys the liquor and puts them in jail."

Whiskey was rife in the Confederate camps, often sparking fights. "The boys are on a general drunk today & the guard house is full," noted a bemused Southerner. "I feel more like throwing down my gun and cursing the hour I was born," a demoralized James Hall jotted in his diary, "I wonder if they at home ever think about us. But I wonder more, what they would think if they were to see me with my large vial filled with whiskey!" Enormous flakes of snow drifted to the ground outside his tent as Hall concluded, "Not to save the life of Gen. Loring, and all the sons of bitches in the Confederate Army, would I volunteer again!"[570]

On November 16, the year's first major snowstorm hit the Alleghenies. Members of the First Georgia Regiment at Camp Bartow were sheltered only by blankets, having lost their tents in the retreat from Laurel Hill. "The snow had fallen during the night to the depth of eight inches," wrote Isaac Hermann. "Not a man was to be seen, the hillocks of snow, however, showed where they lay, so I hollowed, 'look at the snow.' Like jumping out of the graves, the men pounced up in a jiffy, they were wrestling and snowballing and rubbing each other in it."

Many of the Georgians had never seen the stuff. That afternoon, a great snowball "battle" commenced. Members of Hermann's regiment charged the Twelfth Georgia camp with all the fury of a real engagement, pelting their kinsmen with a barrage of icy missiles.[571]

The snow revived debate about a "great question" in the ranks—where would troops spend the winter? In an ominous development, parties had been detailed to erect wooden shanties on the mountain crests. A thousand clanking axe men felled the huge spruces on Cheat Mountain and cut them up in a portable steam saw mill. "Here we slew the forest and builded us giant habitations," boasted Ambrose Bierce, "commodious to lodge an army and fitly loopholed for discomfiture of the adversary." Each company built its cabins just inside the breastworks, forming a ring of houses with stone chimneys at each end. The Confederates built cabins as well; soldiers of both armies winterized their tents. "We took out two widths of the wall of our tent," wrote one, "and have built a fire place of sod with a barrel for a chimney."[572]

The flurry of construction only heightened debate about the great question. "The probable where abouts of our winter quarters is becoming a vital question to us," admitted Billy Davis of the Seventh Indiana. "The great question" wrote a Georgia Confederate, "is what is to become of the remnant of our forces this winter! It is impossible, in my judgment, for the enemy to advance further into Virginia in this direction, this winter; nor can our army move Northward."

Would troops be condemned to a winter in the mountains? An anxious Federal soldier wrote: "The weather being extremely cold, our tents being extremely thin, and our own love for the beauties of this delectable country extremely thinner, it is extremely impossible, I think, for us to winter here." Some feared they might remain "till the snow gets so deep we can't get out, and then we will be content to stay here and starve to death."[573]

A Virginia colonel admonished the Confederate Secretary of War that the weather on Allegheny Mountain was already severe enough "to freeze the tents of my regiment solid." Politicians lobbied to bring the Georgians—so unaccustomed to those latitudes—home for the winter. "Now do, if there is any chance," pleaded one of those Georgians, "try to get us away from these parts, for if we are not moved, we will all die here."

"This country is not worth fighting for," penned a disgruntled Confederate, warning of the "great horror" Southern troops felt at the prospect of remaining in that "bleak, inhospitable climate." When General Loring predicted that the army would remain in those mountains until spring, a tidewater Virginian flatly declared, "Heaven or Hell will have the greater portion."[574]

═══ ▲ ═══

Confederate General Thomas "Stonewall" Jackson, commander of the newly formed Valley District at Winchester, sought Loring's army for a winter offensive. "I have frequently traveled over the road from Staunton to Cheat Mountain," Jackson wrote Secretary of War Judah Benjamin on the fifth of November, "and I hope that you will pardon me for saying that if the withdrawal of the Confederate forces from the Cheat Mountain region shall induce the enemy to advance on Staunton it will be his ruin."

Loring demurred; his intention was to defend the Monterey and Huntersville lines. Secretary Benjamin left the question of retreat to his own discretion. But Stonewall was persistent. Loring had nearly eleven thousand troops, and by his own account needed only forty-five hundred to hold the mountain passes. By late November, more than six thousand members of Loring's Army of the Northwest began to march east.[575]

In the wee hours of November 22, General Henry Jackson's troops abandoned Camp Bartow. Their retreat was a poorly managed thing. Anticipating a return to warmer climes, the Confederates burned clothing and blankets to lighten their load.

Wagon teams churned deep mud in climbing the Staunton-Parkersburg Turnpike, overworked horses dropped dead in their harnesses and were shoved over the bank. A tortuous, nine-mile march led to the windswept summit of Allegheny Mountain. There, many were curtly ordered into winter quarters.

The great question had been answered at last! Angry Georgians swore and fumed at their fate. "It seemed unjust to place us, some of whom are from a climate, almost tropical, upon these bleak, snow-clad mountains, and send Virginia troops, whose homes are here...into other portions of the service," growled a member of the Twelfth Georgia Infantry. Bitterly they pitched tents at Camp Allegheny, in the midst of a driving snowstorm.[576]

General Loring departed for Staunton, leaving a brigade at Huntersville under General Anderson and the brigade at Camp Allegheny under Colonel Ed Johnson. General Henry Jackson left to command state troops in his native Georgia. That reluctant warrior must have been dreaming of home when he encountered a soldier along the road, tinkering with his disassembled musket.

"Who are you?" Jackson inquired sternly.

"I am sort of a sentinel & who are you?" countered the soldier.

"I am sort of a General," replied Jackson.

"Well, Gen.," retorted the sentinel, "if youl wait until I get my old gun together I'll give you a sort of salute?"

The general shook his head and rode on.[577]

════ ▲ ════

By early December, Federal troops also left the mountains in great numbers. General Reynolds resigned his commission and went home to Indiana. General Rosecrans moved department headquarters to Wheeling. Many of the departing troops were bound for Kentucky; all were delirious with excitement. "Virginia, farewell!" became their cry. "[H]ad it rained bullets upon them they would have pushed on," wrote an observer, "so eager were they to get out."[578]

CHAPTER 22
NIGHT CLOTHES
AND A WAR CLUB

*"[O]h, it was heart rending to hear the death
shrieking of the dieing, the groans of the wounded
and to behold the mangled corpses of the slain."*
—Neil Cameron, Twenty-fifth Ohio Infantry

A storm was brewing on Allegheny Mountain. Strong winds lashed across the crest. Whistling out of the northwest, they heralded the arrival of intense cold.

Camp Allegheny, a Confederate stronghold, lay upon that crest. From its windswept meadows, nearly 4,400 feet high, Colonel Edward Johnson stirred a tempest of his own. Tossing boxes from a poorly loaded wagon, Johnson unleashed a torrent of profanity. The cranky colonel was unrivaled in his swearing. On that blustery December day, he turned the air blue. Johnson cursed cowering soldiers, he spat oaths at teamsters and quartermasters, but loudest of all, he damned the Confederate War Department.[579]

Orders to withdraw, dated December 10, had triggered Johnson's ire. While his thin-blooded Georgians were delighted to leave that blustery camp, the colonel was not. His mandate had been to keep Federals out of the Shenandoah Valley, away from vital railroads leading to Richmond. The enemy was active in his front. If the Richmond authorities thought bad roads and severe weather would keep the Yankees from advancing that winter, Ed Johnson swore they had made a "grave mistake."[580]

From the haunting heights of Camp Allegheny, Colonel Johnson overlooked that portal to the Shenandoah, the Staunton-Parkersburg Turnpike, winding through a gap beneath his works. Nearby was the home of John Yeager, the surveyor who had led Colonel Rust to Cheat Mountain. The Confederates had entrenched at Yeager's farm on Buffalo Ridge, just as they had on his brother's property at Travellers Repose, nine miles below. But defensive labors at Camp Allegheny ceased with the order to retreat.

For many days Colonel Johnson had studied the western horizon from his lofty post. The enemy camp on Cheat Mountain was in plain view. Although more than twenty miles distant by road, Johnson could make out details of the fortress with a powerful glass—even to the tents and campfires of his foe.[581]

— ▲ —

Johnson's Confederate lair was also under scrutiny. From the distant horizon, Union General Robert Huston Milroy had watched the faint blue smoke of that camp for long, weary days of his own. Milroy was a newly minted brigadier, commanding the Cheat Mountain District. He was a forty-five-year-old judge from Rensselaer, Indiana, with a restless soul. Prior to leading the Ninth Indiana Infantry in 1861, he had attended a Vermont military academy, held a captaincy in the Mexican War, and toured New England as a fencing instructor. Squinting through a telescope from the parapet of Cheat Fort, General Milroy cut a striking figure.

He was tall and lithe with the look of a biblical prophet. He was stern and deeply religious to match. His thick mane of gray hair rose like the fretted quills of an angry porcupine. His black eyes were piercing and impatient, his nose was aquiline, his bearded countenance swiveled back and forth over the horizon like some gigantic bird of prey.

Milroy was impulsive. His voice broke into a stutter when excited, but his courage and daring were already well established. "No braver warrior than Gen. Milroy ever buckled on a sword," one of his soldiers would declare. The general's wild locks and impetuous character had coined a nickname.[582]

Once, thinking his men were too long in repairing a bridge, Milroy had plunged into waist-deep water to hoist some logs. As he worked, a teamster appeared and began to curse the men for their delay.

The general, shorn of his insignia, gazed up and said, "You look pretty stout; suppose you give us a lift."

"See you damned first!" was the teamster's surly reply.

"Look here," snapped Milroy, "if you give us any more of your abuse, I'll come up there and pummel your head with a stone."

The teamster backed off, stopping to inquire of an acquaintance nearby, "Who is that gray-headed cuss back there at the bridge? He's mighty sassy."

"Why," exclaimed the man, "that's our Old Gray Eagle!"[583]

▲

The Gray Eagle yearned for battle. Anxious to win distinction, he clashed with Colonel Johnson's outposts and probed his flanks. The crisp blue skies of early December begged for action. Milroy grew increasingly restless on his mountain perch. And then, by a miracle, his prayers were answered.

Five Confederate deserters appeared in Milroy's camp. They reported a weak and badly demoralized force at Camp Allegheny. Those defectors offered to serve as guides if Milroy attacked. They assured him that the Rebels were in no mood to fight. Laughed a Confederate in retrospect, it was the "biggest lie that ever tickled the ear of the devil."[584]

Armed with this startling news, General Milroy resolved to strike. The Confederates on that mountain looked to be easy prey. Milroy would "clean out" their camp and earn his first victory. Not

prone to being superstitious, he picked the day of reckoning—
Friday, the thirteenth of December.

Milroy had plenty of guides; a cunning local Unionist named
John Slayton was already employed. Finding enough troops for an
assault was another matter. Many Federal officers were on leave—
so many soldiers were sick or absent from their regiments that the
general was forced to solicit volunteers.[585]

By December 12, Milroy had gathered elements of the Ninth
and Thirteenth Indiana, Twenty-fifth and Thirty-second Ohio
Infantry regiments, the Second (U.S.) Virginia Infantry, and a
detachment of Bracken's Indiana cavalry at Cheat Fort—almost
nineteen hundred men in all. The column was hastily underway.
Those Federals were so confident of victory that seventy-five
members of Rigby's Indiana artillery went along without cannons,
fully expecting to capture and work the Rebel guns![586]

At the head of Milroy's advance that day was a slight, baby-
faced youth named Joseph R.T. Gordon. Just seventeen years old,
"Josie" was the son of Major Jonathan W. Gordon, caretaker of
General Garnett's body at Corricks Ford. The little private had
enlisted in the Ninth Indiana Infantry that summer—after his
father's departure to join the Eleventh United States regulars.

Major Gordon was horrified to learn of his tender son's enlistment. He feared that Josie had "thrown away" his life. A stern letter was addressed to the boy. "You need not be afraid that I shall
interfere with your choice," wrote the Major. "I would...sooner die
than you should do any unworthy act in your new vocation to
bring reproach upon yourself or family. Remember your mother.
Do not forget that you were among her last thoughts....Write to
me often, obey your officers, and die sooner than be a calf or a
coward."

Josie Gordon was so fragile in appearance that General Milroy
took him in as an orderly. But the boy gravitated to danger, proving himself quick-witted and fearless. The amiable Josie soon
became the "pet of the regiment." He was "brave as a lion," it was
said, "and as gentle as a lamb."

Young Gordon narrowly escaped death when hidden Confederates shot into Milroy's advance guard two miles west of old Camp Bartow. The main Federal column reached that point some hours after it was cleared. Curious soldiers peered at the yellow-clad faces of their dead. "How repulsive they looked," recalled Ambrose Bierce, "with their blood-smears, their blank, staring eyes, their teeth uncovered by contraction of the lips! The frost had begun already to whiten their deranged clothing. We were as patriotic as ever, but we did not wish to be that way. For an hour afterward the injunction of silence in the ranks was needless."[587]

That night, the Federals gathered near old Camp Bartow, kindling fires to ward off the cold. General Milroy summoned the officers to his campfire and unfolded a plan. Proposing to split his force in two, the general would send each column, about nine hundred strong, to pounce upon the Confederates from opposite flanks at dawn.

Colonel Gideon Moody, with his Ninth Indiana and the Second (U.S.) Virginia detachment, would march by the Green Bank road, climb Buffalo Ridge, and strike the left flank of Camp Allegheny. General Milroy's column, led by Colonel James Jones's Twenty-fifth Ohio and detachments of the Thirteenth Indiana and Thirty-second Ohio Regiments, would ascend the Staunton-Parkersburg Turnpike to storm the Confederate right. The attacks were to begin at daybreak on December 13.[588]

Colonel Moody's march began at 11 P.M. on December 12, under a brilliant star-lit sky. "How romantic it all was," recalled Ambrose Bierce, "the glades suffused and interpenetrated with moonlight; the long valley of the Greenbrier stretching away...the river itself unseen under its 'astral body' of mist!"

General Milroy's column started up the frozen turnpike at midnight. Within a mile of the enemy camp, Confederate pickets opened fire. A wounded Federal, moaning piteously and covered with blood, was carried through the ranks. Trying to ignore the grim scene, Milroy's troops filed off at a sharp curve and began to scramble up the mountainside.[589]

The Confederates at Camp Allegheny were aroused. Drums beat the call to arms as Colonel Ed Johnson stormed from hut to hut. Clad in his nightclothes and slippers, the colonel was a sight to behold. He donned a teamster's overcoat but had not retrieved his sword. Grabbing a crooked piece of oak root, Johnson waved it menacingly at his men. There was no time for formalities—the Yankees had come calling! "I am of the opinion to this day," John Robson of the Fifty-second Virginia later wrote, "that nobody had to waste time hunting up a fight around old Ed Johnson without getting as much as was good for them before night."⁵⁹⁰

The colonel had only twelve hundred men to cover his mile-long defenses. Lt. Colonel George Hansbrough's Ninth Virginia battalion, Major Albert Reger's Virginia battalion, and the Thirty-first Virginia Infantry occupied the heights on his right, protected only by some felled timber at the edge of a large field. On the Confederate left flank, south of the turnpike, were crude earthworks. Behind them Johnson placed his own Twelfth Georgia, the Fifty-second Virginia Infantry, and Lieutenant C.E. Dabney's Pittsylvania Cavalry. Covering the road from those works were two four-gun batteries, Captain Pierce Anderson's trusty Lee Battery, and the new guns of Captain John Miller, a Presbyterian minister. Miller's Second Rockbridge Artillery had drilled for weeks on the mountain with a makeshift pair of wooden "cannons" until their guns arrived.⁵⁹¹

On the right flank, Confederates braced against a piercing wind as the sky began to glow. From the dark woods came Federal troops, "six files deep at double quick." Lt. Col. Hansbrough's battalion knelt in line at the brow of the mountain and gave them a volley of musketry. Hansbrough's men, badly outnumbered, scattered like a covey of "chased partridges." The Thirty-first Virginia Infantry promptly came to their aid. Rallying, the Confederates broke into a charge.⁵⁹²

The battle was on. "The balls flew thick and fast—I really believe that one thousand passed around me, playing all sorts of music," recalled a Confederate. "We could scarcely see them for the smoke," wrote a Federal officer. "The fight here was almost hand to hand," Lt. Col. Hansbrough declared. "The men fought on their own hook, each loading and firing as fast as possible." Hansbrough fell wounded and was carried from the field. "The roar of the musketry was terrible," wrote an Ohio captain, "and the shouts of the men was like the yelling of fiends."[593]

Colonel Johnson brought up five companies of the Twelfth Georgia Infantry and pitched into the fray. Swinging his oak bludgeon, Johnson led a charge. "Give 'em Hell boys," he roared. "Give 'em Hell." Milroy's Federals melted to the rear. The din of battle overwhelmed sensibilities, shocked mortal flesh. "Stick to the timber, boys, and stand firm," cried a Federal captain attempting to rally his men, "our side is making half that noise."[594]

"Here began a most determined struggle," recalled an Ohio Federal. "They to gain control of the timber, we to keep them out." Bluecoats seized the upper hand. "We suffered much," admitted James Hall, "the enemy having decidedly the advantage, being in the woods,—with us in the open field, and having the sun shining full in our faces." Prostrate forms soon dotted the field. "I fought for more than an hour within a [rod] of two [of] my cabbin mates who lay weltering in their blood," related a member of the Thirty-first Virginia. "It being a very cold frosty morning a fog kept raising from their blood."[595]

Members of the Yeager family were ushered from their home as bullets pattered on the roof like hail. The struggle became desperate. Confederates were driven to their cabins, only to be led back up the slope by the fiery Ed Johnson. "Our boys fought bravely repulsing the enemy three...times," wrote a Federal, "running them at the point of the bayonet...but each time they rallied and drove our boys back." Troops seasoned on the mountain crests now battled like veterans. The Western Virginians under Johnson's command fought with unusual tenacity, for the Federals stood between them and their homes.[596]

"[I]...had my gun shot & dented so that I could scarcely get a load down her & finally threw it down & picked up another," recalled a wounded Virginia Confederate. The battle lines mixed in such confusion that Southern artillerists found it difficult to engage without killing their own men. Muskets were discharged in the very faces of the foe. "I never witnessed harder fighting," avowed Ed Johnson, that veteran of three wars.

The disappearance of skulkers and those aiding the wounded badly thinned Milroy's lines. Federal troops, now low on ammunition, dug frantically through the cartridge boxes of the fallen. Listening in vain for Colonel Moody's attack on the opposite flank, Milroy's remaining troops shot their last rounds and gathered up the wounded. Nearly three hours after the attack commenced, they retreated back down the mountainside.[597]

Just about then, Colonel Moody's column appeared on the Confederate left. Moody's lengthy and difficult circuit had upset the Federal timetable. Worse, his men had tarried at a local mill, guzzling hard apple cider and filling their canteens. Upon climbing the steep mountainside, they found scowling earthworks and acres of slashed timber, "impenetrable to a cat." It did not look like the haunt of a demoralized foe.[598]

Turning from the wreck of Milroy's detachment on the right, Colonel Johnson now joined his men on the left. Captain Pierce Anderson's Lee Battery anchored the Confederate works on that flank. The venerable Anderson saw men in gray jackets clambering through the fallen timber. "Don't shoot," they cried out. "We are your pickets coming in!" Anderson, on horseback a few paces in advance, called out for them to enter the works. He was instantly shot down. Deceiving Federal skirmishers had killed the grizzled veteran of fifty-eight battles![599]

Colonel Moody's Federals—the Ninth Indiana and Second (U.S.) Virginia Regiments—charged up the slope, "whooping like devils." As they closed, Confederates rose from the ditch and poured in a "murderous fire." The charge stalled in a tangle of logs and brush fronting the enemy works. "It was a horrible sight indeed," avowed one Federal. "The balls flew around thick as hail....I felt that I would fall when we were advancing, for I did not see how I could escape their balls....[H]ad we not fell down we would undoubtedly have been killed."[600]

Federals nestled into the slashed timber. "We took cover in it and pot-shotted the fellows behind the parapet," Ambrose Bierce recollected. By slinking through the fallen trees under fire, some drew within twenty yards of the Confederate works. Among them was little Josie Gordon, that darling of the Ninth Indiana Infantry. Tiring of the stalemate, he gathered a storming party, determined to renew the charge. Josie leaped upon a log, boldly exposed to the guns. Comrades watched in horror as the little hero fell, his tender voice still ringing through the timber for them to "Come on!"[601]

The attack devolved into a contest of sharpshooters. Enemy soldiers taunted and cursed—daring each other to hold up their heads! Each man let slip a bullet at anything exposed. "In this position we kept up a regular Indian fight for over four hours," wrote a member of the Second (U.S.) Virginia. "Toward the last the firing became so accurate, that if an inch of one's person was exposed, he was sure to catch it."[602]

Confederate artillerists splintered the fallen timber with round shot and canister to drive out the attackers. Reverend Captain Miller's cannons—no longer the wooden variety—did fine execution. Colonel Moody's brushy nest became too hot to hold. By 2 P.M., nearly seven hours after General Milroy's first shots, the exhausted Federals withdrew. The battle was over.[603]

Colonel Moody's troops rejoined Milroy at the base of the ridge, using swords and bayonets to chisel out graves for the dead. Licking their wounds, the Federals turned back for Cheat Mountain. Large wagons carried off the injured. "This was the saddest trip I ever made," an Ohio captain later mused. "The mountain road was rocky and rough. The moaning of the wounded men and their continual plea for water made the night dismal." Ice in the wagon ruts was often broken for water to quench their thirst.

Upon repassing their unburied dead near Camp Bartow, some Federals noted that the gruesome forms had changed position. "They appeared also to have thrown off some of their clothing,"

Ambrose Bierce recalled, "which lay near by, in disorder. Their expression too, had an added blankness—they had no faces."

"As soon as the head of our straggling column had reached the spot a desultory firing had begun," Bierce wrote. "One might have thought the living paid honors to the dead. No; the firing was a military execution; the condemned, a herd of galloping swine. They had eaten our fallen, but—touching magnanimity!—we did not eat theirs."[604]

═══ ▲ ═══

The Federals had been "most gloriously" thrashed. "Our men discovered at the first fire that a great mistake had been made," editorialized the *Wheeling Intelligencer*. "They had been led to expect a different meeting.—Scouts had reported the enemy only about a thousand strong, and in a place where they could easily be taken. Our men were all eagerness to bag them." Declared a bitter Hoosier, "I think Gen. Milroy placed to[o] much confidence in them damned rebel deserters."[605]

During the fight, Confederates distinctly overheard Federal soldiers grumbling that they had been deceived. General Milroy blamed defeat on a deserter from his own camp, along with the "many base cowards" who left the fight prematurely. But the Gray Eagle had lost his first battle; he alone was to blame. Ironically, had the attack been delayed only two days, Milroy would have found the Confederate camp abandoned.[606]

A War Department commendation praised the Confederates for victory in "combat as obstinate and as hard fought as any that has occurred during the war." Ghastly corpses littered Camp Allegheny's bloodstained crest. "Our victory has been complete but dearly bought," wrote Colonel Johnson of the nearly seven-hour struggle. "I have seen enough of war," wept James Hall. "O my God, how forcibly it illustrates the folly and depravity of the human heart."

The wounded suffered intensely. "Many were groaning from extreme pain," wrote Hall, "with the cold, clammy sweat of death upon their brows." Left in a hospital on the dreary summit, some later died of exposure. The Confederates lost more than 150 men—killed, wounded, or missing in action. Casualties on the Federal side numbered about 140. Bodies turned up in the woods around Camp Allegheny for weeks. "Six were found yesterday," wrote a correspondent on December 21, "with their eyes picked out by the crows."[607]

John Cammack's company of the Thirty-first Virginia Infantry lost eighteen of forty-two men in the fight. "Out of our commissioned and non-commissioned officers," he wrote, "everyone but myself was killed, wounded or missing. I was a corporal at the time and the command of the company devolved on me....We buried six of our men in one grave, and I commanded the firing party."

The clash had truly been a fraternal one. Virginia Confederates recognized some of the Union dead as old neighbors. A Federal captain was said to have drawn a bead on his own brother in the Confederate trenches during that battle.[608]

Little Josie Gordon was greatly mourned. Earlier, in a premonition of death, Josie had asked comrades of the Indiana Ninth to send his body home to Indianapolis. His father, Major Jonathan Gordon, would make a heart-rending discovery upon securing those remains. Found inside the breast pocket of the coat in which Josie fell was an unfinished letter, stained with his blood. The father's trembling hand unfolded a final testament from his son:

> *You seem to be at a loss, my dear Father, to understand my motive for volunteering, but I think, if you will remember the lessons which for years you have endeavored to impress upon my mind, that all will be explained. When you have endeavored ever since I was able to understand you, to instruct me...that I was to prefer Freedom to every thing else in this world, and that I should not hesitate to sacrifice anything, even life itself, upon the altar of my country when required, you surely should not be surprised that I should, in this hour of extreme peril to my country, offer her my feeble aid.*

Josie Gordon was laid to rest with military honors in one of the most imposing funeral ceremonies Indianapolis residents could remember.[609]

▬▬ ▲ ▬▬

Of the many heroes at Camp Allegheny, none stood taller than Colonel Ed Johnson. His stubborn defense allowed the Confederates to claim an unlikely victory, despite being almost twice outnumbered. "The old fellow will die in his tracks before he will consent to a retreat," wrote a Virginian of the colonel, "and the confidence which the troops entertain in his skill and gallantry is worth a thousand men to us."

"My recollections of Col. Edward Johnson, as he appeared that day, is very distinct," wrote John Robson after the war, "because he acted so differently from all my preconceived ideas of how a commander should act on the field of battle." He was "always in the thickest of the fight," marveled a Confederate officer of the musket-toting colonel who could "load and shoot faster than any man he saw." Ed Johnson led the fierce charges in person, infusing his men with courage as he swore defiantly at the bluecoats. His clothes were riddled with bullet holes, yet he came out of the fight without a scratch. With bulldog obstinacy, he drew a line atop the Allegheny that the enemy could not cross.[610]

Colonel Johnson became a bonafide Southern hero. The "immense war club" he carried in the fight appeared on display at the State Library in Richmond. The colonel was awarded a brigadier general's star, to date from the day of battle—Friday the thirteenth! One thing more was earned. The club-wielding defender of those bleak, windswept heights became forever known as "Allegheny" Johnson.[611]

CHAPTER 23
COLD AS THE NORTH POLE

"Of all the places on this earth, there's none I do declare,
That can surpass Cheat mountain top for misery and despair."
—"Colonel" Coe, Thirty-second Ohio Infantry

The Confederate victory at Camp Allegheny doomed soldiers to a winter in the mountains. Southerners under "Allegheny" Johnson were ordered to hold their icy perch, while General Robert Milroy's Federals huddled on Cheat Mountain twenty miles northwest. Deep snow and subzero temperatures could be expected. "Some of the boys are pretty badly scared about it," acknowledged a member of the Thirty-second Ohio Infantry. "They think if [we] stay here the whole regiment will freeze to death." A pragmatic Confederate accepted the inevitable. "[T]here will be no hope of any service," he wrote. "Will lie up and try to keep warm."[612]

Log shanties became their homes. "Well sis we are into winter quarters at last," grumbled a Georgian at Camp Allegheny. "16 men crowded into one little hut—16 ft by 16 ft—one small fireplace to cook, eat, and warm around, and the weather cold, bitter cold, snow all over the ground, and a difficult matter to get wood."[613]

Others were not so fortunate. "We are still living in our tents," Virginian James Hall addressed his diary in late December, "but we make them tolerably comfortable by constructing rude fireplaces to them. At night we do not fare so well. Some mornings when we awaken our blankets are wet…and the inside of our tent lined with hoar frost. Many times our hair is frozen stiff by congealed respiration, and our floor is covered with snow. This is a pleasant life, sure."[614]

Soldiers made desperate pleas for more congenial assignments. "We are…suffering the hardest of all hardships…upon the frigid top of the hateful Alleghany," wrote a shivering captain to Confederate Vice President Alexander Stephens. Indiana Congressman Schuyler Colfax lobbied General McClellan on behalf of the Ninth Indiana Regiment at Cheat Mountain: "I now beg and earnestly entreat you to relieve them…from that Siberia to fields where they will have a chance to fight instead of to freeze."[615]

═══ ▲ ═══

Political intrigue was also rife in the city of Wheeling. Sixty-one delegates had gathered at the Wheeling Custom House since November 26 to frame a constitution for the new "State of Kanawha." The convention opened with acrimonious debate. "Kanawha" proved to be an unpopular name—a county and two rivers within the proposed state already held that title. Many had urged that the name "Virginia" somehow be retained. A poll of members chose the name "West Virginia" for their new state.[616]

Delegates next wrangled over a "proper boundary." A nine-member committee stunned the convention on December 5 by adding thirty-two counties to the thirty-nine included in the original statehood ordinance. The proposal would have pushed the new state's reach to the Blue Ridge Mountains, inflated its slave population, and resulted in a voting majority loyal to the Confederacy! Delegate Gordon Battelle of Ohio County rightfully called it a "delusion and a snare" to defeat the new-state movement.

On December 13, while battle raged at Camp Allegheny, the territorial limits of West Virginia were fixed. Forty-four counties were included unconditionally. The counties of Pendleton, Hardy, Hampshire, Morgan, Berkeley, Jefferson, and Frederick were to be added if their voters ratified the new constitution. Those counties (all but Frederick would ultimately be included), formed a new panhandle—created to place the Baltimore and Ohio Railroad in Union hands. "[It] is the great artery that feeds our country," spoke delegate Waitman Willey. "We cannot do without it."[617]

Little mention had been made of slavery. Anti-slavery feelings pulsed strong in trans-Allegheny Virginia, yet there were influential slaveholders. Few delegates wished to take up the "vexed question"—it might endanger their whole movement. On the morning of December 14, however, Methodist minister Gordon Battelle rose and called for a gradual emancipation clause in the state's new constitution. Most of the delegates were thunderstruck. Exclaimed one, "I discovered on that occasion, as I never had before, the mysterious and over-powering influence 'the peculiar institution' had on men otherwise sane and reliable. Why, when Mr. Battelle submitted his resolutions, a kind of tremor—a holy horror, was visible throughout the house!"

Those vexing resolutions were tabled, but Archibald Campbell's *Wheeling Intelligencer* took the cause public. "We should esteem it far better that the Convention had never assembled that than it should omit to take action of this character," proclaimed the *Intelligencer*. "Congress will hesitate long before it will consent to the subdivision of a slave State simply that two slave States may be made out of it." Anxious to be rid of the subject, delegates voted to exclude slaves or any "free person of color" from taking up permanent residence in the new state following ratification. Most hoped that would be enough to secure Congressional approval. The issue of slavery continued to fester.[618]

The convention approved West Virginia's new constitution by unanimous vote. A public referendum was slated for the first Thursday in April 1862. "[W]inter closes in on the Union people of Western Virginia," noted President Abraham Lincoln in his message to Congress, "leaving them masters of their own country."[619]

▲

Christmas 1861 was unique in America. Troops in the snow-clad Alleghenies spent the day without families or loved ones. There was little holiday cheer. "We are *amusing* ourselves hovering around a fire in our tent," Confederate James Hall wrote from Camp Allegheny. "Though last night was Christmas Eve, I did not sleighride much! Instead of that, we were marched out with the Regt. on the mountain, to guard the batteries and artillery. We spent our Christmas...very gaily, sure."[620]

The new year brought a reprieve from the cold. To celebrate, the armies launched raids. On New Year's Eve, more than seven hundred Federal troops under Major George Webster of the Twenty-fifth Ohio Infantry left Camp Elkwater for Huntersville, nearly forty-five miles south. They drove two hundred and fifty mounted Confederates from the town on January 3, 1862, and captured nearly thirty thousand dollars worth of military provisions. Unable to transport the windfall, Webster consigned it to the flames and nailed a Union flag to the courthouse as his calling card.[621]

From the Shenandoah Valley, Confederate General "Stonewall" Jackson countered with a march on General Kelley's force at Romney, part of his grand strategy to reclaim Western Virginia. Jackson would first march north to strike the B&O Railroad and Chesapeake and Ohio Canal, disrupting Federal supply lines and preventing a junction of United States forces under Generals Frederick Lander and Nathaniel Banks that threatened his base at Winchester, Virginia. Jackson would then turn west for Romney. By claiming the town, he hoped to stack the deck for a spring offensive.

But Jackson needed the Army of the Northwest to strike that blow, and General Loring was slow in coming. His inertia angered the impatient Jackson. When the Army of the Northwest finally slid out of the Alleghenies on roads of mud and snow, they were in no mood to fight. Loring's men had seen enough of war. Veterans of the army intended to seize the pleasures of the holiday season—eggnog, home-cooked meals, and the company of Shenandoah Valley women.[622]

General Jackson was not pleased by what he saw. Nor were Loring's men inspired by their first sight of Stonewall. They laughed at how his mount "looked more like a plow horse than a war steed." Sam Watkins of Tennessee observed Jackson "riding upon his old sorrel horse, his feet drawn up as if his stirrups were much too short for him, and his old dingy military cap hanging well forward over his head, and his nose erected in the air, his old rusty sabre rattling by his side." General Loring was certainly not impressed, and promptly locked horns with Jackson. Loring, six years Jackson's senior, had anticipated a role in planning the offensive, but was told nothing by the secretive Stonewall.[623]

Jackson's mysterious offensive began on New Year's Day under warm and breezy skies. The balmy weather tricked Confederates into dumping their heavy coats and blankets in supply wagons. As the army marched north on Bath (Berkeley Springs), temperatures plummeted. Soft rains turned to driving snow—Old Man Winter was back with a vengeance. The supply wagons were nowhere to be seen. Thinly clad soldiers were punished by the elements. When Loring ordered his suffering men to bivouac after covering eight miles, he was handed a dispatch from Jackson to march on. "By God, sir," the one-armed general exploded, "this is the damnedest outrage ever perpetrated in the annals of history, keeping my men out here in the cold without food."

Loring's pace exasperated Jackson, but the Army of the Northwest showed fight. The First Georgia Regiment stormed into Bath on January 4 with cries of "Remember Laurel Hill!" Detachments under Colonel Rust burned an important railroad bridge over Big Cacapon River and tore up miles of B&O track and telegraph wire.

Following a standoff with troops under General Lander at Hancock, Maryland, Jackson withdrew from the banks of the Potomac and turned on Romney. Severe weather now became his greatest foe. One fierce snowstorm opened with a bizarre thunder and lightning show—"sheet after sheet of wild flames" hissed from the sky. It was said that temperatures plunged to sixteen degrees below zero. Roads turned to solid ice; the wagons lagged far behind as shivering troops again bivouacked without food or shelter. Suffering Confederates robbed parched corn from the horses to ward off death.

Tennessean Marcus Toney watched men drop into "that stupor which precedes death by freezing, and we would have to seize them roughly and keep them moving." Piercing winds chilled the very marrow of their bones. Sam Watkins swore he found eleven pickets who had frozen to death on post—a horrifying "Death Watch!"[624]

As the Confederate offensive ground to a shivering halt, word came that the Yankees under General Kelley had vacated Romney. Jackson gladly took the prize by forfeit and watched Loring's command straggle in on January 17, "very much demoralized."

Romney, a filthy, disgusting place from occupation, now became Confederate winter quarters. Loring's Northwesterners could see little accomplishment for all the suffering. They mistook Stonewall's resolve for insanity. The men became insolent, cursing and abusing him. "They blamed him for the cold weather," wrote Sam Watkins. "They blamed him for everything, and when he would ride by a regiment they would...call him 'Fool Tom Jackson,' and loud enough for him to hear."[625]

When Jackson and his old "Stonewall Brigade" departed for Winchester—a far more desirable post—Loring's troops howled with resentment. On January 23, Colonel Samuel Fulkerson of the Thirty-seventh Virginia Infantry wrote a friend in the Confederate Congress on behalf of Loring's command:

This part of the army, during the last summer and fall,

passed through a campaign in Northwestern Virginia, the character of which in point of suffering, toil, exposure, and deprivations has no parallel in this war....After all this hardship and exposure, and many, with much labor, had built winter huts, a call was made upon them to march some 150 miles to [Jackson's aid]....This was also cheerfully undertaken by the men...with the expectation on every side that after the object of the expedition was accomplished, this force, which had passed through eight months of incessant toil, would be permitted to retire to some convenient point and enjoy a short respite, preparatory to the spring campaign, rendered the more necessary by the terrible exposure since leaving Winchester, which has emaciated the force almost to a skeleton.

"The best army I ever saw of its strength has been destroyed by bad marches and bad management," added Colonel Taliaferro by endorsement. "It is ridiculous to hold this place; it can do no good, and will subject our troops to great annoyance and exposed picket duty, which will destroy them. No one will re-enlist, not one of the whole army. It will be suicidal [for] the Government to keep this command here."

Eleven top-ranking officers of the Army of the Northwest condemned the Romney occupation in similar terms. General Loring endorsed their petition as "expressing the united feeling of the army." He forwarded it to Secretary of War Benjamin with Stonewall's blunt postscript: "Respectfully forwarded, but disapproved."[626]

However, there were potent political forces at work. On January 30, Secretary Benjamin abruptly ordered the Northwestern Army back to Winchester. The move wiped out months of Stonewall Jackson's labor. Infuriated, Jackson submitted his resignation the next day.

Virginia Governor John Letcher and other influential friends scrambled to his support. When the dust settled, Jackson remained in command of the Valley District. He promptly filed court-martial charges against General Loring for "Neglect of duty" and "Conduct subversive of good order and military discipline." The patrician Lee might suffer Loring's agonizing machinations, but the rigid disciplinarian Jackson would not.[627]

Stonewall's charges were never brought to trial. Loring was given a major general's commission and ushered to southwestern Virginia. His Virginia units joined Jackson's Valley Army; most of the other troops were reassigned. All that remained of the original Army of the Northwest was General Ed Johnson's shivering command at Camp Allegheny.[628]

▲

The winter of 1861–1862 was one of the worst old Virginians could remember. The troops suffered terribly in their elevated posts. Weather-beaten cheeks bowed to the howling mountain storms. "Winter is now coming in earnest," wrote Confederate James Hall on January 7. "I never experienced colder weather."

Fierce winds drove blizzards of snow; a bitter chill locked the mountains in its grasp. "[It is] cold, cold, very cold," groaned a Georgia Confederate. A soldier correspondent reported to the *Richmond Daily Dispatch,* "It is snowing; the wind is blowing a hurricane; it is as cold as the North Pole."

Hundreds were victimized by frostbite. The frozen skin of their hands and feet peeled off like onions. "Our suffering was severe from the intense cold," admitted Georgian Parson Parker. "I have seen ice on the barrels of our guns one forth of an inch thick; I have seen the stoutest men of our regiment wrenching their hands and shedding tears from cold, in short, it's almost a matter of impossibility to describe the sufferings of the soldiers on the Alleghany Mountain."[629]

Even when huddled around fires in their makeshift cabins, men could not escape the arctic blasts. Furious winds drove smoke down the rude chimneys and sifted snow through cracks and clapboard roofs. To avoid the miserably crowded huts, some rode out the storms in their tents. "The fireplaces we have constructed do tolerably well while the fire lasts," James Hall wrote, "but at night we suffer considerably, until the snow blows over us enough to cover us, when we sleep quite well." Old Man Winter assailed the Federals on Cheat Mountain with such fury that huge snowdrifts locked the soldiers in their huts.

Just when it appeared that the armies would be sealed in an icy tomb, temperatures spiked, shrouding the mountains in fog. "Dame nature is growing freakish," wrote a Confederate in late January. Black clouds poured rain for days, then sleet, and then snow once more. Rain froze on every surface, rendering the turnpikes impassible and causing overcoats to "rattle like tin."[630]

Long days and nights in the shanties were passed with music and preaching—or with smuggled whiskey and gambling. Whiskey and crowded quarters did not mix. "Men are drunk as usual," wrote a disgusted Confederate from Camp Allegheny. "Decent men must endure it—there is no escape. A feud...found vent this evening....Men were throwing and flourishing knives, bleeding and swearing. It was with difficulty that quiet was restored."

The soldiers learned to cope with winter's onslaught, as they had with previous trials. Pickets stacked rails in tipi fashion, creating elaborate wigwams to keep from freezing at their posts. On Cheat Mountain, tender flapjacks, mess pork, and coffee boosted spirits; interludes of violin and flute music, with homemade tambourines or a crooked bayonet as triangle, revived the soul. Yet every false alarm brought the armies out to mark time in snow-filled trenches, the wind "singing like minie balls" around their ears. "What a life," declared one quaking Confederate. "Would give all I have to be rid of this miserable bargain."[631]

▲

Across the mountains in Washington, General George McClellan also felt an oppressive chill. The weather was far milder there, but McClellan's huge Army of the Potomac remained idle, and the Radical Republicans—those anti-slavery zealots in Congress—grew impatient. Restless newspaper editors joined the politicians in a call for action. McClellan's once-reassuring bulletins of "All quiet on the Potomac" were now mocked by his critics.

President Lincoln stood behind his young general-in-chief. Lincoln had known McClellan from their old railroad days, as an attorney for the Illinois Central. More than once the two had spent long nights at lonely county seats during litigation, where Lincoln spun his many anecdotes. McClellan, however, did not reciprocate the president's support. With each passing day, he became more certain that the Radical leaders sought his ruin. They labored tirelessly, he believed, "sowing the seeds of distrust in Mr. Lincoln's mind." The young general did his best to keep clear of all the "wretched politicians."

McClellan returned home one night and was told that the president awaited, yet he passed the parlor without acknowledgment and retired to bed! Lincoln appeared to ignore the snub. "I will hold McClellan's horse," the president said, "if he will only bring us success."[632]

Lincoln watched as McClellan's Army of the Potomac—the largest and best-equipped fighting force ever assembled on the continent—did nothing. As the clamor for action reached a crescendo at year's end, General McClellan came down with typhoid fever. By January 12, he had recovered enough to attend a council of war at the White House, but would not reveal his plans to subdue the Rebels. McClellan grumbled that neither army generals nor cabinet members could keep a secret, charging that Lincoln even shared them with Tad, his eight-year-old son.

A congressional Joint Committee on the Conduct of the War fueled discontent with General McClellan. Radical Republicans questioned his courage and made subtle allegations of "treason." Newsmen wondered aloud if political ambition clouded McClellan's military sense—that perhaps his heart was not in the war. Critics demanded his resignation.

Still, the Army of the Potomac army did not move. Edwin Stanton, Lincoln's newly appointed Secretary of War, insisted it was time for McClellan and his elegantly furnished troops to "fight or run away." Even the president was heard to remark that if General McClellan did not want to use the army, he would like to *borrow* it.[633]

Lincoln urged McClellan to move against the Confederates at Centreville and Manassas Junction, only twenty-five miles southwest of Washington on the road to Richmond. Week by week, the critics grew louder. Frustrated beyond measure by McClellan's failure to act, the President finally gave February 22—Washington's birthday—as the ultimatum for an advance. But the young general urged another way. To avoid the huge Rebel force he imagined in Northern Virginia, McClellan proposed to ship his vast army down Chesapeake Bay to Urbanna, near the mouth of the Rappahannock River, and from there march west to Richmond before the Confederates could react.

Lincoln was troubled by the plan. If the Potomac Army sailed away, Washington would be left open to attack. When McClellan gave assurances that ample troops would be left to guard the capital, the president acquiesced. But on March 9, news of the withdrawal of Confederates from Centreville and Manassas—just a day's march from Washington—changed everything. General Joseph Johnston's Rebel army had quietly fallen back to new positions behind the Rappahannock River, ruining McClellan's carefully scripted plan to get to Richmond before the enemy did. Left behind for all to see were defenses not so strong as McClellan had feared. Some Confederate works had been armed only with logs painted black to look like cannons—harmless "Quaker guns."

More unpleasant news arrived on March 11. The president had removed McClellan from the post of general-in-chief, ostensibly to focus his attention on the push to Richmond. For the time being, Lincoln and Secretary Stanton would run the war.

Revising his plan to claim Richmond, McClellan proposed to sail to the tip of the Peninsula, a prominent finger of Virginia real estate dividing the James and York Rivers. It had been the scene of the climactic victory at Yorktown in the American Revolution. Landing his army at Union-held Fort Monroe, McClellan would strike overland for Richmond.

The Army of the Potomac was moving at last. From Alexandria, a huge armada set sail: four hundred ships, more than 121,000 men, forty-four batteries of artillery, and all the implements of war. The date was March 17, 1862. McClellan departed with his typical Napoleonic flair. He was thankful to be leaving Washington and his enemies in the rear.[634]

═══ ▲ ═══

Meanwhile, General Robert E. Lee confronted another fleet of Union invaders in his new assignment along the south Atlantic coast. Lee was charged with the defense of nearly three hundred miles of vulnerable South Carolina and Georgia coastline, including the ports of Charleston and Savannah. There were batteries to fortify and waterways to obstruct. It was an unromantic duty of dirt and drudgery. Lee's own competence was in doubt.[635]

In January and February 1862, disaster stalked the Confederacy. General Felix Zollicoffer was killed and his defenses broken at Mill Springs, Kentucky. The irascible Henry Wise lost two-thirds of an army and his own son in defeat at Roanoke Island, North Carolina. On the Tennessee and Cumberland Rivers in Tennessee, Forts Henry and Donelson fell to Union General U.S. Grant. Wise's old antagonist John Floyd had abandoned the latter post, fearing execution as a traitor if captured. The Confederacy lost much of Kentucky and west Tennessee as a result. Southern defenses on the upper Mississippi were crumbling. Confederate hopes of foreign intervention were dashed.

On March 2, President Davis summoned General Lee back to Richmond. Once again, Lee was placed under direction of the Confederate president, serving as liaison with the military authorities. "I do not see either advantage or pleasure in my duties," he admitted to Mary.[636] The *Charleston Mercury* charged that Lee had been reduced "from a commanding general to an orderly sergeant."

The military situation in Richmond was critical. Badly needed shipments of ordnance had been chocked off by the Union blockade. Neither powder nor muskets were available to soldiers in the field. So desperate was the Confederacy that preparations were made to arm the troops with long-handled pikes![637] The news from every front was chilling in the winter of 1861–1862.

CHAPTER 24
ALL'S FAIR IN
LOVE AND WAR

*"[I] could take care of the wounded Federals as
fast as brother Thomas could wound them."*
—attributed to Laura Jackson Arnold

A traveler halted for wagon repairs along the Staunton-Parkersburg Turnpike, eight miles south of Beverly. While he waited, an elderly man appeared at the door of a log cabin opposite. The old fellow, a soldier in the War of 1812, was so crippled by rheumatism that he could scarcely walk.

"They took my two boys from me for the Southern army," he said, "an me an' the old woman are all alone. They promised the boys to take care of me an' the old woman, but they haint done it. We're now livin' on charity. I told the boys not to go an' fight agin the Government."

"Where are they now?" inquired the traveler.

"God only knows, sir," choked the aged cripple, his eyes welling with tears.

"I don't know what's to become of me an' the old woman," he stammered. "We'll never see our boys, an' we can do nothin' for ourselves. I wish I could get clear of this plaguy rheumatiz. I was a mighty good man afore I had this rheumatiz. But no boys, sick, and no money—good God, what'll become of [us]!"[638]

Cruel were the fortunes of war. Many able-bodied men took up arms, leaving women to care for their families. "We meet very few men; the poor women excite our sympathy constantly," wrote Major Rutherford B. Hayes of the Twenty-third Ohio Infantry from the mountains of Western Virginia. "A great share of the calamities of war fall on the women."[639]

Virginia Confederates marching along a road one day happened upon a forlorn family of refugees. The grim-faced matron, her five children, and all of their remaining possessions were strapped aboard a single, jaded horse. "A child's head was looking out each side," recalled one amazed soldier. "Two children were on the horse behind her, and she held a baby in her arms. When she came into our midst…she broke down and commenced to cry."

For civilians, the trials were severe. Andrew Yeager and his son, refugees from Travellers Repose, died from "camp fever" before the close of 1861. John Yeager of Allegheny Mountain was said to have died from being poisoned. Yeager's sons left home in early 1862 to join the Confederate army, but the women of his family remained. To survive, they concealed livestock in the mountains and buried meat, cakes, and jugs of syrup to keep them away from prowling soldiers.[640]

A once-fertile land was devastated by war. "Virginia has suffered more than you could have any idea," wrote an Indiana soldier from the town of Beverly. "Everywhere the army has gone it has been encamped upon the ground of some wealthy secessionist, and whenever it leaves a farm there is scarcely a fence rail upon it, every stalk of Wheat, Corn, Oats, Grass and everything else is completely trodden down or eaten up. We are at present encamped in an Oat field and our horses are grazing in a very large cornfield; and it has been thus all the way."

"Our people will never feel the horrors of war until they have the enemy in their midst," remarked a Confederate of conditions in the upper Greenbrier Valley near Camp Bartow. "When we first passed here…the people of this valley were well fixed, joyful and contented. Now not one of them is to be seen, and their once happy homes are desolate wastes—Poor people!"[641]

Isolated dwellings that escaped the torch were often turned into makeshift hospitals. Such was the mind-numbing scene at a lonely cabin on the slopes of Cheat Mountain: "Lying upon the floor of the only room in the cabin were seven wounded rebels, left there by their fleeing comrades," recalled an Ohio soldier in the aftermath of Lee's attack. "Two sick men had been left to care for them, which they were either not able or unwilling to do, so that the whole burden fell upon a poor woman, who, with her five children, were tenants of the hut. Her husband, a zealous secessionist, had been taken prisoner. *He* was punished, and properly enough, but what crime had the innocent children committed, and the poor mother, in that lonely mountain glen? She moved about in that quiet noiseless step so peculiar to intense sorrow, handing this one water, bathing that one's aching temples, and attending to her household duties. The children stood about the horrid scene—the elder ones in mute despair, the younger prattling away unconscious of the terrors of *bellum, horridum bellum!*"[642]

━━━ ▲ ━━━

Not everyone played the role of victim. In searching a house along the road to Rich Mountain, Federal troops found an indignant old woman, armed with no less than three loaded hunting pieces. She proudly displayed a secession flag, made, as she very frankly told the soldiers, from the tail of an old shirt. Upon it were the letters "J.D." and "S.C.," standing for "Jefferson Davis and the Southern Confederacy."[643]

Soon after the outbreak of hostilities, Union leader Frank Pierpont was absent from his Fairmont home when two gaily-uniformed Confederate officers confronted his beautiful wife, Julia. They sought to claim the state musket issued to Charley Scott, ward of the family and a member of the militia.

Julia Pierpont met them at the door with a gracious smile. In response to their polite inquiry for Mr. Scott, she suavely replied, "Mr. Scott *does not* wish to see you." The fact was put mildly, for Mr. Scott cowered in the room just behind her.

"We have a message for him," answered one of the officers. "Will you ask him to step to the door?"

"*No* Sir, you *cannot* see him *here*. If you wish to see him, you must seek him elsewhere."

The young officers hesitated. They were obviously chivalrous gentlemen, and Julia Pierpont played them to the hilt.

"*Of course*," she waxed, "you will *not intrude* upon a lady?"

They hastened to assure her that nothing was further from their thoughts. And yet there was the matter of that musket, and their orders to retrieve it.

"Will you be kind enough to tell Mr. Scott that Captain Thompson's orders are, that he must deliver up the musket which he received and holds from the state, and if he does not do so by twelve o'clock today he will be arrested."

The gentle play of courtesy was over. Julia Pierpont's defense-less blue eyes now burned with fire. "I understand that matter perfectly well, and young gentlemen," she fended, "*we don't care anything about it, we are not to be intimidated.*"

The two officers were speechless. A flash of crimson spread over the elder's face as they bowed and swiftly walked away. Julia strode to the front room, flung open a window and sang after them in a triumphant voice, "Hail Columbia Happy Land."[644]

▲

Two "rabid" secessionists, known as the Hilleary sisters, resided in a log house at the foot of Rich Mountain. The younger had come from eastern Virginia with her children to escape impending war. Imagine the consternation when General McClellan's army marched up to her front door.

"Surely," she exclaimed to one of the Yankees, "I never imagined men would come to the mountains to fight." Confronting the invader, she rattled vivaciously, "[W]hat do you want to kill us all for?"

"But we don't, Madame!" he replied.

"Well, any how, the Southern men say so, and they are our friends, and we'll have to believe them."

"Well, do you believe them, madame?"

"Why I don't know. They said you'd all abuse us women, kill our children, and burn our houses, and they told dreadful stories until we thought all you Yankees were devils. When you all marched into Roaring Creek we'd a been right down glad to see you all shot down in your tracks."

"Well what do you think of us now?"

"Oh, they lied about you some I 'spose. Your common soldiers even seem gentlemen, and your officers, most of them are mighty agreeable. [I]f the people of Virginia could see us all, they wouldn't want to fight."[645]

—— ▲ ——

Laura Jackson Arnold of Beverly was a woman of conviction—the sister of Confederate General "Stonewall" Jackson. But this determined Jackson pledged allegiance to the *Union* cause. Upon the outbreak of hostilities, she rarely spoke of her famous brother—except to voice regret that he had taken up arms against his country. When war came to her town, Laura served as a nurse. Her graceful form was ever active in the hospitals; her tender hands soothed the aching temples of many a dying soldier far from the loved ones at home.

A Federal surgeon recalled numerous incidents of her loyalty and courage: "Almost alone, amidst a disloyal community, she unflinchingly declared her devotion....Her house was an asylum for the sick soldier, and faithfully she ministered to his wants. Her resources were often taxed to their utmost, and many were her regrets that she was unable to do greater good....We have never heard that she received one farthing from the government, for her generous and loyal out-lay, and have reason to believe that she never made application; but if there is one deserving soul in the great army of patriots that mer-its special recognition...it is Mrs. [Laura] Arnold."[646]

══════ ▲ ══════

A few women actually marched off to war. Betsy Sullivan fol-lowed her husband through the Alleghenies with the First Tennessee Infantry in 1861. While serving the Confederacy, she cared for sick and wounded soldiers, mended, washed, and darned. No trial was too severe, no sacrifice too great on behalf of her "boys." Adored by the regiment as "Mother Sullivan," she marched with a knapsack on her back and slept on the frozen ground with only a blanket—just like the men.[647]

Mother Sullivan was not alone. Nancy Hare campaigned "in real soldier style" with her husband in the Eighth Tennessee Infantry. She could "walk equal to any soldier," recalled a Confederate, and became a leading member of Company K, cooking and washing for the troops. Mary Van Pelt, a "neat, graceful, quiet little woman," accompanied her husband—a sergeant in the Federal army—on active duty with Loomis's Michigan Artillery in Western Virginia. Others intended to fight. A woman named Ann Watson surrepti-tiously enlisted in a Federal company at Wheeling in 1861 before she was discovered in men's clothing and removed.[648]

Some had less wholesome motives. A wide-eyed Confederate wrote of one beguiling female who slinked around camp, "search-ing for her lover." She made quite an impression until sent home as an "abandoned woman."

As Federal soldiers crossed the Ohio River into Western Virginia, the *Wheeling Intelligencer* moralized:

> *Another Runaway—One would think that, in these times*
> *of war and excitement, that wives would behave themselves,*
> *so as not to occasion their husbands any unnecessary trouble.*

But this is not altogether the case, for yesterday, the wife of a farmer in Belmont County (Ohio), passed through the city with a volunteer, with whom she was running away. She had on a Zouave jacket, and her intoxication was barely perceptible to a stranger. For further particulars, the husband will please enquire at Grafton.[649]

━━━━━ ▲ ━━━━━

Attractive women were such a curiosity that the arrival of a Federal officer's wife at Elkwater brought out the entire camp. "That there are good-looking women in Virginia I am confident," wrote a Union soldier from the Tygart Valley, "but they are mighty scarce 'round here, and as a general thing chew snuff and smoke, and are as ignorant as the devil." At least one Ohio foot soldier found the gals more to his liking. "I tell you," wrote that boastful Buckeye, "the fair ones of Virginia are neither slow or scarce. The effect of them upon a soldier is miraculous."[650]

"Some of our boys goes a sparking," wrote another, "married or not." Love was in the air. Fearing that hometown sweethearts would marry someone else while they were away, heartsick soldiers carried on pen-pal courtships. Little Billy Davis, for one, had his eye on a certain Miss Jennie of Hopewell, Indiana. It started innocently with the trading of letters—until the last line of Miss Jennie's latest offered a shocking confession.

"I had never before received a letter of that kind," Billy confessed to his journal, "but I became deeply interested at once; and fully responsive in sentiment." Billy's heart raced as he read her dazzling confession over and over. Ten days of "delightful dreams" and "puzzling questions" passed before he mustered the courage to respond. Once more, Billy savored the magical line of Miss Jennie's letter: "*But I must close lest I love you to[o] much.*" Then he stopped cold—for the word viewed so many times as "love" properly leaped from the page as…"bore"! "I sat dumb," recalled Billy, "while the air castles which I had built, tumbled into one heap and vanished."[651]

An Ohio soldier in Western Virginia mailed the following verse to his distant "Valentine":

> *O, Suzie, don't get married to those that stay at home;*
> *But rather take a soldier, just wait till I get home…*
> *So keep your spirits up, and don't you be afraid,*
> *Because I'm in the army, that you'll be an old maid.*
> *But if you will get married, you needn't wait for me;*
> *There's just as good fish swimming as ever swam the sea.*[652]

———— ▲ ————

A Union telegraph operator named George W. Printz found himself badly smitten by Cupid's arrow. The subject was a Beverly lass named Harriett Crawford. Miss Harriett was fetching and high-spirited. Unfortunately for Printz, she was also a die-hard Rebel.

Printz was hopelessly in love, but Harriett could not bring herself to marry a "Yankee." Inspired by the "mightiest power under heaven," Printz deserted to the Confederate army and returned after the war to marry Miss Harriett.[653]

———— ▲ ————

One day in June of 1861, mail for the Seventh Ohio Infantry arrived in the village of Weston, Lewis County, Virginia. Soldiers crowded around to take in all the news.

"My folks are sending me some shoes," declared one Charles Johns as he slipped an envelope into his pocket. "They think we are in for a first-class war."

Turning, he saw John Wood, the regiment's normally cheerful orderly, holding a letter of his own. Wood's look was tense; his face was pale and drawn.

"What's wrong, fellow? Sick?"

"Nothing at all," snapped Wood, as he disappeared into a tent.

The guard was ordered to be on full alert that night. There were rumors of Confederates about. No one was to pass, not even those Weston girls riding out for social calls.

Guard number ten paced his beat near a covered bridge outside of town. Nothing unusual was observed as night came on. All was peaceful and quiet.

Suddenly, a figure appeared in the gloomy approach to the bridge.

"Halt! Who goes there?"

No answer, only the thump of feet upon wood. A second challenge was offered. No response. And then the sentinel's gun flashed.

A shrill cry, "You can't shoot a rebel," another flash, and all was still.

The anxious sentinel explained the situation to his relief. Fashioning a searchlight, they moved cautiously toward the bridge. Nothing was found.

"Yes, he is seriously wounded. I wish you would send for Dr. Camden," said the physician as he examined John Wood, who lay unconscious at headquarters. Turning to the commanding officer, the physician held up a shattered daguerreotype image. He had found it in a pocket of the wounded man's clothing.

"This no doubt saved his life, if he lives; I wonder who it is. On the back it says 'To John from Evelyn.' But tell me what happened."

"Well, it was like this, replied the officer; the sentry was ordered to shoot and he shot. The second guard after search thought him joking, but when morning came they found blood on the east end of the flooring of the bridge. Further examination showed smears on the top beams of the upper side. All along the great roof beam could be seen the imprint of human hands as though dipped in paint. Lying on it in a precarious situation, fifteen feet above the floor, at the end toward town, was Wood. A detachment of the guard got him down and here he is. I don't know why he did it, for of all persons he knew the orders and that it meant death."

"Well, some things are beyond me," said the physician as he fingered Wood's clothing. "Look, here is a letter. Perhaps it will shed some light on it." Unfolding the paper he read:

> *Elmira, Ohio, June 23, 1861*
> *Dear John: You know all my people are down in Virginia. I simply cannot let you go on making war against many of my loved ones. You have made your choice and I have made mine. Our engagement is to be considered ended.*
> *Evelyn*

"That explains it all, but I hope he will get well anyway. Let Dr. Camden examine him when he comes and leave Johns with him." The physician shook his head and departed.

Wood soon regained consciousness. A few days of careful nursing assured his recovery.

Once again, a courier rode up with the mail. "A letter for you, Wood," he exclaimed. "Brace up, boy, I'll bet its good news."

"Well, give it to Johns and let him read it to me."

With mixed feelings, the letter was opened and its contents read aloud:

> *Elmira, Ohio, June 27, 1861*
> *Dear John: No one will ever know the agony I have gone through since writing a note a few days ago. I know now you were only doing your duty. If you still care and feel unworthy I will be waiting for you. Every day I shall pray that God will spare you, and every moment now I shall look forward to your reply.*
> *Your own ungrateful, Evelyn*[654]

Time has not revealed their fate.

Chapter 25
Lincoln's Odd Trick

*"With our people the Union and the New State are
convertible terms. Crush the one and you, as certain
as death, in my opinion, crush the other."*

—Archibald Campbell

Spring comes slowly to the Alleghenies. The year 1862 was no
exception; snows lingered on the mountain crests even as flowers
blossomed in sequestered coves. The season for active campaigning
was at hand.

On March 11 of that year, President Lincoln included Western
Virginia, parts of Kentucky, and Tennessee in a new "Mountain
Department." General Rosecrans, politically out of favor in
Washington because of a sharp tongue and blunt honesty, was
relieved of command. His replacement was Major General John
Charles Frémont, "the Pathfinder," a flamboyant explorer, and the
1856 Republican candidate for president. On March 29, 1862,
Frémont took command at Wheeling.[655]

General Robert Milroy, commanding the Cheat Mountain
District, promptly begged him for orders to march on Staunton.
Developments in the lower Shenandoah Valley left the
Confederates at Camp Allegheny exposed. On the second of April

1862, General "Allegheny" Johnson reluctantly abandoned that mountaintop post. "All the soldiers are in good spirits," reported native son James Hall as the Confederates marched east, "but Western Virginians think it looks but little like getting home."

At long last, on April 6, General Milroy planted his banner upon the breastworks of Camp Allegheny. Ed Johnson was gone, but the Storm King remained defiant—pummeling Milroy's brigade with a tempest of rain and sleet. Federal soldiers packed into the former Confederate cabins. "But for the shelter they gave us," swore one grateful Unionist, "many would have perished in the storm that prevailed all night."

Dawn unveiled an extraordinary scene. Every surface was coated with a thick layer of glassy ice. As clouds dispersed, the rising sun glittered off millions of frozen crystals—sparkling like the waves of a dazzling silver sea. One of Milroy's soldiers wrote, "The turnpike, after leaving the camp, passed through a dense mountain forest, and as the rain fell upon the trees, freezing as it fell, the tall pines had become freighted with their load of crystal ice, the weight of which inclined them together, forming an arch of fantastic design, under which for miles and miles we marched." Haunting winds emitted "flute-like sounds that contained every note in the scale." Swaying trees creaked and groaned, snapping with a loud report. The percussive crash of falling timber accompanied a "weird, awe-inspiring" serenade to the departing Federals. Ahead lay the Shenandoah Valley and General Stonewall Jackson.[656]

▲

On April 3, the date General Milroy received orders to advance, citizens of the proposed State of West Virginia ratified their new constitution. Governor Frank Pierpont reconvened the General Assembly on May 6 at Wheeling. Pierpont instructed the delegates: "The Constitution of the United States provides that no new State shall be formed or erected within the jurisdiction of any other State, without the consent of the Legislature of the State concerned, as well as of the Congress." Pierpont's Restored Government of Virginia consummated its role on May 13 by including forty-eight counties within the new state border. Certified copies of the West Virginia statehood act and constitution were proudly forwarded to Washington.[657]

Congress was then preoccupied with General McClellan's Army of the Potomac. The general's 135,000-man force had been shipped to the Virginia Peninsula by April 4, but its overland march to Richmond was delayed. The advance had barely commenced when McClellan's juggernaut stalled before an inferior Rebel force at Yorktown. Once again, the general vastly overestimated enemy numbers—thanks in part to Confederate troops that repeatedly marched in circles before his eyes. Badly fooled, the wary McClellan prepared to lay siege. General Joseph Johnston's outmanned Confederates then drew back to within seven miles of Richmond. Again McClellan followed and cautiously laid siege. He was close enough to hear church bells in the Southern capital— bells that might have tolled a death knell for the Confederacy.

As McClellan dallied before Richmond, General Lee saw opportunity. Winning President Davis's distracted approval, Lee encouraged the little army of Stonewall Jackson to launch a coun-teroffensive from the Shenandoah Valley. Jackson's brilliantly exe-cuted "Valley Campaign" appeared to threaten Washington itself, thereby freezing forty thousand Union troops in middle Virginia who were to have joined McClellan for the deathblow at Richmond.

On May 31, a fateful wound at Seven Pines near Richmond knocked Confederate General Joe Johnston out of action and put General Lee in command. Lee promptly reorganized the Army of Northern Virginia and launched a counterattack. Seven days of brutal fighting turned the Federal advance into a humiliating retreat. McClellan's huge army soon cowered under the protection of armored gunboats on the James River. In a matter of weeks, Lee had transformed the war.[658]

===== ▲ =====

While Lee pressed McClellan, the Thirty-seventh Congress debated Senate Bill No. 365, "An Act for the Admission of the State of 'West Virginia' into the Union." On May 29, Waitman Willey presented the formal petition for statehood in the Senate. Privately, he was not optimistic. The Border States were opposed, Senator Willey wrote, because they considered West Virginia statehood "an abolition scheme." Likewise, he feared, "the abolitionists oppose us because they say it is a proslavery scheme."[659]

Willey defended West Virginia statehood in the well of the Senate: "It seems to be supposed that this movement for a new State has been conceived since the breaking out of the rebellion, and was a consequence of it—that it grew alone out of the abhorrence with which the loyal citizens of West Virginia regarded the traitorous proceedings of the conspirators east of the Alleghenies, and that the effort was prompted simply by a desire to dissolve the connection between the loyal and disloyal sections of the State. Not so sir. The question of dividing the State of Virginia...has been mooted for fifty years. It has frequently been agitated with such vehemence as to threaten seriously the public peace....The animosity existing at this time between the North and South is hardly greater than what has at times distinguished the relations between East and West Virginia."[660]

The Committee on Territories, chaired by Benjamin Wade of Ohio, took up the statehood petition. Bullish and bluff in his sixty-second year, Ben Wade was a steadfast anti-slavery man—among the most trenchant of the Radical Republicans. Senator John Carlile was a member of his committee, and so West Virginia's fate appeared to be in able hands.

Nearly a month passed before Senate Bill 365 was reported. Statehood advocates were astonished by its content. The bill *added* fifteen Valley counties to West Virginia's original forty-eight, called for a new state constitutional convention, and contained a provision for the emancipation of all slave children born after July 4, 1863. Citizens of the newly added counties, many with significant numbers of slaves, would never approve such a measure—the bill was a sham!

Angry statehood leaders descended on Washington in protest. "I never saw any question that excited a whole community with the intensity that this question does," marveled chairman Wade. "Perhaps no question of greater importance has ever been presented to the Senate," added Charles Sumner of Massachusetts, a leading Radical. "It concerns the whole question of slavery; it concerns also the question of States rights; it concerns also the results of this war."

On July 14, the West Virginia statehood bill was called up again. Senator Waitman Willey offered an amendment to the bill that omitted the suspect counties and included a constitutional clause for *gradual* emancipation. The Radicals expanded this "Willey Amendment" to free children of slaves at birth after July 4, 1863, to provide a schedule of gradual emancipation for those less than twenty-one years of age, and to prohibit slaves from entering the state for permanent residence. Upon ratification of the Willey Amendment by the residents of West Virginia, President Lincoln would issue a proclamation, to be enacted sixty days later, inaugurating the new state.[661]

Senator Carlile now entered the fray. Angrily seizing the floor, he laid bare the skeletons of the new state movement. Carlile decried the Wheeling conventions as "bogus" affairs. "[T]he people of West Virginia," he alleged, "not only desire an admission to the Union; but they wish to preserve their liberties under the Constitution of the United States, and I shall be mistaken if they surrender the high privilege of freemen, that of forming for themselves, free and untrammeled, their own organic law. They shall never consent that this Congress shall prescribe for them a form of government." The author of the "Trojan Horse" bill was unmasked. John Carlile—the linchpin of West Virginia statehood—had shockingly become its "Judas!"[662]

Carlile's theatrics stunned his colleagues in the Senate. It was the first inkling to many that West Virginia's constitutional convention had not been entirely representative. Chairman Ben Wade called Carlile's behavior "very extraordinary" and concluded there was "something wrong in the matter."

"That there is to be a separation is a foregone conclusion," Wade exclaimed, "and no man has urged it upon the committee more strongly than the Senator who now opposes immediate action. He, of all men in the committee, is the man who penned all these bills....He is the man who has investigated all the precedents....He submitted to the labor; he did it cheerfully; he did it backed by the best men of his State....He is the gentleman who impressed their opinions upon the committee as strongly as anybody else; and what change has come over the spirit of his dream I know not. His conversion is greater than that of St. Paul."[663]

Senator Waitman Willey also denounced his traitorous colleague. "I stand here, where my colleague does not stand," thundered Willey, "representing the voice of the people of [West] Virginia, who ask for freedom, who ask severance from the eastern section of the State....The Almighty, with his own eternal hand, has marked the boundary between us."

Despite John Carlile's "nay" ballot, the West Virginia statehood bill passed the Senate on July 14 by a vote of 23–17.[664]

Carlile had fallen in with the "Copperheads," a movement arising from Northern opposition to President Lincoln's war policy. These conservative Democrats saw the war's object as restoration of the Union. Many became alarmed as the conflict evolved into a crusade to destroy Southern institutions, namely slavery. Their slogan was "The Constitution as it is, the Union as it was, and the Negroes where they are." Abolitionists compared them to venomous snakes, and the "Copperheads" bore that name with pride, displaying the heads of liberty on copper pennies as their badge. Their leader was a seditiously flamboyant Ohio Congressman named Clement Vallandigham. Banished to the Confederacy by

Lincoln and later ejected by Davis, he would become the "man without a country."[665]

Senator Carlile joined Copperheads in loathing the Willey Amendment's emancipation clause, assailing "congressional dictation" and "Abolition influences." Editor Archibald Campbell, in turn, ridiculed Carlile from the pages of the *Wheeling Intelligencer*, charging the impulsive senator with "black hearted" treason.[666]

Against the backdrop of this vitriol, the House of Representatives took fall recess without passing the West Virginia statehood bill. On September 22, following the costly Federal victory at Antietam, President Lincoln unveiled an Emancipation Proclamation, formally announcing his intention to free slaves in the Confederate states on New Year's Day, 1863. That act changed the war. The term "abolitionist," confessed one moderate statehood leader a few weeks later, has lost "all its terrors to me."[667]

On December 9, the House of Representatives again took up the statehood bill. Congressman John Bingham of Ohio spoke eloquently for the bill as "an inroad…into that ancient Bastille of slavery, out of which has come this wild, horrid conflict of arms." Yet the issue was warmly contested. Even Thaddeus Stevens of Pennsylvania, leader of Radical Republicans in the House, questioned the act's legality. "I say then that we may admit West Virginia as a new state," Stevens declared, "not by virtue of any provision of the Constitution but under the absolute power which the laws of war give us." One day later, the House passed the West Virginia statehood bill by a vote of 96–55.

"Glory to God in the highest!" proclaimed the *Wheeling Intelligencer*. Statehood advocates celebrated with speeches, fireworks, and torchlight parades. A formal-looking obituary for Senator John Carlile appeared in the *Intelligencer*, asserting that "the grave has closed over all there was political in this man." All that stood between West Virginians and their long-cherished dream was President Lincoln's signature.[668]

═══ ▲ ═══

Abraham Lincoln was very troubled. His thin, sallow face reflected "pathetic sadness." His gray eyes, sunken and deep-set, cast a faraway look. Furrowed lines of anguish framed his countenance. Lincoln was, in the words of one contemporary, a "long, tall, bony, homely, wiry, sad, gloomy man."[669]

By mid-December 1862, Lincoln had reason to be gloomy. Lee had just crushed his army at Fredericksburg, only the latest in a year of eastern battlefield setbacks. The Republicans had been embarrassed in mid-term elections. Lincoln's statesmanship was in doubt. Radicals disdained him for the limited scope of his Emancipation Proclamation; Democrats accused him of incompetence and abuse of power. Lincoln confessed he was unable to "see a ray of hope."[670]

Passage of the West Virginia statehood bill was untimely news for the forlorn president. Lincoln had viewed Virginia as a pilot state for reconstruction of the Union. The Wheeling experiment, if allowed to ferment, might encourage Unionists in other seceded states to establish loyal governments of their own. But statehood was another matter. The president thought Virginia secessionists would return to the Union "less reluctantly without the division of the old State."[671]

As Lincoln pondered the issue, the White House was deluged with nervous appeals. On December 23, the troubled president sought written opinions from his six-member Cabinet on whether the West Virginia statehood act was "constitutional" and "expedient." Secretary of State William Seward, Secretary of War Edwin Stanton, and Secretary of the Treasury Salmon Chase favored the measure. Attorney General Edward Bates, Navy Secretary Gideon Wells, and Postmaster General Montgomery Blair opposed admission. "A President is as well off without a Cabinet as with one," remarked Lincoln of the deadlock.[672]

The president's signing deadline was midnight, December 31, 1862. As that deadline neared, Governor Pierpont made a last-ditch appeal by telegram from Wheeling: "To His Excellency—The President of the U.S....The Union men of West Va. were not originally for the Union because of the new state. But the sentiment for the two have become identified. If one is stricken down I don't know what is [to] become of the other."[673]

At seven o'clock that evening, Senator Willey and West Virginia Representatives William Brown and Jacob Blair called at the White House. For the next three hours, they huddled with the president. Lincoln read the opinions of his cabinet members; the statehood advocates countered each objection. The president listened studiously but remained poker-faced, his mood undecipherable.

Finally, Mr. Lincoln pulled open the drawer of a small table and retrieved his own written opinion. Referring to the card game Whist, the president declared, "Now, gentlemen, I will give you the 'odd trick'!"

"That is the trick we hope to take," shot back Congressman Blair.[674]

Blair returned the next morning for Lincoln's "New Year's gift," a visit shrouded in myth. He reportedly arrived at daybreak, found the White House locked up, and crawled in through a window. In one version of the tale, he found Mr. Lincoln fully dressed, in another the president had just risen from bed. Whatever Lincoln's state of dress, he greeted Blair cheerfully. "Here is your bill," Lincoln sang out. "You see the signature." It read "Approved—Abraham Lincoln."

Governor Pierpont's eleventh hour plea had won the day. The president would be troubled no longer by constitutional questions—the issue of West Virginia statehood was one of expedience. "The government has been fighting nearly two years for its existence," Lincoln said. "The friends of the bill say it will strengthen the Union cause and will weaken the cause of the Rebels. It is a step and is political."

"We can scarcely dispense with the aid of West Virginia in this struggle," wrote Lincoln. "Much less can we afford to have her against us, in Congress and in the field. Her brave and good men regard her admission into the Union as a matter of life and death. They have been true to the Union under very severe trials....The division of the State is dreaded as a precedent. But a measure made expedient by a war is no precedent for times of peace. It is said that the admission of West Virginia is secession, and tolerated only because it is our secession. Well, if we call it by that name, there is still difference between secession against the Constitution, and secession in favor of the Constitution."

The Willey Amendment, with its gradual emancipation clause, was unanimously approved in convention; on March 26, 1863, West Virginians ratified it by a vote of 28,321 to 572. Opponents of statehood shunned the polls. Reverend Gordon Battelle— champion of the emancipation fight—did not live to see passage of the Willey Amendment. Battelle had died of typhoid fever, contracted while serving as chaplain to the First (U.S.) Virginia Infantry.[675]

Confederate raiders sought to disrupt elections and punish leaders of the statehood movement. The approach of General William "Grumble" Jones's cavalry in late April 1863 chased Senator Willey from his Morgantown home. Defiant Rebels burned the lavish library at Governor Pierpont's vacant Fairmont residence. When a pious Confederate attempted to retrieve the governor's family Bible, his lieutenant, a Wheeling native, consigned it to the flames. "Here goes the word of God," the officer exclaimed, "and I would to God it were Frank Pierpont's body."[676]

Pierpont chose to remain head of the Restored Government of Virginia, then made up of five eastern counties, with a capital in Alexandria. In his stead, Arthur I. Boreman of Parkersburg was elected as West Virginia's first governor. Wheeling's Linsly Institute became the temporary state capitol.

On June 20, 1863, by proclamation of President Lincoln, West Virginia became the nation's thirty-fifth state. She was a creation without parallel in American history—a "child of the storm." Although forged to aid the Union war effort, fully half of West Virginia's counties had voted *for* secession in 1861. Scholars have estimated that as many as 40 percent of her citizens remained loyal to the Confederacy.[677]

The war within her borders was truly "brother against brother." More than twenty-eight thousand West Virginians served in the Union army; perhaps eighteen thousand fought for the Confederacy. A surprising number switched loyalty during the conflict. As Federal troops departed for other campaigns, the new state became a guerrilla battleground. Much of her soil lapsed into anarchy. Partisan bands like the "Moccasin Rangers," "Snake Hunters," "Swamp Dragons," and "Dixie Boys" carried the fight to every hill and hollow.[678]

The scars of that conflict are visible to this day.

EPILOGUE
MEMORIES AND GHOSTS

"After forty-odd years there are neither enemies nor victories, but only gracious mountains & sleepy valleys…hazy & dim as old memories."
—Ambrose Bierce

The epic scale of America's Civil War doomed the first campaign to obscurity. Historians transfixed by the carnage at bloody battle-fields like Shiloh, Antietam, and Gettysburg have neglected it. Yet the little clashes of 1861 in West Virginia's Allegheny Mountains have a significance long unrecognized.

The first campaign was decisive, with great political impact. General George McClellan's army rescued Virginia Unionists and rallied wavering citizens to Mr. Lincoln's government. Building on that success, loyal delegates in Wheeling hammered out a government of their own. Their novel act of defiance, in the face of armed secessionists, resulted in the new state of West Virginia.

Virginia thereby lost forty-eight western counties, nearly one third of her landmass—and perhaps the war. The Confederates lost an opportunity to shift the fight to the upper Ohio Valley. West Virginia's mountainous buffer enabled Federal authorities in Ohio and Pennsylvania to focus on invasions of the South, rather than on defense of their borders. Equally important, the Baltimore and

Ohio Railroad was secured for the Union. That vital link from Washington to Cincinnati and St. Louis would speed Federal armies to both flanks of the Confederacy.

Yet Federal troops pulled up short in the Alleghenies. General McClellan's 1861 victories threw the Confederates into disarray; a few days of hard marching could have taken his army to the heart of the Shenandoah Valley. Had Confederate forces lost control of the Virginia Central or Virginia and Tennessee Railroads—direct lines to Richmond and the Deep South—the result would have been catastrophic. Union arms might then have cut a swath across central Virginia, perhaps ending the war in its second year. Instead, the fertile Shenandoah Valley remained a "breadbasket" for the Confederacy, and a sally port for invasion of the North.

Mountains hindered the movement of armies. Federal troops in Western Virginia dug in along the turnpikes, confounded by the realities of mountain warfare. "It was easy," wrote General Jacob Cox of that region, "sitting at one's office table, to sweep the hand over a few inches of chart showing next to nothing of the topography, and to say, 'We will march from here to here.'" But it was another thing entirely to make that march. The Alleghenies loomed as a towering fortress for armies to pass.[679]

For citizen-soldiers, those mountains were a stern proving ground. Many looked back on their first campaign as the severest of the war. Colonel Samuel Fulkerson of Virginia believed "the history of that remarkable campaign would show, if truly portrayed, a degree of severity, of hardship, of toil, of exposure and suffering that finds no parallel [and]…would have done honor to our sires in the most trying times of the Revolution." A veteran of the Twenty-fifth Ohio Infantry flatly declared, "The history of the Rebellion furnishes no instances of greater suffering, excepting in rebel prisons, than that experienced by the troops on the summit of Cheat Mountain, in the fall and winter of 1861."[680]

General Lee's aide Walter Taylor wrote, "In the subsequent campaigns of the Army of Northern Virginia the troops were subjected to great privations and to many very severe trials—in hunger often; their nakedness scarcely concealed; strength at times almost exhausted—but never did I experience the same heart-sinking emotions as when contemplating the wan faces and the emaciated forms of those hungry, sickly, shivering men of the army at Valley Mountain!"

The toil of mountain warfare chiseled raw recruits into hardy veterans. Many who began the war in Western Virginia went on to perform great feats of bravery and endurance. Their numbers swelled fabled armies North and South, including the Gibraltar Brigade, Stonewall Jackson's "foot cavalry," the Army of the Cumberland, and the Army of Northern Virginia.[681]

The first campaign shaped leaders, notably Generals George McClellan and Robert E. Lee. Each would rise to supreme command of their respective armies, yet each took a different path from the Alleghenies. Here McClellan rocketed to stardom as the "Young Napoleon," while a mud-spattered "Granny" Lee left the mountains in disgrace.

══════ ▲ ══════

Robert E. Lee badly misjudged the political sentiments in Western Virginia, yet gained valuable lessons from defeat. Lee learned to handle troops during the first campaign. His concern for the wants of rank and file soldiers fast became the stuff of legend. He also learned to deal with recalcitrant commanders. The leaders who failed him in Western Virginia—Loring, Rust, Wise, and Floyd—were quietly transferred to distant fields.

Lee never forgot the disappointment on the faces of his volunteers at Cheat and Sewell Mountains when attacks did not come off. In the future, he resolved to strike boldly. Asked of Lee's capacity to make war, a staff officer would later reply, "Lee is audacity personified." There was no more talk of "Granny" Lee.[682]

The cheers for Lee that rang from "Jubilee Mountain" in 1861 were heard again. At Chancellorsville in 1863, Lee rode through flaming woods to the head of his army as the enemy was put to flight. An aide wrote, "One long, unbroken cheer, in which the feeble cry of those who lay helpless on the earth, blended with the strong voices of those who still fought, rose high above the roar of battle, and hailed the presence of the victorious chief. He sat in the full realization of all that soldiers dream of—triumph; and as I looked upon him in the complete fruition of the success....I thought that it must have been from such a scene that men in ancient days rose to the dignity of gods."

Yet the great chieftain remained a man of simplicity. "A more modest man did not live," avowed Walter Taylor. In the full zenith of his fame, Lee wore a plain uniform, kept a simple tent for headquarters, and ate from the same old tinware with which he began the war on Valley Mountain.[683]

When the Army of Northern Virginia surrendered at Appomattox Court House in 1865, weary veterans flocked to their beloved general and his warhorse, Traveller. Lee became an icon of the "Lost Cause." Sheathing his sword, he declined lucrative offers to sell his name and took a modest salary as president of little Washington College in Lexington, Virginia.

Lee's Arlington home was forfeited as a national cemetery. His petition for amnesty went ignored. Nonetheless, until his death in 1870, Lee served as a role model for healing the nation's wounds. One hundred and five years later, Congress restored his citizenship.[684]

George B. McClellan used the first campaign as a springboard to fame. In the mountains of Western Virginia, McClellan won the North's first victories. Soon after his dazzling telegrams reached Washington, Federal hopes were dashed at Manassas and the thirty-four-year-old McClellan was called to save the Union.

But the call proved costly. General McClellan had been miles from the scene of his early triumphs—never "within the range of a hostile cannon," as one of his officers not-so-gently put it. Overlooked in the glow of those little mountain victories were some distressing traits.

"The assumed dash and energy of his first campaign made the disappointment and the reaction more painful, when the excessive caution of his conduct in command of the Army of the Potomac was seen," General Cox would reflect. "But the Rich Mountain affair, when analyzed, shows the same characteristics which became well-known later. There was the same overestimate of the enemy, the same tendency to interpret unfavorably the sights and sounds in front, the same hesitancy to throw in his whole force when he knew that his subordinate was engaged." Remarked a *Cincinnati Daily Gazette* columnist in 1862: "[I]s there any apparent difference in the generalship of Gen. McClellan in Western Virginia and on the Potomac? Did he not show the same reluctance to smell gunpowder then that he has since?"[685]

The talented McClellan organized two great armies. He devised masterful strategy. But, at the moment of truth, he lacked the will to fight. When handed a lost copy of General Lee's orders before Antietam, he failed to seize the opportunity and allowed the Confederates to escape disaster. "Are you acquainted with General McClellan?" Lee had asked one of his subordinates before that epic battle. "He is an able general, but a very cautious one. His enemies among his own people think him too much so."[686]

General-in-Chief Henry Halleck complained that "the lever of Archimedes" was needed to get McClellan moving. Even President Lincoln agonized that the Army of the Potomac was only "McClellan's body-guard." Repeated urgings went unheeded; McClellan was finally relieved of command on November 7, 1862, for what Lincoln called a hopeless case of the "slows."

McClellan went home to New Jersey for orders that never came. Despite his failings on the battlefield, the charismatic general was enormously popular with his troops. In the 1864 election, McClellan failed as the Democratic presidential candidate against Lincoln, resigned his military commission the next day and left for Europe. Returning home in 1868, he served honorably as Governor of New Jersey from 1878–1881, and died there in 1885.

McClellan's rise to command likely prolonged the war—long enough, it could be said, for the abolition of slavery to become a principal aim. General U.S. Grant would use the army McClellan forged to defeat Lee and end the conflict. Yet Grant had been unable to secure an appointment from the young general in 1861! He would later call McClellan "one of the mysteries of the war."[687]

═══ ▲ ═══

As the "Young Napoleon" rocketed to stardom, his luckless opponent **Robert S. Garnett** was buried and forgotten. "[H]ad he lived," wrote Confederate General E.P. Alexander of the dreary-hearted Garnett, "I am sure [he] would have won a reputation no whit behind Stonewall Jackson's." Garnett's body lies unmarked beside those of his wife and child at Green-Wood Cemetery in Brooklyn, New York. He is often confused with a cousin, Confederate General Richard B. Garnett, killed at the battle of Gettysburg—and likewise reposing in an unmarked grave.[688]

Thomas A. Morris, the Indiana brigadier commanding at Laurel Hill, was mustered out of service on July 27, 1861. A promised major-generalship was withheld until the fall of 1862, largely due to McClellan's declaration that Morris was "unfit." When the position was finally tendered, Morris declined it and quietly resumed his duties as a railroad executive. He died in 1904, a leading citizen of Indianapolis.[689]

William S. Rosecrans was appointed a major general to date from March 1862, took command of the Army of the Cumberland that fall, and repulsed the Confederates at Stones River, Tennessee. In 1863, he inaugurated a brilliant campaign to force the Rebels from Chattanooga. However, in September of that year, Rosecrans suffered a crushing defeat at Chickamauga, Georgia, which virtually ended his military career. "Old Rosey" earned a reputation as one of the North's great strategists, but made political enemies he could not overcome. Rosecrans entered business pursuits in California and was elected to Congress before his death in 1898.[690]

Henry W. Benham was arrested for "neglect of duty" while commanding a brigade under Rosecrans during the fall of 1861, but the charges were dropped. Failure at Secessionville, South Carolina in June 1862 caused Benham's removal. Lincoln reinstated his commission in 1863 and Benham went on to lead the engineer brigade of the Army of the Potomac with great skill. He was awarded the brevet of major general, remained in the Corps of Engineers until 1882, and died in New York City two years later.[691]

John Pegram, a prisoner since the battle of Rich Mountain, gained release in 1862 and fought as a brigadier general in the Army of Northern Virginia. On January 19, 1865, Pegram married Hetty Cary, the "Belle of Richmond." Their wedding was marred by omens. First, Hetty broke a mirror; then horses leading a coach sent by President Davis bucked and refused to move. Three weeks later, General Pegram returned to the church where he was married—in a casket. He had been killed in action at Hatcher's Run, Virginia.[692]

David Hart, the Rich Mountain guide, found his life changed by that battle. Feeling unsafe at home, young Hart followed the Tenth Indiana Infantry, a three-month unit, back to Indianapolis for reenlistment. He served as commissary sergeant of that regiment until illness claimed his life near Nashville, Tennessee, in March 1862. His father Joseph served as a delegate in nominating the first state officials of West Virginia.[693]

Charles "Lab" Cox, the wounded Confederate left on Rich Mountain by fleeing comrades, was never seen again. Decades later, a hunter stumbled upon a human skull in the woods about one mile east of the battlefield. Nearby were a rusted musket barrel, bayonet, and enough buttons to identify the remains as those of a Southern soldier.[694]

Benjamin F. Kelley spent the bulk of his war service protecting the vital Baltimore and Ohio Railroad. Brevetted a Federal major general in 1864, he was captured with General George Crook in a brilliant raid by McNeill's Partisan Rangers at Cumberland, Maryland, in February 1865. After the war, Kelley held a number of government positions until his death in 1891.

Confederate Colonel **George A. Porterfield** never escaped his role in the "Philippi Races." He served on General Loring's staff for a time, then retired from the army in 1862 and resumed civilian life as a banker in Charles Town, West Virginia.[695]

James E. Hanger, the Confederate who lost a leg in the war's first amputation, went on to perfect an artificial limb that he manufactured for other veterans. After the war, Hanger appeared at reunions displaying the cannonball that struck him at Philippi, along with his patented "Hanger Limb." J.E. Hanger, Inc. became one of the largest manufacturers of artificial limbs in the world and remains so to this day.

Philippi's covered bridge, the **Monarch of the River**, still stands, having defied the ravages of war, floods, ice jams, and fire. The bridge has been lovingly restored, and remains the only two-lane covered span in America serving a Federal highway.[696]

German soldiers of the **Ninth Ohio Infantry** went on to serve with great distinction. Their dramatic bayonet charge at Mill Springs, Kentucky, in 1862 won the field. In 1863, tenacious fighting by the "Bloody Dutch" at Chickamauga, Georgia, and Missionary Ridge, Tennessee, resulted in the loss of more than half of the regiment. The venerable survivors were mustered out of Federal service in 1864.[697]

Whitelaw Reid, one of the first young newsmen to bring the human tragedy of civil war to northern doorsteps, continued his "Agate" dispatches for the Cincinnati *Gazette*. In 1872, he became principal owner of the New York *Tribune*. Reid was the

Republican vice-presidential candidate on the Harrison ticket in 1892, and served as ambassador to England from 1905 until his death in 1912.[698]

Thomas J. "Stonewall" Jackson became a Confederate lieutenant general in 1862 and went on to immortality as the "right arm" of Lee. On the night of a dramatic flank attack at Chancellorsville, May 2, 1863, Jackson was accidentally shot by his own troops. He died eight days later. Jackson's last words, "Let us cross over the river and rest under the shade of the trees" likely referred to his boyhood home, Jackson's Mill, West Virginia. His estranged sister, **Laura Jackson Arnold**, remained a Unionist until her death in 1911. She was one of two women given honorary membership in a Federal veterans' group, the Grand Army of the Republic.[699]

Mapmaker **Jedediah Hotchkiss** fell victim to typhoid fever at Valley Mountain, but returned to Confederate service in 1862. Valuable contacts made during the first campaign enabled him to secure an appointment with Stonewall Jackson, beginning an association that made Hotchkiss the foremost mapmaker of the Civil War.

Frederick W. Lander was the only unranked and unpaid Union volunteer to receive a general's star. Despite ill health stemming from his Potomac River wound, the intrepid warrior continued to lead with flair. While suffering from "congestive chills" at Paw Paw, Western Virginia, in March 1862, Lander lapsed into a coma and died. Trotting behind the hearse at his Washington funeral was the same gray charger that had carried him on "Lander's Ride" at Philippi and to the battle of Rich Mountain.[700]

Robert H. Milroy, the "Gray Eagle," went on to lock horns with Stonewall Jackson in the Shenandoah Valley. Milroy's suppression of guerrillas in the Alleghenies proved so onerous that the Confederates put a price on his head. As a major general in June

1863, his seven-thousand-man force was virtually "gobbled up" by Lee's army at Winchester, Virginia. Exonerated by a court of inquiry, he commanded defenses of the Nashville and Chattanooga Railroad until the end of the war. Until his death in 1890, Milroy remained a strident abolitionist. The people of Rensselaer, Indiana, later erected a statue of heroic size to his memory.[701]

Ben "Summit," the runaway slave taken in by General Milroy on Cheat Mountain, was freed and sent to the Milroy home in Indiana where he learned to read and write. In 1864, Ben volunteered in a regiment of United States Colored Troops and became a private in the fight for liberty.

Richard "Old Dick" Green, the faithful Tygart Valley slave, remained loyal to the Confederacy. Throughout the war, he piloted gray jackets across the mountains and looked after defenseless neighbors. Years later, a visitor to Green's home was startled to see memorials to Robert E. Lee and Stonewall Jackson on the mantelpiece.[702]

John Elwood of the Ringgold Cavalry (Twenty-second Pennsylvania Cavalry, U.S.A.) eventually traded in his old horse pistol for a new Colt revolver. He also carried a copy of the New Testament in his breast pocket. That testament was later struck by a bullet, saving his life.

John Higginbotham, "lead magnet" of the Twenty-fifth Virginia Infantry, C.S.A., took additional wounds on the Virginia battlefields of McDowell, Cedar Mountain, and Second Manassas. At the tender age of twenty, he was promoted to the rank of colonel for gallantry. Higginbotham was wounded for a *seventh* time at Gettysburg and carried from the field. He returned to lead a brigade at Spotsylvania in 1864, but was killed by a shot through the heart before his commission as brigadier general arrived.[703]

William W. Loring became a Confederate major general in 1862. Assigned to the Army of Mississippi, he escaped capture at Vicksburg, and was a division and corps commander during the Atlanta campaign and at Franklin and Nashville. After the war, Loring went abroad to fight under the Khedive of Egypt. At his 1886 Florida funeral, the body was borne to the grave by three Federal and three ex-Confederate soldiers.[704]

Joseph J. Reynolds returned to active duty as a major general of U.S. volunteers in 1862. He served as chief of staff to George H. Thomas and led U.S. forces in the Department of the Gulf and the Department of Arkansas through the war's end. Remaining in the army, he attacked Crazy Horse's winter hideout in 1876, but withdrew prematurely, thereby contributing to Custer's defeat at Little Bighorn. Reynolds resigned after a court martial and died in 1899.[705]

After besting Lee at Cheat Mountain, **Nathan Kimball** went on to defeat Stonewall Jackson at Kernstown, Virginia, in 1862. For those exploits, he became a brigadier general. Kimball led desperate fighting at Antietam, where more than half of his old Fourteenth Indiana Regiment were casualties. He was badly wounded at Fredericksburg, fought at Vicksburg, Atlanta, Franklin, and Nashville, and was brevetted a major general in 1865. Kimball entered political life and remained there until his death in 1898.[706]

Billy Davis of the Seventh Indiana Infantry—once nearly expelled from the army for his diminutive size—was cited for personal valor at Port Republic, Virginia. Permanently crippled by wounds received at the Wilderness, Billy limped home on July 4, 1864, to discover his family in mourning. He had been reported dead![707]

On more than one occasion, **John H. Cammack** of the Thirty-first Virginia Infantry faced old neighbors on the battlefield. After the war, he became a leading member of the Garnett Camp,

United Confederate Veterans. When citizens of Philippi invited him to an observance of the first land battle, Cammack wrote, "I like a celebration as well as anybody, but as I reviewed the events which transpired…when I went away from Philippi in something of a hurry, leaving a nicely cooked breakfast for some Yankee to eat, I was unable to think of any reason why I should go back to Philippi and celebrate, so I did not go."[708]

Henry R. Jackson, the scholar and diplomat, was recommissioned a brigadier in Confederate service in 1863, saw duty in the Atlanta campaign, and was captured at Nashville. Released in July 1865, Jackson was appointed Minister to Mexico and served as president of the Georgia Historical Society until his death in 1898.

Edward "Allegheny" Johnson had the pleasure of whipping Robert Milroy on two more Virginia battlefields. Severely wounded at McDowell in 1862, Johnson recovered to lead Stonewall Jackson's old division at Gettysburg, the Wilderness, and Spotsylvania until his capture at the "Bloody Angle." Upon exchange, he was captured once again at Nashville. Johnson went back to farming in Virginia after the war and died in 1873, a life-long bachelor.[709]

George R. Latham, supporter of the West Virginia statehood movement with pen and sword, commanded the Second (U.S.) Virginia Infantry (later the Fifth West Virginia Cavalry). He was elected to Congress in 1864, and mustered out of service in 1865 as a brevetted brigadier general of volunteers. Latham served as United States Consul to Australia before his death in 1917. He was said to be the last surviving member of the 1861 Wheeling conventions.[710]

Governor **Francis H. Pierpont's** Restored Government of Virginia moved from Alexandria to Richmond on May 25, 1865. After his term expired in 1868, Pierpont was elected to the West Virginia legislature. He died in 1899 and is honored with a place in the United States Capitol's Statuary Hall. Pierpont is often known as the "Father of West Virginia," yet he was never gover-nor of the state.[711]

Upon the expiration of his term as United States Senator, **Waitman T. Willey** was reelected and served until 1871. The "Grand Old Man" never relinquished his legendary power of speech. At the funeral of Governor Pierpont, he needed assistance to mount the platform, but delivered a magical requiem for his old friend. Willey died in 1900. His half-brother, Confederate Colonel **William J. Willey**, was jailed in 1861 on a charge of treason, but later won parole. "Bridge Burner" Willey was indicted by a Marion County grand jury in 1865 for his part in the railroad vandalism that launched the first campaign. The indictment was dropped and Colonel Willey moved to Missouri, where he died in 1868.[712]

Senator **John S. Carlile's** star glowed brilliantly in 1861, but disdain for the abolition of slavery wrecked his political career. Ignoring calls from the West Virginia legislature to resign, Carlile served out his term and took up residence in Maryland by 1865. He later returned to practice law in Clarksburg and died there in 1878. Carlile's stun-ning reversal on West Virginia statehood is still debated.[713]

The lady guerrilla **Nancy Hart** was arrested by Federal troops in 1862. While in custody, she fashioned a dress from calico, needle, and thread. The jailer was so enchanted by Nancy's new look that he asked her to sit for a photograph. Nervously eying a camera for the first time, she feared it was an execution. As the jailer reassured her, Nancy charmed him out of his gun, shot him down, and rode off into legend. She died in 1902.

Mary Van Pelt campaigned with Loomis's First Michigan Light Artillery beside her soldier husband until removed by military order. Upon learning of her spouse's battlefield death in 1863, Mary volunteered as a nurse. The pallbearers at her Michigan funeral in 1906 were veterans of her husband's battery.[714]

After serving time in Richmond prisons, Dr. **William B. Fletcher**—the Union spy given reprieve by a drunk's penmanship—was exchanged for a Confederate doctor in January 1862. He visited the family of spy Leonard Clark, then returned to Indianapolis and took charge of a hospital serving Confederate prisoners. Fletcher went on to become a leading Indiana physician and humanitarian before his death in 1907.

Fletcher's companion **Leonard Clark** endured nine months of solitary confinement in a Fincastle, Virginia, jail. Only the interposition of old friends in the Confederate army spared his life. Clark spent another year in the notorious Belle Isle prison before he was exchanged in 1863, looking, it was said, "like a man who had come out of the grave." Unbroken in spirit, he joined the Third West Virginia Cavalry and was killed in action at Moorefield, West Virginia, in 1864.[715]

Confederate General **John B. Floyd** was removed from command in 1862 after his humiliating flight from Fort Donelson. He subsequently became a major general of "Virginia State Line" troops, but failing health resulted in his death at home near Abingdon in 1863.

Floyd's old nemesis, General **Henry A. Wise**, later served under P.G.T. Beauregard in South Carolina. Returning to Virginia in 1864, he fought gallantly in the battles around Richmond, Petersburg, and Appomattox. Wise practiced law in Richmond after the war and died there in 1876. He stubbornly refused to seek amnesty. "I never fought under the Confederate flag," Wise claimed, only under the flag of Virginia—and proudly displayed his state buttons to make the point. Defiant as ever, Wise called the new state of West Virginia "the bastard offspring of a political rape."[716]

John Beatty led the Third Ohio Infantry, became a brigadier general in November 1862, and fought courageously at Stones River, Tennessee. He resigned in 1864 and returned to the family bank so that his brother could enter the army. Beatty was later elected to Congress. His splendid diary was published in 1879 as *The Citizen-Soldier.*

Rutherford B. Hayes of the **Twenty-third Ohio Infantry** rose to the rank of brevet major general, served in the Congress, and became governor of Ohio and president of the United States. From his regiment came William McKinley, another U.S. president, and Stanley Matthews, a justice of the Supreme Court.[717]

General Lee's famous warhorse **Traveller** developed lockjaw and died soon after the passing of his master. He is buried near the general's tomb in Lexington, Virginia. It is said that Traveller's ghost haunts his native Greenbrier County, West Virginia. Stories by old Confederate veterans of an equine apparition or the mysterious sounds of a galloping thoroughbred near Lee's old camp on Sewell Mountain are still told.[718]

Marcus Toney, of the First Tennessee Infantry C.S.A., fought in both major theaters of conflict. He was captured at Spotsylvania in 1864 and spent the rest of the war in Union prisons. Of his original company, Toney later asked, "Where are the one hundred and four who marched out so gaily from the old Academy in 1861, when the bands were playing 'The Girl I Left Behind Me?'" Seventy-two of that number had filled soldiers' graves. Toney returned to Tennessee and slept under a quilt in the front yard of his home for nearly a month before he could get used to a bed.[719]

Loyal **West Virginia Regiments**, twenty-nine in number, bore arms in defense of liberty, homeland, and the United States government. Proportionate to their strength in the field, it was said they captured a greater number of enemy battle flags than the troops of any other state.[720]

The **Thirty-first Virginia Infantry**, C.S.A., made up predominately of West Virginians, had mustered eight hundred and fifty men in 1861, but only about fifty-seven remained to answer the roll for their surrender at Appomattox Court House. "On the morning of [April 12, 1865] we were marched out into a large field and heard bands playing on both sides," wrote a member of the regiment. "We saw a large white flag...and knew then that the end had come. The Thirty-first, with its colors, was marched up in front to the New York Zouaves, noted for their blue jackets, red trousers and cap. They saluted at a distance of about 30 feet, sank on their left knee, remaining in this position until we stacked arms. Not a jeer or taunt was heard."[721]

Among the survivors of the Thirty-first Virginia was **James E. Hall**. During the surrender, he recognized several neighbors in the Yankee army. Hall kept up his pocket diary throughout the war. After his long walk home to Barbour County from Appomattox, the last entry, April 28, 1865, reads "Went fishing."[722]

═══ ▲ ═══

Veterans of the armies returned to the scene of their first campaign. "In the summer of 1885," recalled one former Union soldier, "I made a visit to the Tygart's Valley, where we spent so many months during the summer and fall of 1861 and winter of 1862. Then desolation marked the path of war....The condition of the people was pitiable, and their future seemed hopeless. Twenty...years of peace and plenty have worked a marvelous change.

"It seems to me that one of the grandest achievements of this age is the fact that a million men at the word of command left the battle front, and returned without a halt to the pursuit of peace, casting aside the animosities of the strife, and burying all bitterness....To my surprise, I have never received so generous a welcome in my life."

Old foes climbed mountains, visited battlefields, and rode through the country discussing the war as freely as if they had been comrades in arms. Among them was **Ambrose Bierce**, the Indiana volunteer so captivated by that land. He had since become a noted author. In the decade before his 1913 disappearance in Mexico, Bierce returned to the "delectable mountains" of his youth. He wrote in a brief memorial of that trip: "[T]he whole region is wild and grand, and if any one of the men who in his golden youth soldiered through its sleepy valleys and over its gracious mountains will revisit it in the hazy season when it is all aflame with the autumn foliage I promise him sentiments that he will willing entertain and emotions that he will care to feel. Among them will be, I fear, a haunting envy of those of his war comrades whose fall and burial in that enchanted land he once bewailed."[723]

Deep in the wilds of the Alleghenies, a forgotten soldier rests. No flowers, banners, or inscriptions honor his name. Only a sliver of rough fieldstone remains.

> *On the soil of Virginia they laid him to rest,*
> *Where the rude winds of Winter will sweep o'er his breast.*
> *And his comrades will think as deep sighs their breasts rend,*
> *Of the soldier, their brother and brave and true friend.*
>
> *The night watch will pace past his rude lowly grave,*
> *And think how he died his dear country to save,*
> *And his heart will in silence a firm resolve form*
> *To fight till our Union is freed from the storm.*[46]

NOTES

In the following notes, the author's last name, the short title of the work, and the page numbers are cited. Full source information on each work is presented alphabetically in the Bibliography section.

Prelude. The Delectable Mountains

1. Lee, "The First Step of the War," 76; Lang, Loyal West Virginia, 2–3; Hall, The Rending of Virginia, 54, 90.
2. Many primary sources use the capitalized "Western Virginia" in reference to the territory that became West Virginia in 1863. Modern writers have tended to use "western Virginia," a term easily confused with the western part of modern-day Virginia. For a discussion of the evolution of "western Virginia," see Moore, *A Banner in the Hills*, 1–2. Clayton Newell, in *Lee vs. McClellan*, xiii, ably demonstrates that the Western Virginia actions of 1861 were part of a single campaign. General George McClellan waged it "to secure Western Virginia to the Union."
3. Brooks, *The Appalachians*, 12, 17–18.
4. Espenshade, *Pennsylvania Place Names*, 120; Lesser, "Prehistoric Human Settlement," 231–260; Rice and Brown, *West Virginia*, 12–13, 15; Callahan, *Semi-Centennial History*, 14–15.
5. Rice and Brown, *West Virginia*, 16; Wayland, *The Fairfax Line*, 39, 46; Callahan, *Semi-Centennial History*, 17.
6. Callahan, *History of West Virginia, Old and New*, 54–61.
7. Rice and Brown, *West Virginia*, 25–28, 30–31.
8. Callahan, *History of West Virginia, Old and New*, 81; Rice and Brown, *West Virginia*, 38–40; Maxwell, *History of Randolph County*, 183–84.
9. Withers, *Chronicles of Border Warfare*, 209–14, 365; Callahan, *History of West Virginia, Old and New*, 252.
10. Callahan, *Semi-Centennial History*, 48–49, 51, 53–54, 68.
11. Couper, *Claudius Crozet*, 34, 66; Callahan, *Semi-Centennial History*, 91–109; Carnes, *Centennial History of the Philippi Covered Bridge*, 48–56. Claudius

316 ▲ Rebels at the Gate

Crozet, born in 1789, served as a French officer of artillery under Napoleon Bonaparte and immigrated to America in 1816. He promptly secured an appointment as professor of engineering at the U.S. Military Academy. Building the West Point program almost from scratch, Crozet left in 1823 to become "principal engineer" of Virginia.

12. Callahan, *Semi-Centennial History*, 110–25; Summers, *The Baltimore and Ohio*, 18–19.

13. Moore, *A Banner in the Hills*, 2–4, 13–15; Willey, *An Inside View*, 7; Callahan, *History of West Virginia, Old and New*, 256.

14. Hall, *Rending of Virginia*, 77; Moore, *A Banner in the Hills*, 2; Callahan, *History of West Virginia, Old and New*, 247; Siviter, *Recollections of War and Peace*, 84–87.

15. Callahan, *Semi-Centennial History*, 126–28, 129n; Ambler, *Francis H. Pierpont*, 51.

16. Callahan, *Semi-Centennial History*, 130–34; Hall, *The Rending of Virginia*, 34; *Wheeling Gazette*, April 6, 1830 in Rice and Brown, *West Virginia*, 96.

17. Drewry, *The Southampton Insurrection*, 26–28; Ambler, *Sectionalism in Virginia*, 185, 191, 199; Callahan, *Semi-Centennial History*, 136–38.

18. Ibid., 138–39; Lewis, *History of West Virginia*, 307–18.

Chapter 1. A Very God of War
19. Cox, *Military Reminiscences of the Civil War*, vol. 1, 9; McClellan, *McClellan's Own Story*, 20.

20. McClellan, *Report on the Organization and Campaigns of the Army of the Potomac*, 6; Hall, *The Rending of Virginia*, 597; Cox, *Military Reminiscences*, vol. 1, 7.

21. Reid, *Ohio in the War*, vol. 1, 32; Sears, *George B. McClellan*, 66; McClellan, *McClellan's Own Story*, 40–41.

22. Cox, *Military Reminiscences*, vol. 1, 8–9; Sears, *George B. McClellan*, 68; McClellan, *McClellan's Own Story*, 41; Reid, *Ohio in the War*, vol. 1, 275.

23. Sears, *George B. McClellan*, 2–4, 7–8, 12–13.

24. Ibid., 14–15, 21–22.

25. Ibid., 18, 23–24.

26. Ibid., 29, 33, 27, 44, 47–48.

27. Ibid., 51, 58–59, 63–66; Reid, *Ohio in the War*, vol. 1, 278.

28. McClellan, *Report on the Organization*, 6; U.S. War Department, *The War of the Rebellion: A Compilation of the Official Records of the Union and Confederate Armies*. ser. 1, vol. 51, pt. 1, 333–34 (Hereafter, this multivolume work will be cited as *O.R.* Unless specified, all references are to Series I); McClellan, *McClellan's Own Story*, 42–43.

29. Cox, *Military Reminiscences*, vol. 1, 10; Reid, *Ohio in the War*, vol. 1, 33; Sears, *The Civil War Papers of George B. McClellan*, 10.

30. McClellan, *McClellan's Own Story*, 39, 42; *O.R.* ser. 3, pt. 1, 101; McClellan, *Report on the Organization*, 6–7; *O.R.* vol. 51, pt. 1, 370.

31. Ibid., 371; Cox, *Military Reminiscences*, vol. 1, 22–23.

32. *O.R.* vol. 51, pt. 1, 338–39, 369–70; Sears, *Civil War Papers of George McClellan*, 75.

33. McClellan, *McClellan's Own Story*, 42, 44, 46; *O.R.* vol. 51, pt. 1, 334, 339–40, 342–43, 373–74, 376, 384; Reid, *Ohio in the War*, vol. 1, 36.

34. Sears, *Civil War Papers of George McClellan*, 19; O.R. vol. 51, pt. 1, 377, 379; McClellan, *McClellan's Own Story*, 47; Sears, *George B. McClellan*, 73.

35. Cox, *Military Reminiscences*, vol. 1, 19; O.R. vol. 51, pt. 1, 371; *Pinkerton, The Spy of the Rebellion*, vol. 1., 140–41.

36. McClellan, *Report on the Organization*, 11; O.R. vol. 51, pt. 1, 375, 381.

37. Lang, *Loyal West Virginia*, 9, 137; Reid, *Ohio in the War*, vol. 1, 45–46.

38. McClellan, *Report on the Organization*, 9; Reader, *History of the Fifth West Virginia Cavalry*, 28; O.R. vol. 2, 630; G.M. Hagans to G.B. McClellan, May 13, 1861, McClellan Papers, in Summers, *The Baltimore and Ohio*, 70.

39. Reid, *Ohio in the War*, vol. 1, 33, 46–47; Sears, *Civil War Papers of George McClellan*, 24.

40. O.R. vol. 51, pt. 1, 377–78.

Chapter 2. Bury It Deep Within the Hills

41. Hall, *Rending of Virginia*, 119; Curry, *A House Divided*, 28–29.

42. Willey, *An Inside View of the Formation of West Virginia*, 38–39; Hall, *Rending of Virginia*, 124, 520.

43. Willey, *An Inside view*, 207–10; Hall, *Rending of Virginia*, 161, 575–77; Dayton, "Address of Honorable Alston Gordon Dayton," 50.

44. Ambler, *Francis H. Pierpont*, 75; Hall, *Rending of Virginia*, 126; *Wheeling Daily Intelligencer*, February 4, 1861 in Curry, *A House Divided*, 29–30.

45. Hall, *Rending of Virginia*, 151, 183, 522–23.

46. Ibid., 183; Willey, *An Inside View*, 42–43.

47. McGregor, *The Disruption of Virginia*, 176; Siviter, *Recollections of War and Peace*, 45–46, 49; Hall, *Rending of Virginia*, 182–83, 523–24, 528–29.

48. Lewis, *How West Virginia Was Made*, 15–18, 30–31n; McGregor, *Disruption of Virginia*, 182–84.

49. Lewis, *How West Virginia Was Made*, 32–34.

50. Cometti and Summers, ed. *The 35th State*, 297–98; *The Parkersburg Gazette*, April 25, 1861 in McGregor, *Disruption of Virginia*, 186n.

51. McGregor, *Disruption*, 192; Lewis, *How West Virginia Was Made*, 35; Maxwell, *History of Barbour County*, 245–46.

52. McGregor, *Disruption*, 187–88.

53. Hall, *Rending of Virginia*, 231–34; Lewis, *How West Virginia Was Made*, 35–41. McGregor, in *Disruption* 192–93, notes that more than one-third of the delegates were from the district immediately around Wheeling, greatly deceiving reporters as to the mixed sentiments in Western Virginia.

54. Lewis, *How West Virginia Was Made*, 44.

55. Ibid., 48–49.

56. Ibid., 50–51.

57. Willey, *An Inside View*, 181, 188–93; Hall, *Rending of Virginia*, 563–64, Ambler, *Waitman Thomas Willey*, 1, 4–5. In nineteenth century America, the Whig party opposed Democrats by advocating protection of industry and limited government power.

58. Willey, *An Inside View*, 64.

59. Lewis, *How West Virginia Was Made*, 55, 57–58.

60. Ambler, *Francis H. Pierpont*, 3–4, 8–9.

61. Ibid., 17, 28–29, 34, 36–37, 42, 59–60. Originally spelling his name "Pierpoint," Frank Pierpont became convinced of an old family error and changed the spelling in 1881.
62. Lewis, *How West Virginia Was Made*, 59–60.
63. Hall, *Rending of Virginia*, 272–73.
64. Lewis, *How West Virginia Was Made*, 62–66.
65. Ambler, *Waitman Thomas Willey*, 49.
66. Lewis, *How West Virginia Was Made*, 66–71; Hall, *Rending of Virginia*, 270.

Chapter 3. A Tower of Strength
67. Dowdey and Manarin, *Wartime Papers of Robert E. Lee*, 10.
68. Lee, Jr., *Recollections and Letters of General Lee*, 27–28.
69. *Wheeling Daily Intelligencer*, November 2, 1861; Warner, *Generals In Blue*, 429–31; Thomas, *Robert E. Lee*, 110.
70. Freeman, *Lee*, vol. 1, 294, 636–37. For Freeman's discussion of the accuracy of this exchange, see 437n.
71. Ibid., 437.
72. Lee, Jr., *Recollections and Letters*, 26–27; Freeman, *Lee*, vol.1, 372, 421, 440; Nagel, *The Lees of Virginia*, 5.
73. Lee, Jr., *Recollections and Letters*, 24–25.
74. *The Alexandria Gazette*, April 20, 1861 in Freeman, *Lee*, vol. 1, 445.
75. Ibid., 449–50.
76. Ibid., 2, 9, 463–64; Nagel, *The Lees of Virginia*, 161, 166, 182.
77. Freeman, *Lee*, vol. 1, 466–67; Lee, Jr., *Recollections and Letters*, 28; *O.R.* ser. 1, vol. 2, 775–76.
78. Freeman, *Lee*, vol.1, 474, 489; Dowdey and Manarin, *Wartime Papers of Robert E. Lee*, 12; *O.R.* vol. 51, pt. 2, 37, 77, 88; Taylor, *Four Years with General Lee*, 11.
79. Dowdey and Manarin, *Wartime Papers of Robert E. Lee*, 12–13.
80. Warner, *Generals In Gray*, 179, 184; Dowdey and Manarin, *Wartime Papers of Robert E. Lee*, 15.
81. Taylor, *Four Years with General Lee*, 11–12.
82. Freeman, *Lee*, vol. 1, 478.
83. *O.R.* vol. 2, 784, 792, 797–98, 827; *O.R.* vol. 51, pt. 2, 55–56; Taylor, *Four Years with General Lee*, 11; Dowdey and Manarin, *Wartime Papers of Robert E. Lee*, 50–52; Freeman, *Lee*, vol. 1, 478–79.
84. Robertson, *Stonewall Jackson*, 1, 29, 108; *O.R.* vol. 2, 810, 814, 833.
85. *O.R.* vol. 51, pt. 2, 21, 31–32; Summers, *The Baltimore and Ohio in the Civil War*, 17–18, 56; Callahan, *Semi-Centennial History of West Virginia*, 120; *O.R.* vol. 2, 790–91.
86. Ibid., 788, 827.
87. Ibid., 802–03, 830, 837–38, 840, 843, 848, 855–57, 884; Armstrong, *25th Virginia Infantry*, 219.
88. *O.R.* vol. 2, 874.

Chapter 4. The Girl I Left Behind Me
89. Hall, *Diary of a Confederate Soldier*, 11.
90. Robson, *How a One-Legged Rebel Lives*, 9, 14; Toney, *Privations of a Private*, 13; Watkins, "*Company Aytch*," 48.

91. Cammack, *Personal Recollections*, 5–7; Toney, *Privations*, 12–13; Hermann, *Memoirs of a Volunteer*, 8–10.
92. Toney, *Privations*, 12–13.
93. Wood, *The War*, 21; *O.R.* vol. 51, pt. 2, 104; Cammack, *Personal Recollections*, 14–15; Adams, *A Post of Honor: The Pryor Letters*, 115; Marion Harding Diary, June 13, 1861 in Thacker, *French Harding: Civil War Memoirs*, 228.
94. *O.R.* vol. 51, pt. 2, 67–68; Wallace, *Guide to Virginia Military Organizations*, 282–40; Clark, *Under the Stars and Bars*, 10–11.
95. Thompson, "Bound For Glory," 17–18.
96. *O.R.* vol. 51, pt. 2, 97, 100; Robson, *How a One-Legged Rebel Lives*, 8–9; A Member of the Bar, *Cheat Mountain*, 24; Wood, *The War*, 20.
97. Wiley, *Johnny Reb*, 19; Worsham, *One of Jackson's Foot Cavalry*, 1–2.
98. Ibid., 8–9; Robson, *How a One-Legged Rebel Lives*, 9–10.
99. W.B. Tabb to N.S. Bloggs, June 14, 1861, PC; *O.R.* vol. 51, pt. 2, 68, 76.
100. Hermann, *Memoirs of a Veteran*, 13; Poe, *Personal Reminiscences*, 3; *O.R.* vol. 51, pt. 2, 99; Freeman, *Lee*, vol. 1, 497.
101. A Member of the Bar, *Cheat Mountain*, 16–17, 23–24; Watkins, "Company Aytch," 50; Hull, "Recollections," *The Pocahontas Times*, March 5, 1908.
102. *O.R.* vol. 51, pt. 2, 112; Wood, *The War*, 18–20; Worsham, *One of Jackson's Foot Cavalry*, 9.
103. Ibid., 2, 4; Watkins, "Company Aytch," 48; Toney, *Privations*, 14.
104. Rice, "The Letters of John Barret Pendleton," 12.
105. Worsham, *One of Jackson's Foot Cavalry*, 9–10.
106. Clayton Wilson to Joe Wyatt, May 29, 1861, PC; Clark, *Under the Stars and Bars*, 13; Hannaford, *The Story of a Regiment*, 43; Toney, *Privations*, 14; Rice, "The Letters of John Barret Pendleton," 12.
107. Worsham, *One of Jackson's Foot Cavalry*, 9, 11.
108. Wood, *The War*, 20–21; Ruffner, *44th Virginia Infantry*, 7.
109. Worsham, *One of Jackson's Foot Cavalry*, 3; Wood, *The War*, 19.
110. Cammack, *Personal Recollections*, 16. Cammack's Confederates became Company C of the Thirty-first Virginia Infantry. The Unionists at Clarksburg joined the Third (U.S.) Virginia Infantry.
111. Wood, *The War*, 18.
112. Worsham, *One of Jackson's Foot Cavalry*, 10; Watkins, "Company Aytch," 48.
113. Rice, "The Letters of John Barret Pendleton," 19; Toney, *Privations*, 15.
114. Wiley, *Billy Yank*, 20–21; Hannaford, *The Story of a Regiment*, 31; Skidmore, *Civil War Journal of Billy Davis*, 2–3, 8–10; Cox, *Military Reminiscences*, vol. 1, 14.
115. Stevenson, *Indiana's Roll of Honor*, 14, 20–21; Kepler, *Fourth Ohio Volunteer Infantry*, 15.
116. Wiley, *Billy Yank*, 21, 37–38, 40; Skidmore, *Civil War Journal of Billy Davis*, 2; Kepler, *Fourth Ohio Volunteer Infantry*, 13–14; Thomson, *Seventh Indiana Infantry*, 8; Baxter, *Gallant Fourteenth*, 16, 38.
117. Grebner, *We Were The Ninth*, xii, 4–5, 6, 53, 199, 257n; Reid, *Ohio in the War*, vol. 1, 875; Warner, *Generals In Blue*, 294; Cox, *Military Reminiscences*, vol. 1, 36.
118. Skidmore, *Civil War Journal of Billy Davis*, 4, 6; P.R. Galloway to his wife, May 10, 1861, PC; Hannaford, *The Story of a Regiment*, 41; Kepler, *Fourth Ohio Volunteer Infantry*, 17.

119. Baxter, *Gallant Fourteenth*, 41; Skidmore, *Civil War Journal of Billy Davis*, 6, 7, 19; Ben May to Brother Will, June 10, 1861, PC; Merrill, *The Soldier of Indiana*, 15–16.

120. Grebner, *We Were The Ninth*, 14, 52.

121. Thomson, *Seventh Indiana Infantry*, 13; Hannaford, *The Story of a Regiment*, 42–43; Ben May to Brother Will, May 8, 1861, PC.

122. *Cincinnati Gazette*, April 23, 1861 in Hannaford, *The Story of a Regiment*, 34; Thomson, *Seventh Indiana Infantry*, 12.

123. Skidmore, *The Alford Brothers*, 30; P.R. Galloway to wife, May 5, 1861, PC; Skidmore, ed., *The Civil War Journal of Billy Davis*, 26, 28.

124. Ben May to Brother Will, June 10, 1861, PC; Baxter, *Gallant Fourteenth*, 41; Worsham, *One of Jackson's Foot Cavalry*, 5; Rice, *The Letters of John Barret Pendleton*, 12.

125. Wiley, *Billy Yank*, 22; Cox, *Military Reminiscences*, 13; Hannaford, *The Story of a Regiment*, 39; Skidmore, *The Civil War Journal of Billy Davis*, 26.

126. Skidmore, *The Alford Brothers*, 23; Kepler, *Fourth Ohio Volunteer Infantry*, 28; *Indianapolis Daily Journal*, July 5, 1861 in Baxter, *Hoosier Farm Boy in Lincoln's Army*, 16.

127. Sears, *George B. McClellan*, 71; Skidmore, *The Civil War Journal of Billy Davis*, 25.

Chapter 5. McClellan Eyes Virginia

128. Rawling, *History of the First Regiment Virginia Volunteers*, 18–22; Lang, *Loyal West Virginia*, 234–35, 320.

129. Frothingham, *Sketch of the Life of Brig. Gen. B.F. Kelley*, 3–4, 6–8; Strother, *Personal Reminiscences*, 347; Lang, *Loyal West Virginia*, 320, 323.

130. Poe, *Personal Reminiscences of the Civil War*, 3; *O.R.* vol. 51, pt. 2, 109; Callahan, *Semi-Centennial History*, 120; Diary of Charles L. Campbell in Price, *On To Grafton*, 50.

131. Cammack, *Personal Recollections*, 19; Price, *On To Grafton*, 11; Reader, *History of the Fifth West Virginia Cavalry*, 27–28.

132. *O.R.* vol. 51, pt. 2, 109; Powell, "Beginning of the Civil War in West Virginia," 201; Reader, *History of the Fifth West Virginia Cavalry*, 29, 49–50; Cammack, *Personal Recollections*, 18–19; Brinkman, "The War Diary of Fabricus A. Cather," 94.

133. Reader, *History of the Fifth West Virginia Cavalry*, 50; Powell, "Beginning of the Civil War in West Virginia," 200; Murray, "First Soldier Killed in the War," 494; J. Slidell Brown, "Bailey Brown: The First Victim of the Great Rebellion," *The West Virginia Argus*, vol. 33 (May 5, 1904): 1–6, typescript, Stutler Collection, WVSA; Poe, *Personal Reminiscences of the Civil War*, 4; Lang, *Loyal West Virginia*, 211. Bailey Brown was enrolled as a member of the Grafton Guards by May 20, 1861; his comrades were mustered into U.S. service at Wheeling on May 25 as Company B, Second (U.S.) Virginia Infantry. Unlike the Federal troops killed on April 19 by a Baltimore mob, Brown was killed by an officially mustered Confederate—Daniel W.S. Knight of Company A, Twenty-fifth Virginia Infantry. Bailey Brown was buried near Flemington, exhumed in 1903, and reburied at Grafton National Cemetery.

134. Moore, *A Banner in the Hills*, 63; Bird, *Narrative of Two Perilous Adventures*, 9–11; Curry, *A House Divided*, 48, 141–43, 163n. Consensus placed results of the Ordinance of Secession in Western Virginia at 44,000 against to 4,000 in favor. However, scholar Richard Curry has documented that the vote in Western Virginia counties was no greater than 34,000-19,000 against secession. By his tally, some 40 percent of the voters and fully half of the counties later encompassed by the state of West Virginia had supported the Confederacy in 1861.

135. Reader, *History of the Fifth West Virginia Cavalry*, 29, 50; *O.R.* vol. 51, pt. 2, 109. The Confederates occupied Grafton on May 25, 1861, not on May 26 as reported by Lt. Colonel Jonathan Heck in *O.R.* vol. 2, 254. *See also O.R.* vol. 51, pt. 2, 109, and Price, *On To Grafton,* 37.

136. Ambler, *Francis H. Pierpont*, 410–12; Siviter, *Recollections of War and Peace*, 52–53; Reader, *History of the Fifth West Virginia Cavalry*, 13–14.

137. *O.R.* vol. 2, 648; Sears, *The Civil War Papers of George B. McClellan*, 24. In his memoirs, General McClellan insisted: "My movements in West Virginia were, from first to last, undertaken upon my own authority and of my own volition, and without any advice, orders, or instructions from Washington or elsewhere." Delay in his receipt of orders from the War Department may have prompted that assessment. *See also* McClellan, *McClellan's Own Story,* 50, and Sears, *The Civil War Papers of George B. McClellan*, 19.

138. Reid, *Ohio in the War*, vol. 1, 49; *O.R.* vol. 2, 51–52; *Richmond Daily Examiner,* June 11, 1861 in Summers, *The Baltimore and Ohio*, 242.

139. *O.R.* vol. 2, 44–47; McClellan, *Report on the Organization and Campaigns*, 14–15.

140. McClellan, *McClellan's Own Story*, 50; Cox, "McClellan in West Virginia," 135.

141. McClellan, *Report on the Organization and Campaigns*, 16–17.

142. Ibid., 15–16.

143. Ibid., 16–17; Sears, *George B. McClellan*, 79–80.

144. *O.R.* ser. 1, vol. 2, 45; *Wheeling Daily Intelligencer*, May 28, 1861; Rawling, *History of the First Regiment Virginia Infantry*, 22–23; Carnes, *The Tygarts Valley Line*, 45; Leib, *Nine Months in the Quartermaster's Department*, 9.

145. *Wheeling Daily Intelligencer*, May 29, 1861 in Moore, *The Rebellion Record*, vol. 1, 296–298; Summers, *The Baltimore and Ohio*, 73; *O.R.* vol. 2, 45, 49; Lieb, *Nine Months in the Quartermaster's Department*, 10.

146. *O.R.* vol. 2, 49, 51–52; McClellan, *Report on the Organization*, 17. On the morning of May 28, 1861, members of the Second (U.S.) Virginia Infantry under Lieutenant Oliver West clashed with Confederate militia under Captain Christian Roberts at a point midway between Wheeling and Grafton known as Glovers Gap. Fellow Virginians killed Captain Roberts—reputedly the first armed Confederate officer to fall in action. However, Roberts may not have been formally enrolled. See Reader, *History of the Fifth West Virginia Cavalry*, 42; Leib, *Nine Months in the Quartermaster's Department*, 10–11; *Wheeling Daily Intelligencer*, May 30, 1861 in Fansler, *History of Tucker County, West Virginia*, 141.

147. *O.R.* vol. 2, 47; Summers, *The Baltimore and Ohio*, 74–76; J.B. Steedman to F.W. Lander, Lander Papers, LC; F.W. Lander to G.B. McClellan, June 8, 1861, McClellan Papers, LC.

148. *O.R.* vol. 2, 50, 655–56.

Chapter 6. The Philippi Races

149. Reid, *"Agate" Dispatches*, 19; Dayton, "The Beginning—Philippi, 1861," 254–56; Woods, "The First Inland Battle of the Civil War," 7. Philippi (pronounced Fill'-li-pee) was originally named "Philippa." Due to misspellings and confusion with the ancient Macedonian city of "Philippi," the later name has taken hold. See Maxwell, *History of Barbour County*, 279.

150. Maxwell, *History of Barbour County*, 277–78; Carnes, *Centennial History of the Philippi Covered Bridge*, 36–38; Dayton, "The Beginning—Philippi, 1861," 256.

151. Maxwell, *History of Barbour County*, 245; Reid, *"Agate" Dispatches*, 19.

152. "Proclamation of Col. Porterfield," Moore, *Rebellion Record*, vol. 1, Documents, 324–25; Hornbeck, *Upshur Brothers*, 9.

153. Ibid., 9; Phillips, "History of Valley Furnace," IV, V; Poe, *Personal Reminiscences*, 3; Stewart, "First Infantry Fight of the War," 500; *O.R.* 1, vol. 2, 52.

154. Poe, *Personal Reminiscences*, 4–5; *O.R.* vol. 2, 72.

155. Statement of Colonel Porterfield, Haselberger, *Yanks From the South!*, 291; Statement of J.B. Moomau, Ibid., 280; Phillips, "History of Valley Furnace," IV, V.

156. Ibid.; Price, *On To Grafton*, 9; Cammack, *Personal Recollections*, 20.

157. *O.R.* vol. 2, 66; Merrill, *The Soldier of Indiana*, 28; Boatner, *Civil War Dictionary*, 569; Obituary of Thomas Morris, *Indianapolis News*, March 24, 1904, Stutler Collection, WVSA.

158. *O.R.* vol. 2, 66; Rawling, *History of the First Regiment Virginia Infantry*, 24.

159. Merrill, *The Soldier of Indiana*, 25; Beatty, *The Citizen-Soldier*, 90; *O.R.* vol. 2, 66–67; Rawling, *History of the First Regiment Virginia Infantry*, 24. Rawling lists the Federal marching distances as twenty-two miles for Col. Kelley, twelve for Col. Dumont.

160. Thomson, *Narrative of the Service of the Seventh Indiana Infantry*, 20–21; Grayson, *History of the Sixth Indiana Regiment*, 22; Reid, *"Agate" Dispatches*, 16; F.W. Lander to GBM, June 8, 1861, McClellan Papers, LC.

161. *Wheeling Daily Intelligencer*, July 19, 1861; Statement of Jonathan H. Haymond, Haselberger, *Yanks From The South!*, 290–91; J.E. Hanger, Record of Services, Stutler Collection, WVSA.

162. Haselberger, *Yanks From The South!*, 268, 275, 279, 287, 291; *O.R.* vol. 2, 72–74.

163. G.A. Porterfield to Hu Maxwell, August 12, 1899 in Maxwell, *History of Barbour County*, 250; Price, *On To Grafton*, 22; Carnes, *The Tygarts Valley Line*, 42.

164. *O.R.* vol. 2, 67; F.W. Lander to GBM, June 8, 1861, McClellan Papers, LC; Ecelbarger, *Frederick W. Lander*, 1–2, 19–21, 33, 60; Warner, *Generals In Blue*, 274–275; Headley, *Massachusetts in the Rebellion*, 619–620, 629.

165. Stevenson, *Indiana's Roll of Honor*, 45; Carnes, *The Tygarts Valley Line*, 45; Haselberger, *Yanks From The South!*, 71–72; Dayton, "The Beginning—Philippi, 1861," 260.

166. Colonel Ebenezer Dumont, Official Report, June 4, 1861 in Moore, *Rebellion Record*, vol. 1, Documents, 334; *Wheeling Daily Intelligencer*, June 6, 1861.

167. Maxwell, *History of Barbour County*, 255–56n; Reid, *"Agate" Dispatches*, 16–17; J.E. Hanger, Record of Services, Stutler Collection, WVSA; F.W.

Lander to GBM, June 8, 1861, McClellan Papers, LC. Some accounts claim that Mrs. Humphreys fired at Colonel Lander himself, see Stevenson, *Indiana's Roll of Honor*, vol. 1, 44 and *Frank Leslie's Illustrated Newspaper*, June 22, 1861.

168. Statement of Lewis Fahrion, May 17, 1928, PC; Colonel Ebenezer Dumont, Official Report, June 4, 1861 in Moore, *Rebellion Record*, vol. 1, Documents, 334–35; Merrill, *The Soldier of Indiana*, 31; Reid, *"Agate" Dispatches*, 17.

169. Hall, *The Diary of a Confederate Soldier*, 13; Maxwell, *History of Barbour County*, 256n.

170. G.A. Porterfield to Hu Maxwell, August 12, 1899 in Maxwell, *History of Barbour County*, 251; Statement of Daniel A. Stofer in Haselberger, *Yanks From The South!*, 276; "Active Service; or, Campaigning in Western Virginia," 334; Skidmore, *The Civil War Journal of Billy Davis*, 38.

171. Kemper, "The Battle of Philippi," 5; Skidmore, *The Civil War Journal of Billy Davis*, 38; Leib, *Nine Months in the Quartermaster's Department*, 15–16; Colonel Ebenezer Dumont, Official Report, June 4, 1861 in Moore, *Rebellion Record*, vol. 1, Documents, 334; Price, *On To Grafton*, 21.

172. *Wheeling Daily Intelligencer*, August 10, 1906 in Hall, *Lee's Invasion of Northwestern Virginia*, 54; Statement of W.D. Hogshead in Haselberger, *Yanks From The South!*, 286.

173. Kemper, "The Seventh Regiment," 123–24; Moore, *Rebellion Record*, vol. 2, Rumors and Incidents, 82; *Frank Leslie's Illustrated Newspaper*, June 29, 1861, 102–03.

174. *O.R.* vol. 2, 67–68; *Wheeling Daily Intelligencer*, June 6, 1861; F.W. Lander to GBM, June 8, 1861, McClellan Papers, LC; Hall, *Lee's Invasion of Northwestern Virginia*, 56; Stewart, "Battle of Philippi Recounted," 117–18. *See also* Haselberger, *Yanks From the South!*, 72–73 and Maxwell, *History of Barbour County*, 257n for discussion on the circumstances of Colonel Kelley's wounding.

175. *O.R.* vol. 2, 66–67; Cammack, *Personal Recollections*, 21.

176. Ibid., 21; Maxwell, *History of Barbour County*, 251; Moore, *Rebellion Record*, vol. 2, Rumors and Incidents, 82; Statement of Daniel A. Stofer in Haselberger, *Yanks From The South!*, 278; Stewart, "Battle of Philippi Recounted," 118.

177. Kemper, "Seventh Regiment," 124; Colonel Ebenezer Dumont, Official Report, June 4, 1861 in Moore, *Rebellion Record*, vol. 1, Documents 334; Reid, *"Agate" Dispatches*, 19; Moore, *Rebellion Record*, vol. 2, Rumors and Incidents, 82. The term "skedaddle" was soon in common use by Indiana troops at Laurel Hill, see Hannaford, *The Story of a Regiment*, 547.

178. Colonel Ebenezer Dumont, Official Report, June 4, 1861 in Moore, *Rebellion Record*, vol. 1, Documents 334; Maxwell, *History of Barbour County*, 256; Rawling, *History of the First Regiment Virginia Infantry*, 27; Carnes, *The Tygarts Valley Line*, 55. Private Charles Degner, Company I, Seventh Indiana Volunteers, never reached the battlefield. While crossing a foot-log over a small stream during the night march, Degner lost his balance and accidentally shot himself in the thigh, reportedly dying two days later. *See also* Fansler, *History of Tucker County*, 147n and Skidmore, *Civil War Journal of Billy Davis*, 37. Thomson, *Seventh Indiana Infantry*, 37, reports that

Degner was killed on June 15, "while scouting."

179. *O.R.* vol. 2, 67–68; Price, *On To Grafton*, 23; *Wheeling Daily Intelligencer*, June 6, 1861; Rawling, *History of the First Regiment Virginia Infantry*, 234–35, 237–38. The wounded Federals were all members of the First (U.S.) Virginia Infantry.

180. Colonel Ebenezer Dumont, Official Report, June 4, 1861 in Moore, *Rebellion Record*, vol. 1, Documents, 335; San Francisco Examiner, July 19, 1891 in Morris, *Ambrose Bierce*, 26; *Wheeling Daily Intelligencer* June 6, 1861; Lang, *Loyal West Virginia*, 321; *The New York Herald*, June 4, 1861; *O.R.* vol. 2, 65.

181. J.E. Hanger, Record of Services, Stutler Collection, WVSA; Carnes, *J.E. Hanger*; Letter of D.H. Mugridge, November 2, 1960, Stutler Collection, WVSA.

182. Irons, "History of a Noted Physician," 28–29; Carnes, *J.E. Hanger*.

183. *Wheeling Daily Intelligencer*, June 6, 1861; Moore, *Rebellion Record*, vol. 2, Rumors and Incidents, 82; Dayton, "The Beginning—Philippi, 1861," 265; Carnes, *The Tygarts Valley Line*, 50–51.

184. Maxwell, *History of Barbour County*, 259n; Colonel Ebenezer Dumont, Official Report, June 4, 1861 in Moore, *Rebellion Record*, vol. 1, Documents, 335; *O.R.* vol. 2, 71.

185. Ibid., 65; Lang, *Loyal West Virginia*, 321; *The New York Herald*, June 4, 1861; W.S. Rosecrans to GBM, June 5, 1861, McClellan Papers, LC.

186. Lang, *Loyal West Virginia*, 142–43.

187. Reid, *"Agate" Dispatches*, 18–20; Kemper, "The Battle of Philippi," 6, 13.

Chapter 7. Let This Line be Drawn Between Us

188. McClellan, *Report on the Organization*, 18–19; *O.R.* vol. 2, 673–74; *O.R.* ser. 1 vol. 51, pt. 1, 393–94; Reid, *"Agate" Dispatches*, 22–23.

189. Dewitt C. Howard to P.S. Bishop, August 2, 1861, PC; Monfort, "From Grafton to McDowell Through Tygart's Valley," 3.

190. Neal, *Life of Ambrose Bierce*, 33, 35, 37, 53–55; Bierce, *Ambrose Bierce's Civil War*, 4.

191. Brigham, "The Civil War Journal of William B. Fletcher," 51–52, 64. Neatly written in one corner of the apron received by Dr. Fletcher was "Abbie Fleming, Flemington, Taylor, Co. Va."

192. Lewis, *How West Virginia Was Made*, 77, 79–80, 93, 155. It is interesting to note that eighteen counties embracing more than one third of present-day West Virginia were not represented at this convention; *see also* Ambler, *Francis H. Pierpont*, 96.

193. Reid, *"Agate" Dispatches*, 13.

194. Lewis, *How West Virginia Was Made*, 81–82, 155; Ambler, *Waitman Thomas Willey*, 49, 56n. Waitman Willey's stepmother died on June 17, 1861, and his father passed just five days later at the home of Col. William J. "Bridge-burner" Willey in Farmington.

195. Lewis, *How West Virginia Was Made*, 84, 159–70; McGregor, *Disruption*, 209; Hall, *The Rending of Virginia*, 351.

196. Lewis, *How West Virginia Was Made*, 85, 92–93, 171–73.

197. Ibid., 106–10, 125.

198. Ibid., 115, 159–70.

199. Ibid., 134–35, 138; Hall, *The Rending of Virginia*, 331.

200. Lewis, *How West Virginia Was Made*, 139n; Reader, *History of the Fifth West Virginia Cavalry*, 17; *O.R.* ser. 1, vol. 2, 713.

201. Reader, *History of the Fifth West Virginia Cavalry*, 17–18; *Wheeling Daily Intelligencer*, July 3, 1861; Hall, *The Rending of Virginia*, 343; Lewis, *Second Biennial Report*, 190; Moore, *A Banner in the Hills*, 85. An additional sum of $200,000 for Pierpont's government was appropriated by the Lincoln administration; *see also* Curry, *A House Divided*, 166.

202. Hall, *The Rending of Virginia*, 335; Lewis, *How West Virginia Was Made*, 183.

203. *O.R.* vol. 2, 723–24.

Chapter 8. A Dreary-Hearted General

204. *O.R.* vol. 2, 69–70; Arnold, "Battle of Rich Mountain," 46; Cammack, *Personal Recollections*, 21.

205. *O.R.* vol. 2, 72–74. A transcript of Colonel Porterfield's Court of Inquiry is published in Haselberger, *Yanks From the South!*, 267–94.

206. Ibid., 911–12; Taylor, *Four Years*, 13, 15; Freeman, *R.E. Lee*, vol. 1, 518.

207. Moore, *Rebellion Record*, Documents, 290, 295.

208. Guie, *Bugles in the Valley*, 124–25, 149–54; Cullum, *Biographical Register*, 93; Special Orders No. 132. Adjutant General's Office, September 3, 1852, MC; Chesnut, *A Diary from Dixie*, 126.

209. Taylor, *Four Years*, 13; Alexander, *Military Memoirs*, 14; Guie, *Bugles in the Valley*, 126; *O.R.* ser. 1, vol. 2, 72, 915; Chesnut, *Diary from Dixie*, 126.

210. *O.R.* vol. 2, 236; Warner, *Generals In Gray*, 153; Armstrong, *25th Virginia Infantry*, 7. Colonel William L. Jackson was a second cousin of "Stonewall" Jackson.

211. *O.R.* vol. 2, 237–39, 255, 930–31; J.M. Heck to M.G. Harman, July 2, 1861 in The Staunton *Spectator*, July 1861. Captain James Corley, Garnett's West Point-trained adjutant, and later chief quartermaster for Lee's Army of Northern Virginia, selected the position for Camp Garnett.

212. *O.R.* vol. 2, 238; Cammack, *Personal Recollections*, 23–24; Ashcraft, *31st Virginia Infantry*, 121.

213. Rice, "The Letters of John Barret Pendleton," 16; Taliaferro, "Annals of the War," 7; *O.R.* vol. 2, 239–42.

214. McClellan, *Report on the Organization*, 19; *Wheeling Daily Intelligencer*, December 24, 1861; McClellan Papers in Waugh, *Class of 1846*, 177; Sears, *Civil War Papers of George McClellan*, 44; Sears, *George B. McClellan*, 83.

215. Ibid., 83; Sears, *Civil War Papers of George McClellan*, 32–33.

216. Ibid., 34; Hewett, *Supplement to the Official Records*, vol. 2, serial no. 2, 133–34; *O.R.* vol. 2, 195; *Frank Leslie's Illustrated Newspaper*, August 3, 1861, 183.

217. *O.R.* vol. 2, 195.

218. Ibid., 196–97.

219. Sears, *George B. McClellan*, 85; Sears, *Civil War Papers of George McClellan*, 37–40.

220. Grebner, *"We Were the Ninth,"* 61; *Wheeling Daily Intelligencer*, July 10, 1861; Lamers, *The Edge of Glory*, 6, 9, 14, 17–18; Reid, *Ohio in the War*, vol. 1, 314–15, 349, 877; Cox, *Military Reminiscences*, vol. 1, 111–12.

221. *O.R.* vol. 2, 195, 197–98.

222. Plum, *The Military Telegraph*, vol. 1, 44–45, 92–94, 97–98; Rice, "The Military Telegraph in Western Virginia," 25. A description of McClellan's cipher is contained in Plum, 44–47.

223. Sears, *Civil War Papers of George McClellan*, 40; McClellan, *Report on the Organization*, 26; O.R. vol. 2, 199.

224. Elwood, *Elwood's Stories of the Old Ringgold Cavalry*, 30–32.

225. Sears, *Civil War Papers of George McClellan*, 41; O.R. vol. 2, 198–200; Sears, *George B. McClellan*, 19–20.

226. Hornbeck, *Upshur Brothers*, 45.

227. Cox, "McClellan in West Virginia," 131, 137; O.R. vol. 2, 205, 268, 293; Sears, *Civil War Papers of George McClellan*, 43n; Benham, *Recollections of West Virginia Campaign*, 679–80; Hotchkiss, *Virginia*, 47; Sears, *George B. McClellan*, 88. McClellan stubbornly defended his inflated estimate of Garnett's strength; see O.R. vol. 2, 203.

228. O.R. vol. 2, 208–09; Sears, *Civil War Papers of George McClellan*, 44.

229. "Fight at Middle Fork Bridge," Moore, *Rebellion Record*, vol. 2, Documents, 251–52; O.R. vol. 2, 200–01, 255, 259–60; Reid, *Ohio in the War*, vol. 1, 34; Beatty, *The Citizen-Soldier*, 15; Cox, *Military Reminiscences*, vol. 1, 28; John Higginbotham to his grandmother, July 17, 1861 in *Lynchburg Daily Virginian*, July 28, 1861.

230. Griggs, *General John Pegram*, 1–2, 7–8, 23, 25; O.R. vol. 2, 261.

231. O.R. vol. 2, 264; Miller, *Mapping for Stonewall*, 12, 15, 27–29.

232. McClellan, *Report on the Organization*, 25.

233. Sears, *Civil War Papers of George McClellan*, 46; O.R. vol. 2, 200–01.

234. Ibid., 205; Kepler, *History of the Three Months'*, 32–33; Beatty, *The Citizen-Soldier*, 18–19.

235. Merrill, *The Soldier of Indiana*, 36–37, 41–44; O.R. vol. 2, 218–19; Bierce, *Battlefields and Ghosts*, 8–9. Bierce failed to mention that while under fire he carried a mortally wounded comrade, Corporal Dyson Boothroyd, out of those woods.

236. Durham, "The Battle of Belington," 121; R.S. Garnett to G. Deas, July 9, 1861, RG 109, Box 9, # 1940, NA; Skidmore, *Civil War Journal of Billy Davis*, 50; Terrell, *Report of the Adjutant General*, vol. 4, 45. By July 9, General Morris reported the loss of eleven Federals at Laurel Hill; another Federal officer estimated up to five casualties per day on each side. See O.R. vol. 2, 218 and Benham, *Recollections of West Virginia Campaign*, 681.

237. Hall, *The Diary of a Confederate Soldier*, 15; Hermann, *Memoirs of a Veteran*, 16–17. Hermann described some of the works at Laurel Hill as three and one half feet deep, with the dirt thrown towards the front, protecting him up to the shoulders.

238. O.R. vol. 2, 256; G.A. Porterfield to G.D. Hall, February 5, 1904 in Hall, *Lee's Invasion*, 154; R.S. Garnett to G. Deas, July 9, 1861, RG 109, Box 9, # 1940, NA.

Chapter 9. The Whole Earth Seemed to Shake

239. Thompson, "Bound for Glory," 21; Sears, *Civil War Papers of George McClellan*, 50.

240. O.R. vol. 51, pt. 1, 12–15; Grebner, "*We Were the Ninth*," 62–63; Orlando Poe to his wife, July 11, 1861, Poe Papers, LC; *Cincinnati Daily Commercial*,

July 17, 1861; *The Wellsburg Herald*, March 28, 1862. The Ninth Ohio Infantry lost one man killed and two wounded in this reconnaissance, while capturing two Confederate pickets.

241. *O.R.* vol. 51, pt. 1, 13; U.S. Congress, "Rosecrans' Campaigns," 2; *The Hancock Democrat*, July 31, 1861; McClellan, *Report on the Organization*, 28.

242. U.S. Congress, "Rosecrans' Campaigns," 2–3; Frame, "David B. Hart, Rich Mountain Guide," 65–68; Moore, *The Civil War in Song and Story*, 74.

243. U.S. Congress, "Rosecrans' Campaigns," 3,7; Rosecrans, "Rich Mountain," *National Tribune*, February 22, 1883.

244. Beatty, *The Citizen-Soldier*, 22–23; "Woodley's Reminiscence of Rich Mountain," in Bosworth, *A History of Randolph County*, 138–39.

245. *O.R.* vol. 2, 215, 217; U.S. Congress, "Rosecrans' Campaigns," 3, 7; Statement of David Hart, *Wheeling Daily Intelligencer*, July 22, 1861. The Thirteenth Indiana substituted for the Seventeenth Ohio, a unit of Rosecrans's brigade on detached duty.

246. Keifer, "The Battle of Rich Mountain and Some Incidents," 8–10; Keifer, *Slavery and Four Years*, vol. 1: 194–95; *O.R.* vol. 2, 256, 260, 267.

247. *O.R.* vol. 2, 264, 267–69; David P. Curry to R.R. Howison, August 5, 1862, Hench Collection, UVA; Arnold, "Battle of Rich Mountain," 47; Hotchkiss, *Virginia*, 691.

248. *O.R.* vol. 2, 256, 275.

249. U.S. Congress, "Rosecrans' Campaigns," 3–4; *O.R.* 2, 215; Frame, "David B. Hart," 68; Statement of David Hart, *Wheeling Daily Intelligencer*, July 22, 1861; *O.R.* vol. 51, pt. 1, 8–9.

250. *O.R.* vol. 2, 215–16, 270; *O.R.* 51, pt. 1, 9–10; Statement of David Hart, *Wheeling Daily Intelligencer*, July 22, 1861; U.S. Congress, "Rosecrans' Campaigns," 3, 4; David P. Curry to R.R. Howison, August 5, 1862, Hench Collection, UVA.

251. *O.R.* vol. 2, 270–71.

252. Ibid., 207, 216, 270–71; *Cincinnati Daily Commercial*, July 17 and 19, 1861; David P. Curry to R.R. Howison, August 5, 1862, Hench Collection, UVA; Rosecrans, "Rich Mountain," *National Tribune*, Februrary 22, 1883. In the chaos of battle, General Rosecrans's green regimental commanders repeatedly misunderstood his orders.

253. Pool, *Under Canvas*, 15.

254. *O.R.* vol. 2, 216, 271; Statement of David Hart, *Wheeling Daily Intelligencer*, July 22, 1861; *The Hancock Democrat*, July 31, 1861; Zinn, *Battle of Rich Mountain*, 14; U.S. Congress, "Rosecrans' Campaigns," 3, 4; *Cincinnati Daily Commercial*, July 17, 1861.

255. *O.R.* vol. 2, 271; David P. Curry to R.R. Howison, August 5, 1862, Hench Collection, UVA; Arnold, "Battle of Rich Mountain," 48. A 1925 letter by Clyde B. Johnson claims Aleck Hart counted 64 cannon shots. See "That Old Log Cabin," *Randolph Enterprise*, July 16, 1925.

256. U.S. Congress, "Rosecrans' Campaigns," 3, 4; *O.R.* vol. 2, 216; Statement of David Hart, *Wheeling Daily Intelligencer*, July 22, 1861; *O.R.* vol. 51, pt. 1, 11; George Rogers diary, July 12, 1861, IHS; *The Hancock Democrat*, July 31, 1861. The Confederate attempting to kill Rosecrans was said to be Second Lieutenant John G. Boyd, of the Twentieth Virginia Infantry. Private Benjamin Smith of the Thirteenth Indiana killed Boyd.

257. *O.R.* vol. 51, pt. 1, 9, 11; *O.R.* vol. 2, 260, 265, 269, 273; *Richmond Enquirer,* July, 26, 1861; "Woodley's Reminiscence of Rich Mountain" in Bosworth, *History of Randolph County,* 141.

258. *O.R.* vol. 2, 276–80; *Wheeling Daily Intelligencer,* July 18, 1861; David P. Curry to R.R. Howison, August 5, 1862, Hench Collection, UVA; *Richmond Enquirer,* July 26, 1861; *Richmond Daily Dispatch,* August 5, 1861.

259. U.S. Congress, "Rosecrans' Campaigns," 4–5; *Lafayette Daily Journal,* July 19, 1861; Hotchkiss, *Virginia,* 49. A precise chronology of the battle of Rich Mountain is difficult to compile; the opening skirmish with Confederate pickets began around 2:30 P.M., the main engagement was underway by 3 P.M. and—with intermissions—ended sometime before 5:30 P.M. *See also O.R.* vol. 2, 217–18, 257, 260, 270, 272; Rosecrans, "Rich Mountain," *National Tribune,* February 22, 1883; Arnold, "Battle of Rich Mountain," 46; David P. Curry to R.R. Howison, August 5, 1862, Hench Collection, UVA; *Cincinnati Daily Commercial,* July 17, 1861.

260. U.S. Congress, "Rosecrans' Campaigns," 5; Rosecrans, "Rich Mountain," *National Tribune,* February 22, 1883; *O.R.* vol. 2, 216; *O.R.* vol. 51, pt. 1, 9–10.

261. *Cincinnati Daily Commercial,* July 17, 1861; C.R. Boyce to sisters, July 14, 1861, PC; Beatty, *The Citizen-Soldier,* 24–25.

262. McClellan, *Report on the Organization,* 30; Beatty, *The Citizen-Soldier,* 25; *Cincinnati Daily Commercial,* July 17, 1861.

263. McClellan, *Report on the Organization,* 30; *O.R.* vol. 2, 14; Keifer, *Slavery and Four Years,* 197–98; U.S. Congress, "Rosecrans' Campaigns," 6.

264. *O.R.* vol. 2, 257, 261–63, 265–66; C. Tacitus Allen Memoirs, DU.

265. *O.R.* vol. 2, 216–17; U.S. Congress, "Rosecrans' Campaigns," vol. 3, 5, 67; Arnold, "Beverly in the Sixties," 61, 63; Ross, "Old Memories," 154. General Rosecrans's official tally of prisoners included ten officers, five non-commissioned officers, and fifty-four privates.

266. *O.R.* vol. 51, pt. 1, 13–14; *O.R.* vol. 2, 206; Kepler, *Fourth Regiment Ohio Volunteer Infantry,* 33; McClellan, *Report on the Organization,* 30.

267. *Cincinnati Daily Commercial,* July 17, 1861; Keifer, *Slavery and Four Years,* vol. 1, 200; Pool, *Under Canvas,* 13–14; Beatty, *The Citizen-Soldier,* 26; Reid, *Ohio in the War,* vol. 1, 316. Cincinnati newsman W.D. Bickham described the works at Camp Garnett as four feet high and not more than three feet wide, "rude and incomplete." The Federal soldiers thought them more formidable.

268. Letter of Captain T.M. Kirkpatrick, July 21, 1861, Kirkpatrick Family Scrapbook, ISL; Ben May to brother Will, July 17, 1861, PC; *Cincinnati Daily Commercial,* July 17, 1861.

269. Orlando Poe to wife, July 12, 1861, Poe Papers, LC; Haselberger, *Yanks From the South!,* 139, 176; Marcia L. Phillips diary, July 24, 1861, UCHS; *O.R.* vol. 2, 244–45, 267. A number of Federal casualties occurred late in the fight when the Nineteenth Ohio Infantry fired into members of the Indiana Thirteen by mistake. *See also* Landon, "The Fourteenth Indiana Regiment on Cheat Mountain," 352.

270. *Logansport Journal,* July 27, 1861; *Cincinnati Daily Commercial,* July 19, 1861; C.R. Boyce to sisters, July 14, 1861, PC; Augustus Van Dyke to folks, July 17, 1861, IHS. Some accounts refer to a pair of burial trenches. Many of the dead Confederates were shot in the head. See also Statement of David

Hart, *Wheeling Daily Intelligencer*, July 22, 1861; *Hancock Democrat*, July 31, 1861; Pool, *Under Canvas*, 14.

271. *Cincinnati Daily Commercial*, July 19, 1861; *Hancock Democrat*, July 31, 1861; Ross, "Old Memories," 152.

272. C.R. Boyce to sisters, July 14, 1861, PC.

Chapter 10. Death on Jordan's Stormy Banks

273. J.T. Derry to A.S. Garnett, December 27, 1902, Garnett Papers, VHS.

274. Taliaferro, "Annals of the War," 9–10; *O.R.* vol. 2, 206; Stevenson, *Indiana's Roll of Honor*, 55.

275. Taliaferro, "Annals of the War," 10–11; Maxwell, *History of Tucker County*, 327–28; Hannaford, *The Story of a Regiment*, 76. Garnett's own Confederates may have mistakenly felled trees over the road to Beverly. Federal troops did not occupy the town until nearly 1 P.M. on July 12. *See also* McClellan, *Report on the Organization*, 31.

276. Benham, *Recollections*, 681; Cox, *Military Reminiscences*, 89; Warner, *Generals in Blue*, 30.

277. Moore, *Rebellion Record*, vol. 2, Documents, 291–93; R.H. Milroy to S. Colfax, July 19, 1861, Colfax Papers, IHS; Benham, *Recollections*, 681–82; Stevenson, *Indiana's Roll of Honor*, 56; Skidmore, *Civil War Journal of Billy Davis*, 52; Hannaford, *The Story of a Regiment*, 76–77. A *Cincinnati Daily Commercial* account listed Benham's force as follows: Fourteenth Ohio Infantry, 750 men; Seventh Indiana, 550 men; Ninth Indiana, 500 men, and Barnett's First Ohio Light Artillery, 40 men, a total of 1,840.

278. Reid, *"Agate" Dispatches*, 30–31; Stevenson, *Indiana's Roll of Honor*, 56; Hannaford, *The Story of a Regiment*, 77–78; Moore, *Rebellion Record*, vol. 2, Documents, 292; Benham, *Recollections*, 682.

279. Ibid., 682; *O.R.* vol. 2, 222; Reid, *"Agate" Dispatches*, 31–32.

280. *O.R.* vol. 2, 222, 285; Fansler, *History of Tucker County*, 20n; Benham, *Recollections*, 683; Moore, *Rebellion Record*, vol. 2, Documents, 292; Skidmore, *Civil War Journal of Billy Davis*, 53.

281. *O.R.* vol. 2, 222, 285–86; Hermann, *Memoirs*, 19–21; Benham, *Recollections*, 683–684; Reid, *"Agate" Dispatches*, 32.

282. *O.R.* vol. 2, 286; Taliaferro, "Annals of the War," 14.

283. Benham, *Recollections*, 685; Moore, *Rebellion Record*, vol. 2, Documents, 288; Report of Captain L.M. Shumaker, July 20, 1861 in Hewitt, *Supplement*, vol. 1, 143.

284. Benham, *Recollections*, 683; Taliaferro, "Annals of the War," 14–15; *O.R.* vol. 2, 286; Reid, *"Agate" Dispatches*, 34; Moore, *Rebellion Record*, vol. 2, Documents, 292.

285. Ibid., 289, 291, 294; *O.R.* vol. 2, 286–87; Benham, *Recollections*, 684–85; Hall, *Diary*, 16; Skidmore, *Civil War Journal of Billy Davis*, 54; Report of Captain L.M. Shumaker, July 20, 1861 in Hewitt, *Supplement*, vol. 1, 143.

286. *O.R.* vol. 2, 287; Howison, "History of the War," 136; Taliaferro, "Annals of the War," 16–17; Moore, *Rebellion Record*, vol. 2, Documents, 288, 543; Maxwell, *History of Tucker County*, 331. Corricks Ford is spelled "Carricks" in most contemporary accounts. The ford was named for William Corrick, whose home stood above the lower crossing. General Morris later used the Corrick home as headquarters. See Fansler, *History of Tucker County*, 162n.

287. Moore, *Rebellion Record*, vol. 2, Documents, 289, 293; H.C. Ruler to A.S. Garnett, May 17, 1903 and J.W. Gordon to the relatives of the late R.S. Garnett, August 14, 1861, Garnett Papers, VHS; *Indianapolis Star*, November 22, 1928, Dumont Papers, ISL. Sergeant Burlingame of Company E, Seventh Indiana Infantry, was credited with the killing of General Garnett. When later queried of the event, Burlingame would only say, "I was there and was doing a little shooting." He was reported as "a man who evidently does not like the notoriety he has acquired." *See also* Thomson, *Seventh Indiana Infantry*, 34 and *Wheeling Daily Intelligencer*, July 24, 1861.

288. Benham, *Recollections*, 685–86; Moore, *Rebellion Record*, vol. 2, Documents, 289–90, 295; *Wheeling Daily Intelligencer*, July 16, 1861; J.W. Gordon to the relatives of the late R.S. Garnett, August 14, 1861 and H.C. Ruler to A.S. Garnett, May 17, 1903, Garnett Papers, VHS. A second-hand tale of Colonel Dumont throwing up his hands and exclaiming "Poor Bob Garnett!" is contradicted by Dumont's account of the discovery of Garnett's body, in which he avowed no knowledge of the fallen officer's identity. Eyewitnesses suggest that Garnett died almost instantly, rather than after being carried to the Corrick house, as maintained by some historians. See also *Indianapolis Star*, November 22, 1928, Dumont Papers, ISL. The young soldier who fell beside Garnett was not Sam Gaines. He was variously reported as a Georgian or a Virginian, but Sampson Phillips of the "Richmond Sharpshooters," Company H, Twenty-third Virginia Infantry, is listed on a muster roll as "Killed with Gen. Garnett." See William B. Taliaferro Papers, "Muster-Roll of the Richmond Sharpshooters," MC.

289. *O.R.* vol. 2, 223–24; Skidmore, *Civil War Journal of Billy Davis*, 55; Benham, *Recollections*, 686–87; Moore, *Rebellion Record*, vol. 2, Documents, 293; Reid, *"Agate" Dispatches*, 37.

290. Moore, *Rebellion Record*, vol. 2, Documents, 290.

291. Ibid., 290–91. Confederate casualties at Corricks Ford were compiled from the report of Colonel Taliaferro in *O.R.* vol. 2, 288. No members of the First Georgia Infantry are included, so the total may be higher. Federal casualties were compiled from Moore, *Rebellion Record*, vol. 2, Documents, 293. Federal losses: two killed; two later died of wounds; eight wounded; total: twelve. Confederate losses: fourteen killed; fifteen wounded; total: twenty-nine (includes General Garnett). *See also* Haselberger, *Yanks From the South!*, 307–08 for another compilation of losses at Corricks Ford.

292. Fansler, *History of Tucker County*, 162n; Reader, *History of the Fifth West Virginia Cavalry*, 30; Moore, *Rebellion Record*, vol. 2, Documents, 290–95.

293. Taliaferro, "Annals of the War," 17–19; Hagy, "The Laurel Hill Retreat," 172; Benham, *Recollections*, 687.

294. Hermann, *Memoirs*, 20–21; Lane, *"Dear Mother,"* 24–25. The Georgians passed through a portion of what is today the Otter Creek Wilderness.

295. Hermann, *Memoirs*, 23–25, 27; Fansler, History of Tucker County, 165n; Lesser, *Battle at Corricks Ford*, 22–23.

296. *O.R.* vol. 2, 224–30; 233; Report of Adjutant D.W. Marshall, August 6, 1861 in Hewitt, *Supplement*, 137; Sears, *Civil War Papers of George McClellan*, 58.

297. Benham, *Recollections,* 686; Moore, *Rebellion Record,* vol. 2, Documents, 290, 295; *Wheeling Daily Intelligencer,* July 17, 1861; Fansler, *History of Tucker County,* 184; Merrill, *The Soldier of Indiana,* 57.

298. Benham, *Recollections,* 686; Samuel Baldwin to father, July 27, 1861, Margaret A. Baldwin Papers, VHS.

299. Davis, *Rise and Fall,* vol. 1, 294; *O.R.* vol. 2, 253.

Chapter 11. Victory On the Wires

300. Plum, *The Military Telegraph,* vol. 1, 98; *O.R.* vol. 2, 202; Arnold, "Beverly in the Sixties," 65; *Cincinnati Daily Commercial,* July 17, 1861.

301. *O.R.* vol. 2, 203–04; Zinn, *Battle of Rich Mountain,* 35.

302. *O.R.* vol. 2, 260, 262–63, 279–83; Bird, *Two Perilous Adventures,* 33; C. Tacitus Allen Memoirs, DU.

303. *O.R.* vol. 2, 258–66.

304. Ibid., 208, 210, 258–59, 266–67; Sears, *Civil War Papers of George McClellan,* 53; *Cincinnati Daily Commercial,* July 19, 1861. The escape route offered by Captain Moomau was the "Seneca Road," roughly following present-day U.S. Route 33 East. See Hotchkiss, *Virginia,* 54.

305. *O.R.* vol. 2, 267; S. Williams to W.S. Rosecrans, July 14, 1861 RG 393, Box 2, NA; Arnold, "Beverly in the Sixties," 67.

306. Sears, *Civil War Papers of George McClellan,* 53; Howison, "History of the War," 131; *O.R.* vol. 2, 250; Parole of Officers Taken Prisoner…, Beverly C.H., July 16, 1861, RG 109, Entry 212, Box 36 NA; McClellan, *McClellan's Own Story,* 55.

307. Ibid., 55; *O.R.* vol. 2, 251; Maxwell, *History of Randolph County,* 265–66n.

308. Beatty, *The Citizen Soldier,* 27; Sears, *Civil War Papers of George McClellan,* 54–55; Ellen McClellan to G.B. McClellan, July 12, 1861, McClellan Papers, LC.

309. Sears, *Civil War Papers of George McClellan,* 56.

310. *New York Herald,* July 13 and 15, 1861; *New York Tribune,* July 16, 1861; *Louisville Journal,* July 20, 1861; *New York Times,* July 20, 1861 in Moore, *Rebellion Record,* vol. 2, Diary of Events, 31, Documents, 288; *O.R.* ser. 2, vol. 3, 9; Sears, *George B. McClellan,* 93.

311. Rice and Baxter, *Historic Beverly,* 28; Sears, *Civil War Papers of George McClellan,* 53.

312. *O.R.* vol. 2, 236.

313. Kepler, *History of the Fourth Ohio Volunteer Infantry,* 35; *O.R.* vol. 2, 752; *Logansport Weekly Journal,* July 27, 1861; Sears, *Civil War Papers of George McClellan,* 60, 65.

314. Cox, "McClellan in West Virginia," 137–39; *O.R.* vol. 2, 291–92; *Cincinnati Daily Commercial,* July 22, 1861 in Moore, *Rebellion Record,* vol. 2, Documents, 330; Lowry, *Battle of Scary Creek,* 235; Sears, *Civil War Papers of George McClellan,* 61–62. The captured Federal officers at Scary Creek included Col. Jesse S. Norton, Twenty-first Ohio Infantry (wounded), Col. Charles A. De Villers, Eleventh Ohio Infantry, Col. William E. Woodruff and Lt. Col. George W. Neff, Second Kentucky Infantry, along with two captains.

315. Sears, *Civil War Papers of George McClellan,* 65.

316. Catton, *The American Heritage Picture History of the Civil War,* 98, 100, 102; *New York Herald,* July 13, 1861; *New York Tribune,* June 30, 1861; Fry,

"McDowell's Advance to Bull Run," 183–93; Beauregard, "The First Battle of Bull Run," 210.

317. Williams, *Lincoln and His Generals*, 23; *O.R.* vol. 2, 752–53; *O.R.* vol. 51, pt. 1, 491.

Chapter 12. A Fortress in the Clouds

318. Sears, *Civil War Papers of George McClellan*, 67, 70; *Wheeling Daily Intelligencer*, July 24 and 25, 1861; Sears, *George B. McClellan*, 95; Reid, *Ohio in the War*, vol. 1, 283.

319. *O.R.* vol. 2, 759, 767; *O.R.* vol. 5, 6; U.S. Congress, "Rosecrans' Campaigns," 8.

320. Warner, *Generals in Blue*, 397–98; Boatner, *Civil War Dictionary*, 694; Beatty, *The Citizen-Soldier*, 36–37.

321. Stevenson, *Indiana's Roll of Honor*, 154, 156; *Wheeling Daily Intelligencer*, October 7, 1861; Ben May to brother Will, July 29, 1861, PC.

322. Landon, "The Fourteenth Indiana Regiment," 353–54; Stevenson, *Indiana's Roll of Honor*, 154; Beatty, *The Citizen-Soldier*, 43.

323. Ibid., 33.

324. Stevenson, *Indiana's Roll of Honor*, 157–58; Brock, "The Twelfth Georgia Infantry," R.T.D. to editor of the *Savannah Republican*, July 28, 1861, p. 164; J.J.M. to *Cincinnati Daily Press*, September 21, 1861 in Hannaford, *The Story of a Regiment*, 539.

325. Merrill, *The Soldier of Indiana*, 20.

326. Hutton, "A Botanist Visits Tygarts Valley," 23–27; "Letter from the Bracken Rangers," *Indianapolis Daily Journal*, September 10, 1861.

327. Rice, *Randolph 200*, 151.

328. Pool, *Under Canvas*, 16; Warner, *Generals in Blue*, 267; Baxter, *Gallant Fourteenth*, 28, 38; William Houghton Diary, July 16, 1861, IHS. The Fourteenth was reportedly the first Indiana regiment to volunteer for three-year service.

329. Pool, *Under Canvas*, 18, 45, 57; Cobb, "The Huttonsville Vicinity," 59.

330. Pool, *Under Canvas*, 16–17; Van Dyke, "Early Days," 24; Bierce, *Ambrose Bierce's Civil War*, 4–5.

331. Landon, "The Fourteenth Indiana Regiment," 370.

332. Ibid., 357; Ben May to brother Will, August 4 and 5, 1861, PC; Pool, *Under Canvas*, 34–35.

333. Van Dyke, "Early Days," 25; Merrill, *The Soldier of Indiana*, 78; Augustus Van Dyke to Angie, August 18, 1861, Van Dyke Letters, IHS; *Richmond Daily Dispatch*, September 18, 1861; David Beem Papers, narrative history, p. 5, IHS.

334. Hannaford, *The Story of a Regiment*, 104–05; Hewitt, *Supplement to the O.R.*, pt. 2, vol. 16, 257, 260; Beatty, *The Citizen-Soldier*, 44, 48. Col. George D. Wagner's force at Elkwater consisted of his own Fifteenth Indiana Infantry, the Third Ohio Infantry, and two guns of Loomis's First Michigan Light Artillery.

335. Stevenson, *Indiana's Roll of Honor*, 156, 159; *O.R.* vol. 5, 185; Plum, *Military Telegraph*, 98; Pool, *Under Canvas*, 18–19.

336. Ben May to brother Will, August 4, 1861, PC; Landon, "The Fourteenth Indiana Regiment," 355.

337. Ross, "Scouting for Bushwhackers," 399–400; Beatty, *The Citizen-Soldier,* 56.

338. *O.R.* vol. 2, 245, 248, 263; Warner, *Generals in Gray,* 149–50; Freeman, *Robert E. Lee,* vol. 1, 543–44; Dargan, *The Civil War Diary of Martha Abernathy,* 13–14.

339. *O.R.* vol. 2, 984, 988–89, 993, 998; *O.R.* vol. 5, 230; *O.R.* vol. 51 pt. 2, 181, 188; Report on the Condition of the Army of N.Western Va., July 21, 1861, PC. Many war-date dispatches use the spelling "Millborough" for the Virginia Central Railroad terminus.

340. *Southern Confederacy,* August 17, 1861; Albert Rust to H.R. Jackson, July 22, 1861, Army of the Northwest Papers, PC; Hagy, "The Laurel Hill Retreat," 173; *O.R.* vol. 2, 989.

341. Taylor, "War Story of a Confederate Soldier Boy," in Bristol *Herald-Courier,* January 20, 1921, TSLA; Hagy, "The Laurel Hill Retreat," 173; Watkins, *"Company Aytch,"* 50.

342. *O.R.* vol. 2, 993; Toney, *Privations,* 19; Watkins, *"Company Aytch,"* 51–52.

343. Long, *Memoirs of Robert E. Lee,* 119; *O.R.* vol. 51, pt. 2, 197; R.N. Avery to Callie, July 28, 1861, PC.

344. *O.R.* vol. 51, pt. 2, 180–81; Warner, *Generals in Gray,* 193–94; Newell, *Lee vs. McClellan,* 174; John D.H. Ross to Aggie, July 29, 1861 in Oram, "Letters of Colonel John De Hart Ross," 164; *O.R.* vol. 2, 999; Worsham, *One of Jackson's Foot Cavalry,* 14. The disposition of Confederates under General Loring's command in late July was thus: Colonel Edward Johnson's Twelfth Georgia Infantry and three guns of Captain Pierce Anderson's Lee Battery of Virginia held the Staunton-Parkersburg Turnpike on Allegheny Mountain. Colonel Albert Rust's Third Arkansas Infantry was in supporting distance of Johnson at Hightown. The convalescing regiments of Colonel William Taliaferro's Twenty-third Virginia, the remnant of the Twenty-fifth Virginia, Colonel William Jackson's Thirty-first Virginia, Colonel Samuel Fulkerson's Thirty-seventh Virginia, Colonel William Scott's Forty-fourth Virginia, Colonel James Ramsey's shattered First Georgia, a detachment of the Fourteenth Virginia Cavalry under Major George Jackson, and Captain Lindsay Shumaker's Virginia Light Artillery occupied Monterey and points east. Colonel William Gilham's Twenty-first Virginia Infantry was at Huntersville. Colonel Stephen Lee's Sixth North Carolina Infantry and the Bath Cavalry held Elk Mountain, eleven miles north of Huntersville. *See also O.R.* vol. 2, 997–99, 1006; Long, *Memoirs of Robert E. Lee,* 117.

345 *O.R.* vol. 2, 1006, 1009; *O.R.* vol. 51, pt. 2, 206; Long, *Memoirs of Robert E. Lee,* 117–19; Price, *Historical Sketches of Pocahontas County,* 597. General Loring's talented staff consisted of Colonel Carter Stevenson, assistant adjutant general; Major A.L. Long, chief of artillery; Captain James Corley, chief quartermaster; Captain R.G. Cole, chief commissary; Lieutenant H.W. Matthews, *aide-de-camp*; and Colonel W.E. Starke, volunteer *aide-de-camp.* Stevenson later became a major-general; Long became chief of artillery and a brigadier general in the Army of Northern Virginia; Corley and Cole became chief quartermaster and commissary on the staff of General Lee; Starke became a brigadier general and Matthews became governor of West Virginia! *See also* Hotchkiss, *Virginia,* 153.

346. Mills, *History of the Sixteenth North Carolina Regiment*, 3. The Sixth North Carolina later became the Sixteenth North Carolina Infantry. Confederates arriving at Huntersville, finding wet and muddy camp-grounds, would soon call it a "hole of a place."

Chapter 13. Scouts, Spies and Bushwhackers

347. Stevenson, *Indiana's Roll of Honor*, 161; Price, "Guerrilla Warfare," 241–43; *O.R.* vol. 51, pt. 2, 183; "Military History," p. 4, Hugh B. Ewing Papers, OHS; Landon, "The Fourteenth Indiana Regiment," 354. Hanging Rock is adjacent to the present town of Durbin. Accounts vary as to the number of Federal cavalrymen killed and wounded in this incident.

348. Stevenson, *Indiana's Roll of Honor*, 159–61; *O.R.* vol. 2, 984–85; *O.R.* vol. 51, pt. 2, 184–85, 187–88; Pollard, *First Year of the War*, 168.

349. Stevenson, *Indiana's Roll of Honor*, 162; Lang, *Loyal West Virginia*, 8–9; Monfort, "From Grafton to McDowell," 8; Ross, "Scouting for Bushwhackers," 400–01; Leib, *Nine Months*, 126.

350. Monfort, "From Grafton to McDowell," 8; Leib, *Nine Months*, 126–27; Beatty, *The Citizen-Soldier*, 16; *Wheeling Daily Intelligencer*, September 27, 1861; R.B. Hayes to Sardis Birchard, August 17, 1861 and R.B. Hayes to his wife, August 17, 1861 in Curry, *A House Divided*, 74–75. Western Virginia newspapers were filled with stories of guerrilla depredations in 1861.

351. Pool, *Under Canvas*, 25–26; Felix W. Worthington to his father, September 11, 1861 in Wiley, *Billy Yank*, 350.

352. Merrill, *The Soldier of Indiana*, 79–80; Landon, "The Fourteenth Indiana Regiment," 357–58; *Wheeling Daily Intelligencer*, August 2, 1861.

353. *O.R.* vol. 2, 766; Pool, *Under Canvas*, 23, 28; A Member of the Bar, *Cheat Mountain*, 45; John L. Griffin Diary, July 28, 1861, EU.

354. Ben May to brother Will, July 29, 1861, PC; Merrill, *The Soldier of Indiana*, 20–22; Thomson, *The Seventh Indiana Infantry*, 24; Morton, *Sparks From the Camp Fire*, 345–46.

355. Landon, "The Fourteenth Indiana Regiment," 356; Ross, "Old Memories," 152.

356. Beatty, *The Citizen-Soldier*, 51–53; Keifer, *Slavery and Four Years of War*, vol. 1, 208–10; "War Experiences of Colonel DeLagnel," 508; Long, *Memoirs of Robert E. Lee*, 115–16.

357. Stevenson, *Indiana's Roll of Honor*, 73; Hannaford, *The Story of a Regiment*, 94–95; E.D. House Diary, July 18, 1861, PC; *O.R.* vol. 2, 291.

358. Pinkerton, *Spy of the Rebellion*, vol. 1, 210–17; Stutler, *West Virginia in the Civil War*, 54–59.

359. Skidmore, *The Civil War Journal of Billy Davis*, 37; *A Dish of History*, n.p.; Thacker, *French Harding: Civil War Memoirs*, 78.

360. *Wheeling Daily Intelligencer*, July 19 and November 19, 1861; Leib, *Nine Months*, 95–96; Matheny, *Wood County*, 182–88.

361. Stutler, *West Virginia in the Civil War*, 43–48; Plum, *Military Telegraph*, 105.

362. Stevenson, *Indiana's Roll of Honor*, 155; Merrill, *The Soldier of Indiana*, 104–10; Hall, *Lee's Invasion of Northwest Virginia*, 157, 161.

Chapter 14. Mud, Measles and Mutiny

363. Taylor, *Four Years*, 16, 35; Taylor, *General Lee*, 29; Lee, *Recollections*, 41, 50. Lee's cook in Western Virginia, "Meredith," came from a son's residence; his slave "Perry" had worked in the dining room at Arlington.

364. Chesnut, *A Diary from Dixie*, 94–95.

365. Lee, Jr., *Recollections and Letters*, 37; O.R. vol. 5, 767, 828–29; O.R. vol. 51, pt. 2, 254; Taylor, *Four Years*, 16; Freeman, *Lee*, vol. 1, 541–42. The *Richmond Examiner*, July 31, 1861, reported Lee "on a tour of the West, looking after the commands of Generals Loring and Wise...His visit is understood to be one of inspection, and consultation on the plan of campaign." Confusion regarding Lee's role in Western Virginia exists to this day. Biographer Douglas Freeman wrote that Lee "took command with no apologies," yet acknowledged that he was "not in direct command." General Fitzhugh Lee (a nephew) wrote that "General Lee proceeded at once to West Virginia, and for the first time assumed active command of troops in the field." General Loring's chief of artillery and Lee biographer A.L. Long wrote that Lee was appointed "to the command of the department of Western Virginia." An organization chart in the Official Records lists Lee as "Commanding General of the Army of the Northwest." *See also* Freeman, *Lee*, vol. 1, 542n, 600, 640; Lee, *General Lee*, 116, Long, *Memoirs of Robert E. Lee*, 501; O.R. series 4, vol. 1, 631.

366. R.E. Lee to his wife, August 4, 1861 in Dowdey, *Wartime Papers*, 62; Freeman, *Lee*, vol. 1, 543.

367. Hotchkiss, *Virginia*, 155; Armstrong, *25th Virginia Infantry*, 23.

368. R.E. Lee to his wife, August 4, 1861 in Dowdey, *Wartime Papers*, 61; Freeman, *Lee*, vol. 1, 550.

369. Long, *Memoirs of Robert E. Lee*, 117, 119; Hotchkiss, *Virginia*, 154–55; Mills, *History of the Sixteenth North Carolina Infantry*, 4; R.E. Lee to his wife, August 4 and 9, 1861 in Dowdey, *Wartime Papers*, 61, 63. See Freeman, *Lee*, vol. 1, 552–53 for a discussion of the roll played by Lee's sense of *noblesse oblige* in his handling of General Loring.

370. Ibid., 63; Taylor, *Four Years*, 35–36; *Randolph Enterprise*, June 25, 1925.

371. R.E. Lee to his wife, August 9, 1861 in Dowdey, *Wartime Papers*, 63; Warner, *Generals in Gray*, 184; R. Hatton to his wife, August 16, 1861 in Drake, *Life of General Robert Hatton*, 372.

372. O.R. series 2, vol. 3, 25–26; R.E. Lee to his wife, August 9, 1861 in Dowdey, *Wartime Papers*, 63. Joseph Reynolds had been an instructor of philosophy at West Point during Lee's tenure as superintendent of that institution.

373. Merrill, *The Soldier of Indiana*, 110–17.

374. Long, *Memoirs of Robert E. Lee*, 121–22; Freeman, *Lee*, vol. 1, 555.

375. Hermann, *Memoirs*, 39; Watkins, *"Company Aytch,"* 53; Toney, *Privations*, 21.

376. J. Hotchkiss to Fitz Lee, October 22, 1891, Miller, *Mapping for Stonewall*, 42; Worsham, *One of Jackson's Foot Cavalry*, 15–16.

377. Freeman, *Lee*, vol. 1, 577–78.

378. O.R. vol. 5, 552, 554–56, 561, 563–64; Sears, *Civil War Papers of George McClellan*, 79–80.

379. O.R. vol. 5, 7–8; Sears, *Civil War Papers of George McClellan*, 78–79; Sears, *George B. McClellan*, 97–101.

380. Hotchkiss, *Virginia*, 155; S. Pryor to his wife, August 15, 1861 in Adams, *A Post of Honor*, 44; Freeman, *Lee*, vol. 1, 559–60.

381. R.E. Lee to his daughters, August 29, 1861 in Dowdey, *Wartime Papers*, 67; A Member of the Bar, *Cheat Mountain*, 45–46; Worsham, *One of Jackson's Foot Cavalry*, 17.

382. Strider, *The Life and Work of George William Peterkin*, 47; R. Hatton to his wife, August 23, 1861 in Drake, *Life of General Robert Hatton*, 375.

383. *O.R.* vol. 5, 785; Taylor, *Four Years*, 17; Worsham, *One of Jackson's Foot Cavalry*, 17.

384. Hotchkiss, *Virginia*, 156; A Member of the Bar, *Cheat Mountain*, 62; S. Pryor to his wife, August 3, 1861 in Adams, *A Post of Honor*, 33; Toney, *Privations*, 20; Taylor, *Four Years*, 17.

385. Worsham, *One of Jackson's Foot Cavalry*, 16; Strider, *The Life and Work of George William Peterkin*, 48; S. Pryor to his wife, August 9 and September 8, 1861 in Adams, *A Post of Honor*, 38, 63; R.E. Lee to his wife, September 1, 1861 and R.E. Lee to G.W.C. Lee, September 3, 1861 in Dowdey, *Wartime Papers*, 68–70.

386. R. Hatton to his wife, August 14 and 16, 1861 in Drake, *Life of General Robert Hatton*, 370, 373; R.E. Lee to G.W.C. Lee, September 3, 1861 in Dowdey, *Wartime Papers*, 70.

387. Mills, *History of the Sixteenth North Carolina Infantry*, 5; R. Hatton to his wife, August 18, 1861, Drake in *Life of General Robert Hatton*, 374–75.

388. R.E. Lee to his daughters, August 29, 1861 in Dowdey, *Wartime Papers*, 67.

389. Landon, "The Fourteenth Indiana Regiment on Cheat Mountain," 352; Beatty, *The Citizen-Soldier*, 58–60.

390. Pool, *Under Canvas*, 24–25, 33; William Houghton Diary, August 14 and 15, 1861, IHS.

391. Pool, *Under Canvas*, 33; Landon, "The Fourteenth Indiana Regiment on Cheat Mountain, 358–59; "Letter from Cheat Mountain," *Indianapolis Daily Journal*, September 24, 1861. The August snow on Cheat Mountain is well documented. *See also* Augustus Van Dyke to his folks, August 18, 1861, Van Dyke Letters, IHS; Merrill, *The Soldier of Indiana*, 79; J.H. Slaughter to his mother, August 17, 1861 and J.H. Slaughter to J.C. Rawlins, December 5, 1861, PC.

392. Pool, *Under Canvas*, 24, 33, 44; Augustus Van Dyke to his folks, August 23, 1861, Van Dyke Letters, IHS.

393. Augustus Van Dyke to his folks, August 12, 1861, Van Dyke Letters, IHS; Stevenson, *Indiana's Roll of Honor*, 158; George W. Lambert journal, August 1861, IHS; Baxter, *Gallant Fourteenth*, 49.

394. Augustus Van Dyke to Angie, August 18, 1861, Van Dyke Letters, IHS.

395. Baxter, *Gallant Fourteenth*, 59–60; Augustus Van Dyke to his folks, August 12 and 23, 1861, IHS; E.H.C. Cavins to his wife, September 9, 1861 in Smith, *The Civil War Letters of Colonel Elijah H.C. Cavins*, 10; William Houghton diary, August 24, 1861, IHS.

396. E.H.C. Cavins to his father, September 4, 1861 in Smith, *Civil War Letters*, 8; J.R. McClure to his cousin, August 18, 1861 in Baxter, *Hoosier Farm Boy*, 19; Landon, "The Fourteenth Indiana Regiment on Cheat Mountain," 360, 362.

397. Warren Alford to his folks, August 28, 1861 in Skidmore, *The Alford Brothers*, 73; Augustus Van Dyke to Angie, August 18, 1861, Van Dyke Letters, IHS.

Chapter 15. Feuding Generals and Dickering Delegates

398. Boatner, *Civil War Dictionary*, 944; "The Feuding Generals—Floyd and Wise," *The Pocahontas Times*, February 10, 1927 in Phillips, *War Stories*, 254–56; Hall, *Rending of Virginia*, 413; O.R. vol. 2, 290, 293, 908–09; O.R. vol. 5, 151; O.R. series 4, vol. 1, 367; *Richmond Enquirer* in Cohen, *Civil War in West Virginia*, 34.

399. O.R. vol. 2, 291–92, 1012; Jones, Beuhring H. "My First Thirty Days Experience as a Captain," *Southern Literary Messenger*, vol. 37, no. 2, 1863 in Lowry, *The Battle of Scary Creek*, 147–48.

400. O.R. vol. 5, 152–53, 768; O.R. vol. 2, 908–09.

401. Warner, *Generals in Gray*, 89–90; Hotchkiss, *Virginia*, 594; *Wheeling Daily Intelligencer*, October 25, 1861; *New York Times*, September 13, 1861; R.E. Lee to his wife, October 7, 1861 in Dowdey, *Wartime Papers*, 80; Morrison, *Memoirs of Henry Heth*, 152.

402. O.R. vol. 5, 150, 773; O.R. vol. 2, 909; Morrison, *Memoirs of Henry Heth*, 153.

403. O.R. vol. 5, 153, 773–75, 778–81; O.R. vol. 51, pt. 2, 237.

404. O.R. vol. 5, 776, 780–82; Cox, "McClellan in West Virginia," 142–43.

405. O.R. vol. 5, 782–85; O.R. vol. 51, pt. 2, 232.

406. O.R. vol. 5, 785–86, 788.

407. Ibid., 155.

408. Ibid., 789, 791–96; O.R. vol. 51, pt. 2, 237.

409. O.R. vol. 5, 156, 798–99, 802, 813.

410. Ibid., 115–16, 804–05, 810.

411. Pollard, *First Year of the War*, 164; O.R. vol. 51, pt. 2, 256–57; Lowry, *September Blood*, 158; O.R. vol. 5, 158–59.

412. O.R. vol. 5, 127.

413. *Congressional Globe*, 37 Cong., 2 Sess., Appendix in Curry, *A House Divided*, 73. Although originally known as the "Reorganized" Government of Virginia, the term "Restored" Government later gained widespread favor. *See also* Lewis, *Second Biennial Report*, 163.

414. Reorganized Government of Virginia, *Acts of the General Assembly*, 34–35; Hall, *Rending of Virginia*, 338, 342; Lewis, "How West Virginia Became A Member of the Federal Union," 601. A House of Delegates met in the Custom House and the Senate in nearby Linsly Institute. This rump legislature consisted of more than thirty members. *See also* McGregor, *Disruption*, 220, and Curry, *A House Divided*, 73, 166n.

415. Ambler, *Francis H. Pierpont*, 114–15; Hall, *Rending of Virginia*, 347.

416. Lewis, *How West Virginia Was Made*, 183–90, 303, 308, 312; Hall, *Rending of Virginia*, 349–52.

417. Reorganized Government of Virginia, *Journal of the Convention*, 40–41; Lewis, *How West Virginia Was Made*, 192, 208–10, 218–20.

418. Lewis, *How West Virginia Was Made*, 218, 221, 255, 269; Basler, *Collected Works of Abraham Lincoln*, vol. 4, 263.

419. Lewis, *How West Virginia Was Made*, 245, 278, 280–88; Hall, *Rending of Virginia*, 354–57, 372–74; Curry, *A House Divided*, 82–84. The committee

of six appointed to craft a compromise included Daniel Farnsworth, John Carlile, James Paxton, Peter Van Winkle, Lewis Ruffner, and Daniel Lamb. The convention's dismemberment document was titled: "An Ordinance to Provide for the Formation of a New State Out of a Portion of this State." The thirty-nine Virginia counties unconditionally included within the new state boundary were Logan, Wyoming, Raleigh, Fayette, Nicholas, Webster, Randolph, Tucker, Preston, Monongalia, Marion, Taylor, Barbour, Upshur, Harrison, Lewis, Braxton, Clay, Kanawha, Boone, Wayne, Cabell, Putnam, Mason, Jackson, Roane, Calhoun, Wirt, Gilmer, Ritchie, Wood, Pleasants, Tyler, Doddridge, Wetzel, Marshall, Ohio, Brooke, and Hancock.

420. Reorganized Government of Virginia, *Journal of the Convention*, 64–67; Curry, *A House Divided*, 85.

Chapter 16. The Perfect Roll Down

421. R.E. Lee to G.W.C. Lee, September 3, 1861 in Dowdey, *Wartime Papers*, 69–70; O.R. vol. 51 pt. 2, 283–84; Long, *Memoirs of Robert E. Lee*, 123; O.R. series 4, vol. 1, 822; Lang, *Loyal West Virginia*, 47–48. Loring's force on the Huntersville line was said to be six thousand strong, Jackson's on the Monterey line, five thousand. The effective strength of Federal forces under Reynolds may have been no more than six to seven thousand. *See also* Stevenson, *Indiana's Roll of Honor*, vol. 1, 168.

422. General Orders No. 8, Hd. Qts. Army of N.W., Valley Mt. August 28, 1861, PC; R. Hatton to his wife, August 30, 1861 in Drake, *Life of General Robert Hatton*, 378; Clayton Wilson to his mother, August 22, 1861, PC.

423. Taylor, *Four Years*, 22; Hotchkiss, *Virginia*, 156; Hotchkiss to Fitz Lee, October 22, 1891 in Miller, *Mapping for Stonewall*, 42. Hotchkiss lost most of his mapping equipment in the retreat from Rich Mountain.

424. Long, *Memoirs of Robert E. Lee*, 122–23; Taylor, *Four Years*, 22–23; Price, *Historical Sketches of Pocahontas County*, 449–50. John Yeager, Jr. was "the civilian engineer, whose name unfortunately does not appear in the records," in Freeman, *Lee*, vol. 1, 560. William T. Price claimed that Yeager and Rust "succeeded in passing into and throughout the garrison" on Cheat Mountain without arousing suspicion!

425. Barnwell, "The First West Virginia Campaigns," 188; Jones, "The Mountain Campaign Failure," 368; Warner, *Generals in Gray*, 266–67; Collier, *"They'll Do to Tie To!"* 7; Seitz, *Horace Greeley*, 170–71; Taylor, *Four Years*, 23; Long, *Memoirs of Robert E. Lee*, 122.

426. Spec. Order No. 77, Head Qrs. Monterey Line, N.W. Army, August 16, 1861, Willis Papers, HL; Hewitt, *O.R. Supplement*, Record of Events, vol. 2, 321; Jones, "The Mountain Campaign Failure," 368; Barnwell, "The First West Virginia Campaign," 188.

427. Taylor, *Four Years*, 20, 23–27; O.R. vol. 51, pt. 2, 282–83.

428. O.R. vol. 5, 192.

429. O.R. vol. 51, pt. 2, 283; Head, *Campaigns*, 34–35; Hall, *Diary of a Confederate Soldier*, 34–35.

430. O.R. vol. 5, 188–89; Stevenson, *Indiana's Roll of Honor*, vol. 1, 169–70.

431. O.R. vol. 5, 191; Cammack, *Personal Recollections*, 35–36; Carson, "Recollections," 18–19, VHS.

432. Head, *Campaigns*, 30–31; A Member of the Bar, *Cheat Mountain*, 62, 65–66; Warner, *Generals in Gray*, 74–75.

433. Head, *Campaigns*, 33; A Member of the Bar, *Cheat Mountain*, 64.

434. Ibid., 63–67, 69–70; Head, *Campaigns*, 32–33.

435. Ibid., 278–81; J.W. Gray to the Nashville *Union and American*, December 5, 1861 in Head, *Campaigns*, 38–39; A Member of the Bar, *Cheat Mountain*, 70–71, 90. Accounts vary as to the number of Federal pickets captured and killed on Stewart Run. *See also* Head, *Campaigns*, 36; H.H. Dillard, "Sixteenth Tennessee Infantry," in Lindsley, *Military Annals*, vol. 1, 336; Womack, *Civil War Diary*, September 11, 1861.

436. Head, *Campaigns*, 36–37, 41; J.W. Gray to the Nashville *Union and American*, December 5, 1861 in Ibid., 39–40; H.H. Dillard, "Sixteenth Tennessee Infantry," in Lindsley, *Military Annals*, vol. 1, 336–37; D.S. Donelson to R.E. Lee, September 17, 1861 in Hewitt, *O.R. Supplement*, vol. 1, 380–81; Hannaford, *The Story of a Regiment*, 129–30.

437. Head, *Campaigns*, 42; A Member of the Bar, *Cheat Mountain*, 74–77; H.H. Dillard, "Sixteenth Tennessee Infantry," in Lindsley, *Military Annals*, vol. 1, 337. One Federal prisoner reportedly made his escape during the bear's appearance.

438. Toney, *Privations*, 22–23; Warner, *Generals in Gray*, 10; Beard, "The Story of a Five-Dollar Gold Piece," 76; Hotchkiss, *Virginia*, 159–60; J.H. Moore, "Seventh Tennessee Infantry," in Lindsley, *Military Annals*, vol. 1, 228; Dr. J.R. Buist to his uncle, *National Intelligencer*, November 22, 1861 in Freeman, *Lee*, vol. 1, 564. Marcus Toney of the First Tennessee Infantry claimed that General Lee traveled with Anderson's brigade during their march.

439. *Clarksville Jeffersonian*, September 24, 1861; Dr. J.R. Buist to his uncle, *National Intelligencer*, November 22, 1861 in Freeman, *Lee*, vol. 1, 566; Phillips, *Phillips Family History*, 86.

440. *O.R.* vol. 5, 188; Stevenson, *Indiana's Roll of Honor*, vol. 1, 171–72; Worsham, *One of Jackson's Foot Cavalry*, 17. The dead Yankee seen by John Worsham was either Pvt. Alexander Kent or Pvt. George Bealer of the Fifteenth Indiana Infantry.

441. Pool, *Under Canvas*, 37; David Beem narrative, 8, Beem Papers, IHS. Colonel Kimball's force on Cheat Mountain totaled nearly three thousand men, rather than the three hundred often quoted. The mistake originated from wording in the official reports of General Reynolds and Colonel Kimball. Jack Zinn ably documented the error. In early September 1861, Kimball's Federal force on Cheat included the Fourteenth Indiana, Twenty-fourth and Twenty-fifth Ohio Regiments, Bracken's Indiana Cavalry company, and a six gun battery. *See also O.R.* vol. 5, 185, 187; Zinn, *R.E. Lee's Cheat Mountain Campaign*, 149; Augustus Van Dyke to his father, August 29, 1861, Van Dyke Letters, IHS; Taylor, *Four Years*, 21n; "Letter from an Indiana Volunteer," *Cincinnati Gazette*, September 23, 1861 in Moore, *Rebellion Record*, vol. 3, Documents, 136–37.

Chapter 17. Robert E. Lee's Forlorn Hope

442. Taylor, *Four Years*, 27–29n; Jones, "The Mountain Campaign Failure," 305–06; *O.R.* vol. 5, 186, 190–91; Letter to the *Southern Confederacy*, September 25, 1861; Diary of Christian Kuhl, 5, . The captured Federal

wagons, from the Twenty-fourth Ohio Infantry, were en route to Huttonsville for provisions.

443. Hotchkiss, *Virginia*, 165; Pool, *Under Canvas*, 38; *O.R.* vol. 5, 186–87; "Letter from an Indiana Volunteer," *Cincinnati Daily Gazette*, September 23, 1861 in Moore, *Rebellion Record*, vol. 3, Documents, 136–37.

444. Taylor, *Four Years*, 28; A Member of the Bar, *Cheat Mountain*, 78.

445. Levering, "Lee's Advance and Retreat," 25; H.H. Dillard, "Sixteenth Tennessee Infantry," in Lindsley, *Military Annals*, vol. 1, 337; Taylor, *Four Years*, 28–29.

446. Womack, *Civil War Diary*, September 12, 1861; H.H. Dillard, "Sixteenth Tennessee Infantry," in Lindsley, *Military Annals*, vol. 1, 338; A Member of the Bar, *Cheat Mountain*, 79.

447. Savage, "Gen. R.E. Lee at Cheat Mountain," 116–17; R.E. Lee to John Letcher, September 17, 1861 in Dowdey, *Wartime Papers*, 75; Head, *Campaigns*, 46–47.

448. Ibid., 47–49; Levering, "Lee's Advance and Retreat," 23–24; A Member of the Bar, *Cheat Mountain*, 92; Letter of Capt. John Coons, *Indianapolis Daily Journal*, October 29, 1861. This little skirmish on Becky Creek, the baptism of fire for most, "did not exceed ten minutes duration." The Confederates lost one or two killed and as many wounded. The Federals lost at least one killed, seven wounded and seventeen prisoners. *See also* H.H. Dillard, "Sixteenth Tennessee Infantry," in Lindsley, *Military Annals*, vol. 1, 337; Womack, *Civil War Diary*, September 12, 1861; Landon, "The Fourteenth Indiana Regiment on Cheat Mountain," 363.

449. Quintard, *Doctor Quintard*, 22–24; Taylor, *Four Years*, 27; Toney, *Privations*, 23; Phillips, *Phillips Family History*, 87; *O.R.* vol. 5, 190.

450. Levering, "Lee's Advance and Retreat," 24–25; Pool, *Under Canvas*, 41; Van Dyke, "Early Days," 27. Capt. Coons reportedly captured General Anderson's horse in this skirmish. Anderson's Confederates lost two killed, two missing and sixteen wounded. See also Quintard, *Doctor Quintard*, 23.

451. Watkins, "*Company Aytch*," 55.

452. Quintard, *Doctor Quintard*, 24; Merrill, *The Soldier of Indiana*, 87; Levering, "Lee's Advance and Retreat," 24.

453. Letter from "Nestor," *Southern Confederacy*, September 25, 1861; Hermann, *Memoirs*, 52–53; Clayton Wilson to his mother, September 18, 1861, PC; Taylor, *Four Years*, 28.

454. Stevenson, *Indiana's Roll of Honor*, 178–79; *O.R.* vol. 5, 185; Taylor, *Four Years*, 29. Major J. Warren Keifer, commander of the Federal "grand guard" position in front of Camp Elkwater, reported that a small body of Confederates "feebly" assaulted his rear and were driven back on the rainy night of September 12. See Keifer, *Slavery and Four Years*, vol. 1, 222.

455. A Member of the Bar, *Cheat Mountain*, 81–82.

456. Ibid.; Benjamin Randals Journal, 74, PC.

457. R.E. Lee to his wife, September 17, 1861 in Dowdey, *Wartime Papers*, 73; Maxwell, *History of Randolph County*, 297. Generals Lee and Loring reportedly met at the Adam See house, along Tygart Valley River.

458. Ben May to his brother, September 20, 1861, PC; *Coldwater Republican*, May 24, 1878; *Wheeling Daily Intelligencer*, October 7, 1861. The unexploded projectile, a ten-pounder Parrott, was later displayed at a reunion of

Loomis's First Michigan Light Artillery as the shell that almost killed Robert E. Lee. General Loring might have been the lucky officer targeted, instead of Lee. *See also* Tucker Randolph Diary, September 12, 1861, MC.

459. Wright, "Colonel John Augustine Washington," 14–15; Stutler, "Death of Col. John Augustine Washington," 14; Taylor, *General Lee*, 29–30; Moore, *Rebellion Record*, vol. 3, Rumors and Incidents, 37.

460. Wright, "Colonel John Augustine Washington," 15; Levering, "Lee's Advance and Retreat," 30–31; Keifer, *Slavery and Four Years*, vol. 1, 223; R.E. Lee to his wife, September 17, 1861 in Dowdey, *Wartime Papers*, 74. General Lee wrote that Washington and Rooney Lee were fired on from "within twenty yards." *See also* R.E. Lee to John Letcher, September 17, 1861, Ibid., 75.

461. Levering, "Lee's Advance and Retreat," 31–34; Keifer, *Slavery and Four Years*, vol. 1, 223–24; "The Killing of John A. Washington," *Lafayette Daily Courier*, September 20, 1861. Some accounts claim that at least one additional member of Washington's party was wounded. The Federals were dismayed to find an Indiana newspaper article with Washington's belongings that detailed Union strength in the area. *See also* Letter to the editor, *Indianapolis Daily Journal*, September 23, 1861 and "Circumstances of the Death of John A. Washington," *Wheeling Daily Intelligencer*, September 23, 1861.

462. Letter to the editor, *Indianapolis Daily Journal*, September 23, 1861; Lang, *Loyal West Virginia*, 50; Levering, "Lee's Advance and Retreat," 33; Quintard, *Doctor Quintard*, 30.

463. R.E. Lee to his wife, September 17, 1861 in Dowdey, *Wartime Papers*, 74; R.E. Lee to Louisa Washington, September 16, 1861 in Hoover, "Col. John Augustine Washington, C.S.A.," 26; Thomas, *Robert E. Lee*, 207.

464. *O.R.* vol. 5, 191–93. General Reynolds' official report (*O.R.* vol. 5, 184–86), describes action at Camp Elkwater on September 14 that clearly took place the prior day. *See also* Hannaford, *The Story of a Regiment*, 125n, for clarification.

465. Tucker Randolph Diary, September 15, 1861, MC; A Member of the Bar, *Cheat Mountain*, 86–87.

466. Ibid., 84; J.H. Slaughter to his brother, September 21, 1861, PC; "Historical Sketch of the 14th Tenn. Regt. of Infantry C.S.A. 1861–1865" by Sgt. R.T. Mockbee, T-833, MC; McBrien, *The Tennessee Brigade*, 9.

467. J.W. Ross to his wife, September 15, 1861, PC; *O.R.* vol. 5, 186–87; Nathan Kimball to J.J. Reynolds, September 18, 1861, PC; Stevenson, *Indiana's Roll of Honor*, 181; "Letter from Camp Kimball, Va.," *Cincinnati Daily Commercial*, October 8, 1861.

468. Merrill, *The Soldier of Indiana*, 87; R.E. Lee to his wife, September 17, 1861 and R.E. Lee to John Letcher, September 17, 1861 in Dowdey, *Wartime Papers*, 74–75.

469. Hotchkiss, *Virginia*, 165; Taylor, *Four Years*, 29; Lee, Jr., *Recollections and Letters*, 53; R.E. Lee to his daughter Mildred, November 15, 1861 in Dowdey, *Wartime Papers*, 86.

470. *Richmond Daily Dispatch*, September 26, 1861; Quintard, *Doctor Quintard*, 19; Taylor, *Four Years*, 18.

Chapter 18. Mixing Oil and Water

471. Taylor, *Four Years*, 32; U.S. Congress, "Rosecrans' Campaigns," 8–9.
472. O.R. vol. 5, 160–61, 841–45; Reid, *"Agate" Dispatches*, 47.
473. Cox, "McClellan in West Virginia," 145.
474. U.S. Congress, "Rosecrans' Campaigns," 9; O.R. vol. 5, 129–32, 147.
475. Ibid., 146–49, 161. Rosecrans lost two colonels and nearly 150 men at Carnifex Ferry. The entrenched Confederates suffered only about 20 wounded and missing. See Lowry, *September Blood*, 152–58 for amended casualty figures for this battle.
476. O.R. vol. 5, 162, 850, 853–55; Cox, "McClellan in West Virginia," 146; Taylor *General Lee* 33.
477. Morrison, *Memoirs of Henry Heth*, 155; O.R. vol. 5, 859–62, 869.
478. Ibid., 602–03, 868–69, 878; U.S. Congress, "Rosecrans' Campaigns," 10.
479. O.R. vol. 51, pt. 2, 296–97.
480. O.R. vol. 5, 864–66.
481. Ibid., 868.
482. Ibid., 868–69.
483. Ibid., 162; O.R. vol. 51, pt. 2, 318; Long, *Memoirs of Robert E. Lee*, 128; Taylor, *Four Years*, 32–33.
484. O.R. vol. 5, 873–75; O.R. vol. 51, pt. 2, 309.
485. O.R. vol. 5, 163, 78; McKinney, *Lee at Sewell Mountain*, 46; Freeman, *Lee*, vol. 1, 590.
486. Taylor, *Four Years*, 33; T.C. Morton, "Anecdotes of General R.E. Lee," *Southern Historical Society Papers*, vol. 11, 519 in McKinney, *Lee at Sewell Mountain*, 51–52.
487. R.E. Lee to his wife, September 26, 1861 in Dowdey, *Wartime Papers*, 78; O.R. vol. 51, pt. 2, 312.
488. Taylor, *Four Years*, 33; Freeman, *Lee*, vol. 1, 592.
489. Taylor, *General Lee*, 33–34.
490. O.R. vol. 5, 148–49, 163.
491. Taylor, *Four Years*, 34; O.R. vol. 5, 879; O.R. vol. 51, pt. 2, 313.
492. Taylor, *General Lee*, 34; Morrison, *Memoirs of Henry Heth*, 160.

Chapter 19. Too Tender of Blood

493. U.S. Congress, "Rosecrans' Campaigns," 10; Taylor, *Four Years*, 33; *Richmond Daily Dispatch*, October 12, 1861.
494. O.R. vol. 51, pt. 2, 324–26; U.S. Congress, "Rosecrans' Campaigns," 10; O.R. vol. 5, 900; R.E. Lee to his wife, October 7, 1861 in Dowdey, *Wartime Papers*, 80.
495. O.R. vol. 5, 900; Taylor, *General Lee*, 31. The crest of Sewell Mountain is more than three thousand feet above sea level.
496. R.E. Lee to his wife, October 7, 1861 in Dowdey, *Wartime Papers*, 80; O.R. vol. 51 pt. 2, 335; O.R. vol. 5, 253, 615; Freeman, *Lee*, vol. 1, 596–97. The turnpike supply line for Rosecrans was nearly as lengthy as that for Lee. Sewell Mountain was thirty-five miles east of Gauley Bridge and twenty-five miles farther from Rosecrans's steamboat landings on the Kanawha River, leaving about sixty miles of rough wagon road for the Federals. See Cox, "McClellan in West Virginia," 147.

497. *Richmond Examiner*, October 11, 1861; R.E. Lee to his wife, October 7, 1861 in Dowdey, *Wartime Papers*, 80.

498. *O.R.* vol. 51, pt. 2, 337–38, 347; *Richmond Daily Dispatch*, October 22, 1861 in Freeman, *Lee*, vol. 1, 599.

499. *O.R.* vol. 51, pt. 2, 338, 361, 404; *O.R.* vol. 5, 253–59; Cox, "McClellan in West Virginia," 148.

500. *O.R.* vol. 51, pt. 2, 362; Freeman, *Lee*, vol. 1, 577; R.E. Lee to his daughter Mildred, November 15, 1861 in Dowdey, *Wartime Papers*, 86. Biographer Douglas S. Freeman wrote, "It is impossible to say precisely" when Lee stopped shaving, but he had a full beard on October 30 when son Rob met him in Charlottesville.

501. Freeman, *Lee*, vol. 1, 644–47; Broun, "General R.E. Lee's War-Horse," 292; Lee, Jr., *Recollections and Letters*, 82–84.

502. Pollard, *Southern History of the War*, 168; Lee, *General Lee*, 125.

503. J. Cutler Andrews, *The South Reports the Civil War* in McKinney, *Robert E. Lee and the 35th Star*, 98; Freeman, *Lee*, vol. 1, 602.

504. Lee, *General Lee*, 125; Lee, Jr., *Recollections and Letters*, 53.

505. Dowdey, *Wartime Papers*, 84, 86; Lee, Jr. *Recollections and Letters*, 53.

506. Augustus Van Dyke letter, October 18, 1861, IHS; Landon, "The Fourteenth Indiana Regiment," 368–69.

507. Merrill, *The Soldier of Indiana*, 118–23.

508. Ibid., 124–25.

509. Ibid., 126–31.

510. Ibid., 132–34.

Chapter 20. A Touch of Loyal Thunder and Lightning

511. Price, "Plain Tales of Mountain Trails," 461; Taliaferro, "Annals of the War," 5; Hull, "Recollections," *The Pocahontas Times*, March 12, 1908.

512. Osborne Wilson Diary, August 13, 1861 in Price, *On to Grafton*, 47; Stevenson, *Indiana's Roll of Honor*, 189; "The Battle of the Greenbrier," *Augusta Daily Chronicle & Sentinel*, October 8, 1861.

513. Letter to the *Southern Confederacy*, September 19, 1861; *O.R.* vol. 5, 224–25. Camp Bartow, also known as "Greenbrier River" in correspondence, was named for the martyred Colonel Francis S. Bartow of Georgia. Confusion over the origin of the name has resulted from the fact that a West Point-trained officer of the Third Arkansas Infantry named Seth Barton laid out the works. *See also* Robson, *How A One-Legged Rebel Lives*, 17; *O.R.* vol. 5, 228.

514. *O.R.* vol. 5, 603–05; Stevenson, *Indiana's Roll of Honor*, 185–87. Union General Reynolds was reinforced in September by the Seventh and Ninth Indiana Regiments (reenlisted as three-year units), the Thirty-second Ohio Infantry, Howe's Battery of the Fourth U.S. Artillery, Bracken's Indiana cavalry, and Greenfield's Pennsylvania cavalry.

515. U.S. Congress, "Rosecrans' Campaigns," vol. 3, 10; Augustus Van Dyke to Angie, September 29, 1861, Van Dyke Letters, IHS; Stevenson, *Indiana's Roll of Honor*, 184; Skidmore, *The Civil War Journal of Billy Davis*, 78; E.H.C. Cavins to his wife, September 27, 1861 in Smith, *The Civil War Letters of Elijah H.C. Cavins*, 17; Pool, *Under Canvas*, 45.

516. *O.R.* vol. 5, 220; "Armed Reconnaissance on Camp Bartow," *Cincinnati Daily Commercial*, October 9, 1861; "Cincinnati 'Times' Narrative," Moore, *Rebellion Record*, vol. 3, Documents, 161–62; Landon, "The Fourteenth Indiana Regiment," 366; Stevenson, *Indiana's Roll of Honor*, 188. The attacking force, in order of march, consisted of the Ninth and Fourteenth Indiana Infantry, the Twenty-fourth Ohio Infantry, the Seventeenth Indiana Infantry, Captain Loomis's Battery, First Michigan Light Artillery with six 10-pounder Parrott rifles, the Thirteenth Indiana Infantry, Captain Howe's Fourth U.S. Artillery, Battery G, with four bronze 6-pounders and two 12-pounder howitzers, the Seventh Indiana Infantry, Captain Daum's First (U.S.) Virginia Artillery, Battery A with a 6-pounder gun, along with a reserve of the Fifteenth Indiana Infantry, Twenty-fifth Ohio Infantry, parts of Bracken's Indiana, Robinson's Ohio, and Greenfield's Pennsylvania cavalry. The Thirty-second Ohio Infantry and a second gun of Captain Daum's battery were previously detached to hold the "Gum road," a troublesome intersection along the Staunton-Parkersburg Turnpike.

517. "Armed Reconnaissance on Camp Bartow," *Cincinnati Daily Commercial*, October 9, 1861; Hays, *History of the Thirty-second Regiment*, 14; Diary of Co. A., Thirty-second Ohio Infantry, 11–12, Jacob Pinock Papers, WVU.

518. Charles L. Campbell Diary, October 3, 1861 in Price, *On to Grafton*, 56; "Letter from Western Virginia!" *Indianapolis Daily Journal*, October 14, 1861. Three Confederate pickets were reportedly killed in this skirmish; one of the fallen Federals may have been killed by friendly fire.

519. Warner, *Generals in Gray*, 158; Cammack, *Personal Recollections*, 41; Hull, "Recollections," *The Pocahontas Times*, September 10, 1908; Hermann, *Memoirs*, 65; Chesnut, *A Diary From Dixie*, 299–300.

520. Hull, "Recollections," *The Pocahontas Times*, September 10, 1908; *O.R.* vol. 5, 224; "Particulars of the Late Fight," *Southern Confederacy*, October 17, 1861.

521. Hotchkiss, *Virginia*, 169; Phillips, "History of Valley Furnace," *Barbour Democrat*, September 4, 1968.

522. *O.R.* vol. 5, 225–26, 230; "Battle at Camp Bartow," *Lynchburg Daily Virginian*, October 11, 1861. On the Confederate right flank, General Jackson's force consisted of the First and Twelfth Georgia Regiments and a few members of the Churchville (VA) Cavalry. Anchoring the center were the Twenty-third and Forty-fourth Virginia Regiments, along with Major Reger's battalion of the Twenty-fifth Virginia Infantry, led in his absence by Captain John Higginbotham. On the Confederate left were the Third Arkansas Infantry, the Thirty-first Virginia Infantry, and Hansbrough's Ninth Virginia Battalion. Captain Pierce Anderson's Lee Battery posted two guns on the Huntersville (Green Bank) road on the left, while Captain Lindsey Shumaker of the Danville Artillery commanded a battery of four 6-pounder guns and Captain William Rice a single 6-pounder on the center and right flank.

523. "Armed Reconnaissance on Camp Bartow," *Cincinnati Daily Commercial*, October 9, 1861; O.R. vol. 5, 231; Letter to the *Wheeling Daily Intelligencer*, October 7, 1861; Switlik, "Loomis' Battery," 17–18.

524. "Armed Reconnaissance on Camp Bartow," *Cincinnati Daily Commercial*, October 9, 1861; *O.R.* vol. 5, 226, 234; J. T. Wilder to his wife, October 5,

1861 in Williams, "General John T. Wilder," 172; Augustus Van Dyke to his folks, October 6, 1861, Van Dyke Letters, IHS; Clayton Wilson to his father, October 4, 1861, PC. Confederate General Henry Jackson's report described only eight Federal cannons. The 6-pounder gun used by Capt. Daum's battery of the First (U.S.) Virginia Light Artillery was reportedly one captured at the battle of Rich Mountain.

525. "Cincinnati 'Times' Narrative," Moore, *Rebellion Record*, vol. 3, Documents, 163; Landon, "The Fourteenth Indiana Regiment," 367; *O.R.* vol. 5, 226.

526. "Cincinnati 'Times' Narrative," Moore, *Rebellion Record*, vol. 3, Documents, 163; William Houghton to his parents, October 4, 1861, Houghton Papers, IHS; "Description of the Battle of Greenbrier River, October 3d, 1861," manuscript by C.S. Morgan, WVSA.

527. *O.R.* vol. 5, 226–27, 233; "Battle at Camp Bartow," *Lynchburg Daily Virginian*, October 11, 1861.

528. James Atkins Diary, October 3, 1861, GDAH; Stevenson, *Indiana's Roll of Honor*, 192; Thomson, *Narrative of the Seventh Indiana Infantry*, 54.

529. Frank Ingersoll to his sister, October 8, 1861, Ingersoll letters, Lilly Library, IU; "Cincinnati 'Times' Narrative," Moore, *Rebellion Record*, vol. 3, Documents, 165; Landon, "The Fourteenth Indiana Regiment," 368.

530. Irby Scott to his father, October 5, 1861, Irby G. Scott Letters, DU; Cammack, *Personal Recollections*, 38–39; "The Battle of Greenbrier River," *Richmond Daily Dispatch*, October 12, 1861.

531. James Atkins Diary, October 4, 1861, GDAH.

532. *O.R.* vol. 5, 234–35; "Armed Reconnaissance on Camp Bartow," *Cincinnati Daily Commercial*, October 9, 1861; Pool, *Under Canvas*, 49. Confederate Capt. Pierce Anderson's guns on the Huntersville road were not engaged.

533. "Cincinnati 'Times' Narrative," Moore, *Rebellion Record*, vol. 3, Documents, 164; Landon, "The Fourteenth Indiana Regiment," 367–68.

534. *O.R.* vol. 5, 223, 227, 232, 235; Thomson, *Narrative of the Seventh Indiana Infantry*, 55; J.T. Wilder to his wife, October 5, 1861 in Williams, "General John T. Wilder," 173. One correspondent reported that the Seventh Indiana Infantry "broke and ran," sparking controversy that triggered an amusing rebuttal. The ranking officers of three sister regiments ultimately weighed in to swear they had seen "no running" by Dumont's Hoosiers that day! See "Letter to the Editor," *Cincinnati Daily Times*, October 14, 1861 in Harris Milroy Papers, IHS.

535. *O.R.* vol. 5, 221, 227; "Cincinnati 'Times' Narrative," Moore, *Rebellion Record*, vol. 3, Documents, 164; John D.H. Ross to Agnes Reid, October 5, 1861 in Oram, "Letters of Colonel John De Hart Ross," 167; "From the First Georgia Regiment—The Battle of the Greenbrier," *Augusta Daily Chronicle & Sentinel*, October 11, 1861.

536. *O.R.* vol. 5, 221, 224; "The Battle of Greenbrier River," *Augusta Daily Constitutionalist*, October 11, 1861; Letter of Lucian Barber, October 16, 1861, Lucian Barber Papers, LC.

537. Hall, *Diary of a Confederate Soldier*, 29; Irby Scott to his father, October 5, 1861, Irby Scott Letters, DU; "Armed Reconnaissance on Camp Bartow," *Cincinnati Daily Commercial*, October 9, 1861; Cammack, *Personal Recollections*, 38. The Cincinnati Daily Commercial tallied Federal artillery fire as follows: Loomis' Battery—more than six hundred rounds; Howe's

Battery—four hundred rounds; Daum's gun—eighty-five rounds. Other counts placed the total at 1,500 rounds or more. *See also* "Cincinnati 'Times' Narrative," Moore, *Rebellion Record*, vol. 3, Documents, 165; Ben May to his brother, October 5, 1861, PC.

538. *O.R.* vol. 5, 221, 223, 227–29.

539. Pool, *Under Canvas*, 54.

540. "From the First Georgia Regiment—The Battle of the Greenbrier," *Augusta Daily Chronicle and Sentinel*, October 11, 1861; Clayton Wilson to his father, October 4, 1861, PC. A detailed account of the "Lost Flag" story may be found in Thomson, *Narrative of the Seventh Indiana Infantry*, 56–58.

541. Clayton Wilson to his father, October 4, 1861, PC; Bierce, *Ambrose Bierce's Civil War*, 5–6; Hewitt, *Supplement to the Official Records*, pt. 2, vol. 16, 16. Bierce's tale may be embellished, but the circumstances of Abbott's death are well documented.

542. *O.R.* vol. 5, 220–21; Bierce, *Ambrose Bierce's Civil War*, 5; Ben May to his brother, December 2, 1861; "Cincinnati 'Times' Narrative," Moore, *Rebellion Record*, vol. 3, Documents, 166; "From Beverly," *Wheeling Daily Intelligencer*, October 10, 1861.

543. "Special Order No. 15, Army of the Northwest," *Richmond Daily Dispatch*, October 8, 1861; *O.R.* vol. 5, 224–31, 236; Clark, *Under the Stars and Bars*, 32.

544. "From the First Georgia Regiment—The Battle of the Greenbrier," *Augusta Daily Chronicle and Sentinel*, October 11, 1861; Price, *History of Pocahontas County*, 445.

Chapter 21. The Great Question

545. Commeti and Summers, *The Thirty-Fifth State*, 365; Hall, *Rending*, 384–86.

546. Ibid., 387–88; Moore, *Banner*, 134–35; "The Virginia 'Division' Election," *Wheeling Daily Intelligencer*, October 31, 1861; Arnold, "Beverly in the Sixties, 72–73. A total of 273 affirmative votes for the statehood referendum were cast by members of the Third (U.S.) Virginia Infantry, polled in camp at Beverly.

547. Moore, "A Confederate Journal," 207–08; Joseph Snider Diary, October 18, 1861, WVU; Worsham, *One of Jackson's Foot Cavalry*, 20–21.

548. *O.R.* vol. 5, 616, 644; Pool, *Under Canvas*, 56–57.

549. "From Greenbrier River," *Richmond Daily Dispatch*, October 30, 1861; "From Western Virginia," *Cincinnati Daily Gazette*, November 22, 1861; *O.R.* vol. 5, 290–91, 338, 378–80, 625, 644.

550. Sears, *Civil War Papers of George McClellan*, 112; Sears, *George B. McClellan*, 118, 134; Moore, *Rebellion Record*, vol. 3, Diary, 85; *Harper's Weekly*, December 7, 1861.

551. Sears, *George B. McClellan*, 118; Sears, *Civil War Papers of George McClellan*, 81, 87, 103, 112.

552. *O.R.* vol. 51, pt. 1, 491–93; "General Scott Retires from Active Service," *Wheeling Daily Intelligencer*, November 2, 1861; *O.R.* vol. 5, 639.

553. Hay, *Lincoln and the Civil War*, 32–33.

554. Sears, *Civil War Papers of George McClellan*, 106, 113–14, 135–36.

555. Ibid., 112, 114, 122–24; *Wheeling Daily Intelligencer*, November 9, 1861.

556. Hannaford, *The Story of a Regiment*, 145; Beatty, *The Citizen-Soldier*, 80; "From Beverly," *Wheeling Daily Intelligencer*, October 22, 1861.

557. "From Cheat Mountain," *Indianapolis Daily Journal*, September 16, 1861; Ben May to his brother, November 22, 1861, PC; Hall, *Diary of a Confederate Soldier*, 31–32; Adams, *A Post of Honor*, 103, 107.

558. Diary of Co. A, 32nd Ohio Infantry, 14, Jacob Pinock Papers, WVU; Worsham, *One of Jackson's Foot Cavalry*, 21–22; Bierce, *Ambrose Bierce's Civil War*, 6. A large black bear, trapped by a soldier on Cheat Mountain, was transported alive and put on display in Wheeling! *See also* "A Big Black Bear," *Wheeling Daily Intelligencer*, November 29, 1861.

559. Beatty, *The Citizen-Soldier*, 69–70; William Houghton to his father, November 2, 1861, Houghton Papers, IHS; Hall, *Diary of a Confederate Soldier*, 25.

560. Adams, *A Post of Honor*, 107, 117; Beatty, *The Citizen-Soldier*, 78, 80–81; Pool, *Under Canvas*, 54–55.

561. Narrative, 37, Robert H. Milroy Papers, IHS; Alf. Welton Diary, October 21, 1861, LC; "Extracts from a Letter Written Home," *Wheeling Daily Intelligencer*, October 30, 1861.

562. Ben May to his brother, December 12, 1861, PC; Boston *Advertiser* in *Cincinnati Daily Enquirer*, October 11, 1861.

563. Augustus Van Dyke to his father, August 29, 1861, Van Dyke Letters, IHS; James Atkins Diary, December 4, 1861, GDAH.

564. "Letter from the Fourteenth," *Indianapolis Daily Journal*, November 25, 1861; "Our Army in Western Virginia," Kirkpatrick Family Scrapbook, ISL.

565. "Letter from Cheat Mountain," *Cincinnati Daily Commercial*, October 3, 1861; "The Situation in Western Virginia," *Indianapolis Daily Journal*, October 12, 1861; "Blankets for the Oglethorpe Infantry," *Augusta Daily Chronicle & Sentinel*, October 12, 1861.

566. "The War in Virginia," *Cincinnati Daily Gazette*, October 30, 1861; J.W. Ross to his wife, September 15, 1861, PC; Augustus Van Dyke to his father, August 29, 1861, Van Dyke Letters, IHS.

567. "From Camp Bartow," *Richmond Daily Dispatch*, November 13, 1861; "From Cheat Mountain," *Wheeling Daily Intelligencer*, October 22, 1861; Parson Parker, "Sufferings of the Twelfth Georgia Reg't, in the Mountains of Virginia," WVSA; "The Fourteenth Georgia Regiment," *Augusta Daily Constitutionalist*, November 15, 1861.

568. William Houghton Diary, November 8, 1861, Houghton Papers, IHS: Adams, *A Post of Honor*, 99; Ben May to his brother, October 5, 1861, PC.

569. Hannaford, *The Story of a Regiment*, 142; Pool, *Under Canvas*, 57–58; Adams, *The Pryor Letters*, 64, 111; Beatty, *The Citizen-Soldier*, 82; "Our Cheat Mountain Correspondence," *Indianapolis Daily Journal*, October 9, 1861.

570. "A Bad Egg for a Sutler," *Wheeling Daily Intelligencer*, October 25, 1861; Ben May to his brother, December 12, 1861, PC; Joseph Snider Diary, October 30, 1861, Snider Papers, WVU; Hall, *Diary of a Confederate Soldier*, 35–36.

571. Hermann, *Memoirs of a Veteran*, 54–55; Clark, *Under the Stars and Bars*, 37; James Atkins Diary, November 17, 1861, GDAH.

572. Ben May to his brother, November 22, 1861, PC; Hays, *History of the Thirty-second Regiment*, 15; "Report of Rev. Gordon Battelle," *Wheeling Daily Intelligencer*, November 18, 1861; Bierce, *Ambrose Bierce's Civil War*, 6; Diary of Co. A, 32nd Ohio Infantry, 13, Jacob Pinock Papers, WVU; Hermann, *Memoirs of a Veteran*, 55; "From Beverly," *Wheeling Daily*

Intelligencer, November 6, 1861; Augustus Van Dyke to his father, October 26, 1861, Van Dyke Papers, IHS.

573. Skidmore, *The Civil War Journal of Billy Davis*, 80; "The Fourteenth Georgia Regiment," *Augusta Daily Constitutionalist*, November 15, 1861; "Letter from Western Virginia," *Indianapolis Daily Journal*, November 8, 1861; "Letter from the Fourteenth," *Indianapolis Daily Journal*, November 25, 1861.

574. *O.R.* vol. 5, 900, 943; "From Jackson's Brigade," *Augusta Daily Constitutionalist*, October 2, 1861; "The Fourteenth Georgia Regiment," *Augusta Daily Constitutionalist*, November 15, 1861; Tucker Randolph Diary, October 25, 1861, MC.

575. *O.R.* vol. 5, 909, 913, 933, 937–40, 965–66, 968–69. Confederate authorities created the Valley District, Department of Northern Virginia, on October 22, 1861. This new district embraced "the section of country between the Blue Ridge and the Alleghany Mountains."

576. *O.R.* vol. 51, pt. 2, 382–83; James Atkins Diary, November 22, 1861, GDAH; "From the Alleghany Mountains," *Richmond Daily Dispatch*, November 30, 1861; Irby Scott to his father, November 26, 1861, Irby Scott letters, DU; "From the 12th Georgia Regiment," *Augusta Daily Chronicle & Sentinel*, December 17, 1861.

577. *O.R.* vol. 51, pt. 2, 388; *O.R.* vol. 5, 460, 968, 975; Adams, *A Post of Honor*, 117.

578. *O.R.* vol. 5, 644, 669–71, 691; Hannaford, *The Story of a Regiment*, 157; Merrill, *The Soldier of Indiana*, 97; Letter to the *Indianapolis Daily Journal*, December 10, 1861.

Chapter 22. Night Clothes and a War Club

579. James Atkins Diary, December 11, 1861, GDAH; Price, "Guerrilla Warfare," 248. Camp Allegheny, often spelled "Alleghany," was also known as "Camp Baldwin" in honor of John B. Baldwin, colonel of the Fifty-second Virginia Infantry and a respected state politician.

580. Gen. Orders No. 17, Army of N.W., December 10, 1861, Edward Willis Papers, HL; *O.R.* vol. 5, 989–90.

581. "War Recollections," Evelyn Yeager Beard, *The Pocahontas Times*, November 25, 1926; Bierce, *Battlefields and Ghosts*, 16; "The Army of the Northwest," *Richmond Daily Dispatch*, September 7, 1861.

582. Keifer, *Slavery and Four Years*, vol. 1, 311, 316; Boatner, *Civil War Dictionary*, 552; Reader, *History of the Fifth West Virginia Cavalry*, 159.

583. Merrill, *The Soldier of Indiana*, 95.

584. Stevenson, *Indiana's Roll of Honor*, 194–95; *O.R.* vol. 5, 461; Thomas Prickett to Matilda, December 9, 1861, Prickett Papers, IHS; "History of Valley Furnace," *The Barbour Democrat*, September 4, 1968; Poe, *Personal Reminiscences*, 11. The five Confederate deserters, all members of Hansbrough's Ninth Battalion, Virginia Infantry, were said to be Jeff Glenn, Doc Rogers, Wm. Lynn, Eugene Murphy, and Andy Murphy.

585. "The Battle of Alleghany Summit," *Wheeling Daily Intelligencer*, December 24, 1861; Hays, *History of the Thirty-second Regiment*, 16–17; "Full Account of the Late Battle in Western Virginia," *Indianapolis Daily Journal*, December 25, 1861.

586. *O.R.* vol. 51, pt. 1, 51. General Milroy listed his force as follows: seven hundred members of the Ninth Indiana Infantry under Col. Gideon Moody; four hundred of the Twenty-fifth Ohio Infantry, Col. James Jones; two hundred and fifty of the Second (U.S.) Virginia Infantry, Major James Owens; three hundred of the Thirteenth Indiana Infantry, Major Cyrus Dobbs; one hundred and thirty of the Thirty-second Ohio Infantry, Captain William Hamilton; thirty of Captain James Bracken's Indiana cavalry, and seventy-five members of Rigby's Indiana artillery.

587. "Joseph R.T. Gordon," Julia Dumont Gordon Scrapbook, ISL; *O.R.* vol. 51, pt. 1, 51; "Full Account of the Late Battle in Western Virginia," *Indianapolis Daily Journal*, December 25, 1861; Bierce, *Ambrose Bierce's Civil War*, 8.

588. *O.R.* vol. 51, pt. 1, 51; Stevenson, *Indiana's Roll of Honor*, 196–97.

589. Bierce, *Ambrose Bierce's Civil War*, 8; Hays, *History of the Thirty-second Regiment*, 18; Hamilton, *Recollections*, 23.

590. *O.R.* vol. 5, 462; Price, "Rich Mountain in 1861," 42; "A Notable War Club," *Richmond Examiner*, January 7, 1862; James C. Gamble to his brother, December 20, 1861, PC; Robson, *How a One-Legged Rebel Lives*, 20. The *Richmond Daily Dispatch*, December 18, 1861, reported that Colonel Johnson "appeared on the field in the dress of a wagoner."

591. *O.R.* vol. 5, 460, 462–63; Adam W. Kersh to his brother, October 20, 1861, Adam W. Kersh Letters, MML.

592. Hall, *The Diary of a Confederate Soldier*, 41; Poe, *Personal Reminiscences*, 12; *O.R.* vol. 5, 457, 466; James Atkins Diary, December 13, 1861, GDAH.

593. Letter from W.W. Hardwicke, *Richmond Whig*, December 20, 1861; *O.R.* vol. 5, 466; Hays, *History of the Thirty-second Regiment*, 19.

594. *O.R.* vol. 5, 462; Cammack, *Personal Recollections*, 42; *O.R.* vol. 51, pt. 1, 52; Hays, *History of the Thirty-second Regiment*, 19.

595. Ibid., 19; Hall, *The Diary of a Confederate Soldier*, 41; Joseph Snider Diary, December 13, 1861, WVU.

596. "War Recollections," Evelyn Yeager Beard, *The Pocahontas Times*, November 25, 1926; *O.R.* vol. 51, pt. 1, 52; James M. King Journal, 91–92, IHS; Robson, *How a One-Legged Rebel Lives*, 21.

597. Joseph Snider Diary, December 13, 1861, WVU; Letter to the *Richmond Daily Dispatch*, December 18, 1861; *O.R.* vol. 5, 458, 462–63; *O.R.* vol. 51, pt. 1, 52–54; "Battle of Camp Alleghany, Va.," Moore, *Rebellion Record*, vol. 3, Documents, 467. During close-quarters fighting on the Confederate right flank, artillerists fired mostly at Milroy's reserve and wagons along the turnpike.

598. *O.R.* vol. 51, pt. 1, 53; "Greenbank Community History," R.W. Brown, *The Pocahontas Times*, July 18, 1935; "Battle of Camp Alleghany, Va.," Moore, *Rebellion Record*, vol. 3, Documents, 467; Bierce, *Battlefields and Ghosts*, 14; *O.R.* vol. 5, 463.

599. Bierce, *Ambrose Bierce's Civil War*, 7; *O.R.* vol. 5, 463; "The Battle on the Alleghany," *Macon Daily Telegraph*, January 4, 1862; "War Recollections," Evelyn Yeager Beard, *The Pocahontas Times*, November 25, 1926; Letter to the *Richmond Daily Dispatch*, December 23, 1861.

600. Stevenson, *Indiana's Roll of Honor*, 201–02; "The Battle of Alleghany Summit," *Wheeling Daily Intelligencer*, December 24, 1861; Letter from J. Chilcott, *Indianapolis Daily Journal*, January 1, 1862.

601. Bierce, *Battlefields and Ghosts*, 15; "Full Account of the Late Battle in Western Virginia," *Indianapolis Daily Journal*, December 25, 1861; "Joseph R.T. Gordon," Julia Dumont Gordon Scrapbook, ISL: Stevenson, *Indiana's Roll of Honor*, 202; Merrill, *The Soldier of Indiana*, 98. Lt. Colonel Z.T. Connor of the Twelfth Georgia Infantry reported a timber barricade extended to "within 50 paces" of the Confederate earthworks.

602. "The Battle on the Alleghany," *Macon Daily Telegraph*, January 4, 1861; "The Battle of Alleghany Summit," *Wheeling Daily Intelligencer*, December 24, 1861.

603. Robson, *How a One-Legged Rebel Lives*, 21; "Captain John Miller," Letter to *The Pocahontas Times*, February 18, 1904; *O.R.* vol. 5, 460. During the battle, Captain Miller ignored the protests of a Confederate officer, seated in advance, that his guns were "firing too low!" The good captain was later acquitted of a "reckless shooting" charge. Imagine his consternation afterward upon finding a grape shot embedded in a tree not three inches above the offended officer's head. The incriminating tree was promptly chopped down!

604. *O.R.* vol. 51, pt. 1, 53; Hamilton, *Recollections*, 28; Hays, *History of the Thirty-second Regiment*, 20; Bierce, *Ambrose Bierce's Civil War*, 8–9.

605. Bierce, *Battlefields and Ghosts*, 13; "The Battle at Alleghany Summit—Great Exaggerations...," *Wheeling Daily Intelligencer*, December 23, 1861; Frank Ingersoll to his sister, December 15, 1861, Ingersoll Letters, IU.

606. "The Battle of the Alleghany," *Macon Daily Telegraph*, January 4, 1862; *O.R.* vol. 51, pt. 1, 54; Geiger, "Holding the Line," 75.

607. *O.R.* vol. 5, 457, 459–60, 468; Hall, *The Diary of a Confederate Soldier*, 41–42, Robson, *How a One-Legged Rebel Lives*, 24; Geiger, "Holding the Line," 73; *Richmond Dispatch* Account, Moore, *Rebellion Record*, vol. 3, Documents, 470. Most accounts place the engagement at Camp Allegheny between approximately 7 A.M. and 2 P.M. Official returns for the Federals include 20 killed, 107 wounded, and 10 missing for a total of 137. Confederate losses were 20 killed, 98 wounded, and 28 missing, a total of 146. Research by Joe Geiger, Jr. indicates actual Federal losses to have been 143; Confederate, 162.

608. Cammack, *Personal Recollections*, 42; Letter to the *Richmond Daily Dispatch*, December 23, 1861; Ross, "Old Memories," 158–59.

609. "Joseph R.T. Gordon," Julia Dumont Gordon Scrapbook, ISL; J.W. Gordon to G.W. Julian, February 8, 1862, George W. Julian Papers, ISL; "Obsequies," *Indianapolis Daily Journal*, December 21, 1861.

610. Robson, *How a One-Legged Rebel Lives*, 21–22; T.D. Ranson to his cousin, December 27, 1861, Stuart Family Papers, VHS; Letter to the *Richmond Daily Dispatch*, December 18, 1861; "The Battle of Alleghany Mountain," *Augusta Daily Chronicle & Sentinel*, December 19, 1861; Letter to the *Richmond Daily Dispatch*, December 23, 1861. Along with his club, Ed Johnson reportedly carried a musket through much of the battle at Camp Allegheny.

611. "A Notable War Club," *Richmond Examiner*, January 7, 1862; *O.R.* vol. 5, 459; Robson, *How a One-Legged Rebel Lives*, 23; Chesnut, *A Diary From Dixie*, 299.

Chapter 23. Cold as the North Pole

612. *O.R.* vol. 5, 459; Jacob Pinock to William, October 15, 1861, Pinock Papers, WVU; Robert Hatton to his wife, November 2, 1861 in Drake, *Life of General Robert Hatton*, 382.

613. Diary of Co. A, 32nd Ohio Infantry, 14, Pinock Papers, WVU; William Batts to his sister, November 28, 1861, William Batts letters, EU.

614. Hall, *Diary of a Confederate Soldier*, 43.

615. W.A. Hawkins to A.H. Stephens, January 22, 1861, Alexander H. Stephens Papers, EU; Schuyler Colfax to G.B. McClellan, December 12, 1861, Schuyler Colfax Papers, IHS.

616. Lewis, *How West Virginia Was Made*, 318–319; Hall, *Rending of Virginia*, 397, 404; "The New State," *Wheeling Daily Intelligencer*, August 26, 1861.

617. Curry, *A House Divided*, 86–88; Hall, *Rending of Virginia*, 407, 409–10; Ambler, Atwood and Mathews, *Debates and Proceedings*, vol. 1, 438.

618. Hall, *Rending of Virginia*, 415–16, 421, 425, 429; Curry, *A House Divided*, 90–91; *Wheeling Daily Intelligencer*, December 9, 1861.

619. Lewis, *How West Virginia Was Made*, 320–21; Basler, *The Collected Works of Abraham Lincoln*, vol. 5, 50.

620. Hall, *Diary of a Confederate Soldier*, 42–43.

621. *O.R.* vol. 5, 496–99.

622. Dabney, *Life and Campaigns*, 242–43; *O.R.* vol. 5, 965–66, 1004–05; Worsham, *One of Jackson's Foot Cavalry*, 24; Toney, *Privations*, 26.

623. *O.R.* vol. 5, 1004; Toney, *Privations*, 28; Watkins, *"Company Aytch,"* 56; Porterfield, "A Narrative," 90.

624. *O.R.* vol. 5, 390–93, 1066; Walter A. Clark Diary, January 2–4, 1862, PC; Lavender Ray to his brother, January 12, 1862 in Lane, *Letters From Georgia Soldiers*, 90–93; Toney, *Privations*, 31; Watkins, *"Company Aytch,"* 57–58, 62. Moore, *Rebellion Record*, vol. 4, Documents, 15–16. "I ask you in all candor not to doubt the following lines," Sam Watkins wrote of the "Death Watch." Although the story is apocryphal, other accounts give mention of individual soldiers freezing to death that winter. More than one Confederate wrote of temperatures near twenty below zero on the march to Romney, yet weather records do not confirm it. Temperatures can vary greatly in that region. One thing is clear—it was bitterly cold!

625. *O.R.* vol. 5, 392, 1034, 1036, 1047; Watkins, *"Company Aytch,"* 57.

626. *O.R.* vol. 5, 1041–42, 1046–48.

627. Ibid., 1053, 1062–63, 1065–66.

628. Ibid., 1066–68, 1076, 1079; Warner, *Generals in Gray*, 194; Imboden, "Stonewall Jackson," 301.

629. Watkins, *"Company Aytch,"* 56–57; Hall, *Diary of a Confederate Soldier*, 46; James Atkins Diary, January 6, 1862, GDAH; "From the Alleghany Mountains," *Richmond Daily Dispatch*, November 30, 1861; Parker, "Sufferings of the Twelfth Georgia Reg't,…" WVSA.

630. Adam Kersh to his brother, January 29, 1862, Adam W. Kersh Letters, MML; James Atkins Diary, January 3, 19, 24, 1862, GDAH; Hall, *Diary of a Confederate Soldier*, 46–47; Reader, *History of the Fifth West Virginia Cavalry*, 126.

631. James Atkins Diary, January 18, 22, 1862, GDAH; Hall, *Diary of a Confederate Soldier*, 46, 48–49; Reader, *History of the Fifth West Virginia*

Cavalry, 126, 153–54; Parker, "Sufferings of the Twelfth Georgia Reg't,..." WVSA.

632. McClellan, *McClellan's Own Story*, 150–51, 154, 162; Sears, *George B. McClellan*, 131, 135; Hay, *Lincoln and the Civil War*, 34–35; Nicolay and Hay, *Abraham Lincoln*, vol. 4, 469n.

633. Sears, *George B. McClellan*, 136, 140–41, 143–45, 147, 154; McClellan, *McClellan's Own Story*, 195–96.

634. McClellan, *Report on the Organization*, 109, 118; Sears, *George B. McClellan*, 149–50, 154; 163–64, 167–68; *O.R.* vol. 5, 54; Ward, Burns and Burns, *The Civil War*, 92; Sears, *Civil War Papers of George McClellan*, 211.

635. Special Orders, No. 206, November 5, 1861, Dowdey, *Wartime Papers*, 84; Freeman, *Lee*, vol. 1, 606, 609–10; Chesnut, *A Diary From Dixie*, 164.

636. R.E. Lee to his wife, February 23, 1862 and March 14, 1862, Dowdey, *Wartime Papers*, 118, 127–28; Thomas, *Robert E. Lee*, 214; Hawkins, "Early Coast Operations," 645; Freeman, *Lee*, vol. 2, 6. Fort Donelson was named for Confederate General Samuel Donelson, who served under Lee in Western Virginia.

637. *O.R.* vol. 5, 922–33; *O.R.* vol. 51, pt. 2, 158; Freeman, *Lee*, vol. 2, 17.

Chapter 24. All's Fair in Love and War

638. "The War in Western Virginia," *Wheeling Daily Intelligencer*, October 2, 1861.

639. Rutherford B. Hayes to his mother, November 25, 1861 in Williams, *The Life of Rutherford Birchard Hayes*, vol. 1, 154.

640. Worsham, *One of Jackson's Foot Cavalry*, 23–24; Price, *History of Pocahontas County*, 445, 449–51; "War Recollections," Evelyn Yeager Beard, *The Pocahontas Times*, November 25, 1926.

641. Ben May to his brother, July 17, 1861, PC; Samuel V. Fulkerson to his sister, August 22, 1861, PC.

642. Hannaford, *The Story of a Regiment*, 539–41.

643. Beatty, *The Citizen-Soldier*, 16–17.

644. Siviter, *Recollections of War and Peace*, 78–80. Another version of this story can be found in Ambler, *Francis H. Pierpont*, 90–91.

645. "Rebel Ladies," *Cincinnati Daily Commercial*, July 19, 1861.

646. Hamilton, *Recollections of a Cavalryman*, 30; Reader, *History of the Fifth West Virginia Cavalry*, 136; Hannaford, *The Story of a Regiment*, 100–01n.

647. "Mother To the First Tennessee Regiment," 290; Quintard, *Doctor Quintard*, 18. Dr. Quintard recalled how Mrs. Sullivan took off her shoes and gave them to a barefoot soldier during the campaign in Western Virginia.

648. A Member of the Bar, *Cheat Mountain*, 46; *Cincinnati Daily Gazette*, November 26, 1862 in Christen, "Mrs. Van Pelt," 23–24; "Sent Up," *Wheeling Daily Intelligencer*, September 17, 1861.

649. Womack, *Civil War Diary*, July, 24, 1861; "Another Runaway," *Wheeling Daily Intelligencer*, July 19, 1861.

650. "No Women," *Wheeling Daily Intelligencer*, October 31, 1861; "Letter from Alf. Burnett," *Cincinnati Daily Commercial*, November 28, 1861; Dewitt C. Howard to P.S. Bishop, August 2, 1861, PC.

651. Matthew C. Dawson to his brother, January 28, 1862, James Dawson

Papers, OHS; Skidmore, *The Civil War Journal of Billy Davis*, 83–84.

652. Smith, *A View From the Ranks*, 24.

653. Cobb, "Story of Moses and Margaret Phillips," 32; Plum, *The Military Telegraph*, vol. 1, 107.

654. Cook, *Lewis County in the Civil War*, 152–55.

Chapter 25. Lincoln's Odd Trick

655. McClellan, *Report on the Organization*, 125; "Gen. Orders #4, Head-Quarters, Mountain Department. Wheeling, March 29, 1862," PC; Boatner, *Civil War Dictionary*, 314–315; Williams, *Lincoln and His Generals*, 77. General Frémont had been removed from a Missouri command in 1861 for reckless leadership and the unauthorized emancipation of slaves. But the Radicals in Congress declared him a martyr, and Lincoln yielded to their pressure by creating for him the Mountain Department. Abraham Lincoln's "War Order No. 3" defined the Mountain Department as "the country, west of the Department of the Potomac, and east of the Department of the Mississippi."

656. R.H. Milroy to his wife, April 4 and April 7, 1862, Milroy Papers, IHS; Adams, *A Post of Honor*, 152, 161–62; *O.R.* vol. 12, pt. 3, 828, 833–34; Hall, *Diary of a Confederate Soldier*, 50; "From Western Virginia—Milroy Advancing," *Indianapolis Daily Journal*, April 28, 1862; Reader, *History of the Fifth West Virginia Cavalry*, 161; Monfort, "From Grafton to McDowell," 11–12; Lang, *Loyal West Virginia*, 64–65. The vacated Confederate cabins at Camp Allegheny were reportedly left standing by Ed Johnson as a "favor" to the widowed Mrs. Yeager. General Milroy wrote that Johnson had been "courting" her!

657. *O.R.* 51, pt. 1, 566; Lewis, *How West Virginia Was Made*, 321–23; Hall, *Rending of Virginia*, 439. West Virginia's Constitution was ratified by a vote of 18,862 to 514. The small voter turnout was a topic of debate. Also much debated was a straw poll in several counties on the gradual emancipation of slaves. The results indicated nearly ten to one support for the measure—a surprise to many. See Ambler, *Francis H. Pierpont*, 172–73 and Curry, *A House Divided*, 97.

658. McClellan, "The Peninsular Campaign," 168; Downer, *Stonewall Jackson's Valley Campaign*, 24; Dowdey, *Wartime Papers*, 125–27, 179–81.

659. Lewis, *How West Virginia Was Made*, 325; Waitman T. Willey to Harrison Hagans, May 7, 1862 in Curry, *A House Divided*, 100.

660. Ambler, *Waitman Thomas Willey*, 77.

661. Hall, *Rending of Virginia*, 458–59, 463–67, 501; Waugh, *Reelecting Lincoln*, 225; Boatner, *Civil War Dictionary*, 818, 882; Lewis, *How West Virginia Was Made*, 326. The West Virginia statehood bill originally contained the names of forty-eight counties. Berkeley and Jefferson Counties were added to West Virginia in 1866; Mineral, Grant Lincoln, Summers, and Mingo Counties were added later, bringing the modern total to 55. *See also* Cometti and Summers, *The Thirty-fifth State*, 457–58 and Hagans, *Sketch of the Erection and Formation of the State of West Virginia*, 89–96.

662. McGregor, *Disruption*, 293–95, 297; Curry, *A House Divided*, 103; *Congressional Globe*, July 14, 1862 in Cometti and Summers, *The Thirty-fifth State*, 352–53.

663. Willey, *An Inside View*, 112–13; Hall, *Rending of Virginia*, 469.

664. *Congressional Globe*, 37th Congress, 2nd Session in Ambler, *Waitman Thomas Willey*, 86; Lewis, *How West Virginia Was Made*, 327. Ironically, Carlile and Willey had reversed their original positions on West Virginia statehood!

665. McGregor, *Disruption*, 300; Curry, *A House Divided*, 10, 108–09, 114–15, 138–39; *Cincinnati Daily Commercial*, September 4, 1861; Waugh, *Reelecting Lincoln*, 89–90; Smith, *The Borderland in the Civil War*, 329–30; Boatner, *Civil War Dictionary*, 864–65. Clement Vallandigham may have been the model for Edward Everett Hale's *Man Without a Country*.

666. *Wheeling Daily Intelligencer*, November 13, 1862 in Ambler, *Francis H. Pierpont*, 183; Curry, *A House Divided*, 107–08. Other leading figures abandoned the statehood movement upon adoption of the Willey Amendment, including John J. Davis, John S. Burdette, Sherrard Clemens, and Daniel Lamb.

667. Lewis, *How West Virginia Was Made*, 328; Boatner, *Civil War Dictionary*, 265; C.D. Hubbard to William Hubbard, November 11, 1862 in Curry, *A House Divided*, 98.

668. Lewis, *How West Virginia Was Made*, 328; Hall, *Rending of Virginia*, 483; *Congressional Globe*, 37th Congress in Curry, *A House Divided*, 122–23; *Wheeling Daily Intelligencer*, December 11, 1862; Ambler, *Francis H. Pierpont*, 184. The West Virginia legislature passed a resolution demanding Senator Carlile's resignation, but he refused to comply. See Hall, *Rending of Virginia*, 471–72.

669. Waugh, *Reelecting Lincoln*, 76, 79.

670. Shaffer, "Lincoln and the 'Vast Question' of West Virginia," 97–98; Randall and Pease, *The Diary of Orville Hickman Browning*, vol. 1, 600.

671. Edward Bates to A.F. Ritchie, August 12, 1861 in Lewis, *How West Virginia Was Made*, 219–20; *New York Times*, June 27, 1861 in Shaffer, "Lincoln and the 'Vast Question' of West Virginia," 88n; Hall, *Rending of Virginia*, 496.

672. Basler, *The Collected Works of Abraham Lincoln*, vol. 6, 17; Curry, *A House Divided*, 124; Hall, *Rending of Virginia*, 485, 490–94; Lewis, "How West Virginia Became a Member of the Federal Union," 605–06.

673. F.H. Pierpont to Abraham Lincoln, December 30, 1862 in Cometti and Summers, *The Thirty-fifth State*, 368.

674. *Wheeling Daily Intelligencer*, January 22, 1876 in Hall, *Rending of Virginia*, 497–98; Boyd B. Stutler, "Lincoln's Odd Trick," Stutler Collection, WVSA. Whist is a card game, the antecedent of Bridge.

675. Hall, *Rending of Virginia*, 496–98, 500, 504–05; Boyd B. Stutler, "Blair Enters Through White House Window," Stutler Collection, WVSA; Welch, "The Odd Trick," 139; Siviter, *Recollections of War and Peace*, 104–06; Basler, *The Collected Works of Abraham Lincoln*, vol. 6, 27–28; Lewis, *Second Biennial Report*, 201–02; *The Clarksburg Patriot*, March 20, 1863 in Curry, *A House Divided*, 128. Ten of the forty-eight counties included within the new state of West Virginia submitted no voting results on its amended constitution. The Thirteenth Amendment preempted West Virginia's gradual emancipation clause.

676. Ambler, *Waitman Thomas Willey*, 103; Siviter, *Recollections of War and Peace*, 94–95. Governor Pierpont's charred Bible was later pulled from the flames by a neighbor.

677. Ibid., 106, 108–09; Lewis, *How West Virginia Was Made*, 334–37; Curry, *A House Divided*, 137.

678. Lewis, *Third Biennial Report*, 205–06; Dickinson, *Tattered Uniforms*, 1–2, 409–10; Curry, *A House Divided*, 7–8, 53, 76–77, 167–68; Ambler, *Francis H. Pierpont*, 188. The estimate of twenty-eight thousand Federals to eighteen thousand Confederates in service from West Virginia closely matches scholar Richard Curry's calculation of a 60–40 percent split in favor of Unionists within the state.

Epilogue. Memories and Ghosts

679. Smith, *Borderland*, 218–20; Newell, *Lee vs. McClellan*, 266–68, Cox, *Military Reminiscences*, vol. 1, 145; Ambler, *Francis H. Pierpont*, 103.

680. Stevenson, *Indiana's Roll of Honor*, 224; Reader, *History of the Fifth West Virginia Cavalry*, 154; *O.R.* vol. 5, 229–30, 1046; Skidmore, *Civil War Journal of Billy Davis*, 92; Baxter, *Gallant Fourteenth*, 49; Culp, *The 25th Ohio Vet. Vol. Infantry*, 26.

681. Taylor, *Four Years*, 17; Van Dyke, "Early Days," 30.

682. Thomas, *Lee*, 210; Alexander, *Fighting for the Confederacy*, 91.

683. Freeman, *Lee*, vol. 2, 541–42; Taylor, *General Lee*, 32; Lee, *General Lee*, 126.

684. Ibid., 396; "The Monument to General Robert E. Lee," 244; Davis, "Robert E. Lee," 371; Lee, Jr., *Recollections and Letters*, 376–77; Long, *Memoirs of Robert E. Lee*, 456–57; Thomas, *Lee*, 380–81.

685. Cox, "McClellan in West Virginia," 136–37; Benham, *Recollections*, 689; *Cincinnati Daily Gazette*, April 1, 1862.

686. Sears, *George B. McClellan*, 169; Walker, "Jackson's Capture of Harper's Ferry," 605–06.

687. McPherson, *Battle Cry of Freedom*, 568; Sears, *George B. McClellan*, 331, 376, 388; *New York Tribune*, November 10, 1862; Williams, *Lincoln and His Generals*, 177; Waugh, *Class of 1846*, 519.

688. Guie, *Bugles in the Valley*, 145; Alexander, *Fighting for the Confederacy*, 49; Warner, *Generals in Gray*, 99; *Richmond Times-Dispatch*, October 13, 1985.

689. *Indianapolis News*, March 24, 1904, Stutler Collection, WVSA; Hannaford, *The Story of a Regiment*, 88–89; Sears, *George B. McClellan*, 421n.

690. Warner, *Generals in Blue*, 410–11; Reid, *Ohio in the War*, vol. 1, 348–49.

691. *O.R.* vol. 5, 669; Warner, *Generals in Blue*, 30; Boatner, *Civil War Dictionary*, 58–59.

692. Warner, *Generals in Gray*, 232; Griggs, *General John Pegram*, 92, 114.

693. *Lafayette Daily Journal*, April 5, 1862; Frame, "David B. Hart," 73–75.

694. Maxwell, *History of Randolph County*, 309; Fansler, *History of Tucker County*, 154n.

695. Warner, *Generals in Blue*, 260–61; Maxwell, *History of Barbour County*, 250.

696. Carnes, *J.E. Hanger*, n.p.; Carnes, *Centennial History*, 26.

697. Grebner, *"We Were the Ninth,"* xiii; Reid, *Ohio in the War*, vol. 2, 72–75.

698. Boatner, *Civil War Dictionary*, 690; Starr, *Bohemian Brigade*, 356.

699. Warner, *Generals in Gray*, 152; Robertson, *Stonewall Jackson*, 753, 760.

700. Boatner, *Civil War Dictionary*, 411; Ecelbarger, *Frederick W. Lander*, 122, 274, 278; *Cincinnati Daily Commercial*, March 12, 1862.

701. Reader, *History of the Fifth West Virginia Cavalry*, 157–59; Boatner, *Civil War Dictionary*, 552; Keifer, *Slavery and Four Years*, vol. 1, 315–16; Warner, *Generals in Blue*, 326.

702. Robert H. Milroy Papers, 37, IHS; Obituary of Richard Green in Entrepreneurship Class, *A Dish of History*, n.p.

703. Elwood, *Elwood's Stories*, 275; Armstrong, *25th Virginia Infantry*, 176.

704. Warner, *Generals in Gray*, 194; Boatner, *Civil War Dictionary*, 492; Quintard, *Doctor Quintard*, 53–54.

705. Hannaford, *The Story of a Regiment*, 158–59; Warner, *Generals in Blue*, 398; Boatner, *Civil War Dictionary*, 694–95.

706. Warner, *Generals in Blue*, 267–68; Boatner, *Civil War Dictionary*, 381.

707. Skidmore, *The Civil War Journal of Billy Davis*, i, 149, 156.

708. Cammack, *Personal Recollections*, 21–22, 153–56.

709. Warner, Generals in Gray, 150, 159;

710. Reader, *History of the Fifth West Virginia Cavalry*, 30–32; *Upshur Record*, December 20, 1917.

711. Siviter, *Recollections of War and Peace*, xvii, xx–xxiv; Myers, *Myers' History of West Virginia*, vol. 2, 296.

712. Willey, *An Inside View*, 190–97; *O.R.* ser. 2, vol. 3, 813; Ambler, *Waitman Thomas Willey*, 20n.

713. Hall, *Rending of Virginia*, 471–72; Curry, *A House Divided*, 140, 176n; Willey, *An Inside View*, 208–09.

714. Plum, *The Military Telegraph*, vol. 1, 105–06; Stutler, *West Virginia in the Civil War*, 43–48; Christen, "Mrs. Van Pelt," 23–24.

715. *O.R.* ser. 2, vol. 3, 218, 753, 775; Brigham, "The Civil War Journal of William B. Fletcher," 46–47; Hall, *Lee's Invasion*, 161–64; Lang, *Loyal West Virginia*, 195.

716. Warner, *Generals in Gray*, 90, 342; Hall, *Rending of Virginia*, 192; Ambler, *Francis H. Pierpont*, 212.

717. Warner, *Generals in Blue*, 28; Keifer, *Slavery and Four Years*, vol. 1, 208.

718. "Trainer of Traveler," 548–49; Deitz, "Ghost of Traveler," 13–18.

719. Toney, *Privations*, 69, 80, 122, 124.

720. Lang, *Loyal West Virginia*, 243.

721. Ashcraft, *31st Virginia Infantry*, preface; Cook, *Lewis County in the Civil War*, 117.

722. Hall, *Diary of a Confederate Soldier*, 137, 139.

723. Monfort, "From Grafton to McDowell," 19–20; Bierce, *Battlefields and Ghosts*, 16–17.

724. Pool, *Under Canvas*, 49–50. The verse is from "Lines on the Death of Serg't Price and Respectfully Inscribed to Co. A 14th Reg't Ind. V.M." by "W.H.A. Cheat Mountain, Va. Oct. 6, 1861." Sergeant J. Urner Price died of wounds received at the Battle of Greenbrier River.

BIBLIOGRAPHY

A Member of the Bar. *Cheat Mountain; or, Unwritten Chapter of the Late War.* Nashville, TN: Albert B. Tavel, Stationer and Printer, 1885.

"Active Service; or, Campaigning in Western Virginia." *Continental Monthly*, vol. 1 (March 1862): 330–38.

Adams, Charles R., Jr., ed. *A Post of Honor: The Pryor Letters, 1861–63.* Fort Valley, GA: Garret Publications, Inc., 1989.

Alexander, Edward P. *Fighting for the Confederacy: The Personal Recollections of General Edward Porter Alexander.* Edited by Gary W. Gallagher. Chapel Hill, NC: The University of North Carolina Press, 1989.

———. *Military Memoirs of a Confederate: A Critical Narrative.* New York: Charles Scribner's Sons, 1907.

Ambler, Charles H. *Francis H. Pierpont: Union War Governor of Virginia and Father of West Virginia.* Chapel Hill, NC: The University of North Carolina Press, 1937.

———. *Sectionalism in Virginia From 1776 to 1861.* Chicago: The University of Chicago Press, 1910.

———. *Waitman Thomas Willey: Orator, Churchman, Humanitarian.* Huntington, WV: Standard Printing & Publishing Co., 1954.

———, F.H. Atwood and W.B. Mathews, eds. *Debates and Proceedings of the First Constitutional Convention of West Virginia, 1861–1863.* 3 vols. Huntington, WV: Gentry Brothers, 1939.

Alexandria (Va) *Gazette.*

Armstrong, Richard L. *25th Virginia Infantry and 9th Battalion Virginia Infantry.* Lynchburg, VA: H.E. Howard, Inc., 1990.

Arnold, T.J. "Battle of Rich Mountain." *Magazine of History and Biography.* Randolph County Historical Society, Elkins, WV, no. 2 (1925): 46–52.

———. "Beverly in the Sixties." *Magazine of History and Biography.* Randolph County Historical Society, Elkins, WV, no. 13 (June 1969): 59–75.

Ashcraft, John M. *31st Virginia Infantry.* Lynchburg, VA: H.E. Howard, Inc., 1988.

Augusta (GA) *Daily Constitutionalist.*

Augusta (GA) *Daily Chronicle & Sentinel.*

B

Barbour (VA) *Democrat.*

Barnwell, Robert W. "The First West Virginia Campaign." *Confederate Veteran.* vol. 37 (May 1930): 186–189.

Basler, Roy P., ed. *The Collected Works of Abraham Lincoln.* 9 vols. New Brunswick, NJ: Rutgers University Press, 1953.

Baxter, Nancy N. *Gallant Fourteenth: The Story of an Indiana Civil War Regiment.* Traverse City, MI: The Pioneer Study Center Press, 1980.

———, ed. *Hoosier Farm Boy in Lincoln's Army: The Civil War Letters of Pvt. John R. McClure.* Privately published, 1971.

Beauregard, G.T. "The First Battle of Bull Run." *From Sumter to Shiloh: Battles and Leaders of the Civil War,* vol. 1, 196–227, 1887. Reprint. New York: Thomas Yoseloff, 1956.

Beatty, John. *The Citizen-Soldier; or, Memoirs of A Volunteer.* Cincinnati, OH: Wilstach, Baldwin & Co., 1879.

Beard, Richard. "The Story of a Five-Dollar Gold Piece." *Confederate Veteran.* vol. 24 (February 1916): 76–77.

Benham, Henry W. *Recollections of West Virginia Campaign, with the "Three Months Troops." May, June and July, 1861.* Private copy. From the Monthly Magazine, "Old and New," for June 1873. Boston, 1873.

Bierce, Ambrose. *Battlefields and Ghosts.* The Harvest Press, 1931.

———. *Ambrose Bierce's Civil War.* Edited with an introduction by William McCann. Washington, D.C.: Regnery Gateway, 1956.

Bird, Jacob. *Narrative of Two Perilous Adventures Recently Made into Dixie's Land. Also an Account of Six Months' Imprisonment in a Secession Jail.* Pittsburgh, PA: Privately published, 1862.

Boatner, Mark M., III. *The Civil War Dictionary.* New York: David McKay Company, Inc., 1959.

Bosworth, A.S. *A History of Randolph County, West Virginia.* Privately published, 1916.

Brigham, Loriman S., ed. "The Civil War Journal of William B. Fletcher." *Indiana Magazine of History.* vol. 57 (March 1961): 41–76.

Brinkman, Charles, ed. "The War Diary of Fabricus A. Cather." *Brinkman's American Wars and Taylor County, [W] Va. Men.* Grafton, WV: Taylor County Historical and Genealogical Society, 1988.

Brock, R.A., ed. "The Twelfth Georgia Infantry." *Southern Historical Society Papers.* vol. 17 (52 vols.) 160–87. Reprint. Millwood, NY: Kraus Reprint Co., 1977.

Brooks, Maurice. *The Appalachians.* Boston: Houghton Mifflin Company, 1965.

Broun, Thomas L. "Gen. R.E. Lee's War-Horse." *Confederate Veteran.* vol. 6 (June 1898): 292.

C

Callahan, James Morton. *History of West Virginia, Old and New.* Chicago: The American Historical Society, 1923.

———. *Semi-Centennial History of West Virginia.* Semi-Centennial Commission of West Virginia, 1913.

Cammack, John H. *Personal Recollections of Private John Henry Cammack: A Soldier of the Confederacy 1861–1865.* Huntington, WV: Paragon Ptg. & Pub. Co., 1920.

Carnes, Eva Margaret. *Centennial History of the Philippi Covered Bridge, 1852–1952.* Philippi, WV: Barbour County Historical Society, 1952.

————. *The Tygarts Valley Line: June–July 1861*. Philippi, WV: First Land Battle of the Civil War Centennial Commemoration, Inc., 1961.

————. *J.E. Hanger, The First Man to be Injured by a Cannon Ball in the Civil War and the First to Have a Limb Amputated*. Philippi, WV: The Barbour County Historical Society, 1961.

Catton, Bruce. *The American Heritage Picture History of the Civil War*. New York: American Heritage Publishing Co., Inc., 1960.

Chesnut, Mary B. *A Diary From Dixie*. Edited by Ben A. Williams. Boston: Houghton Mifflin Company, 1949.

Christen, William. "Mrs. Van Pelt: A Lady in Camp…" *Civil War Lady* magazine. vol. 1, no. 6: 23–24.

Cincinnati Daily Commercial.

Cincinnati Daily Gazette.

Clark, Walter A. *Under the Stars and Bars or, Memories of Four Years Service with the Oglethorpes, of Augusta, Georgia*. 1900. Reprint. Jonesboro, GA: Freedom Hill Press, Inc., 1987.

Clarksville (TN) *Jeffersonian*

Cobb, William H. "Story of Moses and Margaret Phillips." *Magazine of History and Biography*. Randolph County Historical Society, Elkins, WV, no. 7 (1933): 30–33.

————. "The Huttonsville Vicinity." *Magazine of History and Biography*. Randolph County Historical Society, Elkins, WV, no. 3 (1926): 55–63.

Cohen, Stan. *The Civil War in West Virginia: A Pictorial History*. Charleston, WV: Pictorial Histories Publishing Company, 1995.

Coldwater (MI) *Republican*

Collier, Calvin L. *"They'll Do To Tie To!" The Story of the Third Regiment, Arkansas Infantry, C.S.A.* 1959. Reprint. Little Rock, AR: Eagle Press, 1988.

Cometti, Elizabeth, and Festus P. Summers, eds. *The Thirty-fifth State: A Documentary History of West Virginia*. Morgantown: West Virginia University Library, 1966.

Cook, Roy Bird. *Lewis County in the Civil War, 1861-1865*. Charleston, WV: Jarrett Printing Co., 1924.

Couper, William. *Claudius Crozet: Soldier-Scholar-Educator-Engineer*. Charlottesville, VA: The Historical Publishing Co., Inc., 1936.

Cox, Jacob D. *Military Reminiscences of the Civil War*. 2 vols. New York: Charles Scribner's Sons, 1900.

————. "McClellan In West Virginia." *From Sumter to Shiloh: Battles and Leaders of the Civil War*, vol. 1, 126–48. 1887. Reprint. New York: Thomas Yoseloff, 1956.

Cullum, George W. *Biographical Register of the Officers and Graduates of the U.S. Military Academy at West Point, N.Y. From It's Establishment, in 1802, to 1890*. vol 2. Boston: Houghton, Mifflin and Company, 1891.

Culp, Edward C. *The 25th Ohio Vet. Vol. Infantry in the War for the Union*. Topeka, KS: Geo. W. Crane & Co., 1885.

Curry, Richard O. *A House Divided: A Study of Statehood Politics and the Copperhead Movement in West Virginia*. Pittsburgh, PA: University of Pittsburgh Press, 1964.

D

Dabney, R.L. *Life and Campaigns of Lieut.-Gen. Thomas J. Jackson, (Stonewall Jackson)*. New York: Blelock & Co., 1866.

Dargan, Elizabeth Paisley, ed. *The Civil War Diary of Martha Abernathy; Wife of Dr. C.C. Abernathy of Pulaski, Tennessee.* Beltsville, MD: Professional Printing, Inc., 1994.

Davis, Jefferson. "Robert E. Lee." *Southern Historical Society Papers.* vol. 17 (January-December 1889): 362–72. Reprint. Millwood, NY: Kraus Reprint Co., 1978.

———. *The Rise and Fall of the Confederate Government.* Richmond: Garrett and Massie Inc., n.d.

Dayton, Alston G. "Address of Honorable Alston Gordon Dayton." *Statue of Governor Francis Harrison Pierpont. Proceedings in Statuary Hall and in the Senate and the House of Representatives on the Occasion of the Unveiling, Reception, and Acceptance of the Statue From the State of West Virginia.* Washington, DC: Government Printing Office, 1910.

Dayton, Ruth W. "The Beginning—Philippi, 1861." *West Virginia History.* vol. 13 (July 1952): 254–66.

Deitz, Dennis. "Ghost of Traveler, General Lee's War-Horse." *Greenbrier County in the Civil War, 1861–1865.* Ronceverte, WV: Lee Headquarters Trust, Inc., 1993.

Dickinson, Jack L. *Tattered Uniforms and Bright Bayonets: West Virginia's Confederate Soldiers.* Huntington, WV: Marshall University Library Associates, 1995.

Dowdey, Clifford and Louis H. Manarin, eds. *The Wartime Papers of Robert E. Lee.* 1961. Reprint, New York: Da Capo Press, 1987.

Downer, Edward T. *Stonewall Jackson's Shenandoah Valley Campaign, 1862.* Lexington, VA: Stonewall Jackson Memorial, Inc., 1959.

Drake, James Vaulx. *Life of General Robert Hatton, Including His Most Important Public Speeches, Together, with much of his Washington & Army Correspondence.* 1867. Reprint. Lebanon, TN: Sons of Confederate Veterans, 1996.

Drewry, W.S. *The Southampton Insurrection.* Washington: Neale Company, 1900.

E

Ecelbarger, Gary L. *Frederick W. Lander: The Great Natural American Soldier.* Baton Rouge: Louisiana State University Press, 2000.

Elwood, John W. *Elwood's Stories of the Old Ringgold Cavalry, 1847–1865: The First Three Year Cavalry of the Civil War.* Coal Center, PA: Privately published, 1914.

Entrepreneurship Class. *A Dish of History: A Historical Cookbook Dedicated to Saylie McDonald and Mary Elizabeth Anthony.* Elkins, WV: Randolph County Vocational Technical Center, n.d.

Espenshade, A. Howry. *Pennsylvania Place Names.* State College, PA: The Pennsylvania State University, 1925.

F

Fansler, Homer F. *History of Tucker County, West Virginia.* Parsons, WV: McClain Printing Company, 1962.

Frame, Katharine Hart. "David B. Hart, Rich Mountain Guide." *Magazine of History and Biography.* Randolph County Historical Society, Elkins, WV, no. 12 (April 1961): 64–75.

Frank Leslie's Illustrated Newspaper.

Freeman, Douglas S. *R.E. Lee: A Biography.* 4 vols. New York: Charles Scribner's Sons, 1934–1935.

Frothingham, John B. *Sketch of the Life of Brig. Gen. B.F. Kelley.* Boston: L. Prang & Co., 1862.

Fry, James B. "McDowell's Advance to Bull Run." *From Sumter to Shiloh: Battles and Leaders of the Civil War*, vol. 1, 167–93, 1887. Reprint. New York: Thomas Yoseloff, 1956.

G

Geiger, Joe, Jr. "Holding the Line: Confederate Defense of the Staunton-Parkersburg Turnpike in the Fall of 1861." Master's Thesis. Department of History, Marshall University, Huntington, WV, 1995.

Grayson, Andrew J. *History of the Sixth Indiana Regiment in the Three Months' Campaign in Western Virginia*. Madison, IN: Courier Print, ca. 1875.

Grebner, Constantine. *"We Were the Ninth": A History of the Ninth Regiment, Ohio Volunteer Infantry April 17, 1861 to June 7, 1864*. Translated and edited by Frederic Trautmann. 1907. Reprint. Kent, OH: The Kent State University Press, 1987.

Griggs, Walter S., Jr. *General John Pegram, C.S.A.* Lynchburg, VA: H.E. Howard, Inc., 1993.

Guie, H. Dean. *Bugles in the Valley: Garnett's Fort Simcoe*. Portland, OR: Oregon Historical Society, 1956.

H

Hagans, John Marshall. *Sketch of the Erection and Formation of the State of West Virginia From the Territory of Virginia*. Reprinted from vol. 1, West Virginia Supreme Court Report, Charleston, WV: 1927.

Hagy, P.S. "The Laurel Hill Retreat in 1861." *Confederate Veteran*. vol. 24 (April 1916): 169–73.

Hall, Granville D. *The Rending of Virginia*. Chicago: Mayer & Miller, 1901.

———. *Lee's Invasion of Northwest Virginia in 1861*. Chicago: The Mayer & Miller Company, 1911.

Hall, James E. *The Diary of a Confederate Soldier*. Edited by Ruth Woods Dayton. Privately printed, 1961.

Hamilton, William Douglas. *Recollections of a Cavalryman of the Civil War After Fifty Years, 1861–1865*. Columbus, OH: The F.J. Heer Printing Co., 1915.

Hancock (IN) Democrat.

Hannaford, E. *The Story of a Regiment: A History of the Campaigns, and Associations in the Field, of the Sixth Regiment Ohio Volunteer Infantry*. Cincinnati, OH: Privately published, 1868.

Harper's Weekly.

Haselberger, Fritz. *Yanks From the South! (The First Land Campaign of the Civil War: Rich Mountain, West Virginia)*. Baltimore, MD: Past Glories, 1987.

Hawkins, Rush C. "Early Coast Operations in North Carolina." *From Sumter to Shiloh: Battles and Leaders of the Civil War*, vol. 1, 632–59, 1887. Reprint. New York: Thomas Yoseloff, 1956.

Hay, John. *Lincoln and the Civil War in the Diaries and Letters of John Hay*. Edited by Tyler Dennett. New York: Dodd, Mead & Company, 1939.

Hays, E.Z. ed. *History of the Thirty-second Regiment Ohio Veteran Volunteer Infantry*. Columbus, OH: Cott & Evans, 1896.

Head, Thomas A. *Campaigns and Battles of the Sixteenth Regiment, Tennessee Volunteers*. 1885. Reprint. McMinnville, TN: Womack Printing Company, 1961.

Headley, P.C. *Massachusetts In The Rebellion*. Boston: Walker, Fuller and Company, 1866.

Hermann, Isaac. *Memoirs of a Veteran.* 1911. Reprint. Lakemont, GA: CSA Press, 1974.

Hewitt, Janet B. et al., ed. *Supplement to the Official Records of the Union and Confederate Armies.* 100 vols. Wilmington, NC: Broadfoot Publishing Company, 1994–?

Hoover, Sallie W.S. "Col. John Augustine Washington, C.S.A." *Magazine of History and Biography.* Randolph County Historical Society, Elkins, WV, no. 3 (1926): 19–28.

Hornbeck, Betty. *Upshur Brothers of the Blue and The Gray.* 1967. Reprint. Parsons, WV: McClain Printing Company, 1995.

Hotchkiss, Jedediah. *Virginia,* vol. 3 of Clement A. Evans, ed. *Confederate Military History.* Atlanta: Confederate Publishing Company, 1899.

Howison, Robert R. "History of the War." *Southern Literary Messenger.* vol. 37 (March 1863).

Hull, W.H. "Some Recollections of the Civil War." *The Pocahontas Times,* various dates, 1908–09.

Hutton, E.E., Jr. "A Botanist Visits Tygarts Valley." *Magazine of History and Biography.* Randolph County Historical Society, Elkins, WV, no. 11 (December 1954): 23–27.

I

Imboden, John D. "Stonewall Jackson in the Shenandoah." *North To Antietam: Battles and Leaders of the Civil War,* vol. 2, 282–301, 1887. Reprint. New York: Thomas Yoseloff, 1956.

Irons, J.C. "History of a Noted Physician of Central West Virginia, Dr. John Taylor Huff, 1833–1925." *Magazine of History and Biography.* Randolph County Historical Society, Elkins, WV, no. 9 (1937): 27–33.

Indianapolis Daily Journal.

J

Jones, A.C. "The Mountain Campaign Failure." *Confederate Veteran.* vol. 22 (July 1914): 305–06.

———. "The Mountain Campaign Failure." *Confederate Veteran.* vol. 22 (August 1914): 368.

K

Keifer, J. Warren. *Slavery and Four Years of War.* 2 vols. New York: G.P. Putnam's Sons, 1900.

———. "The Battle of Rich Mountain and Some Incidents." Paper Read Before the Ohio Commandery of the Loyal Legion, December 6, 1911.

Kemper, G.W.H. "The Seventh Regiment." *War Papers Read Before The Indiana Commandery, Military Order of the Loyal Legion of the United States,* 117–131. 1898. Reprint. Wilmington, NC: Broadfoot Publishing Company, 1992.

———. "The Battle of Philippi as Experienced and Written at the Time." *Souvenir Booklet of Home-Coming Week and Blue and Gray Re-Union.* Philippi, WV. (May 29–June 3, 1911): 5–6.

Kepler, William. *History of the Three Months' and Three Years' Service of the Fourth Regiment Ohio Volunteer Infantry in the War for the Union.* 1886. Reprint. Huntington, WV: Blue Acorn Press, 1992.

L

Lafayette (IN) Daily Courier.

Lafayette (IN) Daily Journal.

Lamers, William M. *The Edge of Glory: A Biography of General William S. Rosecrans, U.S.A.* New York: Harcourt, Brace & World, Inc., 1961.

Lane, Mills, ed. *"Dear Mother: Don't grieve about me. If I get killed, I'll only be dead." Letters from Georgia Soldiers in the Civil War.* Savannah, GA: The Beehive Press, 1977.

Landon, William. "The Fourteenth Indiana Regiment on Cheat Mountain: Letters to the Vincennes *Sun*. *Indiana Magazine of History*, vol. 29 (December 1933): 350–71.

Lang, Theodore F. *Loyal West Virginia From 1861 to 1865*. Baltimore, MD: The Deutsch Publishing Co., 1895.

Lee, Fitzhugh. *General Lee.* The Great Commanders Series. New York: D. Appleton and Company, 1894.

Lee, Robert E., Jr. *Recollections and Letters of General Robert E. Lee.* 1905. Reprint. Wilmington, NC: Broadfoot Publishing Company, 1988.

Lee, Stephen D. "The First Step in the War." *From Sumter to Shiloh: Battles and Leaders of the Civil War*, vol. 1, 74–81. 1887. Reprint. New York: Thomas Yoseloff, 1956.

Leib, Charles. *Nine Months in the Quartermaster's Department; or The Chances for Making a Million.* Cincinnati: Moore, Wistach, Keys & Co., 1862.

Lesser, W. Hunter. *Battle at Corricks Ford: Confederate Disaster and Loss of a Leader.* Parsons, WV: McClain Printing Company, 1993.

———. "Prehistoric Human Settlement in the Upland Forest Region." *Upland Forests of West Virginia.* Edited by Steven L. Stephenson. Parsons, WV: McClain Printing Co., 1993.

Levering, John. "Lee's Advance and Retreat in the Cheat Mountain Campaign in 1861: Supplemented by the Tragic Death of Colonel John A. Washington of His Staff." Military Order of the Loyal Legion of the United States, Illinois Commandery. *Military Essays and Recollections.* vol. 4: 11–35. Chicago: Cozzens & Beaton Co., 1907.

Lewis, Virgil A. *History of West Virginia.* In Two Parts. Philadelphia, Hubbard Brothers, Publishers, 1889.

———. *How West Virginia Was Made: Proceedings of the First Convention...and the Journal of the Second Convention of the People of Northwestern Virginia...* Charleston, WV: News-Mail Company Public Printers, 1909.

———. *Second Biennial Report of the Department of Archives and History of the State of West Virginia.* Charleston, WV: 1908.

———. *Third Biennial Report of the Department of Archives and History of the State of West Virginia.* Charleston, WV: The News-Mail Company, 1911.

———. "How West Virginia Became a Member of the Federal Union." *West Virginia History.* vol. 30 (July 1969): 598–606.

Lindsley, John Berrien, ed. *The Military Annals of Tennessee. Confederate.* 2 vols. 1886. Reprint. Wilmington, NC: Broadfoot Publishing Company, 1995.

Logansport (IN) *Weekly Journal.*

Long, A.L. *Memoirs of Robert E. Lee, His Military and Personal History.* London: Sampson Low, Marston, Searle and Rivington, 1886.

Louisville Journal.

Lowry, Terry. *The Battle of Scary Creek: Military Operations in the Kanawha Valley, April–July 1861.* Revised Edition. Charleston, WV: Quarrier Press, 1998.

————. *September Blood: The Battle of Carnifex Ferry*. Charleston, WV: Pictorial Histories Publishing Company, 1985.

Lynchburg Daily Virginian.

M

McBrien, Joe Bennett. *The Tennessee Brigade*. Chattanooga, TN: Privately published, 1977.

McClellan, George B. *McClellan's Own Story*. Edited by William C. Prime. New York: Charles L. Webster & Company, 1887.

————. *Report on the Organization and Campaigns of the Army of the Potomac, to Which Is Added an Account of the Campaign in Western Virginia...* New York: Sheldon & Co., 1864.

————. "The Peninsular Campaign," *North To Antietam: Battles and Leaders of the Civil War*. vol. 2, 160–187, 1887. Reprint. New York: Thomas Yoseloff, 1956.

McGregor, James C. *The Disruption of Virginia*. New York: The Macmillan Company, 1922.

McKinney, Tim. *Robert E. Lee at Sewell Mountain: The West Virginia Campaign*. Charleston, WV: Pictorial Histories Publishing Co., 1990.

————. *Robert E. Lee and the 35th Star*. Charleston, WV: Pictorial Histories Publishing Co., 1993.

McPherson, James M. *Battle Cry of Freedom: The Civil War Era*. New York: Oxford University Press, 1988.

Macon (GA) Daily Telegraph.

Matheny, H.E. *Wood County, West Virginia, in Civil War Times; With an Account of the Guerrilla Warfare in the Little Kanawha Valley*. Parkersburg, WV: Trans-Allegheny Books, Inc., 1987.

Maxwell, Hu. *The History of Barbour County, West Virginia*. 1899. Reprint. Parsons, WV: McClain Printing Company, 1968.

————. *The History of Randolph County, West Virginia*. 1898. Reprint. Parsons, WV: McClain Printing Company, 1961.

Merrill, Catherine. *The Soldier of Indiana in the War for the Union*. Indianapolis, IN: Merrill and Company, 1864.

Miller, William J. *Mapping for Stonewall: The Civil War Service of Jed Hotchkiss*. Washington, D.C.: Elliott & Clark, 1993.

Mills, George Henry. *History of the Sixteenth North Carolina Infantry Regiment in the Civil War*. Reprint. Hamilton, NY: Edmonston Publishing, Inc., 1992.

Monfort, E.R. "From Grafton To McDowell Through Tygart's Valley." *Sketches of War History 1861–1865. Papers Read Before the Ohio Commandery of the Military Order of the Loyal Legion of the United States*. vol. 2, 1–23. Cincinnati: Robert Clarke & Co., 1888.

Moore, Frank, ed. *The Civil War in Song and Story*. New York: P.F. Collier, 1889.

————. *The Rebellion Record: A Diary of American Events*. 12 vols. New York: G.P. Putnam, 1861–1868.

Moore, George E. *A Banner in the Hills: West Virginia's Statehood*. New York: Appleton-Century-Crofts, 1963.

————. ed. "A Confederate Journal." *West Virginia History*. vol. 22 (July 1961): 201–16.

Morris, Roy, Jr. *Ambrose Bierce: Alone in Bad Company*. New York: Crown Publishers, Inc., 1995.

Morrison, James L. Jr., ed. *The Memoirs of Henry Heth*. Westport, CT: Greenwood

Press, 1974.

Morton, Joseph W. Jr., ed. *Sparks From the Camp Fire*. Philadelphia: Keystone Publishing Company, 1892.

"Mother to the First Tennessee Regiment." *Confederate Veteran*. vol. 34 (August 1926): 290.

Murray, J. Ogden. "First Soldier Killed in the War." *Confederate Veteran*. vol. 16 (October 1908): 494.

Myers, S. *Myers' History of West Virginia*. 2 vols. New Martinsville, WV: 1915.

N

Nagel, Paul C. *The Lees of Virginia: Seven Generations of an American Family*. New York: Oxford University Press, 1990.

New York Herald.

New York Times.

New York Tribune.

Newell, Clayton R. *Lee vs. McClellan: The First Campaign*. Washington, DC: Regnery Publishing Inc., 1996.

Nicolay, John G. and John Hay. *Abraham Lincoln: A History*. 10 vols. New York: Century Co., 1886.

O

Oram, Richard W. ed. "Harpers Ferry to the Fall of Richmond: Letters of Colonel John De Hart Ross, C.S.A., 1861–1865." *West Virginia History*. vol. 45, no. 1–4: 159–74.

P

Phillips, David L. *War Stories: Civil War in West Virginia*. Leesburg, VA: Gauley Mount Press, 1991.

Phillips, Harry. *Phillips Family History*. Lebanon, TN: The Lebanon Democrat, Inc., 1935.

Phillips, John R. "History of Valley Furnace." *The Barbour Democrat* (1968), in 15 parts, typescript.

Pinkerton, Allan. *The Spy of the Rebellion; Being a True History of the Spy System of the United States Army During the Late Rebellion*. New York: G.W. Dillingham, 1883.

Plum, William R. *The Military Telegraph during the Civil War in the United States*. 2 vols. Chicago: Jansen, McClurg & Company, 1882.

Poe, David. *Personal Reminiscences of the Civil War*. Buckhannon, WV: Upshur-Republican Print, 1911.

Pollard, Edward A. *Southern History of the War. The First Year of the War*. New York: Charles B. Richardson, 1863.

Pool, J.T. *Under Canvas; or, Recollections of the Fall and Summer Campaign of the 14th Regiment Indiana Volunteers, Col. Nathan Kimball, in Western Virginia, in 1861*. Terre Haute, IN: Oliver Bartlett, 1862.

Porterfield, George A. "A Narrative of the Service of Colonel Geo. A. Porterfield in Northwestern Virginia in 1861–'2." *Southern Historical Society Papers*. vol. 16 (January–December 1888): 82–91. Reprint. Broadfoot Publishing Company, 1990.

Powell, William S. "Beginning of the Civil War In West Virginia." *The West Virginia Review* (March 1937): 200–17.

Price, Andrew. "Plain Tales of Mountain Trails." *West Virginia Blue Book*. vol. 13 (1928): 323–511.

Price, Henry M. "Rich Mountain in 1861. An Account of that Memorable Campaign and How General Garnett Was Killed." *Southern Historical Society Papers.* vol. 27 (January–December 1899): 38–48.

Price, William T. *Historical Sketches of Pocahontas County, West Virginia.* Marlinton, WV: Price Brothers, 1901.

———. "Guerrilla Warfare; The Ambush on Greenbrier River in Which Seven Troopers Were Killed." *West Virginia Historical Magazine Quarterly*, vol. 4 (July 1904): 241–249.

———. *On To Grafton: An Account of One of the First Campaigns of the Civil War, May, 1861.* Marlinton, WV: Privately published, 1901.

Q

Quintard, Charles Todd. *Doctor Quintard, Chaplain, C.S.A. and Second Bishop of Tennessee; Being His Story of the War (1861–1865).* Edited and Extended by the Rev. Arthur Howard Noll. 1905. Reprint. Harrisonburg, VA: Sprinkle Publications, 1999.

R

Randall, James G. and T.C. Pease, eds. *The Diary of Orville Hickman Browning.* 2 vols. Springfield, IL: Illinois State Historical Library, 1933.

Randolph (WV) Enterprise.

Rawling, C.J. *History of the First Regiment Virginia Infantry.* Philadelphia: J.B. Lippincott Company, 1887.

Reader, Frank S. *History of the Fifth West Virginia Cavalry, Formerly the Second Virginia Infantry, and of Battery G, First West Va. Light Artillery.* New Brighton, PA: Daily News, 1890.

Reid, Whitelaw. *Ohio in the War: Her Statesmen, Generals and Soldiers.* 2 vols. 1868. Reprint. Columbus: Bergman Books, n.d.

———. *A Radical View: The "Agate" Dispatches of Whitelaw Reid, 1861–1865.* Edited by James G. Smart. 2 vols. Memphis, TN: Memphis State University Press, 1976.

Reorganized Government of Virginia. *Journal of the Convention, Assembled at Wheeling on the 11th of June, 1861.* Wheeling, VA: The Daily Press Book and Job Office, 1861.

———. *Acts of the General Assembly, Passed at the Extra Session, Held July, First, 1861 at the City of Wheeling.* Wheeling: Daily Press Book and Job Office, 1861.

Rice, Donald L. ed. "The Letters of John Barret Pendleton." *Magazine of History and Biography.* Randolph County Historical Society, Elkins, WV, no. 12 (April 1961): 10–20.

———. "The Military Telegraph in Western Virginia." *Magazine of History and Biography.* Randolph County Historical Society, Elkins, WV, no. 12 (April 1961): 25–28.

———, ed. *Randolph 200: A Bicentennial History of Randolph County, West Virginia.* Elkins, WV: Randolph County Historical Society, 1987.

———, and Phyllis Baxter. *Historic Beverly: A Guide Book.* Elkins, WV: Randolph County Historical Society, 1993.

Rice, Otis K. and Stephen W. Brown. *West Virginia: A History.* Lexington, KY: The University Press of Kentucky, 1985.

Richmond Daily Dispatch.

Richmond Enquirer.

Richmond Examiner.

Richmond Times-Dispatch.

Richmond Whig.

Robertson, James I., Jr. *Stonewall Jackson: The Man, The Soldier, The Legend.* New York: Macmillan Publishing USA, 1997.

Robson, John S. *How a One-Legged Rebel Lives: Reminiscences of the Civil War.* 1898. Reprint. Gaithersburg, MD: Butternut Press, 1984.

Ross, Charles H. "Old Memories." *War Papers.* Military Order of the Loyal Legion of the United States, Wisconsin Commandery. Vol. 1, 149–163. Milwaukee: Burdick, Armitage & Allen, 1891.

———. "Scouting for Bushwhackers in West Virginia in 1861." *War Papers.* Military Order of the Loyal Legion of the United States, Wisconsin Commandery. vol. 3, 399–412. Milwaukee: Burdick & Allen, 1903.

Ruffner, Kevin C. *44th Virginia Infantry.* Lynchburg, VA: H.E. Howard, Inc., 1987.

S

Savage, John H. "Gen. R.E. Lee at Cheat Mountain." *Confederate Veteran.* vol. 7 (March 1899): 116–18.

Sears, Stephen W. *George B. McClellan: The Young Napoleon.* New York: Ticknor & Fields, 1988.

———, ed. *The Civil War Papers of George B. McClellan.* New York: Ticknor & Fields, 1989.

Seitz, Don C. *Horace Greeley, Founder of the New York Tribune.* Indianapolis, IN: The Bobbs-Merrill Company, 1926.

Shaffer, Dallas S. "Lincoln and the 'Vast Question' of West Virginia." *West Virginia History.* vol. 32 (January 1971): 86–100.

Siviter, Anna Pierpont. *Recollections of War and Peace 1861–1868.* Edited by Charles H. Ambler. New York: G.P. Putnam's Sons, 1938.

Skidmore, Richard S., ed. *The Civil War Journal of Billy Davis.* Greencastle, IN: The Nugget Publishers, 1989.

———, ed. *The Alford Brothers: "We All Must Dye Sooner or Later."* Hanover, IN: The Nugget Publishers, 1995.

Smith, Barbara A., compiler. *The Civil War Letters of Col. Elijah H.C. Cavins, 14th Indiana.* Owensboro, KY: Cook-McDowell Publications, 1981.

Smith, Charles E. *A View From the Ranks: The Civil War Diaries of Corporal Charles E. Smith.* Compiled by George E. Cryder and Stanley R. Miller. Delaware, OH: Delaware County Historical Society, Inc., 1999.

Smith, Edward Conrad. *The Borderland in the Civil War.* New York: The Macmillan Company, 1927.

Southern Confederacy (GA).

Starr, Louis M. *Bohemian Brigade: Civil War Newsmen in Action.* 1954. Reprint. Madison, WI: The University of Wisconsin Press, 1987.

Staunton (VA) *Spectator.*

Stevenson, David. *Indiana's Roll of Honor.* vol. 1. Indianapolis, IN: Privately published, 1864.

Stewart, D.B. "First Infantry Fight of the War." *Confederate Veteran.* vol. 17 (October 1909): 500.

———. "Battle of Philippi Recounted." *Confederate Veteran.* vol. 18 (March 1910): 116–18.

Strider, Robert E. Lee. *The Life and Work of George William Peterkin.* Philadelphia: George W. Jacobs & Company, 1929.

Strother, David H. "Personal Recollections of the War. By a Virginian." *Harper's New Monthly Magazine*. vol. 33 (October 1866): 339–61. Reprinted in *Port Crayon Sampler*, edited by Jim Comstock. Richwood, WV: Privately published, 1974.

Stutler, Boyd B. *West Virginia in the Civil War*. Charleston, WV: Education Foundation, Inc. 1963.

———. "Death of Col. John Augustine Washington, C.S.A." *Magazine of History and Biography*. Randolph County Historical Society, Elkins, WV, no. 11 (December 1954): 11–18.

Summers, Festus P. *The Baltimore and Ohio in the Civil War*. New York: G.P. Putnam's Sons, 1939.

Switlik, Matthew C. "Loomis' Battery, First Michigan Light Artillery, 1859–1865." Master's Thesis. Department of History, Wayne State University, Detroit, MI, 1975.

T

Taliaferro, William B. "Annals of the War. Chapters of Unwritten History. Garnett in West Virginia..." Typescript from *The Philadelphia Weekly Times*, March 11, 1882.

Taylor, Walter H. *Four Years with General Lee*. New York: D. Appleton and Company, 1878.

———. *General Lee: His Campaigns in Virginia, 1861–1865, with Personal Reminiscences*. 1906. Reprint. Lincoln, NE: University of Nebraska Press, 1994.

Terrell, W.H.H. *Report of the Adjutant General of the State of Indiana*. 8 vols. Indianapolis, IN: Samuel M. Douglass, 1866.

Thacker, Victor L., ed. *French Harding: Civil War Memoirs*. Parsons, WV: McClain Printing Company, 2000.

"The Monument to General Robert E. Lee." *Southern Historical Society Papers*. vol. 17 (January–December 1889): 187–335. Reprint. Millwood, NY: Kraus Reprint Co., 1978.

Thomas, Emory M. *Robert E. Lee: A Biography*. New York: W.W. Norton & Company, 1995.

Thompson, William E. "Bound for Glory...But Headed Nowhere: Story of the 'Hampden-Sydney Boys,' Company G, 20th VA. Infantry, C.S.A." *The Record of Hampden-Sydney College*, vol. 68, no. 2 (Autumn 1992): 17–24.

Thomson, Orville. *Narrative of the Service of the Seventh Indiana Infantry in the War for the Union*. n.d. Reprint, Baltimore, MD: Butternut and Blue, 1993.

Toney, Marcus B. *The Privations of a Private*. Nashville, TN: Privately published, 1905.

"Trainer of Traveler—Frank Page." *Confederate Veteran*. vol. 15 (December 1907): 548–49.

U

Upshur (WV) *Record*.

U.S. Congress. "Rosecrans' Campaigns," *Report on the Joint Committee on the Conduct of the War at the Second Session of the Thirty-Eighth Congress*. Washington: Government Printing Office, 1865.

U.S. War Department. *The War of the Rebellion: A Compilation of the Official Records of the Union and Confederate Armies*. 70 vols. in 128 parts. Washington, DC: Government Printing Office, 1880–1901.

V

Van Dyke, Augustus M. "Early Days; Or, the School of the Soldier." *Sketches of War History, 1861–1865*. Papers Prepared for the Commandery of the State of Ohio, Military Order of the Loyal Legion of the United States. vol. 5, 18–31. Cincinnati: Robert Clarke, 1903.

W

Walker, John G. "Jackson's Capture of Harper's Ferry." *North to Antietam: Battles and Leaders of the Civil War*. vol. 2, 604–11. 1887. Reprint. New York: Thomas Yoseloff, 1956.

Wallace, Lee A. Jr. *A Guide to Virginia Military Organizations 1861–1865*. Lynchburg, VA: H.E. Howard, Inc., 1986.

"War Experiences of Colonel DeLagnel." *Confederate Veteran*. vol. 18 (November 1910): 508.

Ward, Geoffrey C., with Ric Burns and Ken Burns. *The Civil War: An Illustrated History*. New York: Alfred A. Knopf, 1990.

Warner, Ezra J. *Generals In Blue: Lives of the Union Commanders*. Baton Rouge, LA: Louisiana State University Press, 1964.

———. *Generals In Gray: Lives of the Confederate Commanders*. Baton Rouge, LA: Louisiana State University Press, 1959.

(Washington, D.C.) *National Tribune*.

Watkins, Sam R. *"Company Aytch:" Maury Grays First Tennessee Regiment or A Side Show of the Big Show*. 1882. Reprint, Wilmington, NC: Broadfoot Publishing Company, 1990.

Waugh, John C. *Reelecting Lincoln: The Battle for the 1864 Presidency*. New York: Crown Publishers, Inc., 1997.

———. *The Class of 1846: From West Point to Appomattox: Stonewall Jackson, George McClellan and their Brothers*. New York: Warner Books, 1994.

Wayland, John W. ed. *The Fairfax Line: Thomas Lewis's Journal of 1746*. New Market, VA: The Henkel Press, 1925.

Welch, Lewis. "The Odd Trick." *The West Virginia Review*. (January 1937): 139.

Wellsburg (VA) *Herald*.

Wheeling (VA) *Daily Intelligencer*.

Wiley, Bell I. *The Life of Billy Yank: The Common Soldier of the Union*. Baton Rouge, LA: Louisiana State University Press, 1952.

———. *The Life of Johnny Reb: The Common Soldier of the Confederacy*. Baton Rouge, LA: Louisiana State University Press, 1943.

Willey, William P. *An Inside View of the Formation of the State of West Virginia*. Wheeling, WV: The News Publishing Company. 1901.

Williams, Charles Richard. *The Life of Rutherford Birchard Hayes, Nineteenth President of the United States*. 2 vols. Boston: Houghton Mifflin Company, 1914.

Williams, Samuel C. "General John T. Wilder." *Indiana Magazine of History*, vol. 31 (September 1935): 169–203.

Williams, T. Harry. *Lincoln and His Generals*. New York: Alfred A. Knopf, 1952.

Withers, Alexander Scott. *Chronicles of Border Warfare*. A New Edition. Reuben Gold Thwaites, ed. 1895. Reprint. Parsons, WV: McClain Printing Company, 1961.

Womack, J.J. *The Civil War Diary of Capt. J.J. Womack. Co. E, Sixteenth Regiment, Tennessee Volunteers (Confederate)*. McMinnville, TN: Womack Printing Company, 1961.

Wood, James H. *The War.* Cumberland, MD: The Eddy Press Corporation, 1910.
Woods, J.H. "The First Inland Battle of the Civil War." *Souvenir Booklet of Home-Coming Week and Blue and Gray Re-Union.* Philippi, WV. (May 29–June 3, 1911): 7–12.
Worsham, John H. *One of Jackson's Foot Cavalry.* Edited by James I. Robertson, Jr. Jackson, TN: McCowat-Mercer Press, Inc., 1964.
Wright, Juanita E. "Colonel John Augustine Washington, CSA." *UDC Magazine, Virginia Division Special Issue.* (March 1991): 14–16.
Z
Zinn, Jack. *The Battle of Rich Mountain.* Parsons, WV: McClain Printing Company, 1971.
———. *R.E. Lee's Cheat Mountain Campaign.* Parsons, WV: McClain Printing Company, 1974.'

World Wide Web

Diary of Christian Kuhl of the Gilmer Rifles. 2002.
www.rootsweb.com/~hcpd/kuhl.htm

Edward "Alleghany" Johnson Home Page. 1995.
www.fsu.edu/~ewoodwar

Manuscript Collections

Duke University (DU)
C. Tacitus Allen Memoirs
Irby G. Scott Letters

Emory University (EU)
William Batts Letters
John L. Griffin Diary
Alexander H. Stephens Papers

Georgia Department of Archives and History (GDAH)
James Atkins Diary, transcript

Huntington Library (HL)
Edward Willis Papers

Indiana Historical Society (IHS)
David Beem Papers
Schuyler Colfax Papers
William Houghton Papers
James M. King Journal
George W. Lambert Journal
Harris Milroy Papers
Robert H. Milroy Papers

Thomas Prickett Papers
George Rogers Diary
Augustus Van Dyke Letters

Indiana State Library (ISL)
Ebenezer Dumont Papers
Julia Dumont Gordon Scrapbook
George W. Julian Papers
Kirkpatrick Family Scrapbook

Library of Congress (LC)
Lucian Barber Papers
Frederick W. Lander Papers
George B. McClellan Papers
Orlando Poe Papers
Alf. Welton Diary

Lilly Library, Indiana University (IU)
Frank Ingersoll Letters

Alexander Mack Memorial Library, Bridgewater College, Virginia (MML)
Adam W. Kersh Letters, typescript

Museum of the Confederacy, Eleanor S. Brockenbrough Library (MC)

R.T. Mockbee, "Historical Sketch of the 14ᵗʰ Tenn. Regt. of Infantry, C.S.A. 1861–1865"
Tucker Randolph Diary
William B. Taliaferro Papers

National Archives (NA)
Record Group 109
Record Group 393

Ohio Historical Society (OHS)
James Dawson Papers
Hugh B. Ewing Papers

Tennessee State Library and Archives (TSLA)
Oliver Taylor, "The War Story of a Confederate Soldier Boy," extracts from the Bristol (TN, VA) *Herald-Courier*, January 23–February 27, 1921

Upshur County Historical Society, Buckhannon, WV (UCHS)
Marsha L. Phillips Diary, typescript

University of Virginia (UVA)
A.L. Hench Collection

Virginia Historical Society (VHS)
Margaret A. Baldwin Papers
Robert P. Carson, "Recollections," typescript
William Garnett Chisholm Papers
R.S. Garnett Papers
Stuart Family Papers

West Virginia State Archives (WVSA)
C.S. Morgan Manuscript
Parson Parker, "Sufferings of the Twelfth Georgia Reg't, in the Mountains of Virginia"
Boyd B. Stutler Collection

West Virginia University (WVU)
Roy Bird Cook Collection
Jacob Pinock Papers
Joseph Snider Diary

Private Collections (PC)
Army of the Northwest Papers
R.N. Avery Letter
C.R. Boyce Letter
Walter A. Clark Diary
Samuel V. Fulkerson Letters
P.R. Galloway Letters
James C. Gamble Letters
E.D. House Diary
Dewitt C. Howard Letter
Nathan Kimball Letter
Ben May Letters
Benjamin Randals Journal
J.W. Ross Letter
J.H. Slaughter Letters
W.B. Tabb Letter
U.S. General Orders
Clayton Wilson Letters

INDEX

ABOUT THE AUTHOR

W. Hunter Lesser has had a twenty-year career as an archaeologist and historical interpreter. His writings on America's past have spanned topics from ancient Native American sites to Kentucky moonshine stills. A lifelong student of the Civil War, he served as a technical advisor for the Conservation Fund's *The Civil War Battlefield Guide*. He resides in the Allegheny Mountains of West Virginia.